COMPUTE! Publications,Inc.abc

Part of ABC Consumer Magazines, Inc.
One of the ABC Publishing Companies

Greensboro, North Carolina

ISBN 0-87455-053-X

The author and publisher have made every effort in the preparation of this book to insure the accuracy of the programs and information. However, the information and programs in this book are sold without warranty, either express or implied. Neither the author nor COMPUTE! Publications, Inc., will be liable for any damages caused or alleged to be caused directly, indirectly, incidentally, or consequentially by the programs or information in this book.

The opinions expressed in this book are solely those of the author and are not necessarily those of COMPUTE! Publications, Inc.

COMPUTE! Publications, Inc., Post Office Box 5406, Greensboro, NC 27403, (919) 275-9809, is part of ABC Consumer Magazines, Inc., one of the ABC Publishing Companies, and is not associated with any manufacturer of personal computers. Amiga is a trademark of Commodore-Amiga, Inc.

Contents

Foreword v

Chapter 1. Introduction 1

Chapter 2. Games of Skill 7
  Enigma 14
  Elementary, Watson 26
  Knights Errant 39
  Pharaoh's Pyramid 52
  Roman Checkers 62
  Falstaff 73
  Mosaic Puzzle 86
  Hi-Q 96
  Solitaire Checkers 105
  Bunny's and Piglet's Tic-Tac-Toe 114

Chapter 3. Stop, Look, and Learn 129
  Crazy Critters 135
  Let's Add and Subtract 148
  Let's Multiply 165
  Fun with Fractions 181
  Foreign Language Flash Cards 198

Chapter 4. Household Helpers 211
  IRA Planner 217
  Loan Payments 225
  Multifunction Calculator 236
  Paycheck Analysis 249

Chapter 5. Business and Finance 259
  Electronic Spreadsheet 265
  Least-Squares Forecasting 291
  Future Worth 305
  Computer Cash Register 314

Chapter 6. Science and Math 323
  Chemistry Basics 329
  Weather Forecasting 352

Simultaneous Equation Solver 366
Matrix Manipulator (MatMan) 377

Chapter 7. Statistics 393
Scatter Diagram 399
Super Curve-Fitter 419

Index 437

Disk Coupon 439

Foreword

COMPUTE!'s Amiga Applications has something for every member of the family. With 29 different applications—from games to finance—it's an instant library of easy-to-use programs for your Amiga.

Game players will enjoy the vivid graphics and challenge of games like "Knights Errant" and "Pharaoh's Pyramid." Children will enjoy learning using "Crazy Critters," "Fun with Fractions," and "Let's Multiply."

COMPUTE!'s Amiga Applications also includes practical programs that help with home and business financial matters, statistics, and science. There's even an easy-to-use spreadsheet program.

Each program is written in Amiga BASIC and takes advantage of the advanced features of the Amiga including pull-down menus and crisp, colorful graphics. We've even included menu programs that make loading programs easy.

Written by an experienced programmer and writer, *COMPUTE!'s Amiga Applications* includes all the information you need to use each of the applications included here. Each program has been fully tested and is ready to type in and enjoy. It's the perfect introduction to the power within your computer.

> All the programs included in *COMPUTE!'s Amiga Applications* are ready to type in and run. All you need is an Amiga computer, a monitor, and a copy of Amiga BASIC. Also recommended, but not necessary, are a color monitor and 512K Random Access Memory. If you prefer not to type in the programs, however, you can purchase a 3-1/2-inch disk which includes all the programs in this book by calling toll-free 1-800-346-6767 (in NY, call 212-887-8525), or by using the coupon found in the back of this book.)

CHAPTER 1

Introduction

CHAPTER 1

Introduction

The Amiga is one of the most impressive personal computers ever built. With amazing graphics, sound, color, speed, and mouse and icon operations, it's a computer that's powerful, useful, and fun to run.

This book is designed to take advantage of some of the Amiga's handiest and most entertaining features. The programs use pull-down menus, multicolored high-resolution graphics, icon displays, and mouse selection of program options. The educational programs use multivoice sound to produce some nice tunes.

This book focuses on six different topics, ranging from challenging games to business and scientific applications. The programs have been carefully designed for ease of use, entertainment, and practicality. Even if you don't think you're interested in a particular subject, try some of the programs. You might change your mind.

Equipment Required

Each program is written in Amiga BASIC, and for best results, each should be run on a system with a color monitor and 512K Random Access Memory, or more. Some of the programs will run with just 256K RAM, but the longer ones, such as "Electronic Spreadsheet," require the additional memory. To prevent system crashes, 512K is recommended.

The Spreadsheet has the capability of producing two types of reports, and you'll need a printer to use this option. None of the other programs requires a printer.

Amiga BASIC and Workbench

None of the programs uses line numbers. Having the option of using or not using line numbers is a fantastic feature. Indeed, the Amiga dialect of BASIC is one of the most powerful versions available on a microcomputer. So, in addition to running the programs in the book, you may want to examine some of the code in detail to pick up ideas for your own projects.

Communications between Amiga BASIC and the disk drives are handled by software known as an operating system. To run the programs in the book, you should have Kickstart 1.1 and Workbench 1.1, or later updates.

Typing In the Programs

Typing in the programs and getting them running can be instructive. Each program is modular in design. Each generally consists of three parts: a definition of shapes, menus, and variables; a main routine; and a series of subroutines.

Once you get used to the modular design, you'll begin to understand the internal structure of the programs. Armed with this knowledge, you should be able to modify any of the routines to suit your fancy.

Table 1-1 is a list of the programs in the book. Save each program to a disk *that contains a copy of Amiga BASIC* with the filename shown in Table 1-1. You will notice that starting with Chapter 2 each chapter begins with a "Menu Driver" program, selected from Workbench level, which uses these filenames. If you like, you can ignore the Menu Drivers altogether, but they can be really handy. The choice is up to you. Each of the six Menu Driver program listings is printed at the start of the chapter. Most of the code for each of the Menu Driver programs is exactly the same. The only differences appear in three sections of the program: The second line of the SETSCREEN routine contains the title of the chapter; the value for N in the second line of the KEYVALUES routine is set to the number of programs in the chapter; and a list of the programs appears in DATA statements at the very end of the program.

Therefore it's necessary to type the Menu Driver program only once. When you're ready to prepare new Menu Drivers for subsequent chapters, simply load the first copy and make the necessary changes. Once the changes have been made, save the new version with the appropriate filename as in Table 1-1. *Be sure to save a copy of the Menu Driver for each chapter before running it.* Note: The menu drivers will not operate properly unless Amiga BASIC is also present on the same disk.

Finally, if your disk becomes too cluttered with icon names, such as ENIGMA, WATSON, and so on, simply execute a statement like KILL "ENIGMA.info" from BASIC. This removes the icon from your disk, but not the program.

If you prefer you can purchase a disk containing all the programs and Menu Drivers. To purchase *COMPUTE!'s Amiga Applications* disk, please use the coupon in the back of this book. If you purchase the disk, please read the special note below for instructions on disk duplication and on copying Amiga BASIC.

General Operating Instructions

To load and run a program, use the Menu Driver for each chapter. You can do this in one of two ways. From BASIC, key in RUN, followed by the name of the Menu Driver, such as "GAMES". Then press the RETURN key. Or from Workbench, simply click the mouse on the appropriate icon, such as SCIENCE.

After you're through with a program, use a pull-down menu to go to (1) BASIC, (2) Menu Driver, or (3) System. If you're in Amiga BASIC and want to go to the Workbench, type in SYSTEM and press RETURN.

The chapters describe how to use each program. Read the instructions before running a program.

Most of the programs use a little white bar on the bottom of the screen. The bar contains two circles, one green with a *Y* on it and the other red with an *N* on it. This is a button bar, with the *Y* standing for *Yes* and the *N* for *No*. Make your selection either by clicking the mouse on the appropriate circle or by simply pressing Y or N.

Many of the programs will display the message *Click Mouse* or *Press any Key*. In both cases, you can either click or press to continue program execution.

Every program in *COMPUTE!'s Amiga Applications* uses 60 columns on your screen. Make sure that the Preferences drawer on the Workbench disk is set to this value rather than to 80 columns.

Table 1-1. Program Names

Program Title	Filename
Games of Skill (Menu Driver)	GAMES
Enigma	ENIGMA
Elementary, Watson	WATSON
Knights Errant	KNIGHTS
Pharaoh's Pyramid	PYRAMID
Roman Checkers	ROMAN
Falstaff	FALSTAFF
Mosaic Puzzle	MOSAIC
Hi-Q	HI-Q
Solitaire Checkers	SOLITAIRE
Bunny's and Piglet's Tic-Tac-Toe	TTT
Stop, Look, and Learn (Menu Driver)	LEARNING
Crazy Critters	CRITTERS
Let's Add and Subtract	ADD
Let's Multiply	MULTIPLY
Fun with Fractions	FRACTIONS
Foreign Language Flash Cards	CARDS

Household Helpers (Menu Driver)	HELPERS
IRA Planner	IRA
Loan Payments	LOAN
Multifunction Calculator	CALCULATOR
Paycheck Analysis	PAYCHECK
Business and Finance (Menu Driver)	FINANCE
Electronic Spreadsheet	SPREADSHEET
Least-Squares Forecasting	LSF
Future Worth	WORTH
Computer Cash Register	REGISTER
Science and Math (Menu Driver)	SCIENCE
Chemistry Basics	CHEMISTRY
Weather Forecasting	WEATHER
Simultaneous Equation Solver	SES
Matrix Manipulator	MATMAN
Statistics (Menu Driver)	STATISTICS
Scatter Diagram	SCATTER
Super Curve-Fitter	SUPER

If You Purchased a *COMPUTE!'s Amiga Applications* Disk

Before you use the programs on a disk purchased directly from COMPUTE! Publications you should do two things:

• Put Amiga BASIC on the disk.
• Make a back-up copy of the disk.

Amiga BASIC is not on the *Applications* disk simply because it's copyrighted software. But putting it there is easy. Just follow these instructions:

1. Load your Amiga Extras disk, and then click on it.
2. By holding down the left button of the mouse, move the AmigaBASIC icon to any convenient place outside the window. Then close the Extras window to give yourself plenty of space on the screen.
3. Insert your *COMPUTE!'s Amiga Applications* disk.
4. Using the mouse, move the AmigaBASIC icon on top of the icon that represents the *Amiga Applications* disk.
5. Follow the Amiga's prompts as it asks you to alternately insert the Extras disk and then the *Amiga Applications* disk. Two complete swaps are required.

With this accomplished, duplicate *COMPUTE!'s Amiga Applications* disk. If you don't recall how to do this, follow the instructions on pages 3-14 to 3-16 in your *Introduction to Amiga* manual. By the way, before duplicating a disk, it's a good idea to always slip the little black tab of the disk to be duplicated to the open position. This write-protects it, thus eliminating all possibility of accidental loss of data.

CHAPTER 2

Games of Skill

CHAPTER 2

Games of Skill

In some of these games you'll play against yourself (examples are "Enigma," "Knights Errant," and "Pharaoh's Pyramid"). The Amiga will present you with some sort of puzzle, contest, or riddle, and you'll have to achieve a goal in as few moves as possible. In other games ("Roman Checkers" and "Falstaff") you'll compete against the computer, and the Amiga is a very formidable opponent.

No matter which type of game you play, however, all have one thread in common. Each challenges your intellect, memory, concentration, and persistence. What you accomplish is up to you rather than to luck.

Enigma. The Amiga scrambles a secret phrase chosen randomly from its library of 75 entries. Your job is to decipher the message as quickly as possible.

Elementary, Watson. The Amiga creates a hidden code consisting of four items chosen from these six: a horse, a monkey, a duck, a rabbit, a witch, and a kitten. Employing your high powers of logic, you've got to deduce the code in short order.

Knights Errant. A dozen Don Quixotes face a legion of harmless windmills. Try to transfer each group of pieces from one side of the board to the other in as few moves as possible.

Pharaoh's Pyramid. On the Giza plateau, ten miles west of the city of Cairo, Egypt, stands the Great Pyramid of Cheops. The Amiga draws Cheops using 14 blocks. Try to remove as many blocks as possible, with a piece lifted from play when it's jumped.

Roman Checkers. Try to line up five of your chariots in a row on an 8 × 8 board before the Amiga lines up five of its markers.

Falstaff. You're pitted against the Amiga in this version of what's been called one of the most entertaining games of logic ever invented. Place one of your markers on an empty square so that a string of the Amiga's pieces is capped at both ends; then watch as the Amiga's markers turn into yours.

Mosaic Puzzle. A version of the old sliding-squares game. Rearrange the shapes of a 3 × 3 square, using as few moves as possible. Two levels of play are available: Easy (with numbers drawn on each piece) and Hard (without the numbers).

Hi-Q. The famous European solitaire game of finesse and foresight. Try to remove as many pegs as possible from a cross-shaped board, with only horizontal and vertical jumps allowed.

Solitaire Checkers. Eliminate as many checkers as possible from a standard 8 × 8 board, filled along the outer two borders with 48 pieces.

Bunny's and Piglet's Tic-Tac-Toe. Play against the Amiga in this delightful version of an old favorite. Kids and grownups will enjoy the lovable bunny and the lively animation.

Games of Skill Menu Driver

Save using the filename **GAMES**

```
REM GAMES OF SKILL
  GOSUB INITIALIZE
  GOSUB MAIN.MENU
  RUN TITLE.SHORT$(PICK)
END

INITIALIZE:
  GOSUB SETSCREEN
  GOSUB KEYVALUES
  GOSUB SETMENUS
  GOSUB SETCOLORS
  GOSUB SHAPES
RETURN

SETSCREEN:
  SCREEN 1,640,200,3,2
  WINDOW 2,"Games of Skill",,0,1
RETURN

KEYVALUES:
  DEFINT A-Z
  N = 10
  DIM TITLE.LONG$(N),TITLE.SHORT$(N)
  DIM CIRCLES(150)
  CIRCLE.I(1) = 1: CIRCLE.I(2) = 75
  READ CHAPTER$
  FOR I=1 TO N
    READ TITLE.LONG$(I),TITLE.SHORT$(I)
  NEXT
RETURN
```

```
SETMENUS:
 FOR I=2 TO 4
  MENU I,0,0,""
 NEXT
 MENU 1,0,1,"STOP"
 MENU 1,1,1," Go to BASIC"
 MENU 1,2,1," Go to System"
 MENU ON
 ON MENU GOSUB GOODBYE
RETURN

GOODBYE:
 WINDOW CLOSE 2: WINDOW 1: MENU RESET
 SCREEN CLOSE 1
 ITEM = MENU(1)
 IF ITEM = 2 THEN SYSTEM
 CLS
 PRINT "Bye-Bye"
 STOP
RETURN

SETCOLORS:
 REM TAN, GREEN, & RED
  PALETTE 4,.95,.7,.53
  PALETTE 5,.14,.43,0
  PALETTE 6,.93,.2,0
RETURN

SHAPES:
 X=313: Y=80: X1=X-7: X2=X+7: Y1=Y-3: Y2=Y+3
 LINE(X1,Y1)-(X2,Y2),4,BF
 FOR I=1 TO 2
  K = 7-I
  CIRCLE(X,Y),7,K: PAINT(X,Y),K
  GET(X1,Y1)-(X2,Y2),CIRCLES(CIRCLE.I(I))
 NEXT
RETURN

MAIN.MENU:
 CLS
 RTN$ = "OFF": PICK = 1
 S$ = CHAPTER$: L = LEN(S$)
 LINE(313-10*L/2-15,15)-(313+10*L/2+15,27),1,B
 PAINT(313,20),6,1
 COLOR 1,6: LOCATE 3: PRINT PTAB(313-10*L/2)S$
 LINE(135,32)-(495,130),2,B: PAINT(313,80),4,2
 COLOR 2,4
 FOR I=1 TO N
  IF I = PICK THEN INX = 2 ELSE INX = 1
```

```
   CALL DRAW.CIRCLE(I,INX)
   LOCATE I+4,23: PRINT TITLE.LONG$(I)
  NEXT
  LINE(263,141)-(360,153),2,B: PAINT(313,145),3,2
  COLOR 2,3
  LOCATE 17: PRINT PTAB(282)"Return"
  COLOR 1,0
  LOCATE 19,11: PRINT "Click Mouse on Choice,";
  PRINT " then Click on Return"
  GOSUB CHOOSE
RETURN

SUB DRAW.CIRCLE(R,INX) STATIC
  SHARED CIRCLES(),CIRCLE.I()
  Y = 9*R+27
  PUT(182,Y),CIRCLES(CIRCLE.I(INX)),PSET
END SUB

CHOOSE:
  GOSUB GURGLE
  GOSUB CLICKIT
  IF S$ = "" THEN GOSUB LOCATION
  IF ASC(S$+" ") <> 13 AND RTN$ = "OFF" THEN
   GOTO CHOOSE
  END IF
RETURN

GURGLE:
  FREQ = 300
  FOR G=1 TO 5
   FREQ = 500 - FREQ
   SOUND FREQ,1,50
  NEXT
RETURN

CLICKIT:
  S$ = ""
  WHILE MOUSE(0) = 0 AND S$ = ""
   S$ = INKEY$
  WEND
  X = MOUSE(1)
  Y = MOUSE(2)
  WHILE MOUSE(0)<> 0: WEND: REM RESET
RETURN

LOCATION:
  IF X>263 AND X<360 AND Y>141 AND Y<153 THEN
   RTN$ = "ON"
  ELSE
```

12

```
  P = INT((Y-35)/9) + 1
  IF X>170 AND X<210 AND P>0 AND P<= N THEN
   CALL DRAW.CIRCLE(PICK,1)
   CALL DRAW.CIRCLE(P,2)
   PICK = P
  END IF
 END IF
RETURN

REM PROGRAMS
 DATA Games of Skill
 DATA Enigma, ENIGMA
 DATA "Elementary, Watson", WATSON
 DATA Knights Errant, KNIGHTS
 DATA Pharaoh's Pyramid, PYRAMID
 DATA Roman Checkers, ROMAN
 DATA Falstaff, FALSTAFF
 DATA Mosaic Puzzle, MOSAIC
 DATA Hi-Q, HI-Q
 DATA Solitaire Checkers, SOLITAIRE
 DATA Bunny's Tic-Tac-Toe, TTT
```

Enigma

In this exciting game of cryptography, the Amiga selects a message from its lex-icon of 75 famous phrases. Then it garbles the message by interchanging a let-ter in the expression with a random selection from the alphabet. *GOOSE* might end up *KMMGD*, for example.

Your goal is to decipher the scrambled message in fewer than 25 moves by choosing a letter in the garbled code (use the mouse to make your selection) and entering what you think is the correct character.

Figure 2-1 illustrates the setup. The top bar in each group holds the cryptogram, the middle space your entries, and the bottom bar the correct let-ters that you've identified.

A good place to begin deciphering this message is with the double-letter sequence *ZZ*. Two *N*'s or *S*'s or *T*'s are possibilities here, and on the third try, we find that *T* is correct.

Next, the two-letter word *BZ* is ripe for solution. Since the *Z* is a *T*, the *B* must be either an *A* or an *I*, giving us *AT* or *IT*. As it turns out, *A* is correct.

Now we're somewhat at a loss. Since *E* is the most popular letter in the English language, however, and since four *H*'s and three *Q*'s appear in the gar-bled message, perhaps the *E* is one of these. We try the *Q*, and as luck would have it, the *H* is actually the *E*.

Where do we go from here? The second letter in the first word must be a consonant since it's surrounded by *E*'s. Trial and error reveals an *N*.

We proceed in this fashion for the rest of the code, using commonsense guesses based on our knowledge of the English language. We eventually come up with this translation:

ENEMY ATTACK-NE ROUTE, AT DAWN

Figure 2-1. Enigma

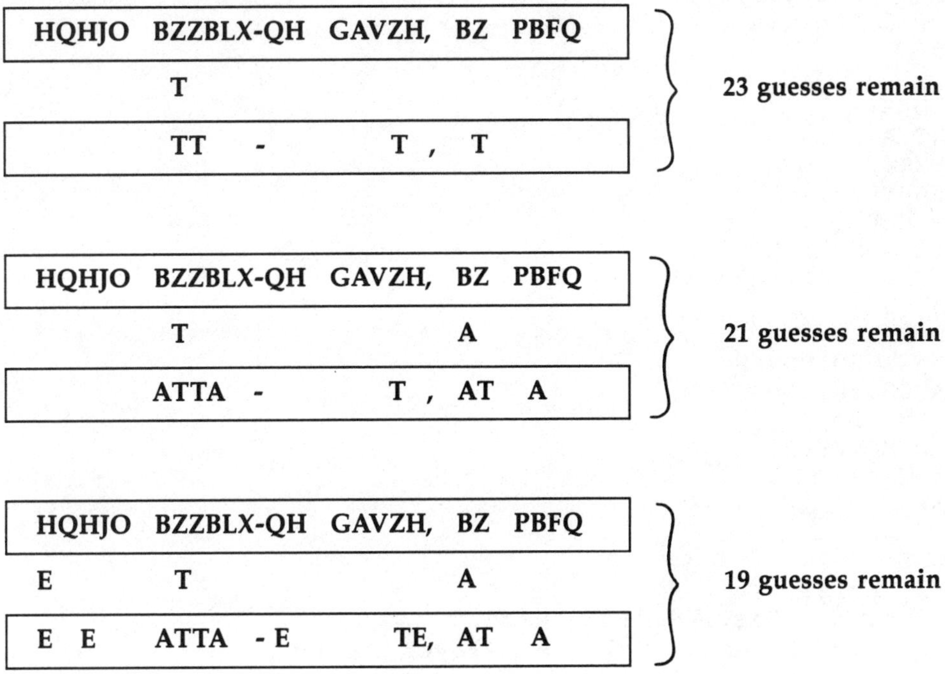

```
┌─────────────────────────────────────┐
│ HQHJO  BZZBLX-QH  GAVZH,  BZ  PBFQ   │
│              T                        │        ⎫
├─────────────────────────────────────┤        ⎬  23 guesses remain
│        TT   -        T , T           │        ⎭
└─────────────────────────────────────┘
```

```
┌─────────────────────────────────────┐
│ HQHJO  BZZBLX-QH  GAVZH,  BZ  PBFQ   │
│        T                 A            │        ⎫
├─────────────────────────────────────┤        ⎬  21 guesses remain
│       ATTA  -        T , AT  A       │        ⎭
└─────────────────────────────────────┘
```

```
┌─────────────────────────────────────┐
│ HQHJO  BZZBLX-QH  GAVZH,  BZ  PBFQ   │
│ E      T                 A            │        ⎫
├─────────────────────────────────────┤        ⎬  19 guesses remain
│ E  E    ATTA  - E       TE, AT  A    │        ⎭
└─────────────────────────────────────┘
```

Program 2-1. Enigma
Save using the filename **ENIGMA**

```
REM ENIGMA
 GOSUB INITIALIZE
PLAYGAME:
 GOSUB GAME
PLAYAGAIN:
 LOCATE 20,21: PRINT "Play Again ? ";
 ROW=20: X0=337: GOSUB DECIDE
 IF BUTTON = 1 THEN PLAYGAME
 GOSUB GOODBYE
END

INITIALIZE:
 GOSUB SETSCREEN
 GOSUB KEYVALUES
 GOSUB SETMENUS
 GOSUB SETCOLORS
 GOSUB HEADING
RETURN
```

```
SETSCREEN:
 SCREEN 1,640,200,3,2
 WINDOW 2,"Enigma",,0,1
RETURN

KEYVALUES:
 DEFINT A-Z
 RANDOMIZE TIMER
 DIM ALBT(26)
 BK$ = CHR$(32)
 LT$(1) = "Y": LT$(2) = "N"
 REM NUMBER OF PHRASES
  DATA 75
  READ NP
 REM MAXIMUM MOVES
  DATA 25,20,15
  FOR I=1 TO 3
   READ MOVES(I)
  NEXT
RETURN

SETMENUS:
 DATA 2, Rules, Yes, No
 DATA 3, Game, Easy, Medium, Hard
 DATA 2, Secret, Amiga Selects, Player Selects
 DATA 3, Stop, Go to BASIC
 DATA Go to Games Menu, Go to System
 FOR I=1 TO 4
  READ NUMBER
  FOR J=0 TO NUMBER
   READ TITLE$
   IF J<>0 THEN TITLE$ = SPACE$(3) + TITLE$
   STATUS = 1
    IF I<>4 AND J=1 THEN STATUS = 2
   MENU I,J,STATUS,TITLE$
 NEXT J,I
 RULES = 1: GAME = 1: SELECTOR = 1
 MENU ON
 ON MENU GOSUB OPTIONS
RETURN

SETCOLORS:
 REM GREEN AND RED
  PALETTE 5,.14,.43,0
  PALETTE 6,.93,.2,0
RETURN

HEADING:
 LINE(233,78)-(393,108),2,BF
```

16

```
    COLOR 6,2
    LOCATE 11: PRINT PTAB(284)"Enigma"
    COLOR 1,0
    LOCATE 17,24:PRINT "Please use menus,"
    LOCATE 19,23:PRINT "Click mouse to play"
    GOSUB CLICKIT
RETURN

OPTIONS:
  ID = MENU(0): ITEM = MENU(1)
  ON ID GOSUB MENU1,MENU2,MENU3,GOODBYE
  ITEM = 0
RETURN

MENU1:
  MENU 1,RULES,1: MENU 1,ITEM,2
  RULES = ITEM
RETURN

MENU2:
  MENU 2,GAME,1: MENU 2,ITEM,2
  GAME = ITEM
RETURN

MENU3:
  MENU 3,SELECTOR,1: MENU 3,ITEM,2
  SELECTOR = ITEM
RETURN

GOODBYE:
  WINDOW CLOSE 2: WINDOW 1: MENU RESET
  SCREEN CLOSE 1
  IF ITEM = 2 THEN RUN "GAMES"
  IF ITEM = 3 THEN SYSTEM
  COLOR 1,0: CLS
  PRINT "Bye-Bye"
  STOP
RETURN

CLICKIT:
  S$ = ""
  WHILE MOUSE(0) = 0 AND S$ = ""
   S$ = INKEY$
  WEND
  X = MOUSE(1)
  Y = MOUSE(2)
  WHILE MOUSE(0)<> 0: WEND: REM RESET
RETURN
```

```
GAME:
 IF RULES = 1 THEN GOSUB RULES
 ON SELECTOR GOSUB AMIGA, HUMAN
 GOSUB LABEL
 GOSUB PUNCTUATION
 GOSUB SCRAMBLE
 GOSUB PLAY
 COLOR 1,Ø
 IF GAME$ = "WIN" THEN
   LOCATE 17,23: PRINT "Congratulations !"
   SOUND 9ØØ,2
 ELSE
   GOSUB DEFEAT
 END IF
RETURN

RULES:
 CLS
 PRINT
 PRINT "    Department G2 has intercepted a ";
 COLOR 6,2: PRINT "SECRET";: COLOR 1,Ø
 PRINT " enemy transmission."
 PRINT
 PRINT "    Your goal is to decode it by:"
 PRINT
 PRINT "    -- Clicking the mouse on a letter in";
 PRINT " the garbled message."
 PRINT
 PRINT "    -- Entering what you think is the";
 PRINT " correct character."
 LOCATE 2Ø,26:PRINT "Click Mouse";
 GOSUB CLICKIT
RETURN

AMIGA:
 RESTORE PHRASES
 Z = INT(RND*NP) + 1
 FOR I=1 TO Z
   READ SECRET$
 NEXT
RETURN

HUMAN:
 CLS
 SOUND 44Ø,2
 LOCATE 2,3: PRINT "Please enter your secret.";
 PRINT "  Use the Back Space key to"
 PRINT " correct a mistake."
 ROW=6: L=45: GOSUB ENTER.PHRASE
```

```
  SECRET$ = PHRASE$
RETURN

ENTER.PHRASE:
 YØ = ROW*9-15
 LINE (16,YØ)-((L+3)*1Ø,YØ+18),2,BF
 S$ = "": C=3: COLOR 6,2
 GOSUB KEY
RETURN

KEY:
 LOCATE ROW,C: PRINT CHR$(124);
 L$ = INKEY$: IF L$ = "" THEN KEY
 A = ASC(L$)
 IF C = 3 AND (A = 8 OR A = 13) THEN
   SOUND 9ØØ,2: GOTO KEY
 END IF
 IF A = 8 THEN
  S$ = LEFT$(S$,LEN(S$)-1)
  PRINT CHR$(8);
  C = C - 1
  GOTO KEY
 END IF
 IF C=L+3 AND A<>13 THEN SOUND 9ØØ,2: GOTO KEY
 IF A <> 13 THEN
  PRINT CHR$(8);UCASE$(L$)
  S$ = S$ + UCASE$(L$)
  C = C + 1
  GOTO KEY
 END IF
 PHRASE$ = S$
RETURN

LABEL:
 COLOR 1,Ø
 CLS
 LINE(15,5)-(16Ø,29),1,BF
 COLOR 6,1
 LOCATE 2,3: PRINT "Guesses"
 LOCATE 3,3: PRINT "Remaining:"
RETURN

PUNCTUATION:
 GUESS$ = ""
 L = LEN(SECRET$)
 FOR I=1 TO L
  L$ = MID$(SECRET$,I,1): A = ASC(L$)
  IF A > 64 AND A < 91 THEN L$ = BK$
  GUESS$ = GUESS$ + L$
```

```
  NEXT
RETURN

SCRAMBLE:
  COLOR 1,Ø
  FOR I=1 TO 26: ALBT(I)=Ø: NEXT
  LOCATE 1Ø,27: PRINT "Scrambling ..."
  SCRAMBLE$ = GUESS$
  FOR I=1 TO L
   LT$ = MID$(SECRET$,I,1)
   S$ = MID$(SCRAMBLE$,I,1)
   IF LT$ <> BK$ AND S$ = BK$ THEN
     GOSUB RANDOM.LETTER
     GOSUB SUBSTITUTE
   END IF
  NEXT I
RETURN

RANDOM.LETTER:
  SOUND 2ØØ,1
  SEARCH$ = "ON"
  WHILE SEARCH$ = "ON"
   V = INT(26*RND) + 1
   IF ALBT(V) <> 1 THEN SEARCH$ = "OFF"
  WEND
  RL$ = CHR$(64+V): ALBT(V) = 1
RETURN

SUBSTITUTE:
  FOR J=I TO L
   IF MID$(SECRET$,J,1) = LT$ THEN
     MID$(SCRAMBLE$,J,1) = RL$
   END IF
  NEXT J
RETURN

PLAY:
  GOSUB DRAWBARS
  GOSUB INITIAL.VALUES
  WHILE GAME$ = "ON" AND N < MAX.MOVES
   GOSUB ENTER.LETTER
   GOSUB CHECK.FOR.MATCH
   IF GUESS$ = SECRET$ THEN GAME$ = "WIN"
   IF GAME$ = "ON" AND AN$ = "Right" THEN
     GOSUB ASK.TO.DECODE
   END IF
  WEND
RETURN
```

```
INITIAL.VALUES:
 N = Ø: REM NUMBER OF WRONG GUESSES
 MAX.MOVES = MOVES(GAME)
 COLOR 6,1
 LOCATE 3,13: PRINT MAX.MOVES
 GAME$ = "ON"
 REM HIGHLIGHT FIRST LETTER
  COL =3: COL.HOLD = 3: P = 1
  COLOR 1,3
  LOCATE 8,3: PRINT MID$(SCRAMBLE$,1,1)
RETURN

DRAWBARS:
 COLOR 1,Ø
 LOCATE 10,27: PRINT SPACE$(14)
 LOCATE 6,3: PRINT "Secret Code:"
 LINE(16,57)-(22+L*10,75),3,BF
 COLOR 2,3
 LOCATE 8,3: PRINT SCRAMBLE$
 LINE(16,93)-(22+L*10,111),1,BF
 COLOR Ø,1
 LOCATE 12,3: PRINT GUESS$
RETURN

ENTER.LETTER:
 COLOR 1,Ø
 LOCATE 6,16: PRINT "(Click on letter;";
 PRINT " enter guess)"
 ACTION$ = "OK"
 WHILE ACTION$ <> "LETTER"
  GOSUB CLICKIT
  IF S$="" THEN GOSUB LOCATION ELSE GOSUB LETTER
  IF ACTION$ = "BAD" THEN SOUND 9ØØ,2
 WEND
 COLOR 1,Ø
 LOCATE 10,COL: PRINT C$
RETURN

LOCATION:
 ACTION$ = "OK"
 C1 = INT(X/1Ø)+1
 IF Y<57 OR Y>75 OR C1<3 OR C1 > L+2 THEN
  ACTION$ = "BAD"
 ELSE
  COL = C1: P = COL-2
  COLOR 2,3
  LOCATE 8,COL.HOLD
  PRINT MID$(SCRAMBLE$,COL.HOLD-2,1)
  COLOR 1,3
```

21

```
      LTR$ = MID$(SCRAMBLE$,P,1)
      IF LTR$ = BK$ THEN LTR$ = CHR$(124)
      LOCATE 8,COL: PRINT LTR$
      COL.HOLD = COL
   END IF
RETURN

LETTER:
   ACTION$ = "LETTER"
   S$ = UCASE$(S$): A = ASC(S$): C$ = CHR$(A)
   L1$ = MID$(GUESS$,P,1)
   L2$ = MID$(SECRET$,P,1)
   IF A<65 OR A>90 OR L1$<>BK$ OR L2$=BK$ THEN
    ACTION$ = "BAD"
   END IF
RETURN

CHECK.FOR.MATCH:
   IF L2$=C$ THEN AN$ = "Right" ELSE AN$ = "Wrong"
   LOCATE 6,16: PRINT SPACE$(30)
   LOCATE 6,16: PRINT AN$;" Letter."
   GOSUB GURGLE
   IF AN$ = "Right" THEN GOSUB HIT ELSE GOSUB MISS
RETURN

HIT:
   FOR J=1 TO L
     S$ = MID$(SECRET$,J,1)
     IF S$ = C$ THEN MID$(GUESS$,J,1) = C$
   NEXT
   COLOR 0,1
   LOCATE 12,3: PRINT GUESS$
RETURN

MISS:
   COLOR 6,1
   N = N+1
   LOCATE 3,13: PRINT MAX.MOVES-N
   FOR PAUSE=1 TO 7500: NEXT
RETURN

GURGLE:
   FREQ = 300
   FOR G=1 TO 7
     FREQ = 500-FREQ
     SOUND FREQ,1,50
   NEXT G
RETURN
```

```
ASK.TO.DECODE:
 COLOR 1,0
 LOCATE 16,20: PRINT "Decode ?"
 ROW=16: X0=275: GOSUB DECIDE
 LOCATE 16,20: PRINT SPACE$(8)
 LINE(X0,Y0)-(X0+96,Y0+14),0,BF
 IF BUTTON = 1 THEN GOSUB GET.ANSWER
RETURN

DECIDE:
 BUTTON = 0
 GOSUB DRAWBUTTON
 GOSUB PUSHBUTTON
 COLOR 1,0
RETURN

DRAWBUTTON:
 Y0 = 9*ROW-13
 XB(1) = X0+27: XB(2) = X0+69: YB = Y0+7
 LINE (X0,Y0)-(X0+96,Y0+14),1,BF
 FOR I=1 TO 2
   CIRCLE (XB(I),YB),12,I+4
   PAINT (XB(I),YB),I+4
   COLOR 1,I+4
   LOCATE ROW: PRINT PTAB(XB(I)-4);LT$(I);
 NEXT I
RETURN

PUSHBUTTON:
 SOUND 440,2
 GOSUB CLICKIT
 S$ = UCASE$(S$)
 IF S$ = "Y" THEN BUTTON = 1
 IF S$ = "N" THEN BUTTON = 2
 FOR I=1 TO 2
   XD = ABS(X-XB(I)): YD = ABS(Y-YB)
   IF XD<13 AND YD<7 THEN BUTTON = I: I=2
 NEXT
 IF BUTTON = 0 THEN PUSHBUTTON
RETURN

GET.ANSWER:
 ROW = 15
 GOSUB ENTER.PHRASE
 IF PHRASE$ = SECRET$ THEN
  GAME$ = "WIN"
 ELSE
  COLOR 1,0
  LOCATE 18,23: PRINT "Wrong translation."
```

```
   SOUND 150,9: SOUND 130,9
   LOCATE 20,26: PRINT "Click Mouse";
   GOSUB CLICKIT
   LOCATE 18,23: PRINT SPACE$(18)
   LOCATE 20,26: PRINT SPACE$(11);
   LINE(16,YØ)-((L+3)*1Ø,YØ+18),Ø,BF
 END IF
RETURN

DEFEAT:
 COLOR 1,Ø
 LOCATE 16,16: PRINT "View Secret ?"
 ROW=16: XØ=285: GOSUB DECIDE
 LOCATE 16,16: PRINT SPACE$(13)
 LINE(XØ,YØ)-(XØ+96,YØ+14),Ø,BF
 IF BUTTON = 1 THEN LOCATE 1Ø,3: PRINT SECRET$
RETURN

PHRASES:
 DATA GOD SAVE THE QUEEN
 DATA "THE FEW, THE PROUD, THE MARINES !"
 DATA A FEW GOOD MEN
 DATA "I CAME, I SAW, I CONQUERED"
 DATA I SHALL NOT DEAL IN MALICE
 DATA LOVE THY NEIGHBOR
 DATA TAKE IT EASY
 DATA EVERY WHICH WAY BUT LOOSE
 DATA THE RUSSIANS ARE COMING
 DATA JACK AND JILL WENT UP A HILL
 DATA THE COW JUMPED OVER THE MOON
 DATA HEY DIDDLE DIDDLE
 DATA THE OLD GRAY MARE
 DATA "TINKER, TAILOR, SOLDIER, SPY"
 DATA THE GRAPES OF WRATH
 DATA GONE WITH THE WIND
 DATA THE GULAG ARCHIPELAGO
 DATA TIE ME KANGAROO DOWN MATE
 DATA MY LITTLE CHICKADEE
 DATA THE LAST OF THE MOHICANS
 DATA NICE GUYS FINISH LAST
 DATA THE WHOLE NINE YARDS
 DATA I LOVE NEW YORK
 DATA DON QUIXOTE AND SANCHO PANZA
 DATA HONEST ABE LINCOLN
 DATA "EAST SIDE, WEST SIDE"
 DATA SUGAR AND SPICE AND EVERYTHING NICE
 DATA OF MICE AND MEN
 DATA ALICE IN WONDERLAND
 DATA THERE'S SOMETHING ROTTEN IN DENMARK
```

```
DATA WHAT A REVOLTING PREDICAMENT
DATA A ROLLING STONE GATHERS NO MOSS
DATA BEAM ME ABOARD SCOTTY
DATA IT'S A LONG WAY TO TIPPERARY
DATA THE ANSWER IS BLOWING IN THE WIND
DATA GIVE ME LIBERTY OR GIVE ME DEATH
DATA DIVIDE AND CONQUER
DATA IT'S THE REAL THING
DATA I THINK THEREFORE I AM
DATA A STITCH IN TIME SAVES NINE
DATA THERE'S NO FREE LUNCH
DATA TWAS THE NIGHT BEFORE CHRISTMAS
DATA "RED SKY AT NIGHT, SAILOR'S DELIGHT"
DATA IN THE LONG RUN, WE'RE ALL DEAD
DATA "HAIL TO THE REDSKINS, HAIL VICTORY"
DATA "TO ERR IS HUMAN, TO FORGIVE DIVINE"
DATA THE MOUSE RAN UP THE CLOCK
DATA A CAT HAS NINE LIVES
DATA THE JOLLY GREEN GIANT
DATA THE AMAZING AMIGA
DATA "ELEMENTARY, MY DEAR WATSON"
DATA MARY HAD A LITTLE LAMB
DATA HE WHO HESITATES IS LOST
DATA "COLUMBIA, THE GEM OF THE OCEAN"
DATA THIS LAND IS MADE FOR YOU AND ME
DATA "MOBY DICK, THE GREAT WHITE WHALE"
DATA THE HOUND OF THE BASKERVILLES
DATA THE BRONX BOMBER
DATA I AM THE GREATEST
DATA SLOW AS MOLASSES
DATA THE LAND OF THE RISING SUN
DATA "ALMOST HEAVEN, WEST VIRGINIA"
DATA FROM THE HALLS OF MONTEZUMA
DATA TOO MANY COOKS SPOIL THE BROTH
DATA "HARK THE RAVEN, NEVERMORE ↓"
DATA TOM SAWYER AND HUCKLEBERRY FINN
DATA WHERE'S THE BEEF ?
DATA "TWINKLE, TWINKLE, LITTLE STAR"
DATA IT'S A GRAND SLAM HOME RUN
DATA E PLURIBUS UNUM
DATA NO TAXATION WITHOUT REPRESENTATION
DATA ONCE UPON A MIDNIGHT DREARY
DATA E EQUALS MC SQUARED
DATA THE HUNCHBACK OF NOTRE DAME
DATA AND THEY LIVED HAPPILY EVER AFTER
```

Elementary, Watson

Image that you're Watson sitting by the fire. Suddenly the door flies open and Holmes appears along with the Thames fog and the cold night air. "The game's afoot, Watson!" he cries. "This note holds the key to the Farmingdale frame-up."

You leap to your feet and take the page from his hand, and exclaim in utter surprise, "But Holmes, this sheet is blank!"

"That, my dear Watson, is precisely what makes the game interesting."

The secret code in this brain-busting game of logic consists of a column of four items chosen randomly from these six: a horse, a duck, a witch, a rabbit, a kitten, and a monkey. An item might appear more than once or not at all. The code remains invisible while you play, and your goal is to figure it out based on clues that the Amiga provides.

Play begins with the computer asking you to select an item for each of the four positions in the column. You guess a rabbit, a monkey, a duck, and a witch, in that order (Figure 2-2).

The Amiga grades your guess using two kinds of markers, one red and one white. The number of red markers indicates how many objects are of the right kind and in the right location. The number of white markers indicates how many objects are of the right kind but in the wrong location.

Each item in the secret code receives one marker at most. You'll therefore never see more than four circles in your score. Four red markers means victory, and a quartet of white ones means that you've identified all the right objects, but none of them is in the right place. A complete absence of markers, on the other hand, means that none of the objects you've selected is in the hidden code. This is often fortunate, for it eliminates a number of objects from further consideration.

Figure 2-2. Elementary, Watson

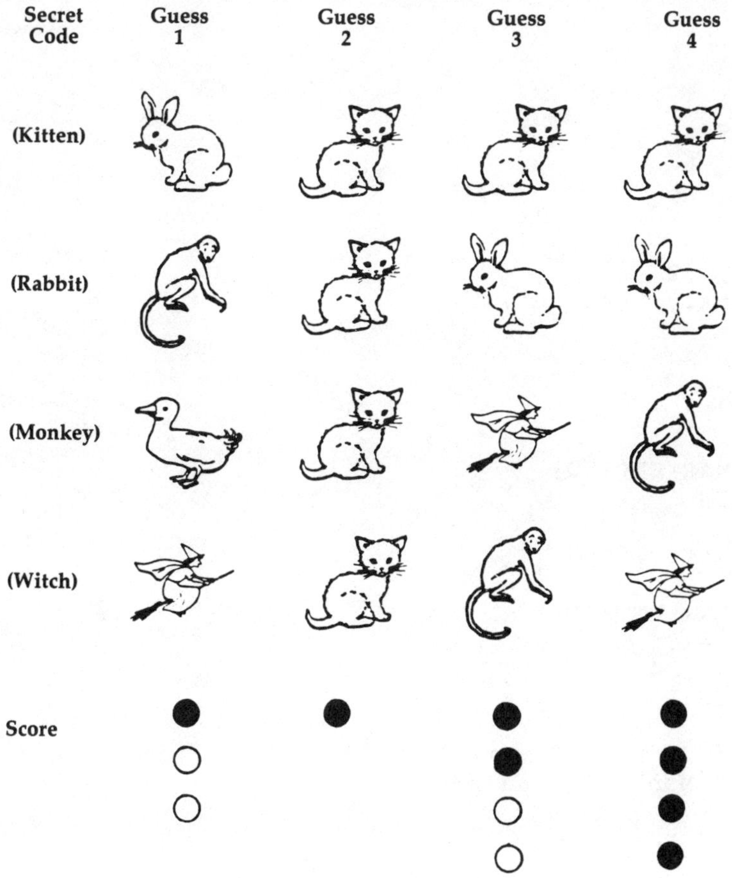

Secret Code	Guess 1	Guess 2	Guess 3	Guess 4
(Kitten)				
(Rabbit)				
(Monkey)				
(Witch)				

Program 2-2. Elementary, Watson
Save using the filename **WATSON**

```
REM ELEMENTARY, WATSON
 GOSUB INITIALIZE
PLAYGAME:
 GOSUB PLAY
PLAYAGAIN:
 LOCATE 20,21: PRINT "Play Again ? ";
 GOSUB DECIDE
 IF BUTTON = 1 THEN PLAYGAME
 GOSUB GOODBYE
END
```

```
INITIALIZE:
 GOSUB SETSCREEN
 GOSUB KEYVALUES
 GOSUB SETMENUS
 GOSUB SETCOLORS
 GOSUB DRAWSHAPES
 GOSUB DRAWCIRCLES
 GOSUB HEADING
RETURN

SETSCREEN:
 SCREEN 1,640,200,3,2
 WINDOW 2,"Elementary, Watson",,0,1
RETURN

KEYVALUES:
 DEFINT A-Z
 RANDOMIZE TIMER
 DIM SHAPE(1561),MARKER(150)
 REM VECTOR INDICES
  FOR I=1 TO 6
    INDEX(I) = 1 + (I-1)*260
  NEXT
 REM BUTTON HOLES & LETTERS
  XB(1)=364: YB(1)=174
  XB(2)=406: YB(2)=174
  LT$(1) = "Y": LT$(2) = "N"
 REM NAMES
  DATA " Horse "," Duck  "," Witch "
  DATA " Bunny "," Monkey"," Kitten"
  FOR I=1 TO 6
    READ NM$(I)
  NEXT
RETURN

SETMENUS:
 DATA 2, Rules, Yes, No
 DATA 2, Game, Easy, Hard
 DATA 3, Stop, Go to BASIC
 DATA Go to Games Menu, Go to System
 FOR I=1 TO 3
  READ NUMBER
  FOR J=0 TO NUMBER
   READ TITLE$
   IF J<>0 THEN TITLE$ = SPACE$(3) + TITLE$
   STATUS = 1
    IF I<>3 AND J=1 THEN STATUS = 2
   MENU I,J,STATUS,TITLE$
 NEXT J,I
```

```
   MENU 4,Ø,1,""
   RULES = 1: GAME = 1
 RETURN

 SETCOLORS:
  REM PINK, BROWN, RED, GRAY
    PALETTE 4,1,.51,.64
    PALETTE 5,.82,.37,.Ø7
    PALETTE 6,.93,.2,Ø
    PALETTE 7,.73,.83,.73
 RETURN

 DRAWSHAPES:
  MENU ON
  ON MENU GOSUB OPTIONS
  GOSUB HORSE
  GOSUB DUCK
  GOSUB WITCH
  GOSUB BUNNY
  GOSUB MONKEY
  GOSUB KITTEN
  GOSUB GETSHAPES
 RETURN

 HORSE:
  XØ=1Ø6: YØ=76
  CALL DRAWLINE(1,XØ,YØ,151)
  PAINT (XØ,YØ+3)
  CALL DRAWPOINT(Ø,XØ,YØ,4)
 RETURN

 SUB DRAWLINE(K,X.C,Y.C,T) STATIC
  COLOR K
  PSET(X.C,Y.C)
  FOR I=1 TO T
   READ X,Y
   LINE -STEP(X,Y)
  NEXT
 END SUB

 SUB DRAWPOINT(K,X.C,Y.C,T) STATIC
  COLOR K
  FOR I=1 TO T
   READ X,Y
   PSET(X.C+X,Y.C+Y)
  NEXT
 END SUB
```

```
DUCK:
 XØ=183: YØ=8Ø
 CALL DRAWLINE(3,XØ,YØ,73)
 PAINT (XØ-9,YØ+4)
 PAINT (XØ+17,YØ+4)
 CALL DRAWPOINT(2,XØ,YØ,12)
 REM BILL
  COLOR 1
  PSET(XØ+23,YØ+5)
  LINE -STEP(Ø,1): LINE -STEP(4,Ø)
RETURN

WITCH:
 REM DRESS/SHOES
  XØ=263
  CALL DRAWLINE(2,XØ,YØ,59)
  PAINT (XØ+2,YØ+4)
  PAINT (XØ-3,YØ-2)
 REM HAIR
  CALL DRAWPOINT(2,XØ,YØ-6,7)
 REM BROOM
  LINE(XØ-15,YØ+8)-(XØ+30,YØ-5)
  CALL DRAWLINE(2,XØ-15,YØ+8,9)
 REM CAPE
  CALL DRAWLINE(6,XØ+4,YØ-5,26)
  PAINT (XØ-12,YØ-3)
 REM HAT
  CALL DRAWLINE(6,XØ+1,YØ-7,10)
 REM FACE
  CALL DRAWLINE(4,XØ+4,YØ-6,8)
 REM ARMS
  CALL DRAWLINE(4,XØ+11,YØ-1,3)
RETURN

BUNNY:
 XØ=343
 CALL DRAWLINE(4,XØ,YØ,80)
 PAINT (XØ,YØ+3)
 CALL DRAWPOINT(2,XØ,YØ,41)
RETURN

MONKEY:
 XØ=423
 CALL DRAWLINE(5,XØ,YØ,36)
 CALL DRAWLINE(5,XØ,YØ,68)
 PAINT (XØ+3,YØ+2)
 CALL DRAWLINE(5,XØ+18,YØ+4,8)
 CALL DRAWPOINT(Ø,XØ,YØ,10)
 CALL DRAWPOINT(2,XØ,YØ,6)
RETURN
```

```
KITTEN:
 X0=503
 CALL DRAWLINE(7,X0,Y0,140)
 PAINT(X0,Y0-3)
 CALL DRAWPOINT(2,X0,Y0,16)
 CALL DRAWPOINT(6,X0,Y0,4)
RETURN

GETSHAPES:
 FOR I=1 TO 6
  X1 = 80*I-7: X2 = 80*I+53
  GET(X1,70)-(X2,90),SHAPE(INDEX(I))
 NEXT
RETURN

DRAWCIRCLES:
 X0=193: X1=428: Y0=110
 COLOR 6: CIRCLE (X0,Y0),10: PAINT(X0,Y0)
 COLOR 1: CIRCLE (X1,Y0),10: PAINT(X1,Y0)
 GET(X0-10,Y0-5)-(X0+10,Y0+5),MARKER(1)
 GET(X1-10,Y0-5)-(X1+10,Y0+5),MARKER(75)
RETURN

HEADING:
 COLOR 1,0
 LOCATE 13,23:PRINT "Elementary, Watson"
 LOCATE 17,24:PRINT "Please use menus,"
 LOCATE 19,23:PRINT "Click mouse to play"
 GOSUB CLICKIT
RETURN

OPTIONS:
 ID = MENU(0): ITEM = MENU(1)
 ON ID GOSUB MENU1,MENU2,GOODBYE
 ITEM = 0
RETURN

MENU1:
 MENU 1,RULES,1: MENU 1,ITEM,2
 RULES = ITEM
RETURN

MENU2:
 MENU 2,GAME,1: MENU 2,ITEM,2
 GAME = ITEM
RETURN

GOODBYE:
 WINDOW CLOSE 2: WINDOW 1: MENU RESET
```

```
 SCREEN CLOSE 1
 IF ITEM = 2 THEN RUN "GAMES"
 IF ITEM = 3 THEN SYSTEM
 COLOR 1,0: CLS:
 PRINT "Bye-Bye"
 STOP
RETURN

CLICKIT:
 S$ = ""
 WHILE MOUSE(0) = 0 AND S$ = ""
  S$ = INKEY$
 WEND
  X = MOUSE(1)
  Y = MOUSE(2)
 WHILE MOUSE(0)<> 0: WEND: REM RESET
RETURN

PLAY:
 IF RULES = 1 THEN GOSUB RULES
 GOSUB RECORD
 GOSUB DRAWBOARD
 WHILE GAME$ = "ON" AND N > 0
  GOSUB ENTERMOVE
  GOSUB GRADEMOVE
  IF RR = 4 THEN GAME$ = "OVER"
 WEND
 GOSUB GAMEOVER
RETURN

RULES:
 CLS
 PRINT
 PRINT "   The game's afoot, Watson !  And your";
 PRINT " job is to guess"
 PRINT " the Amiga's secret code using these";
 PRINT " markers:"
 PUT(100,42),MARKER(1),PSET
 LOCATE 6,15:
 PRINT "Right item in the right location"
 PUT(100,69),MARKER(75),PSET
 LOCATE 9,15
 PRINT "Right item in the wrong location."
 PRINT: PRINT
 PRINT "    When play begins, click the mouse on";
 PRINT " the name of the"
 PRINT " item you'd like to choose (say HORSE or";
 PRINT " WITCH)."
 LOCATE 20,26:PRINT "Click Mouse";
```

```
    GOSUB CLICKIT
  RETURN

  RECORD:
   ITEMS = GAME + 4
   FOR I=1 TO 4
     SECRET(I) = INT(ITEMS*RND) + 1
   NEXT
   GAME$ = "ON"
   N = 7: REM TURNS LEFT
  RETURN

  DRAWBOARD:
   CLS
   COLOR 6,1
   FOR I=1 TO 4
     LOCATE 3*I-1,2: PRINT I
     Y = 27*I-19
     LINE(10,Y)-(39,Y),1
   NEXT
   COLOR 2
   FOR I=1 TO ITEMS
     LOCATE 18,9*I-3
     PRINT NM$(I)
     LINE(I*90-40,152)-(I*90+29,161),6,B
   NEXT
   COLOR 1,0: S$ = "Score"
   FOR I=1 TO 5
     LOCATE I+12,3: PRINT MID$(S$,I,1)
   NEXT
  RETURN

  ENTERMOVE:
   COLOR 1,0
   S$ = STR$(N) + " turns left."
   IF N=1 THEN S$ = "Your last chance !"
   LOCATE 20,32-LEN(S$)/2: PRINT S$;
   SOUND 440,2
   HZ = (7-N)*76 + 102
   FOR I=1 TO 4
     GOSUB GUESS
   NEXT
  RETURN

  GUESS:
   LOCATE 3*I-1: PRINT PTAB(HZ+30)"?";
   GOSUB CLICKIT
   P = INT( (X-39)/90 ) + 1
   IF Y<152 OR Y>161 OR P<1 OR P > ITEMS THEN
```

```
    SOUND 900,2
    GOTO GUESS
  END IF
  PUT(HZ,27*I-26),SHAPE(INDEX(P)),PSET
  GUESS(I) = P
RETURN

GRADEMOVE:
  GOSUB GURGLE
  FOR I=1 TO 4: CODE(I)=SECRET(I): NEXT
  REM RIGHT ITEM, RIGHT PLACE
    GOSUB RIGHT.RIGHT
  REM RIGHT ITEM, WRONG PLACE
  FOR I=1 TO 4
    IF GUESS(I) <> -9 THEN GOSUB RIGHT.WRONG
  NEXT I
  N = N - 1
RETURN

RIGHT.RIGHT:
  Y = 107: RR = 0
  FOR I=1 TO 4
    IF GUESS(I) = CODE(I) THEN
      PUT(HZ+20,Y),MARKER(1),PSET
      Y = Y+11
      GUESS(I) = -9
      CODE(I) = -9
      RR = RR + 1
    END IF
  NEXT
RETURN

RIGHT.WRONG:
  FOR J=1 TO 4
    IF GUESS(I) = CODE(J) THEN
      PUT(HZ+20,Y),MARKER(75),PSET
      Y = Y+11
      CODE(J) = -9: J=4
    END IF
  NEXT J
RETURN

GURGLE:
  FREQ = 300
  FOR G=1 TO 5
    FREQ = 500-FREQ
    SOUND FREQ,1,50
  NEXT G
RETURN
```

```
GAMEOVER:
 G = 7-N: REM NUMBER OF GUESSES
 LOCATE 20,23: PRINT SPACE$(18);
 LINE(50,152)-(570,161),0,BF
 IF RR = 4 THEN GOSUB VICTORY ELSE DEFEAT
RETURN

VICTORY:
 RK$ = "Amateur"
 IF G = 6 THEN RK$ = "Scotland Yarder"
 IF G<= 5 THEN RK$ = "Holmes, the Master !"
 S$ = "Rank: " + RK$
 LOCATE 18,32-LEN(S$)/2: PRINT S$
RETURN

DEFEAT:
 LOCATE 20,21: PRINT "View Secret ?";
 GOSUB DECIDE
 IF BUTTON = 1 THEN GOSUB SECRET
RETURN

SECRET:
 LINE(10,0)-(88,105),0,BF
 LINE(10,0)-(88,105),6,B
 FOR I=1 TO 4
  S = SECRET(I)
  PUT(20,27*I-26),SHAPE(INDEX(S)),PSET
 NEXT
RETURN

DECIDE:
 BUTTON = 0
 GOSUB DRAWBUTTON
 GOSUB PUSHBUTTON
 COLOR 1,0
RETURN

DRAWBUTTON:
 LINE (337,167)-(433,181),1,BF
 FOR I=1 TO 2
  CIRCLE (XB(I),YB(I)),12,I*3
  PAINT (XB(I),YB(I)),I*3
  COLOR 1,I*3
  LOCATE 20: PRINT PTAB(XB(I)-4);LT$(I);
 NEXT I
RETURN

PUSHBUTTON:
 SOUND 440,2
```

```
GOSUB CLICKIT
S$ = UCASE$(S$)
IF S$ = "Y" THEN BUTTON = 1
IF S$ = "N" THEN BUTTON = 2
FOR I=1 TO 2
  XD = ABS(X-XB(I)): YD = ABS(Y-YB(I))
  IF XD<13 AND YD<7 THEN BUTTON = I: I=2
NEXT
IF BUTTON = Ø THEN PUSHBUTTON
RETURN

REM HORSE
  DATA -1Ø,Ø,Ø,-1,-9,Ø,Ø,1,-4,Ø,Ø,1,-1,Ø,Ø,1,-2,Ø
  DATA Ø,-1,-3,Ø,Ø,1,-2,Ø,Ø,2,1,Ø,Ø,3,-3,Ø,Ø,1
  DATA 1,Ø,Ø,-1,2,Ø,Ø,-1,1,Ø,Ø,-1,1,Ø,Ø,-1,-1,Ø
  DATA Ø,-2,4,Ø,Ø,2,1,Ø,Ø,1,2,Ø,Ø,3,-1,Ø,Ø,1
  DATA -3,Ø,Ø,5,3,Ø,-1,Ø,Ø,-4,2,Ø,Ø,-1,2,Ø,Ø,-1
  DATA 3,Ø,Ø,-1,3,Ø,Ø,2,-1,Ø,Ø,2,3,Ø,Ø,1,4,Ø,Ø,1
  DATA 2,Ø,Ø,1,3,Ø,-2,Ø,Ø,-1,-2,Ø,Ø,-1,-2,Ø,Ø,-1
  DATA -2,Ø,Ø,-2,1,Ø,Ø,-1,1,Ø,Ø,-1,1,Ø,Ø,-1,1,Ø
  DATA Ø,-1,2,Ø,Ø,1,1Ø,Ø,Ø,2,-1,Ø,Ø,4,-1,Ø,Ø,1
  DATA -1,Ø,1,Ø,Ø,1,4,Ø,-2,Ø,Ø,-4,1,Ø,Ø,-1,1,Ø
  DATA Ø,-1,1,Ø,Ø,-1,2,Ø,Ø,-2,3,Ø,Ø,1,3,Ø,Ø,1
  DATA 1,Ø,Ø,1,-1,Ø,Ø,1,-1,Ø,Ø,1,-2,Ø,Ø,1,1,Ø
  DATA Ø,-1,2,Ø,Ø,-1,1,Ø,Ø,-1,1,Ø,Ø,-1,1,Ø,Ø,-1
  DATA -1,Ø,Ø,-1,-3,Ø,Ø,-2,1,Ø,Ø,-1,-1,Ø,Ø,-3
  DATA 2,Ø,Ø,2,1,Ø,Ø,1,2,Ø,Ø,-1,1,Ø,Ø,-1,2,Ø
  DATA Ø,-3,-1,Ø,Ø,-1,-2,Ø,Ø,-1,-8,Ø,Ø,1,-4,Ø
  DATA Ø,1,-3,Ø,Ø,1,-1,Ø,Ø,1,-1,Ø,Ø,1,-3,Ø
  DATA -2Ø,6,-19,7,2Ø,-2,21,-2

REM DUCK
  DATA 3,Ø,-1,Ø,Ø,2,-1,Ø,Ø,2,3,Ø,Ø,1,7,Ø,Ø,-1
  DATA 2,Ø,Ø,-1,7,Ø,Ø,1,1,Ø,Ø,1,1,Ø,-2,Ø
  DATA Ø,1,-5,Ø,Ø,-1,-5,Ø,Ø,1,-4,Ø,Ø,1,-4,Ø
  DATA Ø,1,-13,Ø,Ø,-1,-6,Ø,Ø,-1,-5,Ø,Ø,-1
  DATA -4,Ø,9,Ø,Ø,-1,2,Ø,Ø,-2,1,Ø,Ø,-1,1,Ø,Ø,-1
  DATA 1,Ø,Ø,-2,-1,Ø,Ø,-1,-1,Ø,Ø,-2,-1,Ø,Ø,-2
  DATA 1,Ø,Ø,-1,1,Ø,Ø,1,2,Ø,Ø,1,2,Ø,Ø,1,2,Ø,Ø,1
  DATA 1,Ø,Ø,1,1,Ø,Ø,1,2,Ø,Ø,-2,2,Ø,Ø,1,1,Ø
  DATA Ø,1,1,Ø,Ø,1,1,Ø,Ø,1
  DATA -4,-1,-3,Ø,-3,1,-2,2,-2,3,-1,4,1,5,2,6
  DATA 1,7,Ø,7,18,4,19,4

REM WITCH
  DATA Ø,1,2,Ø,1,Ø,1Ø,Ø,Ø,3,-2,Ø,Ø,1,-2,Ø,Ø,1
  DATA -2,Ø,Ø,1,-2,Ø,Ø,1,-1,Ø,Ø,-1,-2,Ø,Ø,2,Ø,-1
  DATA -1,Ø,Ø,-1,-6,Ø,1,Ø,Ø,-1,2,Ø,Ø,-1,2,Ø,Ø,-2
  DATA -4,Ø,Ø,-1,-1,Ø,Ø,-1,1,Ø,Ø,-3,1,Ø,Ø,-1,1,Ø
```

```
    DATA 0,-1,2,0,0,-1,8,0,0,1,1,0,0,1,1,0,0,1,2,0
    DATA -3,0,0,1,-1,0,0,1,0,-1,-2,0,0,-2,-2,0,0,1
    DATA -1,0,0,1,-2,0,0,1
    DATA -1,0,1,0,2,0,3,0,3,-1,4,-1,5,-1
    DATA -2,0,0,1,-4,0,0,1,-5,0,9,0,0,-1,2,0,0,-1
    DATA -6,0,0,-1,-7,0,0,1,-7,0,0,1,-4,0,0,1,-9,0
    DATA 1,0,0,1,11,0,0,1,3,0,0,1,3,0,0,-1,1,0
    DATA 0,-1,1,0,0,-1,2,0,0,-1,2,0,0,-1,3,0
    DATA 1,0,0,-1,8,0,-3,0,0,-1,-3,0,0,-1,-2,0
    DATA 1,0,0,1
    DATA 3,0,0,1,1,0,0,-1,2,0,-2,0,0,-1,-1,0
    DATA 1,0,1,0,0,1

REM BUNNY
    DATA 0,-1,3,0,0,-1,8,0,0,1,4,0,0,1,3,0,0,1,1,0
    DATA 0,1,1,0,0,3,3,0,0,1,1,0,0,1,-1,0,0,1,-12,0
    DATA 0,1,-16,0,1,0,0,-2,-2,0,0,1,-3,0,1,0,0,-1
    DATA 2,0,0,-2,-1,0,0,-1,-3,0,0,-1,-1,0,0,-1
    DATA -1,0,0,-1,-7,0,0,-1,-1,0,0,-1,-1,0,1,0
    DATA 0,-1,2,0,0,-1,2,0,0,-2,-1,0,0,-1,-1,0,0,-2
    DATA -1,0,1,0,0,-1,1,0,0,1,3,0,0,1,1,0,0,3,4,0
    DATA 0,-2,1,0,0,-1,4,0,0,-1,2,0,0,2,-1,0,0,1
    DATA -2,0,0,1,-1,0,0,2,2,0,0,1,4,0,-15,-5
    DATA -14,-5,-15,-6,-14,-6,-15,-7,-8,-4,-8,-5
    DATA -7,-6,-6,-6,-15,-1,-14,-1,-13,-1,-14,-2
    DATA -13,-2,-11,1,-10,1,-9,0,-8,0,-8,8,-3,9
    DATA -2,7,-1,6,4,8,3,8,2,8,1,7,0,6,0,5,0,4,2,3
    DATA 4,2,8,2,9,2,10,2,12,3,17,6,18,5,19,5
    DATA -19,1,-18,1,-17,1

REM MONKEY
    DATA -4,0,0,1,-1,0,0,1,-1,0,0,5,-3,0,0,1,-10,0
    DATA 0,-1,-4,0,0,-1,-2,0,0,-1,-2,0,0,-1,-1,0
    DATA 0,-4,1,0,0,-1,1,0,0,-1,5,0,0,2,-3,0,3,0
    DATA 0,-1,1,0,-1,0,0,-1,-5,0,0,1,-2,0,0,1,-1,0
    DATA 0,3,-2,0,0,-1,3,0,0,-1,3,0,0,-1,4,0,0,-2
    DATA 2,0,0,-1,1,0,0,-1,4,0,0,1,2,0,0,2,-1,0,0,2
    DATA -2,0,0,-1,-3,0,0,2,1,0,0,2,1,0,0,1,3,0,0,-1
    DATA 2,0,0,-1,2,0,0,-1,3,0,0,-1,3,0,0,1,1,0,-6,0
    DATA 0,1,-2,0,0,1,-2,0,0,3,-1,0,0,-1,-3,0,0,-1
    DATA -2,0,0,-1,-4,0,0,2,4,0,0,1,-2,0,0,1,-2,0
    DATA 0,1,-4,0,0,1,6,0,-2,0,0,1,-8,0,1,0,0,-2
    DATA -2,0,0,1,-3,0,1,0,0,1,2,0,0,2,0,-1,2,0,0,1
    DATA 1,0,0,5,2,4,3,3,4,3,3,6,5,5,8,4,7,0,8,1
    DATA 16,3,12,-5,13,-5,15,-5,16,-5,15,-3,9,-5

REM KITTEN
    DATA 0,1,3,0,0,-1,2,0,0,1,2,0,0,2,1,0,0,3,-2,0
    DATA 0,1,-2,0,0,1,-3,0,5,0,0,-1,2,0,0,-1,2,0
```

```
DATA 0,-1,3,0,-1,0,0,-3,2,0,0,1,1,0,0,1,1,0,0,2
DATA -1,0,0,1,-1,0,0,1,-3,0,4,0,0,-1,1,0,0,-1
DATA 2,0,0,-1,1,0,0,-1,1,0,-1,0,0,-1,-1,0,0,-1
DATA -1,0,0,-4,1,0,0,-2,6,0,0,1,2,0,0,1,2,0,0,4
DATA -1,0,0,1,1,0,0,2,2,0,-1,0,0,-3,1,0,0,-1,1,0
DATA 0,-2,-1,0,0,-1,-1,0,0,-1,-2,0,0,-1,-4,0
DATA 0,-1,-3,0,0,-1,-3,0,0,-1,-3,0,0,-1,-5,0
DATA 0,-1,-7,0,0,1,-6,0,0,1,-2,0,0,1,-2,0,0,1
DATA -6,0,0,-1,-1,0,0,-1,0,1,-7,0,0,1,-5,0,0,-1
DATA 0,1,1,0,0,2,1,0,0,1,1,0,0,1,2,0,0,1,1,0
DATA 0,1,1,0,0,1,2,0,0,1,2,0,0,1,1,0,0,2,1,0,0,3
DATA -2,0,3,0,0,-1,1,0,0,-3,2,0,0,3,3,0,-1,0
DATA 0,-3,1,0,0,-1,1,0,0,-1,2,0,0,-1,3,0,-2,0
DATA -10,3,-11,4,-11,5,13,2,14,1
DATA 16,0,5,0,6,-1,5,-2,-17,-1,-16,-1,-15,-1
DATA -12,-2,-11,-3,-11,-4,-12,-5,-21,-3,-20,-3
DATA -16,-4,-15,-4
```

Knights Errant

"God help us!" exclaimed Sancho, *"Did I not tell Your Grace to look well, that those were nothing but windmills, a fact which no one could fail to see unless he had mills of the same sort in his head?"*

Don Quixote by Cervantes

A dozen Don Quixotes face a legion of harmless windmills in this solitaire game of logic. Your goal is to transfer each group of pieces from one side of the board (Figure 2-3) to the other in as few moves as possible. Each piece moves as in chess: one square forward or backward and two sideways, or vice versa.

To move a piece, simply click the mouse on the appropriate square of the board. Since there's only one blank position, the Amiga always knows where you want to move.

Completing the game in fewer than 43 moves is genius-level play, worthy indeed of our chivalrous Man from La Mancha.

Figure 2-3. Knights Errant

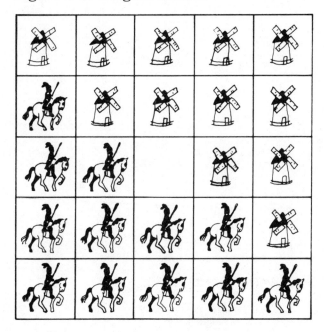

Program 2-3. Knights Errant
Save using the filename **KNIGHTS**

```
REM KNIGHTS ERRANT
 GOSUB INITIALIZE
PLAYGAME:
 GOSUB PLAY
PLAYAGAIN:
 LOCATE 20,21: PRINT "Play Again ?";
 GOSUB DECIDE
 IF BUTTON = 1 THEN PLAYGAME
 GOSUB GOODBYE
END

INITIALIZE:
 GOSUB SETSCREEN
 GOSUB KEYVALUES
 GOSUB SETMENUS
 GOSUB SETCOLORS
 GOSUB START
RETURN

SETSCREEN:
 SCREEN 1,640,200,3,2
 WINDOW 2,"Knights Errant",,0,1
RETURN

KEYVALUES:
 GOSUB FUNCTIONS
 GOSUB ARRAYS
 GOSUB RANKINGS
 REM DATA FOR SHAPES
  GOSUB MILL
  GOSUB VANE
  GOSUB HORSE
  GOSUB SADDLE
  GOSUB MAN
  GOSUB HELMET
  GOSUB PLUME
RETURN

FUNCTIONS:
 DEFINT A-J,L-Z
 RANDOMIZE TIMER
 DEF FNEVENODD(I,J) = ( (I+J)/2=INT((I+J)/2) )
 DEF FNX(V) = 75*V - 62
 DEF FNY(V) = 32*V - 77
RETURN
```

```
ARRAYS:
 DIM B(9,9),SQODD(1500),SQEVEN(1500)
 DIM MILL.X(45),MILL.Y(45),VANE.X(28),VANE.Y(28)
 DIM HORSE.X(151),HORSE.Y(151),MAN.X(53)
 DIM MAN.Y(53),HELMET.X(13),HELMET.Y(13)
 DIM PLUME.X(13),PLUME.Y(13)
 REM VECTOR INDICES
  DATA 1,500,1000
  READ INDEX(0),INDEX(1),INDEX(2)
 REM BUTTON VALUES
  XB(1)=364: YB(1)=174
  XB(2)=406: YB(2)=174
  LT$(1) = "Y": LT$(2) = "N"
 REM OFF-BOARD SQUARES
  FOR I=1 TO 2
   FOR J=1 TO 9
    B(I,J) = -9: B(I+7,J) = -9
    B(J,I) = -9: B(J,I+7) = -9
   NEXT J,I
 REM DELTAS FOR LEGAL MOVES
  N = 8
  DATA -2,1, -2,-1, -1,2, -1,-2
  DATA 2,1, 2,-1, 1,2, 1,-2
  FOR I=1 TO N
   READ DR(I), DC(I)
  NEXT
RETURN

RANKINGS:
 DATA King ↓,Duke,Knight,Vassal,Knave,Clown
 FOR I=1 TO 6
  READ RK$(I)
 NEXT
RETURN

MILL:
 DATA -2,0,0,1,-1,0,0,1,-1,0,0,1,-1,0,0,1
 DATA -1,0,0,1,-1,0,0,1,-2,0,0,1,-1,0,0,1
 DATA -1,0,0,1,-1,0,0,2,-1,0,0,2,27,0,0,-2
 DATA -1,0,0,-2,-1,0,0,-1,-1,0,0,-1,-1,0
 DATA 0,-1,-2,0,0,-1,-1,0,0,-1,-1,0,0,-1
 DATA -1,0,0,-1,-1,0,0,-1,-1,0,0,-1,-3,0
 FOR I=1 TO 45
  READ MILL.X(I),MILL.Y(I)
 NEXT
RETURN

VANE:
 DATA 0,-1,-3,0,0,-1,-1,0,0,-1,-1,0,0,-1
```

```
DATA -1,0,0,-1,-1,0,0,-1,-1,0,0,-1,-1,0
DATA 0,1,-1,0,0,1,-2,0,0,1,-2,0,0,1,5,0
DATA 0,1,4,0,0,1,2,0,0,1,3,0
FOR I=1 TO 28
  READ VANE.X(I),VANE.Y(I)
NEXT
REM SIGNS & OFFSETS FOR DRAWING 4 VANES
  DATA 1,1, -1,1, 1,-1, -1,-1
  FOR I=1 TO 4
  READ SX(I),SY(I)
  NEXT
  DATA 0,0, 1,0, 0,1, 1,1
  FOR I=1 TO 4
  READ XFSET(I),YFSET(I)
  NEXT
RETURN

HORSE:
  DATA -10,0,0,-1,-9,0,0,1,-4,0,0,1,-1,0,0,1,-2,0
  DATA 0,-1,-3,0,0,1,-2,0,0,2,1,0,0,3,-3,0,0,1
  DATA 1,0,0,-1,2,0,0,-1,1,0,0,-1,1,0,0,-1,-1,0
  DATA 0,-2,4,0,0,2,1,0,0,1,2,0,0,3,-1,0,0,1
  DATA -3,0,0,5,3,0,-1,0,0,-4,2,0,0,-1,2,0,0,-1
  DATA 3,0,0,-1,3,0,0,2,-1,0,0,2,3,0,0,1,4,0,0,1
  DATA 2,0,0,1,3,0,-2,0,0,-1,-2,0,0,-1,-2,0,0,-1
  DATA -2,0,0,-2,1,0,0,-1,1,0,0,-1,1,0,0,-1,1,0
  DATA 0,-1,2,0,0,1,10,0,0,2,-1,0,0,4,-1,0,0,1
  DATA -1,0,1,0,0,1,4,0,-2,0,0,-4,1,0,0,-1,1,0
  DATA 0,-1,1,0,0,-1,2,0,0,-2,3,0,0,1,3,0,0,1
  DATA 1,0,0,1,-1,0,0,1,-1,0,0,1,-2,0,0,1,1,0
  DATA 0,-1,2,0,0,-1,1,0,0,-1,1,0,0,-1,1,0,0,-1
  DATA -1,0,0,-1,-3,0,0,-2,1,0,0,-1,-1,0,0,-3
  DATA 2,0,0,2,1,0,0,1,2,0,0,-1,1,0,0,-1,2,0
  DATA 0,-3,-1,0,0,-1,-2,0,0,-1,-8,0,0,1,-4,0
  DATA 0,1,-3,0,0,1,-1,0,0,1,-1,0,0,1,-3,0
  FOR I=1 TO 151
  READ HORSE.X(I),HORSE.Y(I)
  NEXT
RETURN

SADDLE:
  DATA 4,0,0,1,1,0,0,2,-13,0,0,-3,8,0
  FOR I=1 TO 7
  READ SADDLE.X(I),SADDLE.Y(I)
  NEXT
RETURN

MAN:
  DATA 2,0,0,1,1,0,0,1,1,0,0,1,1,0,0,1,-1,0,0,3
```

```
  DATA 4,0,-5,0,0,-2,-1,0,0,-2,-1,0,0,-1,-1,0
  DATA 0,-1,-2,0,0,-1,-1,0,0,-1,-3,0,0,1,-1,0
  DATA 0,1,-1,0,0,1,-3,0,1,0,0,-1,1,0,0,-1,1,0
  DATA 0,-2,1,0,0,-1,1,0,0,-3,1,0,0,-1,3,0,0,-1
  DATA 3,0,0,2,1,0,0,2,3,0,-5,0,0,2,1,0,0,2
  FOR I=1 TO 53
   READ MAN.X(I),MAN.Y(I)
  NEXT
 RETURN

 HELMET:
  DATA -3,0,0,-1,1,0,0,-1,3,0,0,1,1,0,-1,0,0,2
  DATA 1,0,0,-1,-1,0,0,-1
  FOR I=1 TO 13
   READ HELMET.X(I),HELMET.Y(I)
  NEXT
 RETURN

 PLUME:
  DATA -1,0,0,-1,-5,0,0,1,-2,0,2,0,0,1,0,-1,2,0
  DATA 0,1,0,-1,1,0,0,-1
  FOR I=1 TO 13
   READ PLUME.X(I),PLUME.Y(I)
  NEXT
 RETURN

 SETMENUS:
   DATA 2, Rules, Yes, No
   DATA 5, Quixote, Brown, Blue, Green
   DATA Purple, Random
   DATA 3, Stop, Go to BASIC
   DATA Go to Games Menu, Go to System
   FOR I=1 TO 3
    READ NUMBER
    FOR J=0 TO NUMBER
     READ TITLE$
     IF J<>0 THEN TITLE$ = SPACE$(3) + TITLE$
     STATUS = 1
      IF I<>3 AND J=1 THEN STATUS = 2
     MENU I,J,STATUS,TITLE$
    NEXT J,I
   MENU 4,0,1,""
   RULES = 1: QCOLOR = 1
 RETURN

 SETCOLORS:
  REM BROWN, BLUE, DULL GREEN, PURPLE
   DATA .58,.11,.2,  .2,.09,.8
   DATA .14,.33,.25,  .02,0,.45
```

```
   FOR I=1 TO 4
    FOR J=1 TO 3
      READ KOLOR(I,J)
   NEXT J,I
  REM GRAY, VIOLET, BROWN, GREEN, & RED
   PALETTE 2,.32,.39,.61
   PALETTE 3,.75,.36,.75
   PALETTE 4,.58,.11,.2
   PALETTE 5,.14,.43,0
   PALETTE 6,.93,.2,0
RETURN

START:
 MENU ON
 ON MENU GOSUB OPTIONS
 GOSUB DRAWSQUARES
 GOSUB MAKEPIECES
 GOSUB HEADING
RETURN

DRAWSQUARES:
 X1=201: X2=275: X3=351: X4=425
 Y1=35: Y2=66: Y3=67: Y4=98
 REM EVEN
   LINE (X1,Y1)-(X2,Y2),2,BF
   GET (X1,Y1)-(X2,Y2),SQEVEN(1)
   CALL DRAWIT(4,6,0)
   CALL DRAWIT(5,5,0)
 REM ODD
   LINE (X1,Y3)-(X2,Y4),3,BF
   GET (X1,Y3)-(X2,Y4),SQODD(1)
   CALL DRAWIT(5,6,0)
   CALL DRAWIT(4,5,0)
RETURN

SUB DRAWIT(ROW,COL,Z) STATIC
 SHARED SQEVEN(),SQODD(),INDEX()
 IDX = INDEX(Z)
 X = FNX(COL) - 37
 Y = FNY(ROW) - 16
 V = FNEVENODD(ROW,COL)
 IF V = -1 THEN
  PUT(X,Y),SQEVEN(IDX),PSET
 ELSE
  PUT(X,Y),SQODD(IDX),PSET
 END IF
END SUB
```

```
MAKEPIECES:
 REM WINDMILL
  CALL MAKEMILL(238,49)
  GET (X1,Y1)-(X2,Y2),SQEVEN(500)
  CALL MAKEMILL(238,81)
  GET (X1,Y3)-(X2,Y4),SQODD(500)
 REM KNIGHT
  X0 = 392: Y0 = 50: GOSUB MAKEKNIGHT
  GET (X3,Y1)-(X4,Y2),SQEVEN(1000)
  Y0 = 82: GOSUB MAKEKNIGHT
  GET (X3,Y3)-(X4,Y4),SQODD(1000)
RETURN

SUB MAKEMILL(X0,Y0) STATIC
 REM MILL
  SHARED MILL.X(),MILL.Y(),VANE.X(),VANE.Y()
  SHARED SX(),SY(),XFSET(),YFSET()
  PSET (X0,Y0)
  COLOR 1
  FOR J=1 TO 45
   LINE -STEP(MILL.X(J),MILL.Y(J))
  NEXT
  PAINT (X0,Y0+7)
 REM VANES
  Y0 = Y0-3: COLOR 6
  FOR D=1 TO 4
   SX = SX(D): SY = SY(D)
   X = X0 + XFSET(D)
   Y = Y0 + YFSET(D)
   PSET (X,Y)
   FOR J=1 TO 28
    LINE -STEP(SX*VANE.X(J),SY*VANE.Y(J))
   NEXT J
   PAINT (X-SX*7,Y-SY*3)
  NEXT D
END SUB

MAKEKNIGHT:
 GOSUB MAKEHORSE
 GOSUB MAKESADDLE
 GOSUB MAKEMAN
 GOSUB MAKEHELMET
 GOSUB MAKEPLUME
 REM LANCE
  COLOR 1
  LINE (X0-2,Y0-1)-(X0+14,Y0-13)
RETURN
```

```
MAKEHORSE:
 COLOR 1
 PSET (XØ,YØ)
 FOR J=1 TO 151
  LINE -STEP(HORSE.X(J),HORSE.Y(J))
 NEXT
 PAINT (XØ,YØ+3)
 COLOR Ø
 PSET (XØ-2Ø,YØ+6): PSET (XØ-19,YØ+7)
RETURN

MAKESADDLE:
 PSET (XØ,YØ)
 FOR J=1 TO 7
  LINE -STEP(SADDLE.X(J),SADDLE.Y(J))
 NEXT
 PAINT (XØ,YØ+1)
RETURN

MAKEMAN:
 PSET (XØ,YØ)
 COLOR 4
 FOR J=1 TO 53
  LINE -STEP(MAN.X(J),MAN.Y(J))
 NEXT
 PAINT (XØ-3,YØ-3): PAINT (XØ+2,YØ+2)
RETURN

MAKEHELMET:
 COLOR Ø
 PSET (XØ,YØ-9)
 FOR J=1 TO 13
  LINE -STEP(HELMET.X(J),HELMET.Y(J))
 NEXT
 PAINT (XØ,YØ-1Ø)
RETURN

MAKEPLUME:
 COLOR 6
 PSET (XØ-1,YØ-12)
 FOR J=1 TO 13
  LINE -STEP(PLUME.X(J),PLUME.Y(J))
 NEXT
RETURN

HEADING:
 COLOR 1,4: LOCATE 18,3Ø:PRINT " then "
 COLOR 1,Ø
 LOCATE 13: PRINT PTAB(243)"Knights Errant"
```

```
   LOCATE 17,24:PRINT "Please use menus,"
   LOCATE 19,23:PRINT "Click mouse to play"
   GOSUB CLICKIT
RETURN

OPTIONS:
  ID = MENU(Ø): ITEM = MENU(1)
  ON ID GOSUB MENU1,MENU2,GOODBYE
  ITEM = Ø
RETURN

MENU1:
  MENU 1,RULES,1: MENU 1,ITEM,2
  RULES = ITEM
RETURN

MENU2:
  K1 = KOLOR(ITEM,1): K2 = KOLOR(ITEM,2)
  K3 = KOLOR(ITEM,3)
  IF ITEM=5 THEN K1=RND: K2=RND: K3=RND
  PALETTE 4,K1,K2,K3
  MENU 2,QCOLOR,1: MENU 2,ITEM,2
  QCOLOR = ITEM
RETURN

GOODBYE:
  WINDOW CLOSE 2: WINDOW 1: MENU RESET
  SCREEN CLOSE 1
  IF ITEM = 2 THEN RUN "GAMES"
  IF ITEM = 3 THEN SYSTEM
  COLOR 1,Ø: CLS
  PRINT "Bye-Bye"
  STOP
RETURN

CLICKIT:
  S$ = ""
  WHILE MOUSE(Ø) = Ø AND S$ = ""
   S$ = INKEY$
  WEND
   X = MOUSE(1)
   Y = MOUSE(2)
  WHILE MOUSE(Ø)<> Ø: WEND: REM RESET
RETURN

PLAY:
  IF RULES = 1 THEN GOSUB RULES
  GOSUB RECORD
  GOSUB DRAWBOARD
```

```
      GOSUB MOVESCARD
      WHILE GAME$ = "ON"
        GOSUB ENTERMOVE
        GOSUB MAKEMOVE
        GOSUB CHECK.FOR.END
      WEND
      GOSUB GAMEOVER
    RETURN

    RULES:
      CLS
      PRINT
      PRINT "    A dozen Don Quixotes face a legion";
      PRINT " of harmless windmills,"
      PRINT " thought to be lawless giants."
      PRINT
      PRINT "    Your goal is to transfer each group";
      PRINT " from one side of the"
      PRINT " board to the other in as few moves as";
      PRINT " possible."
      PRINT
      PRINT "    Each piece moves as in chess: one";
      PRINT " square forward and two"
      PRINT " sideways, or vice versa."
      LOCATE 20,26:PRINT "Click Mouse";
      GOSUB CLICKIT
    RETURN

    RECORD:
      REM 0 = VACANT; 1 = WINDMILL; 2 = KNIGHT
      FOR I=3 TO 7
        FOR J=3 TO 7
          V = 2
          IF I=3 OR (I=4 AND J>3) THEN V = 1
          IF (I=5 AND J>5) OR (I=6 AND J=7) THEN V=1
          B(I,J) = V
      NEXT J,I
      B(5,5) = 0: REM CENTER
      GAME$ = "ON"
      MOVES = 0
    RETURN

    DRAWBOARD:
      CLS
      LINE (125,2)-(501,163),1,B
      FOR R=3 TO 7
        FOR C=3 TO 7
          CALL DRAWIT(R,C,B(R,C))
      NEXT C,R
    RETURN
```

```
MOVESCARD:
 LINE (21,15)-(95,49),1,BF
 COLOR 6,1: LOCATE 3,4: PRINT "MOVES:"
RETURN

ENTERMOVE:
  COLOR 1,Ø
  LOCATE 2Ø,26:PRINT "Select piece ...";
  GOSUB CLICKIT
 REM FIND SQUARE (its Row and Column)
  R1 = INT( (Y-3)/32 ) + 3
  C1 = INT( (X-126)/75 ) + 3
  IF R1<3 OR R1>7 OR C1<3 OR C1>7 THEN
   SOUND 9ØØ,2
   GOTO ENTERMOVE
  END IF
  IF B(R1,C1)=Ø THEN SOUND 9ØØ,2: GOTO ENTERMOVE
 REM CHECK LEGALITY
  MOVE$ = ""
  FOR I=1 TO N
   R2 = R1 + DR(I): C2 = C1 + DC(I)
   IF B(R2,C2) = Ø THEN MOVE$ = "OK": I=N
  NEXT
  IF MOVE$ = "" THEN SOUND 9ØØ,2: GOTO ENTERMOVE
RETURN

MAKEMOVE:
 PIECE = B(R1,C1)
 CALL DRAWIT(R1,C1,Ø)
 GOSUB GURGLE
 CALL DRAWIT(R2,C2,PIECE)
 B(R1,C1) = Ø: B(R2,C2) = PIECE
 MOVES = MOVES + 1
 COLOR 6,1
 LOCATE 5,5: PRINT MOVES
RETURN

GURGLE:
 FREQ = 3ØØ
 FOR G=1 TO 5
  FREQ = 5ØØ-FREQ
  SOUND FREQ,1,5Ø
 NEXT G
RETURN

CHECK.FOR.END:
 GAME$ = "OVER": R = 3
 WHILE GAME$ = "OVER" AND R<=6
  C = 3
```

```
   WHILE GAME$ = "OVER" AND C<=7
    IF B(R,C) = 1 THEN
      IF R=3 OR (R=4 AND C>3) THEN GAME$="ON"
      IF R=5 AND C>5 THEN GAME$="ON"
      IF R=6 AND C=7 THEN GAME$="ON"
    END IF
    C = C+1
   WEND
   R = R+1
  WEND
  IF B(5,5) <> Ø THEN GAME$ = "ON"
RETURN

GAMEOVER:
 V = INT(MOVES/1Ø)-2
 IF MOVES > 89 THEN V = 6
 IF MOVES < 43 THEN V = 1
 COLOR 6,1
 LINE(533,15)-(6Ø9,49),1,BF
 LOCATE 3,55: PRINT "RANK:"
 LOCATE 5,55: PRINT RK$(V)
 COLOR 1,Ø
 LOCATE 2Ø,26: PRINT SPACE$(16);
RETURN

DECIDE:
 BUTTON = Ø
 GOSUB DRAWBUTTON
 GOSUB PUSHBUTTON
 COLOR 1,Ø
RETURN

DRAWBUTTON:
 LINE (337,167)-(433,181),1,BF
 FOR I=1 TO 2
  CIRCLE (XB(I),YB(I)),12,4+I
  PAINT (XB(I),YB(I)),4+I
  COLOR 1,4+I
  LOCATE 2Ø: PRINT PTAB(XB(I)-4);LT$(I);
 NEXT
RETURN

PUSHBUTTON:
 SOUND 44Ø,2
 GOSUB CLICKIT
 S$ = UCASE$(S$)
 IF S$ = "Y" THEN BUTTON = 1
```

```
 IF S$ = "N" THEN BUTTON = 2
 FOR I=1 TO 2
  XD = ABS(X-XB(I)): YD = ABS(Y-YB(I))
   IF XD<13 AND YD<7 THEN BUTTON = I: I=2
 NEXT
 IF BUTTON = 0 THEN PUSHBUTTON
RETURN
```

Pharaoh's Pyramid

On the Giza plateau, ten miles west of the city of Cairo, Egypt, stands the Great Pyramid of Cheops. The Amiga reproduces the ancient wonder on your video screen in this solitaire game of skill (Figure 2-4).

Your goal is to remove as many of the 14 square markers as possible. A piece is lifted from play when it's jumped.

To play the game, first choose one of the 14 positions to make blank. Then start to move, with the only legal move a jump.

You're crowned the new pharaoh if you wind up with one piece left at the end of the game. You win a sphinx if two pieces remain. But four left means back to the quarry. And five or more means you've just been entombed.

Figure 2-4. Pharaoh's Pyramid

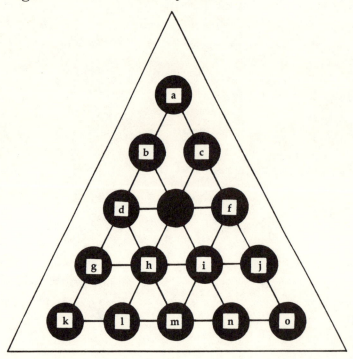

Program 2-4. Pharaoh's Pyramid
Save using the filename **PYRAMID**

```
REM PHARAOH'S PYRAMID
 GOSUB INITIALIZE
PLAYGAME:
 GOSUB PLAY
PLAYAGAIN:
 GOSUB DECIDE
 IF BUTTON = 1 THEN PLAYGAME
 GOSUB GOODBYE
END

INITIALIZE:
 GOSUB SETSCREEN
 GOSUB HOLES
 GOSUB LINES
 GOSUB LEGALMOVES
 GOSUB OUTCOMES
 GOSUB SETMENUS
 GOSUB SETCOLORS
 GOSUB START
RETURN

SETSCREEN:
 SCREEN 1,640,200,3,2
 WINDOW 2,"PHARAOH'S PYRAMID",,0,1
RETURN

HOLES:
 DEFINT A,B,D-Z
 N = 15
 DIM X(N),Y(N),R(N),LM(18,3)
 DIM SQ(70),SQK(70),PYMD(70)
 RANDOMIZE TIMER
 REM Y, & X COORDINATES FOR EACH HOLE (BY ROW)
  DATA 25,   310
  DATA 55,   275,345
  DATA 85,   240,310,380
  DATA 115,  205,275,345,415
  DATA 145,  170,240,310,380,450
  HOLE = 0
  FOR ROW = 1 TO 5
   READ Y
   FOR J=1 TO ROW
    HOLE = HOLE + 1
    READ X(HOLE)
    Y(HOLE) = Y
  NEXT J,ROW
```

```
 REM BUTTON HOLES
   XB(1)=136: YB(1)=39
   XB(2)=136: YB(2)=57
RETURN

LINES:
 DATA 1,11, 3,12, 6,13
 DATA 1,15, 2,14, 4,13
 DATA 4,6, 7,10, 11,15
 FOR I=1 TO 9
   READ LINEFROM(I),LINETO(I)
 NEXT
RETURN

LEGALMOVES:
 REM (from, to, middle)
 REM POSITIVE SLANT
   DATA 1,4,2:    DATA 2,7,4
   DATA 4,11,7:   DATA 3,8,5
   DATA 5,12,8:   DATA 6,13,9
 REM NEGATIVE SLANT
   DATA 1,6,3:    DATA 3,10,6
   DATA 6,15,10:  DATA 2,9,5
   DATA 5,14,9:   DATA 4,13,8
 REM HORIZONTAL
   DATA 11,13,12: DATA 12,14,13
   DATA 13,15,14: DATA 7,9,8
   DATA 8,10,9:   DATA 4,6,5
 FOR I=1 TO 18
   FOR J=1 TO 3
     READ LM(I,J)
 NEXT J,I
RETURN

OUTCOMES:
 DATA "You're the new Pharaoh !"
 DATA "You win a sphinx !"
 DATA "Not too shabby."
 DATA "Back to the quarry, slave."
 DATA "You've just been entombed."
 FOR I=1 TO 5
   READ OUTCOME$(I)
 NEXT
RETURN

SETMENUS:
   DATA 2, Rules, Yes, No
   DATA 5, Pyramid, Yellow, Red, Green, Aqua
   DATA Random
```

```
    DATA 2, Initial Hole, Player Chooses
    DATA Amiga Chooses
    DATA 3, Stop, Go to BASIC
    DATA Go to Games Menu, Go to System
    FOR I=1 TO 4
      READ K
      FOR J=0 TO K
        READ TITLE$
        IF J<>0 THEN TITLE$ = SPACE$(3) + TITLE$
        STATUS = 1
        IF I<>4 AND J=1 THEN STATUS = 2
        MENU I,J,STATUS,TITLE$
      NEXT J,I
      RULES$="ON":PYDCOLOR=1: FIRSTHOLE$="PLAYER"
RETURN

SETCOLORS:
  REM YELLOW, RED, GREEN, AQUA
    DATA .79,.41,.08, .93,.20,0   ,.50,.50,0
    DATA 0,.93,.87
    FOR I=1 TO 4
      FOR J=1 TO 3
        READ CLR(I,J)
    NEXT J,I
  REM YELLOW, LIGHT GREEN, & RED
    PALETTE 4,.79,.41,.08
    PALETTE 5,.25,.9,0
    PALETTE 6,.93,.2,0
RETURN

START:
  MENU ON
  ON MENU GOSUB OPTIONS
  COLOR 4
  AREA (315,40): AREA (195,130): AREA (435,130)
  AREAFILL
  COLOR 2,4
  LOCATE 14,24:PRINT "Pharaoh's Pyramid"
  COLOR 3,2: LOCATE 18,30:PRINT "then"
  COLOR 1,0
  LOCATE 17,24:PRINT "Please use menus,"
  LOCATE 19,23:PRINT "Click mouse to play"
  GOSUB CLICKIT
RETURN

OPTIONS:
  ID = MENU(0): ITEM = MENU(1)
  ON ID GOSUB MENU1, MENU2, MENU3, GOODBYE
  ITEM = 0
RETURN
```

```
MENU1:
 IF ITEM = 1 THEN RULES$="ON" ELSE RULES$="OFF"
 MENU 1,ITEM,2: MENU 1,3-ITEM,1
RETURN

MENU2:
 C1=CLR(ITEM,1): C2=CLR(ITEM,2): C3=CLR(ITEM,3)
 IF ITEM=5 THEN C1=RND: C2=RND: C3=RND
 PALETTE 4,C1,C2,C3
 MENU 2,PYDCOLOR,1: MENU 2,ITEM,2
 PYDCOLOR = ITEM
RETURN

MENU3:
 FIRSTHOLE$ = "PLAYER"
 IF ITEM=2 THEN FIRSTHOLE$ = "AMIGA"
 MENU 3,ITEM,2: MENU 3,3-ITEM,1
RETURN

GOODBYE:
 WINDOW CLOSE 2: WINDOW 1: MENU RESET
 SCREEN CLOSE 1
 IF ITEM = 2 THEN RUN "GAMES"
 IF ITEM = 3 THEN SYSTEM
 COLOR 1,0: CLS
 PRINT "Bye-Bye"
 STOP
RETURN

CLICKIT:
 WHILE MOUSE(0) = 0: WEND: REM CLICK
 X = MOUSE(1)
 Y = MOUSE(2)
 WHILE MOUSE(0)<> 0: WEND: REM RESET
RETURN

PLAY:
 IF RULES$="ON" THEN GOSUB RULES
 GOSUB SETBOARD
 WHILE GAME$ = "ON"
  GOSUB ENTERMOVE
  GOSUB MAKEMOVE
  GOSUB CHECKEND
 WEND
 GOSUB GAMEOVER
RETURN

RULES:
 CLS
```

```
   PRINT
   PRINT "    On the Giza Plateau, ten miles ";
   PRINT "west of the city of Cairo,"
   PRINT " Egypt, stands the Great ";
   PRINT "Pyramid of Cheops.":PRINT
   PRINT " I'm about to fill this ancient ";
   PRINT "wonder with 14 blocks.":PRINT
   PRINT " Try to remove as many as possible, ";
   PRINT "with a piece lifted"
   PRINT " from play when it's jumped."
   LOCATE 20,26:PRINT "Click Mouse";
   GOSUB CLICKIT
RETURN

SETBOARD:
 GOSUB RECORD
 GOSUB PYRAMID
 GOSUB DRAWHOLES
 GOSUB DRAWLINES
 GOSUB MARKERS
 GOSUB FIRSTHOLE
RETURN

RECORD:
 FOR I=1 TO N
  R(I) = 1
 NEXT
 TALLY = 14
 GAME$ = "ON"
RETURN

PYRAMID:
 CLS
 COLOR 4
 AREA (310,3): AREA (110,160): AREA (510,160)
 AREAFILL
RETURN

DRAWHOLES:
 COLOR 2
 FOR I=1 TO N
  X = X(I): Y = Y(I)
  CIRCLE (X,Y),21
  PAINT (X,Y)
 NEXT
RETURN

DRAWLINES:
 FOR I=1 TO 9
```

```
    HOLE1 = LINEFROM(I): HOLE2 = LINETO(I)
    LINE (X(HOLE1),Y(HOLE1))-(X(HOLE2),Y(HOLE2))
  NEXT
RETURN

MARKERS:
  REM BACKGROUND SQUARE
    X1 = 300: X2 = 320
    Y1 = 20:  Y2 = 30
    GET (X1,Y1)-(X2,Y2),SQK
  REM PYRAMID
    COLOR 6
    AREA (310,20): AREA (301,29): AREA (319,29)
    AREAFILL
    GET (X1,Y1)-(X2,Y2),PYMD
    PUT (300,20),SQK,PSET
  REM FIRST SQUARE
    COLOR 1
    LINE (X1+1,Y1+1)-(X2-1,Y2-1),,BF
    GET (X1,Y1)-(X2,Y2),SQ
  REM OTHER SQUARES
    FOR I=2 TO N
      PUT (X(I)-10,Y(I)-5),SQ,PSET
    NEXT
RETURN

FIRSTHOLE:
  HOLE = INT(15*RND)+1
  IF FIRSTHOLE$ = "PLAYER" THEN
    LOCATE 20,26:PRINT "Initial Hole ? ";
    GOSUB USEMOUSE
  END IF
  PUT (X(HOLE)-10,Y(HOLE)-5),SQK,PSET
  R(HOLE) = 0
RETURN

USEMOUSE:
  GOSUB CLICKIT
  REM FIND HOLE
    HOLE = 0: I=1
    WHILE HOLE = 0 AND I <= N
     XD = ABS(X-X(I)): YD = ABS(Y-Y(I))
     IF XD<15 AND YD<15 THEN HOLE=I:X=X(I):Y=Y(I)
     I = I+1
    WEND
    IF HOLE = 0 THEN USEMOUSE
RETURN
```

```
ENTERMOVE:
 GOSUB ENTERPIECE
 GOSUB ENTERHOLE
 GOSUB LEGALITY
 IF MOVE$ = "BAD" THEN
  PUT(XFROM,YFROM),SQ,PSET
  SOUND 900,2
  GOTO ENTERMOVE
 END IF
RETURN

ENTERPIECE:
 LOCATE 20,26:PRINT "Piece to Move ?";
 GOSUB USEMOUSE
 IF R(HOLE) = Ø THEN ENTERPIECE
 XFROM = X-1Ø: YFROM = Y-5: HOLEFROM = HOLE
 PUT(XFROM,YFROM),PYMD,PSET
RETURN

ENTERHOLE:
 LOCATE 20,26:PRINT "Hole to Fill ? ";
 GOSUB USEMOUSE
 IF R(HOLE) <> Ø THEN ENTERHOLE
 XTO = X-1Ø: YTO = Y-5: HOLETO = HOLE
RETURN

LEGALITY:
 MOVE$ = "BAD": I = 1
 H1 = HOLEFROM: H2 = HOLETO
 REM F = From, T = To, M = Middle
 WHILE MOVE$ = "BAD" AND I < 19
  F = LM(I,1): T = LM(I,2): M = LM(I,3)
  IF F=H1 AND T=H2 AND R(M)=1 THEN MOVE$ = "OK"
  IF F=H2 AND T=H1 AND R(M)=1 THEN MOVE$ = "OK"
  I = I+1
 WEND
RETURN

MAKEMOVE:
 PUT (XFROM,YFROM),SQK,PSET
 PUT (X(M)-1Ø,Y(M)-5),SQK,PSET
 PUT (XTO,YTO),SQ,PSET
 R(HOLEFROM) = Ø: R(M) = Ø: R(HOLETO) = 1
 TALLY = TALLY - 1
 GOSUB GURGLE
RETURN
```

```
GURGLE:
 FREQ = 300
 FOR I=1 TO 5
  FREQ = 500-FREQ
  SOUND FREQ,1,50
 NEXT
RETURN

CHECKEND:
 REM F=from; T=to; M=middle
 GAME$ = "OVER": I=1
 WHILE GAME$="OVER" AND I < 19
  F=R(LM(I,1)): T=R(LM(I,2)): M=R(LM(I,3))
  IF F=1 AND T=0 AND M=1 THEN GAME$="ON"
  IF F=0 AND T=1 AND M=1 THEN GAME$="ON"
  I = I+1
 WEND
RETURN

GAMEOVER:
 S1$ = STR$(TALLY)+" LEFT:"
 IF TALLY > 5 THEN TALLY = 5
 S2$ = " " + OUTCOME$(TALLY)
 S$ = S1$+S2$: L = LEN(S$)
 LOCATE 20,26:PRINT SPACE$(14);
 COLOR 3,2
 LOCATE 20,32-L/2:PRINT S1$;
 COLOR 1,0: PRINT S2$;
 FOR PAUSE=1 TO 5000: NEXT
RETURN

DECIDE:
 BUTTON = 0
 GOSUB DRAWBUTTON
 GOSUB PUSHBUTTON
 COLOR 1,0
RETURN

DRAWBUTTON:
 LINE (20,15)-(160,66),2,BF
 COLOR 3,2
 LOCATE 3,4:PRINT "Play Again ?"
 COLOR 1,2
 LOCATE 5,9:PRINT "Yes"
 LOCATE 7,10:PRINT "No"
 FOR I=1 TO 2
  CIRCLE (XB(I),YB(I)),12,4+I
  PAINT (XB(I),YB(I)),4+I
 NEXT
RETURN
```

```
PUSHBUTTON:
 SOUND 440,2
 GOSUB CLICKIT
 FOR I=1 TO 2
  XD = ABS(X-XB(I)): YD = ABS(Y-YB(I))
   IF XD<8 AND YD<8 THEN BUTTON = I: I=2
 NEXT
 IF BUTTON = 0 THEN PUSHBUTTON
RETURN
```

Roman Checkers

Your goal in this exciting game of wits is to line up five of your chariots in a row on an 8 × 8 board before the Amiga lines up five of its pieces, which are replicas of the Pantheon.

Either side goes first, and you and the Amiga alternate turns. You're allowed to place a chariot on any vacant square, no matter what color (Figure 2-5). The first side to get five markers in a row, either vertically, horizontally, or diagonally, wins the contest.

The Amiga plays exceedingly well in this game. After the first couple of turns, it takes about 20 seconds to search the board for an optimal move. You'll have to really think ahead in order to win.

Figure 2-5. Roman Checkers

Program 2-5. Roman Checkers
Save using the filename **ROMAN**

```
REM ROMAN CHECKERS
  GOSUB INITIALIZE
PLAYGAME:
  GOSUB PLAY
PLAYAGAIN:
  LOCATE 20,21: PRINT "Play Again ?";
  GOSUB DECIDE
  IF BUTTON = 1 THEN PLAYGAME
  GOSUB GOODBYE
END

INITIALIZE:
  GOSUB SETSCREEN
  GOSUB KEYVALUES
  GOSUB SETMENUS
  GOSUB SETCOLORS
  GOSUB START
RETURN

SETSCREEN:
  SCREEN 1,640,200,3,2
  WINDOW 2,"Roman Checkers",,0,1
RETURN

KEYVALUES:
  GOSUB FUNCTIONS
  GOSUB ARRAYS
  REM DATA FOR SHAPES
   GOSUB PANTHEON
   GOSUB CHARIOT
RETURN

FUNCTIONS:
  DEFINT A-J,L-Z
  RANDOMIZE TIMER
  DEF FNEVENODD(I,J) = ( (I+J)/2=INT((I+J)/2) )
  DEF FNX(V) = 48*V + 98
  DEF FNY(V) = 20*V - 7
RETURN

ARRAYS:
  DIM B(100),R(100),SQODD(600),SQEVEN(600)
  DIM PTH.X(54),PTH.Y(54),BODY.X(26),BODY.Y(26)
  DIM WHEEL.X(22),WHEEL.Y(22)
  REM VECTOR INDICES
   DATA 1,200,400
```

```
 READ INDEX(Ø),INDEX(1),INDEX(2)
REM BUTTON VALUES
 XB(1)=364: YB(1)=174
 XB(2)=4Ø6: YB(2)=174
 LT$(1) = "Y": LT$(2) = "N"
REM OFF-BOARD SQUARES
 FOR I=1 TO 1Ø
  B(I) = -9: B(9Ø+I) = -9
  B(1Ø*I) = -9: B(1Ø*I-9) = -9
 NEXT
REM RANDOM FIRST MOVES
 DATA 34,37,45,46,55,56,64,67
 FOR I=1 TO 8: READ RM(I): NEXT
REM DIRECTION DELTAS
 DATA 1,9,1Ø,11
 FOR I=1 TO 4: READ DR(I): NEXT
RETURN

PANTHEON:
 DATA Ø,13,-16,Ø,Ø,-1,1,Ø,Ø,-8,1,Ø,Ø,8,1,Ø
 DATA Ø,-8,1,Ø,Ø,8,4,Ø,Ø,-8,1,Ø,Ø,8,1,Ø,Ø,-8
 DATA 1,Ø,Ø,8,4,Ø,Ø,-8,2,Ø,Ø,9,16,Ø,Ø,-1,-1,Ø
 DATA Ø,-8,-1,Ø,Ø,8,-1,Ø,Ø,-8,-1,Ø,Ø,8,-4,Ø
 DATA Ø,-8,-1,Ø,Ø,8,-1,Ø,Ø,-8,-1,Ø,Ø,8,-4,Ø
 DATA Ø,-9,15,Ø,-33,Ø,5,Ø,Ø,-1,23,Ø,-4,Ø,Ø,-1
 DATA -15,Ø,4,Ø,Ø,-1,7,Ø
 FOR I=1 TO 54
  READ PTH.X(I),PTH.Y(I)
 NEXT
RETURN

CHARIOT:
 REM BODY
  DATA Ø,9,16,Ø,Ø,-2,1,Ø,Ø,3,-34,Ø,Ø,-1,16,Ø
  DATA Ø,-1,-15,Ø,Ø,-1,15,Ø,Ø,-1,-13,Ø,4,Ø
  DATA Ø,-1,9,Ø,Ø,-1,-4,Ø,2,Ø,Ø,-1,2,Ø,Ø,-1
  DATA -1,Ø,1,Ø,Ø,-2
  FOR I=1 TO 26
   READ BODY.X(I),BODY.Y(I)
  NEXT
 REM WHEEL
  DATA 5,1,6,1,7,1,8,1,9,1,1Ø,1,2,2,3,2,4,2
  DATA 5,2,1Ø,2,11,2,12,2,13,2,1,3,2,3
  DATA 6,3,7,3,8,3,9,3,13,3,14,3
  FOR I=1 TO 22
   READ WHEEL.X(I),WHEEL.Y(I)
  NEXT
RETURN
```

```
SETMENUS:
  DATA 2, Rules, Yes, No
  DATA 5, Chariot, Brown, Blue, Green
  DATA Purple, Random
  DATA 2, First Move, Amiga, Human
  DATA 3, Stop, Go to BASIC
  DATA Go to Games Menu, Go to System
  FOR I=1 TO 4
   READ N
   FOR J=Ø TO N
    READ TITLE$
    IF J<>Ø THEN TITLE$ = SPACE$(3) + TITLE$
    STATUS = 1
     IF I<>4 AND J=1 THEN STATUS = 2
    MENU I,J,STATUS,TITLE$
  NEXT J,I
  RULES = 1: CHCOLOR = 1: FMOVE = 1
RETURN

SETCOLORS:
 REM BROWN, BLUE, DULL GREEN, PURPLE
  DATA .58,.11,.2,  .2,.Ø9,.8
  DATA .14,.33,.25,  .Ø2,Ø,.45
  FOR I=1 TO 4
   FOR J=1 TO 3
    READ KOLOR(I,J)
  NEXT J,I
 REM GRAY, VIOLET, BROWN, GREEN, & RED
  PALETTE 2,.32,.39,.61
  PALETTE 3,.75,.36,.75
  PALETTE 4,.58,.11,.2
  PALETTE 5,.14,.43,Ø
  PALETTE 6,.93,.2,Ø
RETURN

START:
 MENU ON
 ON MENU GOSUB OPTIONS
 GOSUB DRAWSQUARES
 GOSUB MAKEPIECES
 GOSUB HEADING
RETURN

DRAWSQUARES:
 REM EVEN
  X1=266: Y1=63: X2=313: Y2=82
  LINE (X1,Y1)-(X2,Y2),2,BF
  GET (X1,Y1)-(X2,Y2),SQEVEN(1)
  CALL DRAWIT(5,5,Ø)
```

```
  REM ODD
   X3=314: X4=361
   LINE (X3,Y1)-(X4,Y2),3,BF
   GET (X3,Y1)-(X4,Y2),SQODD(1)
   CALL DRAWIT(5,4,0)
RETURN

SUB DRAWIT(ROW,COL,Z) STATIC
 SHARED SQEVEN(),SQODD(),INDEX()
 IDX = INDEX(Z)
 X = FNX(COL) - 24
 Y = FNY(ROW) - 10
 V = FNEVENODD(ROW,COL)
 IF V = -1 THEN
  PUT(X,Y),SQEVEN(IDX),PSET
 ELSE
  PUT(X,Y),SQODD(IDX),PSET
 END IF
END SUB

MAKEPIECES:
 REM PANTHEON
   CALL MAKEPANTHEON(289,66)
   GET (X1,Y1)-(X2,Y2),SQEVEN(200)
   CALL MAKEPANTHEON(289,86)
   GET (X1,83)-(X2,102),SQODD(200)
 REM CHARIOT
   CALL MAKECHARIOT(337,66)
   GET (X3,Y1)-(X4,Y2),SQODD(400)
   CALL MAKECHARIOT(337,86)
   GET (X3,83)-(X4,102),SQEVEN(400)
RETURN

SUB MAKEPANTHEON(X0,Y0) STATIC
 SHARED PTH.X(),PTH.Y()
 PSET (X0,Y0)
 COLOR 1
 FOR J=1 TO 54
  LINE -STEP(PTH.X(J),PTH.Y(J))
 NEXT
END SUB

SUB MAKECHARIOT(X0,Y0) STATIC
 SHARED BODY.X(),BODY.Y(),WHEEL.X(),WHEEL.Y()
 REM BODY
  PSET (X0,Y0)
  COLOR 4
  FOR J=1 TO 26
   LINE -STEP(BODY.X(J),BODY.Y(J))
```

```
    NEXT
   REM WHEEL (TOP AND BOTTOM)
    COLOR 1
    FOR J=1 TO 22
     X = XØ - 16 + WHEEL.X(J)
     YT= YØ + 7  + WHEEL.Y(J)
     YB= YØ + 14 - WHEEL.Y(J)
     PSET (X,YT)
     PSET (X,YB)
    NEXT
 END SUB

 HEADING:
  COLOR 1,4: LOCATE 18,30:PRINT " then "
  COLOR 1,Ø
  LOCATE 13: PRINT PTAB(243)"Roman Checkers"
  LOCATE 17,24:PRINT "Please use menus,"
  LOCATE 19,23:PRINT "Click mouse to play"
  GOSUB CLICKIT
 RETURN

 OPTIONS:
  ID = MENU(Ø): ITEM = MENU(1)
  ON ID GOSUB MENU1,MENU2,MENU3,GOODBYE
  ITEM = Ø
 RETURN

 MENU1:
  MENU 1,RULES,1: MENU 1,ITEM,2
  RULES = ITEM
 RETURN

 MENU2:
  K1 = KOLOR(ITEM,1): K2 = KOLOR(ITEM,2)
  K3 = KOLOR(ITEM,3)
  IF ITEM=5 THEN K1=RND: K2=RND: K3=RND
  PALETTE 4,K1,K2,K3
  MENU 2,CHCOLOR,1: MENU 2,ITEM,2
  CHCOLOR = ITEM
 RETURN

 MENU3:
  MENU 3,FMOVE,1: MENU 3,ITEM,2
  FMOVE = ITEM
 RETURN

 GOODBYE:
  WINDOW CLOSE 2: WINDOW 1: MENU RESET
  SCREEN CLOSE 1
```

```
 IF ITEM = 2 THEN RUN "GAMES"
 IF ITEM = 3 THEN SYSTEM
 COLOR 1,0: CLS
 PRINT "Bye-Bye"
 STOP
RETURN

CLICKIT:
 S$ = ""
 WHILE MOUSE(0) = 0 AND S$ = ""
  S$ = INKEY$
 WEND
  X = MOUSE(1)
  Y = MOUSE(2)
 WHILE MOUSE(0)<> 0: WEND: REM RESET
RETURN

PLAY:
 IF RULES = 1 THEN GOSUB RULES
 GOSUB RECORD
 GOSUB DRAWBOARD
 WHILE GAME = 0 AND N <> 64
  ON PLAYER GOSUB AMIGA, HUMAN
  GOSUB MAKEMOVE
  GOSUB CHECK.FOR.END
  PLAYER = 3 - PLAYER
 WEND
 GOSUB GAMEOVER
RETURN

RULES:
 CLS
 PRINT
 PRINT
 PRINT "   My marker is the Pantheon, an ancient";
 PRINT " Roman temple.  And"
 PRINT " yours is Caesar's chariot."
 PRINT
 PRINT "   Try to get five of your pieces in a";
 PRINT " row, in any direction,"
 PRINT " before I line up five of mine."
 LOCATE 20,26:PRINT "Click Mouse";
 GOSUB CLICKIT
RETURN

RECORD:
 REM 0 = VACANT; 1 = AMIGA; 2 = HUMAN
 FOR I=1 TO 100
  IF B(I) <> -9 THEN B(I) = 0
 NEXT
```

```
   PLAYER = FMOVE
   GAME = Ø
   N = Ø: REM NUMBER OF MOVES
RETURN

DRAWBOARD:
 CLS
 LINE (121,2)-(5Ø6,163),1,B
 FOR R=1 TO 8
  FOR C=1 TO 8
    CALL DRAWIT(R,C,Ø)
 NEXT C,R
RETURN

AMIGA:
 LOCATE 2Ø,28: PRINT " My turn ... ";
 MOVE = Ø
 IF N <= 2 THEN GOSUB FIRSTMOVES
 IF MOVE=Ø THEN GOSUB RANKBOARD
 IF MOVE=Ø THEN GOSUB CHANCE
 R = INT(MOVE/1Ø): C = MOVE - R*1Ø - 1
RETURN

FIRSTMOVES:
 V = INT(RND*8) + 1
 MOVE = RM(V)
 IF B(MOVE) <> Ø THEN FIRSTMOVES
RETURN

RANKBOARD:
 HPTS = -999
 FOR I=12 TO 89
  IF B(I) = Ø THEN
    GOSUB RANKSQUARE
    IF PTS = HPTS THEN
     IF RND > .5 THEN MOVE = I
    END IF
    IF PTS > HPTS THEN HPTS = PTS: MOVE = I
  END IF
 NEXT I
RETURN

RANKSQUARE:
 FOR J=1 TO 2
  GOSUB SEARCH
 NEXT J
 REM COMPARE
  PTS = SCR(1)
  IF SCR(2) > SCR(1) THEN PTS = SCR(2)
RETURN
```

```
SEARCH:
 SCR(J) = -J
 FOR D=1 TO 4
  T=Ø: DLT = DR(D)
  REM FIRST HALF
   L$ = "ON": SQ = I
   WHILE L$ = "ON"
    SQ = SQ + DLT
    IF B(SQ) = J THEN T=T+1 ELSE L$ = "OFF"
   WEND
   V1 = -(B(SQ) = Ø)
  REM SECOND HALF
   L$ = "ON": SQ = I
   WHILE L$ = "ON"
    SQ = SQ - DLT
    IF B(SQ) = J THEN T=T+1 ELSE L$ = "OFF"
   WEND
   V2 = -(B(SQ) = Ø)
   F = -(T>Ø)
   SCR(J) = SCR(J) + F*V1*V2*3^T - 1ØØØ*(T>=4)
 NEXT D
RETURN

CHANCE:
 REM VACANT SQUARES
  CNT = Ø
  FOR I=12 TO 89
   IF B(I)=Ø THEN CNT=CNT+1:R(CNT)=I
  NEXT
 REM CHOOSE
  V = INT(RND*CNT) + 1
  MOVE = R(V)
RETURN

HUMAN:
  LOCATE 2Ø,28:PRINT "Your turn ...";
  GOSUB CLICKIT
 REM FIND SQUARE (its Row and Column)
  R = INT( (Y-3)/2Ø ) + 1
  C = INT( (X-122)/48 ) + 1
  IF R<1 OR R>8 OR C<1 OR C>8 THEN HUMAN
  MOVE = R*1Ø + C + 1
  IF B(MOVE) <> Ø THEN SOUND 9ØØ,2: GOTO HUMAN
RETURN

MAKEMOVE:
 CALL DRAWIT(R,C,PLAYER)
```

```
   GOSUB GURGLE
   CALL DRAWIT(R,C,Ø)
   FOR PAUSE=1 TO 5ØØ: NEXT PAUSE
   CALL DRAWIT(R,C,PLAYER)
   B(MOVE) = PLAYER
   N = N + 1
RETURN

GURGLE:
 FREQ = 3ØØ
 FOR G=1 TO 5
  FREQ = 5ØØ-FREQ
  SOUND FREQ,1,5Ø
 NEXT G
RETURN

CHECK.FOR.END:
 I = MOVE
 J = PLAYER
 GOSUB SEARCH
 IF SCR(J) > 997 THEN GAME = PLAYER
RETURN

GAMEOVER:
 LOCATE 8,55: PRINT "WINNER:"
 W$ = "Cat"
 IF GAME = 1 THEN W$ = "Me"
 IF GAME = 2 THEN W$ = "You"
 LOCATE 9,55: PRINT W$
 LOCATE 2Ø,28: PRINT SPACE$(13);
RETURN

DECIDE:
 BUTTON = Ø
 GOSUB DRAWBUTTON
 GOSUB PUSHBUTTON
 COLOR 1,Ø
RETURN

DRAWBUTTON:
 LINE (337,167)-(433,181),1,BF
 FOR I=1 TO 2
  CIRCLE (XB(I),YB(I)),12,4+I
  PAINT (XB(I),YB(I)),4+I
  COLOR 1,4+I
  LOCATE 2Ø: PRINT PTAB(XB(I)-4);LT$(I);
 NEXT
RETURN
```

```
PUSHBUTTON:
 SOUND 440,2
 GOSUB CLICKIT
 S$ = UCASE$(S$)
 IF S$ = "Y" THEN BUTTON = 1
 IF S$ = "N" THEN BUTTON = 2
 FOR I=1 TO 2
  XD = ABS(X-XB(I)): YD = ABS(Y-YB(I))
  IF XD<13 AND YD<7 THEN BUTTON = I: I=2
 NEXT
 IF BUTTON = Ø THEN PUSHBUTTON
RETURN
```

Falstaff

Oh, Falstaff! Poor, portly Shakespearean squire;
Just when you've almost won this game,
Your goodly fortune does expire.

You're pitted against the Amiga in this version of what's been called one of the most entertaining games of logic ever invented. Your marker is the diamond and the Amiga's is the disc. The object of each side is to have more pieces on the board at the end of the game than the opponent.

Either side goes first. To move, place a diamond on any vacant square (of either color) so that a string of discs is sandwiched between two of your markers. The discs will turn into diamonds (Figure 2-6).

Note that each move *must* be a capture, and that captures in any direction are allowed so long as you're on a straight line. Press the ESCape key if no such move is available when it's your turn. If the Amiga can't move either, the game ends.

What makes "Falstaff" so exciting is that fortunes can change radically in just one move. You might be enjoying a four-point advantage during most of the game, for example, then the Amiga captures five of your pieces. Well, not only does your count go down by five, but the computer's goes up by the same amount, for a total swing in score of ten points. This can be disastrous if only a couple of moves remain.

The Amiga plays well and aggressively. It uses about 20 seconds to search the board for a good move, and you'll have to think ahead to beat it.

Three versions of the game are available: short, medium, and long. These lengths correspond to the maximum number of moves allowed both sides in total (25, 40, and 60). In the long game, the entire board will eventually fill up with discs and diamonds, assuming, of course, that you and the computer never reach the point where neither can move.

Use the pull-down menus to choose the length of the game and who goes first.

Figure 2-6. Capturing Discs in Falstaff

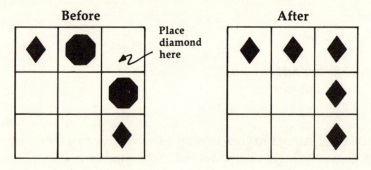

Program 2-6. Falstaff
Save using the filename **FALSTAFF**

```
REM FALSTAFF
 GOSUB INITIALIZE
PLAYGAME:
 GOSUB PLAY
PLAYAGAIN:
 LOCATE 20,21: PRINT "Play Again ?";
 GOSUB DECIDE
 IF BUTTON = 1 THEN PLAYGAME
 GOSUB GOODBYE
END

INITIALIZE:
 GOSUB SETSCREEN
 GOSUB KEYVALUES
 GOSUB SETMENUS
 GOSUB SETCOLORS
 GOSUB START
RETURN

SETSCREEN:
 SCREEN 1,640,200,3,2
 WINDOW 2,"Falstaff",,0,1
RETURN

KEYVALUES:
 GOSUB FUNCTIONS
 GOSUB ARRAYS
 GOSUB XYOFFSETS
 GOSUB DIRECTIONS
RETURN
```

```
FUNCTIONS:
 DEFINT A-J,L-S,U-Z
 RANDOMIZE VAL(RIGHT$(TIME$,2))
 DEF FNEVENODD(I,J) = ( (I+J)/2=INT((I+J)/2) )
 DEF FNX(V) = 48*V + 98
 DEF FNY(V) = 20*V - 7
RETURN

ARRAYS:
 DIM B(9,9),SQODD(600),SQEVEN(600)
 REM VECTOR INDICES
  DATA 1,200,400
  READ INDEX(0),INDEX(1),INDEX(2)
 REM BUTTON VALUES
  XB(1)=364: YB(1)=174
  XB(2)=406: YB(2)=174
  LT$(1) = "Y": LT$(2) = "N"
 REM OFF-BOARD SQUARES
  FOR I=0 TO 9 STEP 9: FOR J=0 TO 9
   B(I,J) = -9: B(J,I) = -9
  NEXT J,I
 REM GAME LENGTH
  DATA 25,40,60
  FOR I=1 TO 3: READ LENGTH(I): NEXT
RETURN

XYOFFSETS:
 REM DISC
  DATA -9,4, 0,5, 9,4, 13,0, 9,-4
  DATA 0,-5, -9,-4
 REM DIAMOND
  DATA -14,7, 0,0, 14,7, 1,0
  DATA 14,-7, 0,0, -14,-7
 FOR I=1 TO 2
  FOR J=1 TO 7
  READ X.OFFSET(I,J),Y.OFFSET(I,J)
 NEXT J,I
RETURN

DIRECTIONS:
 DATA 0,1, -1,1, -1,0, -1,-1
 DATA 0,-1, 1,-1, 1,0, 1,1
 FOR I=1 TO 8
  READ DR(I),DC(I)
 NEXT
RETURN
```

```
SETMENUS:
  DATA 2, Rules, Yes, No
  DATA 5, Diamond, Brown, Blue, Green
  DATA Purple, Random
  DATA 3, Game, Short, Medium, Long
  DATA 2, First Move, Amiga, Human
  DATA 3, Stop, Go to BASIC
  DATA Go to Games Menu, Go to System
  FOR I=1 TO 5
    READ N
    FOR J=Ø TO N
      READ TITLE$
      IF J<>Ø THEN TITLE$ = SPACE$(3) + TITLE$
      STATUS = 1
        IF I<>5 AND J=1 THEN STATUS = 2
      MENU I,J,STATUS,TITLE$
    NEXT J,I
  RULES = 1: DMCOLOR = 1: GAME = 1: FMOVE = 1
RETURN

SETCOLORS:
 REM BROWN, BLUE, DULL GREEN, PURPLE
  DATA .7,.28,.15,   .2,.Ø9,.8
  DATA .14,.43,Ø,   .52,Ø,.57
  FOR I=1 TO 4
    FOR J=1 TO 3
      READ KOLOR(I,J)
  NEXT J,I
 REM LT. BLUE, VIOLET, BROWN, GREEN, & RED
  PALETTE 2,.29,.66,.94
  PALETTE 3,.75,.46,.85
  PALETTE 4,.7,.28,.15
  PALETTE 5,.14,.43,Ø
  PALETTE 6,.93,.2,Ø
RETURN

START:
 MENU ON
 ON MENU GOSUB OPTIONS
 GOSUB DRAWSQUARES
 GOSUB DRAWPIECES
 GOSUB HEADING
RETURN

DRAWSQUARES:
 REM EVEN
  X1=266: Y1=63: X2=313: Y2=82
```

```
    LINE (X1,Y1)-(X2,Y2),2,BF
    GET (X1,Y1)-(X2,Y2),SQEVEN(1)
    CALL DRAWIT(5,5,0)
  REM ODD
    X3=314: X4=361
    LINE (X3,Y1)-(X4,Y2),3,BF
    GET (X3,Y1)-(X4,Y2),SQODD(1)
    CALL DRAWIT(5,4,0)
RETURN

SUB DRAWIT(ROW,COL,Z) STATIC
  SHARED SQEVEN(),SQODD(),INDEX()
  IDX = INDEX(Z)
  X = FNX(COL) - 24
  Y = FNY(ROW) - 10
  V = FNEVENODD(ROW,COL)
  IF V = -1 THEN
   PUT(X,Y),SQEVEN(IDX),PSET
  ELSE
   PUT(X,Y),SQODD(IDX),PSET
  END IF
END SUB

DRAWPIECES:
  REM DISCS
    COLOR 0: X=283: Y=66: I=1: GOSUB SHAPE
    GET (X1,Y1)-(X2,Y2),SQEVEN(200)
    Y=86: GOSUB SHAPE
    GET (X1,83)-(X2,102),SQODD(200)
  REM DIAMONDS
    COLOR 4: X=337: Y=66: I=2: GOSUB SHAPE
    GET (X3,Y1)-(X4,Y2),SQODD(400)
    Y=86: GOSUB SHAPE
    GET (X3,83)-(X4,102),SQEVEN(400)
RETURN

SHAPE:
  AREA (X,Y)
  FOR J=1 TO 7
   AREA STEP(X.OFFSET(I,J),Y.OFFSET(I,J))
  NEXT
  AREAFILL
RETURN

HEADING:
  COLOR 1,4: LOCATE 18,30:PRINT " then "
  COLOR 1,0
```

```
 LOCATE 13: PRINT PTAB(276)"Falstaff"
 LOCATE 17,24:PRINT "Please use menus,"
 LOCATE 19,23:PRINT "Click mouse to play"
 GOSUB CLICKIT
RETURN

OPTIONS:
 ID = MENU(Ø): ITEM = MENU(1)
 ON ID GOSUB MENU1,MENU2,MENU3,MENU4,GOODBYE
 ITEM = Ø
RETURN

MENU1:
 MENU 1,RULES,1: MENU 1,ITEM,2
 RULES = ITEM
RETURN

MENU2:
 K1 = KOLOR(ITEM,1): K2 = KOLOR(ITEM,2)
 K3 = KOLOR(ITEM,3)
 IF ITEM=5 THEN K1=RND: K2=RND: K3=RND
 PALETTE 4,K1,K2,K3
 MENU 2,DMCOLOR,1: MENU 2,ITEM,2
 DMCOLOR = ITEM
RETURN

MENU3:
 MENU 3,GAME,1: MENU 3,ITEM,2
 GAME = ITEM
RETURN

MENU4:
 MENU 4,FMOVE,1: MENU 4,ITEM,2
 FMOVE = ITEM
RETURN

GOODBYE:
 WINDOW CLOSE 2: WINDOW 1: MENU RESET
 SCREEN CLOSE 1
 IF ITEM = 2 THEN RUN "GAMES"
 IF ITEM = 3 THEN SYSTEM
 COLOR 1,Ø: CLS
 PRINT "Bye-Bye"
 STOP
RETURN
```

```
CLICKIT:
 S$ = "": ESC = Ø
 WHILE MOUSE(Ø)=Ø AND S$ = ""
  S$ = INKEY$
 WEND
  X = MOUSE(1)
  Y = MOUSE(2)
 IF S$ <> "" THEN ESC = ASC(S$)
 WHILE MOUSE(Ø)<> Ø: WEND: REM RESET
RETURN

PLAY:
 IF RULES = 1 THEN GOSUB RULES
 GOSUB SETUP
 WHILE GAME$ = "ON" AND MOVES > Ø
  MOVE$ = "ON"
  ON PLAYER GOSUB AMIGA, HUMAN
  IF MOVE$ = "ON" THEN GOSUB MAKEMOVE
  SWAP PLAYER, ENEMY
 WEND
 GOSUB GAMEOVER
RETURN

RULES:
 CLS
 PRINT
 PRINT "    I'm the Disc and you're the Diamond."
 PRINT
 PRINT "    To move, place a Diamond on an empty";
 PRINT " square of either"
 PRINT " color so that a string of my pieces is";
 PRINT " sandwiched between"
 PRINT " two of yours."
 PRINT
 PRINT "    - My Discs will become your Diamonds."
 PRINT
 PRINT "    In the rare event that no capture is";
 PRINT " available when it's"
 PRINT " your turn to move, hit the ESCape key."
 PRINT
 PRINT "    I'll try to 'turn' your pieces just";
 PRINT " as you try to"
 PRINT " 'turn' mine."
 PRINT
 PRINT "    You'll win if you end up with more";
 PRINT " markers than me."
 LOCATE 20,26:PRINT "Click Mouse";
 GOSUB CLICKIT
RETURN
```

```
SETUP:
 GOSUB RECORD
 GOSUB DRAWBOARD
 GOSUB SCORECARD
 GOSUB MOVESCARD
 GOSUB STATUS
RETURN

RECORD:
 REM Ø = VACANT; 1 = AMIGA; 2 = HUMAN
 FOR R=1 TO 8
  FOR C=1 TO 8
   B(R,C) = Ø
 NEXT C,R
 B(4,4)=1: B(4,5)=2
 B(5,4)=2: B(5,5)=1
 SCORE(1)=2: SCORE(2)=2
 MOVES = LENGTH(GAME): GAME$ = "ON"
 PLAYER = FMOVE: ENEMY = 3-PLAYER
 FORFEITS = Ø
RETURN

DRAWBOARD:
 CLS
 LINE (121,2)-(506,163),1,B
 FOR R=1 TO 8
  FOR C=1 TO 8
   CALL DRAWIT(R,C,B(R,C))
 NEXT C,R
RETURN

SCORECARD:
 COLOR 6,1
 LINE (533,15)-(609,54),1,BF
 LOCATE 3,55:PRINT "SCORE:"
 COLOR Ø: LOCATE 5,56: PRINT "Me"
 LOCATE 6,55: PRINT "You"
RETURN

MOVESCARD:
 LINE (21,15)-(95,54),1,BF
 COLOR 6: LOCATE 3,4: PRINT "MOVES:"
RETURN

STATUS:
 REM SCORE
  FOR I=1 TO 2
```

```
      COLOR 1,1: LOCATE I+4,58: PRINT SPACE$(2)
      COLOR 6,1: LOCATE I+4,58: PRINT SCORE(I)
    NEXT
  REM MOVES
    COLOR 1,1: LOCATE 5,5: PRINT SPACE$(2)
    COLOR 6,1: LOCATE 5,5: PRINT MOVES
    COLOR 1,0
RETURN

AMIGA:
  LOCATE 20,28: PRINT " My turn ... ";
  TALLYHOLD = -9
  FOR I=1 TO 8
   FOR J=1 TO 8
    IF B(I,J) = 0 THEN GOSUB SEARCH
  NEXT J,I
  IF TALLYHOLD = 0 THEN GOSUB NOMOVE
RETURN

SEARCH:
  GOSUB TALLYSCORE
  GOSUB ADJUSTSCORE
  GOSUB COMPARESCORE
RETURN

TALLYSCORE:
  TALLY = 0
  FOR L=1 TO 8
   CNT = 0
   R = I: C = J: SEQ$ = "ON"
   WHILE SEQ$ = "ON"
     SEQ$ = "OFF"
     R = R + DR(L)
     C = C + DC(L)
     IF B(R,C) = 2 THEN CNT=CNT+1: SEQ$="ON"
   WEND
   IF B(R,C) = 1 THEN TALLY = TALLY + CNT
  NEXT L
RETURN

ADJUSTSCORE:
  IF I=1 OR I=8 OR J=1 OR J=8 THEN TALLY=2*TALLY
  IF I=2 OR I=7 OR J=2 OR J=7 THEN TALLY=TALLY/2
RETURN
```

```
COMPARESCORE:
  IF TALLY > TALLYHOLD THEN
    TALLYHOLD = TALLY
    ROW = I: COL = J
  END IF
  IF TALLY = TALLYHOLD AND RND > .5 THEN
    ROW = I: COL = J
  END IF
RETURN

NOMOVE:
  IF PLAYER = 1 THEN
    LOCATE 20,10
    PRINT "SORRY: I can't move.";
    PRINT " Click mouse to continue.";
    SOUND 900,2
    GOSUB CLICKIT
    LOCATE 20,10: PRINT SPACE$(45);
  END IF
  MOVE$ = "OFF"
  FORFEITS = FORFEITS + 1
  IF FORFEITS = 2 THEN GAME$ = "OVER"
RETURN

HUMAN:
  GOSUB ENTERSQUARE
  IF ESC = 27 THEN
    GOSUB DOUBLECHECK
    IF BUTTON = 1 THEN GOSUB NOMOVE
    IF BUTTON = 2 THEN GOTO HUMAN
  END IF
  IF MOVE$ = "ON" THEN
    GOSUB CHECKCAPTURE
    IF CAP$="NO" THEN SOUND 900,2: GOTO HUMAN
  END IF
RETURN

ENTERSQUARE:
  LOCATE 20,28:PRINT "Your turn ...";
  GOSUB CLICKIT
  REM FIND SQUARE (its Row and Column)
  R = INT( (Y-3)/20 ) + 1
  C = INT( (X-122)/48 ) + 1
  IF ESC = 0 THEN
    IF R<1 OR R>8 OR C<1 OR C>8 THEN ENTERSQUARE
    IF B(R,C) <> 0 THEN ENTERSQUARE
    ROW = R: COL = C
  END IF
RETURN
```

```
DOUBLECHECK:
 LOCATE 20,28: PRINT SPACE$(13);
 LOCATE 20,19: PRINT "Forfeit Turn ?";
 GOSUB DECIDE
 LOCATE 20,19: PRINT SPACE$(14);
 LINE (337,167)-(433,181),0,BF
RETURN

DECIDE:
 BUTTON = 0
 GOSUB DRAWBUTTON
 GOSUB PUSHBUTTON
 COLOR 1,0
RETURN

DRAWBUTTON:
 LINE (337,167)-(433,181),1,BF
 FOR I=1 TO 2
  CIRCLE (XB(I),YB(I)),12,4+I
  PAINT (XB(I),YB(I)),4+I
  COLOR 1,4+I
  LOCATE 20: PRINT PTAB(XB(I)-4);LT$(I);
 NEXT
RETURN

PUSHBUTTON:
 SOUND 440,2
 GOSUB CLICKIT
 S$ = UCASE$(S$)
 IF S$ = "Y" THEN BUTTON = 1
 IF S$ = "N" THEN BUTTON = 2
 FOR I=1 TO 2
  XD = ABS(X-XB(I)): YD = ABS(Y-YB(I))
  IF XD<13 AND YD<7 THEN BUTTON = I: I=2
 NEXT
 IF BUTTON = 0 THEN PUSHBUTTON
RETURN

CHECKCAPTURE:
 CAP$ = "NO": I=1
 WHILE CAP$ = "NO" AND I<9
  CNT = 0: R = ROW: C = COL: SEQ$ = "ON"
  WHILE SEQ$ = "ON"
   SEQ$ = "OFF"
   R = R + DR(I)
   C = C + DC(I)
   IF B(R,C)=1 THEN CNT=CNT+1: SEQ$ = "ON"
  WEND
  IF B(R,C) = 2 AND CNT>0 THEN CAP$="YES"
```

83

```
   I = I+1
 WEND
RETURN

MAKEMOVE:
 REM INITIAL SQUARE
  R = ROW: C = COL: GOSUB FLASH
  SCORE(PLAYER) = SCORE(PLAYER) + 1
 REM OTHERS
  FOR I=1 TO 8
    CNT = 0
    R = ROW: C = COL: SEQ$ = "ON"
   WHILE SEQ$ = "ON"
    SEQ$ = "OFF"
    R = R + DR(I)
    C = C + DC(I)
    IF B(R,C)=ENEMY THEN CNT=CNT+1: SEQ$="ON"
   WEND
   IF B(R,C)=PLAYER AND CNT>0 THEN GOSUB FLIP
  NEXT I
 REM SHOW SCORE/MOVES
  MOVES = MOVES - 1: FORFEITS = 0
  GOSUB STATUS
RETURN

FLASH:
 CALL DRAWIT(R,C,PLAYER)
 GOSUB GURGLE
 CALL DRAWIT(R,C,0)
 FOR PAUSE=1 TO 500: NEXT PAUSE
 CALL DRAWIT(R,C,PLAYER)
 B(R,C) = PLAYER
RETURN

FLIP:
 R = ROW: C = COL
 FOR J=1 TO CNT
  R = R + DR(I): C = C + DC(I)
  GOSUB FLASH
 NEXT J
 SCORE(PLAYER) = SCORE(PLAYER) + CNT
 SCORE(ENEMY)  = SCORE(ENEMY)  - CNT
RETURN

GURGLE:
 FREQ = 300
 FOR G=1 TO 5
  FREQ = 500-FREQ
```

```
   SOUND FREQ,1,50
  NEXT G
RETURN

GAMEOVER:
  LOCATE 8,55: PRINT "WINNER:"
  W$ = "Cat"
  IF SCORE(1) > SCORE(2) THEN W$ = "Me"
  IF SCORE(1) < SCORE(2) THEN W$ = "You"
  LOCATE 9,55: PRINT W$
  LOCATE 20,28: PRINT SPACE$(13);
RETURN
```

Mosaic Puzzle

Sliding-square puzzles have been challenging minds for years. "Mosaic Puzzle" is an electronic version of those rectangular brainteasers that you may have spent hours trying to figure out. Unlike the plastic version, however, this computer game keeps track of the number of moves you make, and it has numerical aids that you can turn on and off with the click of a mouse. You can even save an uncompleted board to disk and return to it later.

The Amiga draws an octagon, on a 3 × 3 board. Then it scrambles the pieces (Figure 2-7). Your job is to make it whole again.

To move, click the mouse on a piece, and it will slide onto the empty gold square. Vertical and horizontal moves are allowed. But reaching your goal isn't easy. You'll constantly have to think ahead, or you will find yourself rearranging pieces endlessly.

To make things easier, you can use a pull-down menu while the game is in progress to number each piece of the puzzle (1–8). After you're oriented, you can then turn off the numbers. And if you despair of finding a solution, you can save the game to disk and resume play later.

Try playing Mosaic Puzzle with your friends. The player using the fewest moves is the winner.

Figure 2-7. Mosaic Puzzle

Your Goal

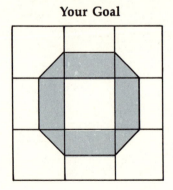

Good Luck!

Program 2-7. Mosaic Puzzle
Save using the filename **MOSAIC**

```
REM MOSAIC PUZZLE
 CLEAR ,40000&
 GOSUB INITIALIZE
PLAYGAME:
 GOSUB PLAY
PLAYAGAIN:
 COLOR 1,0
 LOCATE 20,26: PRINT SPACE$(16);
 LOCATE 20,21: PRINT "Play Again ?";
 X0=337: Y0=167: GOSUB DECIDE
 IF BUTTON = 1 THEN PLAYGAME
 GOSUB GOODBYE
END

INITIALIZE:
 GOSUB SETSCREEN
 GOSUB FUNCTIONS
 GOSUB ARRAYS
 GOSUB SETMENUS
 GOSUB SETCOLORS
 GOSUB START
RETURN

SETSCREEN:
 SCREEN 1,640,200,3,2
 WINDOW 2,"Mosaic Puzzle",,0,1
RETURN

FUNCTIONS:
 DEFINT A-J,L-Z
 RANDOMIZE TIMER
 DEF FNX(V) = 112*V + 33
 DEF FNY(V) = 50*V - 41
RETURN

ARRAYS:
 DIM SQ(11071),NR(1531)
 REM VECTOR INDICES
  FOR I=1 TO 9
   INDEX.SQ(I) = 1 + (I-1)*1230
   INDEX.NR(I) = 1 + (I-1)*170
  NEXT
 REM X COORDINATES FOR NUMBERS
  XN(1)=158: XN(2)=298: XN(3)=438
 REM OFFSETS FOR CIRCLES
  FOR I=1 TO 3
```

```
    YFSET(I) = -13:     YFSET(I+6) = 13
    XFSET(3*I-2) = -28: XFSET(3*I) = 28
  NEXT
 REM BUTTON LETTERS
  LT$(1) = "Y": LT$(2) = "N"
RETURN

SETMENUS:
 DATA 2, Rules, Yes, No
 DATA 5, Washer, Brown, Blue, Green
 DATA Purple, Random
 DATA 2, Aid, Numbers On, Numbers Off
 DATA 4, Stop, Go to BASIC, Go to Games Menu
 DATA Go to System, Save Board
 FOR I=1 TO 4
  READ NUMBER
  FOR J=Ø TO NUMBER
   READ TITLE$
   IF J<>Ø THEN TITLE$ = SPACE$(3) + TITLE$
    STATUS = 1
    IF I < 3 AND J = 1 THEN STATUS = 2
   MENU I,J,STATUS,TITLE$
 NEXT J,I
 MENU 4,4,Ø: MENU 3,Ø,Ø
 RULES = 1: WCOLOR = 1: AID = 2
RETURN

SETCOLORS:
 REM BROWN, BLUE, DULL GREEN, PURPLE
  DATA .58,.11,.2,   .2,.Ø9,.8
  DATA .14,.33,.25,  .Ø2,Ø,.45
  FOR I=1 TO 4
   FOR J=1 TO 3
    READ KOLOR(I,J)
  NEXT J,I
 REM VIOLET, GOLD, BROWN, GREEN, & RED
  PALETTE 2,.75,.36,.75
  PALETTE 3,.99,.4,.Ø3
  PALETTE 4,.58,.11,.2
  PALETTE 5,.14,.43,Ø
  PALETTE 6,.93,.2,Ø
RETURN

START:
 MENU ON
 ON MENU GOSUB OPTIONS
 CALL OCTAGON(246,58,45,18)
 GOSUB HEADING
RETURN
```

```
SUB OCTAGON(X1,Y1,XD,YD) STATIC
 X2 = X1+3*XD: Y2 = Y1+3*YD
 LINE (X1,Y1)-(X2,Y2),2,BF
 REM WASHER
  COLOR 4
  AREA (X1+XD,Y1+YD/2)
  AREA STEP(-XD/2,YD/2): AREA STEP(0,YD)
  AREA STEP(XD/2,YD/2): AREA STEP(XD,0)
  AREA STEP(XD/2,-YD/2): AREA STEP(0,-YD)
  AREA STEP(-XD/2,-YD/2): AREAFILL
 REM HOLE
  LINE (X1+XD,Y1+YD)-(X2-XD,Y2-YD),3,BF
 REM GRID
  COLOR 1
  FOR I = X1 TO X2 STEP XD
   LINE (I,Y1)-(I,Y2)
  NEXT
  FOR I = Y1 TO Y2 STEP YD
   LINE (X1,I)-(X2,I)
  NEXT
END SUB

HEADING:
 COLOR 1,4: LOCATE 18,30:PRINT " then "
 COLOR 1,0
 LOCATE 14: PRINT PTAB(249)"Mosaic Puzzle"
 LOCATE 17,24:PRINT "Please use menus,"
 LOCATE 19,23:PRINT "Click mouse to play"
 GOSUB CLICKIT
RETURN

OPTIONS:
 ID = MENU(0): ITEM = MENU(1)
 ON ID GOSUB MENU1,MENU2,MENU3,GOODBYE
 ITEM = 0
RETURN

MENU1:
 MENU 1,RULES,1: MENU 1,ITEM,2
 RULES = ITEM
RETURN

MENU2:
 K1 = KOLOR(ITEM,1): K2 = KOLOR(ITEM,2)
 K3 = KOLOR(ITEM,3)
 IF ITEM=5 THEN K1=RND: K2=RND: K3=RND
 PALETTE 4,K1,K2,K3
 MENU 2,WCOLOR,1: MENU 2,ITEM,2
 WCOLOR = ITEM
RETURN
```

```
MENU3:
 MENU 3,AID,1: MENU 3,ITEM,2
 AID = ITEM
 INDEX = INDEX.NR(5)
 REM DRAW OR ERASE
  FOR L=1 TO 3
   FOR M=1 TO 3
    V = B(L,M)
    IF AID = 1 THEN INDEX = INDEX.NR(V)
    X.C = FNX(M)+38+XFSET(V)
    Y.C = FNY(L)+17+YFSET(V)
    IF V <> 5 THEN PUT(X.C,Y.C),NR(INDEX),PSET
  NEXT M,L
RETURN

GOODBYE:
 COLOR 1,Ø
 IF ITEM = 4 THEN GOSUB ASK.TO.SAVE
 WINDOW CLOSE 2: WINDOW 1: MENU RESET
 SCREEN CLOSE 1
 IF ITEM = 2 THEN RUN "GAMES"
 IF ITEM = 3 THEN SYSTEM
 CLS
 PRINT "Bye-Bye"
 IF ITEM = 4 AND BUTTON = 1 THEN
  PRINT FILE$;" is saved."
 END IF
 STOP
RETURN

ASK.TO.SAVE:
 CLS
 LOCATE 7,15
 PRINT "Would you like to save your board ?"
 XØ=265: YØ=68: GOSUB DECIDE
 IF BUTTON = 1 THEN GOSUB SAVEGAME
RETURN

DECIDE:
 BUTTON = Ø
 GOSUB DRAWBUTTON
 GOSUB PUSHBUTTON
 COLOR 1,Ø
RETURN

DRAWBUTTON:
 ROW = (YØ+13)/9
 XB(1)=XØ+27: XB(2)=XØ+69: YB=YØ+7
 LINE (XØ,YØ)-(XØ+96,YØ+14),1,BF
```

```
    FOR I=1 TO 2
      CIRCLE (XB(I),YB),12,4+I
      PAINT (XB(I),YB),4+I
      COLOR 1,4+I
      LOCATE ROW: PRINT PTAB(XB(I)-4);LT$(I);
    NEXT
RETURN

PUSHBUTTON:
  SOUND 440,2
  GOSUB CLICKIT
  S$ = UCASE$(S$)
  IF S$ = "Y" THEN BUTTON = 1
  IF S$ = "N" THEN BUTTON = 2
  FOR I=1 TO 2
    XD = ABS(X-XB(I)): YD = ABS(Y-YB)
    IF XD<13 AND YD<7 THEN BUTTON = I: I=2
  NEXT
  IF BUTTON = 0 THEN PUSHBUTTON
RETURN

SAVEGAME:
  SOUND 440,2
  LOCATE 13,15
  INPUT "File name: ";FILE$
  IF FILE$="" THEN SAVEGAME
  REM SAVE DATA
    OPEN "O",#1,FILE$
    WRITE #1,MOVES,RGOLD,CGOLD
    FOR R=1 TO 3
      FOR C=1 TO 3
        WRITE #1,B(R,C)
    NEXT C,R
    CLOSE
RETURN

CLICKIT:
  S$ = ""
  WHILE MOUSE(0) = 0 AND S$ = ""
    S$ = INKEY$
  WEND
  X = MOUSE(1)
  Y = MOUSE(2)
  WHILE MOUSE(0)<> 0: WEND: REM RESET
RETURN

PLAY:
  MENU 3,0,0
  IF RULES = 1 THEN GOSUB RULES
```

```
 GOSUB CHECK.FOR.OLD.GAME
 ON BUTTON GOSUB OLDGAME, NEWGAME
 GOSUB DRAWBOARD
 GOSUB MOVESCARD
 WHILE GAME$ = "ON"
  GOSUB ENTERMOVE
  GOSUB MAKEMOVE
  GOSUB CHECK.FOR.END
 WEND
RETURN

RULES:
 CLS
 PRINT
 PRINT "    This 3x3 square holds an eight-sided";
 PRINT " washer, or octagon."
 PRINT
 PRINT "    I'm going to scramble the pieces";
 PRINT " of the washer, and"
 PRINT " your job is to make it whole again,";
 PRINT " just like you see here."
 CALL OCTAGON(246,58,45,18)
 LOCATE 15,1
 PRINT "    When play begins, 'click' a piece";
 PRINT " and it will slide"
 PRINT " onto the empty (gold) square.";
 PRINT "   Vertical and horizontal"
 PRINT " moves are allowed.  If you'd like,";
 PRINT " I'll number the squares"
 PRINT " to help you."
 LOCATE 20,27:PRINT "Click Mouse";
 GOSUB CLICKIT
RETURN

CHECK.FOR.OLD.GAME:
 CLS
 LOCATE 7,18
 PRINT "Are you resuming an old game ?"
 X0=265: Y0=68: GOSUB DECIDE
RETURN

OLDGAME:
 SOUND 440,2
 LOCATE 13,18
 INPUT "File name: ";FILE$
 IF FILE$="" THEN OLDGAME
 REM READ DATA
  OPEN "I",#1,FILE$
  INPUT #1,MOVES,RGOLD,CGOLD
```

```
    FOR R=1 TO 3
     FOR C=1 TO 3
       INPUT #1,B(R,C)
     NEXT C,R
     CLOSE
  RETURN

  NEWGAME:
   LOCATE 12,27: PRINT "Scrambling ..."
   FOR I=1 TO 9: Y(I) = -9: NEXT
   REM RANDOM INTEGERS
    FOR I=1 TO 9
     SEARCH$ = "ON"
     WHILE SEARCH$ = "ON"
      V = INT(9*RND) + 1
      IF Y(V) = -9 THEN Y(V) = I: SEARCH$="OFF"
     WEND
    NEXT
   REM RECORD
    CNT = 1
    FOR R=1 TO 3
     FOR C=1 TO 3
      B(R,C) = Y(CNT)
      IF Y(CNT) = 5 THEN RGOLD=R: CGOLD=C
      CNT = CNT + 1
     NEXT C,R
    MOVES = Ø
  RETURN

  DRAWBOARD:
   CLS
   CALL OCTAGON(145,9,112,5Ø)
   GOSUB GETPIECES
   GOSUB NUMBERS
   COLOR 1,3
   LOCATE 9: PRINT PTAB(295)"Your"
   LOCATE 1Ø: PRINT PTAB(295)"Goal"
   COLOR 1,Ø
   LOCATE 2Ø,27: PRINT "Click Mouse";
   GOSUB CLICKIT
   GOSUB GAMEBOARD
  RETURN

  GETPIECES:
   FOR R=1 TO 3
    FOR C=1 TO 3
     X = FNX(C): Y = FNY(R)
     CNT = (R-1)*3 + C
     INX = INDEX.SQ(CNT)
```

93

```
    GET(X,Y)-(X+112,Y+50),SQ(INX)
  NEXT C,R
RETURN

NUMBERS:
  REM BLANK SQUARE
  GET(155,13)-(191,29),NR(INDEX.NR(5))
  FOR R=1 TO 3
   FOR C=1 TO 3
    X0 = FNX(C) + 56: Y0 = FNY(R) + 25
    N = (R-1)*3 + C
    IF N <> 5 THEN
     COLOR 6
     X = X0+XFSET(N): Y = Y0+YFSET(N)
     CIRCLE (X,Y),18: PAINT (X,Y)
     COLOR 1,6
     REM NUMBER
      LOCATE 7*R-4: PRINT PTAB(XN(C));N
      GET(X-18,Y-8)-(X+18,Y+8),NR(INDEX.NR(N))
    END IF
  NEXT C,R
RETURN

GAMEBOARD:
  CLS
  FOR R=1 TO 3
   FOR C=1 TO 3
    CALL DRAWIT(R,C,B(R,C))
  NEXT C,R
  GAME$ = "ON"
  MENU 3,0,1: MENU 3,AID,2: MENU 4,4,1
RETURN

SUB DRAWIT(ROW,COL,Z) STATIC
  SHARED SQ(),NR(),INDEX.SQ(),INDEX.NR()
  SHARED XFSET(),YFSET(),AID
  ISQ = INDEX.SQ(Z)
  INR = INDEX.NR(Z)
  X = FNX(COL)
  Y = FNY(ROW)
  PUT(X,Y),SQ(ISQ),PSET
  IF AID = 1 AND Z <> 5 THEN
   PUT(X+38+XFSET(Z),Y+17+YFSET(Z)),NR(INR),PSET
  END IF
END SUB

MOVESCARD:
  LINE (21,15)-(95,49),1,BF
  COLOR 6,1: LOCATE 3,4: PRINT "MOVES:"
```

```
    LOCATE 5,4: PRINT MOVES
  RETURN

  ENTERMOVE:
    COLOR 1,Ø
    LOCATE 2Ø,26:PRINT "Select piece ...";
    GOSUB CLICKIT
   REM FIND SQUARE (its Row and Column)
    R1 = INT( (Y-9)/5Ø ) + 1
    C1 = INT( (X-145)/112 ) + 1
    IF R1<1 OR R1>3 OR C1<1 OR C1>3 THEN
     SOUND 9ØØ,2
     GOTO ENTERMOVE
    END IF
    IF B(R1,C1)=5 THEN SOUND 9ØØ,2: GOTO ENTERMOVE
   REM CHECK LEGALITY
    MOVE$ = ""
    RD = RGOLD-R1: CD = CGOLD-C1
    IF ABS(RD)=1 AND CD=Ø THEN MOVE$="OK"
    IF ABS(CD)=1 AND RD=Ø THEN MOVE$="OK"
    IF MOVE$ = "" THEN SOUND 9ØØ,2: GOTO ENTERMOVE
  RETURN

  MAKEMOVE:
   PIECE = B(R1,C1)
   CALL DRAWIT(R1,C1,5)
   GOSUB GURGLE
   CALL DRAWIT(RGOLD,CGOLD,PIECE)
   B(R1,C1) = 5: B(RGOLD,CGOLD) = PIECE
   RGOLD = R1: CGOLD = C1
   MOVES = MOVES + 1
   COLOR 6,1
   LOCATE 5,4: PRINT MOVES
  RETURN

  GURGLE:
   FREQ = 3ØØ
   FOR G=1 TO 5
    FREQ = 5ØØ-FREQ
    SOUND FREQ,1,5Ø
   NEXT G
  RETURN

  CHECK.FOR.END:
   GAME$ = "OVER"
   FOR R=1 TO 3
    FOR C=1 TO 3
     IF B(R,C) <> (R-1)*3+C THEN GAME$ = "ON"
   NEXT C ,R
  RETURN
```

Hi-Q

"Hi-Q" is a peg game of thought and skillful movement. Thirty-two pegs appear on a cross-shaded board, with only the center position empty (Figure 2-8). By jumping one peg over another, a piece is removed from the board. Your goal is to remove as many pegs as possible.

You get a perfect score in Hi-Q if only one peg remains. It's somewhat like pitching a shutout. The ultimate thrill is leaving the one peg in the center of the board; that's like a no-hitter.

To make a move, click the mouse on the peg of your choice. Then click the mouse on the square where you'd like the peg to go. Every move must be a jump, and only horizontal and vertical leaps are allowed.

One of the nice features of this game is that you can undo your last move simply by using one of the pull-down menus.

Figure 2-8. Hi-Q Game Board

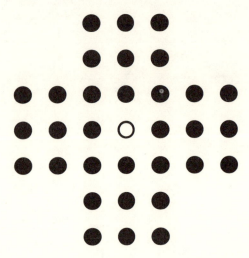

Program 2-8. Hi-Q
Save using the filename **HI-Q**

```
REM HI-Q
 GOSUB INITIALIZE
PLAYGAME:
 GOSUB PLAY
```

```
PLAYAGAIN:
 GOSUB DECIDE
 IF BUTTON = 1 THEN PLAYGAME
 GOSUB GOODBYE
END

INITIALIZE:
 GOSUB SETSCREEN
 GOSUB KEYVALUES
 GOSUB OUTCOMES
 GOSUB SETMENUS
 GOSUB SETCOLORS
 GOSUB START
RETURN

SETSCREEN:
 SCREEN 1,640,200,3,2
 WINDOW 2,"HI-Q",,0,1
RETURN

KEYVALUES:
 DEFINT A-J,L-Z
 RANDOMIZE VAL(RIGHT$(TIME$,2))
 DEF FNHX(V) = 53*V + 100
 DEF FNHY(V) = 23*V - 7
 DIM B(9,9),PEG(70),PEGK(70),CROSS(70)
 REM BUTTON HOLES
  XB(1)=81: YB(1)=85
  XB(2)=81: YB(2)=102
 REM OFF-BOARD SQUARES
  FOR R=1 TO 7
   FOR C=1 TO 7
    IF C<3 OR C>5 THEN
     IF R<3 OR R>5 THEN B(R,C) = -9
    END IF
   NEXT C,R
  FOR I=8 TO 9: FOR J=1 TO 9
   B(I,J) = -9: B(J,I) = -9
  NEXT J,I
RETURN

OUTCOMES:
 DATA "You're a genius !"
 DATA "Superb play; I'm impressed !"
 DATA "Not bad."
 DATA "You can do better than that."
 DATA "Gobble, gobble, turkey."
 FOR I=1 TO 5
  READ OUTCOME$(I)
```

```
  NEXT
RETURN

SETMENUS:
  DATA 2, Rules, Yes, No
  DATA 5, Board, Yellow, Violet, Green
  DATA Sky Blue, Random
  DATA 1, Last Move, Un-do
  DATA 3, Stop, Go to BASIC
  DATA Go to Games Menu, Go to System
  FOR I=1 TO 4
   READ K
   FOR J=0 TO K
    READ TITLE$
    IF J<>0 THEN TITLE$ = SPACE$(3) + TITLE$
    STATUS = 1
      IF I<3 AND J=1 THEN STATUS = 2
      IF I=3 AND J=1 THEN STATUS = 0
    MENU I,J,STATUS,TITLE$
  NEXT J,I
  RULES = 1: BRDCOLOR = 1
RETURN

SETCOLORS:
 REM YELLOW, VIOLET, GREEN, SKY BLUE
  DATA 0.79,0.41,0.08, 0.97,0.32,0.96
  DATA 0.50,0.50,0,    0.29,0.66,0.94
  FOR I=1 TO 4
   FOR J=1 TO 3
     READ KOLOR(I,J)
  NEXT J,I
 REM TAN, YELLOW, LIGHT GREEN, & RED
  PALETTE 3,.95,.7,.53
  PALETTE 4,.79,.41,.08
  PALETTE 5,.25,.9,0
  PALETTE 6,.93,.2,0
RETURN

START:
 MENU ON
 ON MENU GOSUB OPTIONS
 COLOR 4
 LINE (258,30)-(368,120),,BF
 LINE (208,53)-(418,97),,BF
 COLOR 2,4
 LOCATE 9: PRINT PTAB(296)"Hi-Q"
 COLOR 3,2: LOCATE 18,30:PRINT " then "
 COLOR 1,0
 LOCATE 17,24:PRINT "Please use menus,"
```

```
      LOCATE 19,23:PRINT "Click mouse to play"
      GOSUB CLICKIT
   RETURN

   OPTIONS:
      ID = MENU(Ø): ITEM = MENU(1)
      ON ID GOSUB MENU1, MENU2, MENU3, GOODBYE
      ITEM = Ø
   RETURN

   MENU1:
      RULES = ITEM
      MENU 1,ITEM,2: MENU 1,3-ITEM,1
   RETURN

   MENU2:
      K1 = KOLOR(ITEM,1): K2 = KOLOR(ITEM,2)
      K3 = KOLOR(ITEM,3)
      IF ITEM=5 THEN K1=RND: K2=RND: K3=RND
      PALETTE 4,K1,K2,K3
      MENU 2,BRDCOLOR,1: MENU 2,ITEM,2
      BRDCOLOR = ITEM
   RETURN

   MENU3:
      CALL XY(R1HOLD,C1HOLD): PUT(X,Y),PEG,PSET
      CALL XY(RMHOLD,CMHOLD): PUT(X,Y),PEG,PSET
      CALL XY(R2HOLD,C2HOLD): PUT(X,Y),PEGK,PSET
      B(R1HOLD,C1HOLD) = 1: B(RMHOLD,CMHOLD) = 1
      B(R2HOLD,C2HOLD) = Ø
      PEGS = PEGS + 1
      MENU 3,1,Ø
   RETURN

   GOODBYE:
      WINDOW CLOSE 2: WINDOW 1: MENU RESET
      SCREEN CLOSE 1
      IF ITEM = 2 THEN RUN "GAMES"
      IF ITEM = 3 THEN SYSTEM
      COLOR 1,Ø: CLS
      PRINT "Bye-Bye"
      STOP
   RETURN

   CLICKIT:
      WHILE MOUSE(Ø) = Ø: WEND: REM CLICK
      X = MOUSE(1)
      Y = MOUSE(2)
      WHILE MOUSE(Ø)<> Ø: WEND: REM RESET
   RETURN
```

```
PLAY:
 IF RULES = 1 THEN GOSUB RULES
 GOSUB SETBOARD
 WHILE GAME$ = "ON"
  GOSUB ENTERMOVE
  GOSUB MAKEMOVE
  GOSUB CHECKEND
 WEND
 GOSUB GAMEOVER
RETURN

RULES:
 CLS
 PRINT
 PRINT "    I'm about to place 32 pegs on a ";
 PRINT "cross-shaped board, with"
 PRINT " the center empty.":PRINT
 PRINT "    Try to remove as many pegs as ";
 PRINT "possible, with a peg lifted "
 PRINT " from the board when it's jumped."
 LOCATE 20,26:PRINT "Click Mouse";
 GOSUB CLICKIT
RETURN

SETBOARD:
 GOSUB RECORD
 GOSUB DRAWCROSS
 GOSUB DRAWHOLES
 GOSUB DRAWLINES
 GOSUB MARKERS
RETURN

RECORD:
 REM 1 = Filled; Ø = Vacant
 FOR R=1 TO 7
  FOR C=1 TO 7
   IF B(R,C) <> -9 THEN B(R,C) = 1
 NEXT C,R
 B(4,4) = Ø: REM CENTER
 PEGS = 32
 GAME$ = "ON"
RETURN

DRAWCROSS:
 CLS
 COLOR 4
 LINE (219,3)-(407,166),,BF
 LINE (124,47)-(502,123),,BF
RETURN
```

```
DRAWHOLES:
 COLOR 2
 FOR R=1 TO 7
  FOR C=1 TO 7
   X = FN HX(C): Y = FN HY(R)
   IF B(R,C) <> -9 THEN
    CIRCLE (X,Y),19
    PAINT (X,Y)
   END IF
 NEXT C,R
RETURN

DRAWLINES:
 REM VERTICAL
  FOR C=1 TO 7
   ROW1 = 1: ROW2 = 7
   IF B(1,C) = -9 THEN ROW1 = 3: ROW2 = 5
   X = FNHX(C): Y1 = FNHY(ROW1): Y2 = FNHY(ROW2)
   LINE (X,Y1)-(X,Y2)
  NEXT
 REM HORIZONTAL
  FOR R=1 TO 7
   COL1 = 1: COL2 = 7
   IF B(R,1) = -9 THEN COL1 = 3: COL2 = 5
   Y = FNHY(R): X1 = FNHX(COL1): X2 = FNHX(COL2)
   LINE (X1,Y)-(X2,Y)
  NEXT
RETURN

MARKERS:
 REM BLANK
  X = FNHX(3): Y = FNHY(1)
  X1=X-12: X2=X+12: Y1=Y-5: Y2=Y+5
  GET (X1,Y1)-(X2,Y2),PEGK
 REM CROSS
  LINE (X-5,Y-5)-(X+5,Y+5),6,BF
  LINE (X-11,Y-2)-(X+11,Y+2),6,BF
  GET (X1,Y1)-(X2,Y2),CROSS
  PUT (X1,Y1),PEGK,PSET
 REM PEG
  CIRCLE (X,Y),10,3: PAINT (X,Y),3
  GET (X1,Y1)-(X2,Y2),PEG
 REM DRAW PEGS
  FOR R=1 TO 7
   FOR C=1 TO 7
    IF B(R,C) = 1 THEN
     CALL XY(R,C): PUT(X,Y),PEG,PSET
    END  IF
```

```
   NEXT C,R
   COLOR 1
RETURN

SUB XY(ROW,COL) STATIC
 SHARED X,Y
 X = FNHX(COL) - 12
 Y = FNHY(ROW) - 5
END SUB

ENTERMOVE:
 GOSUB ENTERPIECE
 GOSUB ENTERHOLE
 GOSUB LEGALITY
 IF MOVE$ = "BAD" THEN
  CALL XY(R1,C1): PUT(X,Y),PEG,PSET
  BEEP
  GOTO ENTERMOVE
 END IF
RETURN

ENTERPIECE:
 LOCATE 20,26:PRINT "Piece to Move ?";
 GOSUB USEMOUSE
 IF B(R,C) = 0 THEN ENTERPIECE
 MENU 3,1,0: REM TURN OFF 'UN-DO LAST MOVE'
 CALL XY(R,C): PUT (X,Y),CROSS,PSET
 R1 = R: C1 = C
RETURN

USEMOUSE:
  GOSUB CLICKIT
 REM FIND SQUARE (its Row and Column)
  R = INT( (Y-4.5)/23 ) + 1
  C = INT( (X-126.5)/53 ) + 1
 REM CHECK FOR ON BOARD
  SQ$ = "BAD"
  IF C>2 AND C<6 AND R>0 AND R<8 THEN SQ$="OK"
  IF R>2 AND R<6 AND C>0 AND C<8 THEN SQ$="OK"
  IF SQ$ = "BAD" THEN USEMOUSE
RETURN

ENTERHOLE:
 LOCATE 20,26:PRINT "Hole to Fill ? ";
 GOSUB USEMOUSE
 IF B(R,C) <> 0 THEN ENTERHOLE
 R2 = R: C2 = C
RETURN
```

```
LEGALITY:
 MOVE$ = "BAD"
 RM = R1 - (R1-R2)/2
 CM = C1 - (C1-C2)/2
 IF B(RM,CM) = 1 THEN
  IF R1=R2 AND ABS(C1-C2)=2 THEN MOVE$="OK"
  IF C1=C2 AND ABS(R1-R2)=2 THEN MOVE$="OK"
 END IF
RETURN

MAKEMOVE:
 CALL XY(R1,C1): PUT(X,Y),PEGK,PSET
 CALL XY(RM,CM): PUT(X,Y),PEGK,PSET
 CALL XY(R2,C2): PUT(X,Y),PEG,PSET
 B(R1,C1) = 0: B(RM,CM) = 0: B(R2,C2) = 1
 PEGS = PEGS - 1
 GOSUB GURGLE
 REM REMEMBER IT
  R1HOLD=R1: C1HOLD=C1: R2HOLD=R2: C2HOLD=C2
  RMHOLD=RM: CMHOLD=CM
  MENU 3,1,1
RETURN

GURGLE:
 FREQ = 300
 FOR I=1 TO 5
  FREQ = 500-FREQ
  SOUND FREQ,1,50
 NEXT
RETURN

CHECKEND:
 GAME$ = "OVER": R = 0
 WHILE GAME$ = "OVER" AND R < 8
  R = R + 1: C = 0
  WHILE GAME$ = "OVER" AND C < 8
   C = C + 1
   REM HORIZONTAL CHECK
    IF B(R,C+1) = 1 THEN
     IF B(R,C)=1 AND B(R,C+2)=0 THEN GAME$="ON"
     IF B(R,C)=0 AND B(R,C+2)=1 THEN GAME$="ON"
    END IF
   REM VERTICAL CHECK
    IF B(R+1,C) = 1 THEN
     IF B(R,C)=1 AND B(R+2,C)=0 THEN GAME$="ON"
     IF B(R,C)=0 AND B(R+2,C)=1 THEN GAME$="ON"
    END IF
  WEND
 WEND
RETURN
```

103

```
GAMEOVER:
 MENU 3,1,0
 S1$ = STR$(PEGS)+" LEFT:"
 IF PEGS > 5 THEN PEGS = 5
 S2$ = " " + OUTCOME$(PEGS)
 S$ = S1$+S2$: L = LEN(S$)
 LOCATE 20,26:PRINT SPACE$(14);
 COLOR 3,2
 LOCATE 20,32-L/2:PRINT S1$;
 COLOR 1,0: PRINT S2$;
 FOR PAUSE=1 TO 5000: NEXT
RETURN

DECIDE:
 BUTTON = 0
 GOSUB DRAWBUTTON
 GOSUB PUSHBUTTON
 COLOR 1,0
RETURN

DRAWBUTTON:
 LINE (10,47)-(105,112),2,BF
 COLOR 3,2
 LOCATE 7,3:PRINT "Play"
 LOCATE 8,3:PRINT "Again ?"
 COLOR 1,2
 LOCATE 10,3:PRINT "Yes"
 LOCATE 12,4:PRINT "No"
 FOR I=1 TO 2
   CIRCLE (XB(I),YB(I)),12,4+I
   PAINT (XB(I),YB(I)),4+I
 NEXT
RETURN

PUSHBUTTON:
 SOUND 440,2
 GOSUB CLICKIT
 FOR I=1 TO 2
   XD = ABS(X-XB(I)): YD = ABS(Y-YB(I))
   IF XD<12 AND YD<7 THEN BUTTON = I: I=2
 NEXT
 IF BUTTON = 0 THEN PUSHBUTTON
RETURN
```

Solitaire Checkers

A challenging contest of logic, "Solitaire Checkers" places 48 pieces around the edges of an 8 × 8 board. You try to eliminate as many as possible by leaping over the checkers diagonally, just as in the traditional board game.

Removing all but 11 or 12 checkers is relatively easy. Ending up with only a handful requires the insight of a mathematician and the foresight of a soothsayer.

To make a move, first click the mouse on the piece you want to move. It will change shape before your very eyes. Next, click the mouse on a vacant square. Every move must be a jump, and only diagonal leaps are permitted (Figure 2-9).

If you decide to jump a checker and then change your mind, don't worry. Simply enter an illegal position as the destination square. The Amiga will buzz at you for a few seconds, but that's all. You can then make your desired move. Furthermore, just like in the game of Hi-Q, you can always undo your last move.

Figure 2-9. Jumping in Solitaire Checkers

Before

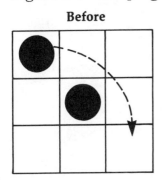

After

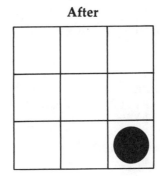

Program 2-9. Solitaire Checkers
Save using the filename **SOLITAIRE**

```
REM SOLITAIRE CHECKERS
 GOSUB INITIALIZE
PLAYGAME:
 GOSUB PLAY
PLAYAGAIN:
```

```
    GOSUB DECIDE
    IF BUTTON = 1 THEN PLAYGAME
    GOSUB GOODBYE
  END

  INITIALIZE:
    GOSUB SETSCREEN
    GOSUB KEYVALUES
    GOSUB RATINGS
    GOSUB SETMENUS
    GOSUB SETCOLORS
    GOSUB START
  RETURN


  SETSCREEN:
    SCREEN 1,640,200,3,2
    WINDOW 2,"Solitaire Checkers",,0,1
  RETURN


  KEYVALUES:
    DEFINT A-J,L-Z
    RANDOMIZE TIMER
    DEF FNEVENODD(I,J) = ( (I+J)/2=INT((I+J)/2) )
    DEF FNX(V) = 48*V + 98
    DEF FNY(V) = 20*V - 7
    DIM B(9,9),SQODD(600),SQEVEN(600)
    REM ARRAY INDICES
    DATA 1,200,400
    READ INDEX(0),INDEX(1),INDEX(2)
    REM BUTTON HOLES
    XB(1)=81: YB(1)=85
    XB(2)=81: YB(2)=102
    REM OFF-BOARD SQUARES
    FOR I=0 TO 9 STEP 9: FOR J=0 TO 9
      B(I,J) = -9: B(J,I) = -9
    NEXT J,I
    REM X & Y OFFSETS FOR CHECKER
    DATA -9,4, 0,5, 9,4, 13,0, 9,-4
    DATA 0,-5, -9,-4
    FOR I=1 TO 7
      READ XFSET(I),YFSET(I)
    NEXT
  RETURN


  RATINGS:
    DATA Magician, Master, Journeyman
    DATA Apprentice, Novice, Turkey
    FOR I=1 TO 6
      READ RANK$(I)
```

```
   NEXT
RETURN

SETMENUS:
  DATA 2, Rules, Yes, No
  DATA 5, Checker, Brown, Blue, Green
  DATA Purple, Random
  DATA 1, Last Move, Un-do
  DATA 3, Stop, Go to BASIC
  DATA Go to Games Menu, Go to System
  FOR I=1 TO 4
   READ K
   FOR J=0 TO K
    READ TITLE$
    IF J<>0 THEN TITLE$ = SPACE$(3) + TITLE$
    STATUS = 1
      IF I<3 AND J=1 THEN STATUS = 2
      IF I=3 AND J=1 THEN STATUS = 0
    MENU I,J,STATUS,TITLE$
   NEXT J,I
  RULES = 1: CKCOLOR = 1
RETURN

SETCOLORS:
 REM BROWN, BLUE, DULL GREEN, PURPLE
  DATA .7,.28,.15,   .2,.09,.8
  DATA .14,.43,0,   .52,0,.57
  FOR I=1 TO 4
   FOR J=1 TO 3
    READ KOLOR(I,J)
  NEXT J,I
 REM LT. BLUE, VIOLET, BROWN, GREEN, & RED
  PALETTE 2,.29,.66,.94
  PALETTE 3,.75,.46,.85
  PALETTE 4,.7,.28,.15
  PALETTE 5,.14,.43,0
  PALETTE 6,.93,.2,0
RETURN

START:
 MENU ON
 ON MENU GOSUB OPTIONS
 COLOR 4
 AREA(269,30): AREA(208,55): AREA(208,95)
 AREA(269,120): AREA(357,120): AREA(418,95)
 AREA(418,55): AREA(357,30)
 AREAFILL
 COLOR 1,4
 LOCATE 9: PRINT PTAB(224)"Solitaire Checkers"
```

```
   COLOR 1: LOCATE 18,30:PRINT " then "
   COLOR 1,0
   LOCATE 17,24:PRINT "Please use menus,"
   LOCATE 19,23:PRINT "Click mouse to play"
   GOSUB CLICKIT
RETURN

OPTIONS:
  ID = MENU(0): ITEM = MENU(1)
  ON ID GOSUB MENU1, MENU2, MENU3, GOODBYE
  ITEM = 0
RETURN

MENU1:
  RULES = ITEM
  MENU 1,ITEM,2: MENU 1,3-ITEM,1
RETURN

MENU2:
  K1 = KOLOR(ITEM,1): K2 = KOLOR(ITEM,2)
  K3 = KOLOR(ITEM,3)
  IF ITEM=5 THEN K1=RND: K2=RND: K3=RND
  PALETTE 4,K1,K2,K3
  MENU 2,CKCOLOR,1: MENU 2,ITEM,2
  CKCOLOR = ITEM
RETURN

MENU3:
  CALL DRAWIT(R1HOLD,C1HOLD,1)
  CALL DRAWIT(RMHOLD,CMHOLD,1)
  CALL DRAWIT(R2HOLD,C2HOLD,0)
  B(R1HOLD,C1HOLD) = 1: B(RMHOLD,CMHOLD) = 1
  B(R2HOLD,C2HOLD) = 0
  CHECKERS = CHECKERS + 1
  MENU 3,1,0
RETURN

GOODBYE:
  WINDOW CLOSE 2: WINDOW 1: MENU RESET
  SCREEN CLOSE 1
  IF ITEM = 2 THEN RUN "GAMES"
  IF ITEM = 3 THEN SYSTEM
  COLOR 1,0: CLS
  PRINT "Bye-Bye"
  STOP
RETURN

CLICKIT:
  WHILE MOUSE(0) = 0: WEND: REM CLICK
```

```
 X = MOUSE(1)
 Y = MOUSE(2)
 WHILE MOUSE(Ø)<> Ø: WEND: REM RESET
RETURN

PLAY:
 IF RULES = 1 THEN GOSUB RULES
 GOSUB SETBOARD
 WHILE GAME$ = "ON"
  GOSUB ENTERMOVE
  GOSUB MAKEMOVE
  GOSUB CHECKEND
 WEND
 GOSUB GAMEOVER
RETURN

RULES:
 CLS
 PRINT
 PRINT "    I'm going to place 48 markers";
 PRINT " on the outer two borders"
 PRINT " of a standard-sized checker board."
 PRINT
 PRINT "    Try to remove as many pieces as you";
 PRINT " can.": PRINT
 PRINT "    A checker is lifted from play";
 PRINT " when it's jumped diagonally,"
 PRINT " just like in the regular game."
 LOCATE 20,26:PRINT "Click Mouse";
 GOSUB CLICKIT
RETURN

SETBOARD:
 GOSUB RECORD
 GOSUB EVENSQUARE
 GOSUB ODDSQUARE
 GOSUB DRAWBOARD
RETURN

RECORD:
 REM 1 = Filled; Ø = Vacant
 FOR R=1 TO 8
  FOR C=1 TO 8
   V = 1
    IF R>2 AND R<7 AND C>2 AND C<7 THEN V=Ø
   B(R,C) = V
 NEXT C,R
 CHECKERS = 48
 GAME$ = "ON"
RETURN
```

```
EVENSQUARE:
 CLS
 REM BACKGROUND
  X1=122: Y1=3: X2=169: Y2=22
  LINE (X1,Y1)-(X2,Y2),2,BF
  GET (X1,Y1)-(X2,Y2),SQEVEN(1)
 REM BOX
  LINE (132,7)-(159,18),6,BF
  LINE (136,9)-(155,16),1,BF
  LINE (142,11)-(149,14),0,BF
  GET (X1,Y1)-(X2,Y2),SQEVEN(400)
 REM CHECKER
  CALL DRAWIT(1,1,0)
  X=139: Y=6: GOSUB CREATEPIECE
  GET (X1,Y1)-(X2,Y2),SQEVEN(200)
RETURN

SUB DRAWIT(ROW,COL,Z) STATIC
 SHARED SQEVEN(),SQODD(),INDEX()
 IDX = INDEX(Z)
 X = FNX(COL) - 24
 Y = FNY(ROW) - 10
 V = FNEVENODD(ROW,COL)
 IF V = -1 THEN
  PUT(X,Y),SQEVEN(IDX),PSET
 ELSE
  PUT(X,Y),SQODD(IDX),PSET
 END IF
END SUB

CREATEPIECE:
 COLOR 4: AREA (X,Y)
 FOR I=1 TO 7
  AREA STEP(XFSET(I),YFSET(I))
 NEXT
 AREAFILL
RETURN

ODDSQUARE:
 REM BACKGROUND
  X3=170: X4=217
  LINE (X3,Y1)-(X4,Y2),3,BF
  GET (X3,Y1)-(X4,Y2),SQODD(1)
 REM BOX
  LINE (180,7)-(207,18),6,BF
  LINE (184,9)-(203,16),1,BF
  LINE (190,11)-(197,14),0,BF
  GET (X3,Y1)-(X4,Y2),SQODD(400)
 REM CHECKER
```

```
   CALL DRAWIT(1,2,0)
   X=187: Y=6: GOSUB CREATEPIECE
   GET (X3,Y1)-(X4,Y2),SQODD(200)
RETURN

DRAWBOARD:
 LINE (121,2)-(506,163),1,B
 FOR R=1 TO 8
  FOR C=1 TO 8
    INDEX = B(R,C)
    CALL DRAWIT(R,C,INDEX)
 NEXT C,R
 COLOR 1
RETURN

ENTERMOVE:
 GOSUB ENTERPIECE
 GOSUB ENTERHOLE
 GOSUB LEGALITY
 IF MOVE$ = "BAD" THEN
  CALL DRAWIT(R1,C1,1)
  SOUND 900,2
  GOTO ENTERMOVE
 END IF
RETURN

ENTERPIECE:
 LOCATE 20,26:PRINT "Piece to Move ?";
 GOSUB USEMOUSE
 IF B(R,C) = 0 THEN ENTERPIECE
 MENU 3,1,0: REM TURN OFF 'UN-DO LAST MOVE'
 CALL DRAWIT(R,C,2)
 R1 = R: C1 = C
RETURN

USEMOUSE:
  GOSUB CLICKIT
 REM FIND SQUARE (its Row and Column)
  R = INT( (Y-3)/20 ) + 1
  C = INT( (X-122)/48 ) + 1
  IF R<1 OR R>8 OR C<1 OR C>8 THEN USEMOUSE
RETURN

ENTERHOLE:
 LOCATE 20,26:PRINT "Hole to Fill ? ";
 GOSUB USEMOUSE
 IF B(R,C) <> 0 THEN ENTERHOLE
 R2 = R: C2 = C
RETURN
```

```
LEGALITY:
 MOVE$ = "BAD"
 RM = R1 - (R1-R2)/2
 CM = C1 - (C1-C2)/2
 IF ABS(R1-R2)=2 AND ABS(C1-C2)=2 THEN
  IF B(RM,CM) = 1 THEN MOVE$ = "OK"
 END IF
RETURN

MAKEMOVE:
 CALL DRAWIT(R1,C1,Ø)
 CALL DRAWIT(RM,CM,Ø)
 CALL DRAWIT(R2,C2,1)
 B(R1,C1) = Ø: B(RM,CM) = Ø: B(R2,C2) = 1
 CHECKERS = CHECKERS - 1
 GOSUB GURGLE
 REM REMEMBER IT
  R1HOLD=R1: C1HOLD=C1: R2HOLD=R2: C2HOLD=C2
  RMHOLD=RM: CMHOLD=CM
  MENU 3,1,1
RETURN

GURGLE:
 FREQ = 3ØØ
 FOR I=1 TO 5
  FREQ = 5ØØ-FREQ
  SOUND FREQ,1,5Ø
 NEXT
RETURN

CHECKEND:
 GAME$ = "OVER": R = 1
 WHILE GAME$ = "OVER" AND R <= 6
  C = 1
  WHILE GAME$ = "OVER" AND C <= 8
   REM NEGATIVE SLANT
    IF B(R+1,C+1) = 1 THEN
     IF B(R,C)=1 AND B(R+2,C+2)=Ø THEN GAME$="ON"
     IF B(R,C)=Ø AND B(R+2,C+2)=1 THEN GAME$="ON"
    END IF
   REM POSITIVE SLANT
    IF B(R+1,C-1) = 1 THEN
     IF B(R,C)=1 AND B(R+2,C-2)=Ø THEN GAME$="ON"
     IF B(R,C)=Ø AND B(R+2,C-2)=1 THEN GAME$="ON"
    END IF
    C = C + 1
  WEND
   R = R + 1
 WEND
RETURN
```

```
GAMEOVER:
 MENU 3,1,0
 S1$ = STR$(CHECKERS) + " LEFT"
 RANK = INT(CHECKERS/2)
 IF RANK > 6 THEN RANK = 6
 S2$ = "  Rank: " + RANK$(RANK)
 S$ = S1$ + S2$
 LOCATE 20,26: PRINT SPACE$(14);
 COLOR 0,1
 LOCATE 20,32-LEN(S$)/2: PRINT S1$;
 COLOR 1,0: PRINT S2$;
 FOR PAUSE=1 TO 5000: NEXT
RETURN

DECIDE:
 BUTTON = 0
 GOSUB DRAWBUTTON
 GOSUB PUSHBUTTON
 COLOR 1,0
RETURN

DRAWBUTTON:
 LINE (10,47)-(105,112),1,BF
 COLOR 0,1
 LOCATE 7,3:PRINT "Play"
 LOCATE 8,3:PRINT "Again ?"
 LOCATE 10,3:PRINT "Yes"
 LOCATE 12,4:PRINT "No"
 FOR I=1 TO 2
  CIRCLE (XB(I),YB(I)),12,4+I
  PAINT (XB(I),YB(I)),4+I
 NEXT
RETURN

PUSHBUTTON:
 SOUND 440,2
 GOSUB CLICKIT
 FOR I=1 TO 2
  XD = ABS(X-XB(I)): YD = ABS(Y-YB(I))
  IF XD<12 AND YD<7 THEN BUTTON = I: I=2
 NEXT
 IF BUTTON = 0 THEN PUSHBUTTON
RETURN
```

Bunny's and Piglet's Tic-Tac-Toe

Play against the Amiga in this delightful version of an old favorite. The computer is the Piglet, and you're the Bunny. Try to get three of your markers in a row, in any direction, before the Piglet gets three of his.

Two versions of the game are available: Easy and Hard. The easy version is recommended for beginners, such as children in grammar school and adults who've never played before.

In the hard version the computer plays a perfect game. This doesn't mean that you'll always lose, but you will have to play perfectly to win.

Use a pull-down menu to select a version. To make a move, simply click the mouse on a vacant square.

Finally, the game uses some nice animation. Both the Piglet and the Bunny dance, and children will love to see this.

Program 2-10. Bunny's and Piglet's Tic-Tac-Toe
Save using the filename **TTT**

```
REM BUNNY'S AND PIGLET'S TIC-TAC-TOE
  GOSUB INITIALIZE
PLAYGAME:
  GOSUB PLAY
PLAYAGAIN:
  LOCATE 20,21: PRINT "Play Again ? ";
  GOSUB DECIDE
  IF BUTTON = 1 THEN PLAYGAME
  GOSUB GOODBYE
END

INITIALIZE:
  GOSUB SETSCREEN
  GOSUB KEYVALUES
  GOSUB SETMENUS
  GOSUB SETCOLORS
  GOSUB DRAWSHAPES
  GOSUB HEADING
RETURN

SETSCREEN:
  SCREEN 1,640,200,3,2
  TITLE$ = "Bunny's and Piglet's Tic-Tac-Toe"
```

```
      WINDOW 2,TITLE$,,0,1
   RETURN

   KEYVALUES:
    DEFINT A-Z
    RANDOMIZE TIMER
    DEF FNX(V) = V*124 + 31
    DEF FNY(V) = V*52 - 41
    DIM SHAPE(2501),R(49)
    REM VECTOR INDICES
     FOR I=1 TO 4
       INDEX(I) = 1 + (I-1)*625
     NEXT
    REM BUTTON HOLES & LETTERS
     XB(1)=364: YB(1)=174
     XB(2)=406: YB(2)=174
     LT$(1) = "Y": LT$(2) = "N"
    REM OFF-BOARD SQUARES
     FOR I=1 TO 14
       R(I) = -9: R(I+35) = -9
     NEXT
     FOR I=15 TO 29 STEP 7
       R(I) = -9: R(I+1) = -9
       R(I+5) = -9: R(I+6) = -9
     NEXT
    REM DIRECTION DELTAS
     DATA 1,6,7,8
     FOR I=1 TO 4: READ DR(I): NEXT
    REM WINNER
     DATA Nobody, Bunny, Piglet
     FOR I=0 TO 2: READ W$(I): NEXT
   RETURN

   SETMENUS:
    DATA 2, Rules, Yes, No
    DATA 2, Game, Easy, Hard
    DATA 2, First Move, Bunny (Amiga), Piglet (You)
    DATA 3, Stop, Go to BASIC
    DATA Go to Games Menu, Go to System
    FOR I=1 TO 4
     READ NUMBER
     FOR J=0 TO NUMBER
      READ TITLE$
      IF J<>0 THEN TITLE$ = SPACE$(3) + TITLE$
      STATUS = 1
       IF I<>4 AND J=1 THEN STATUS = 2
      MENU I,J,STATUS,TITLE$
    NEXT J,I
    RULES = 1: DIFF.GAME = 1: FMOVE = 1
   RETURN
```

```
SETCOLORS:
 REM GRAY, PINK, FLESH, RED, BLUE
   PALETTE 3,.32,.39,.61
   PALETTE 4,1,.51,.64
   PALETTE 5,1,.87,.73
   PALETTE 6,.93,.2,Ø
   PALETTE 7,.4,.6,1
RETURN

DRAWSHAPES:
 MENU ON
 ON MENU GOSUB OPTIONS
 GOSUB DRAWBOX
 GOSUB BUNNY1
 GOSUB BUNNY2
 GOSUB PIGLET1
 GOSUB PIGLET2
 GOSUB GETSHAPES
RETURN

DRAWBOX:
 LINE(188,3Ø)-(438,13Ø),3,BF
 LINE(3Ø9,3Ø)-(317,13Ø),1,BF
 LINE(188,78)-(438,82),1,BF
RETURN

BUNNY1:
 REM SHIRT
  XØ=38Ø: YØ=53
  CALL DRAWLINE(4,XØ,YØ,67)
  PAINT(XØ,YØ+3): PAINT(XØ+12,YØ+1)
  CALL DRAWPOINT(2,XØ,YØ,11)
 REM PANTS
  CALL DRAWLINE(7,XØ+6,YØ+7,34)
  PAINT(XØ,YØ+1Ø)
  CALL DRAWPOINT(2,XØ,YØ,5)
 REM FEET
  CALL DRAWLINE(5,XØ+8,YØ+14,17)
  PAINT(XØ+11,YØ+16)
  CALL DRAWPOINT(2,XØ,YØ,5)
  CALL DRAWLINE(5,XØ-1,YØ+15,18)
  PAINT(XØ-16,YØ+15)
  CALL DRAWPOINT(2,XØ,YØ,3)
 REM HANDS
  CALL DRAWLINE(5,XØ+16,YØ+6,14)
  CALL DRAWLINE(5,XØ-19,YØ+4,17)
 REM FACE
  CALL DRAWLINE(5,XØ,YØ-2,7Ø)
  PAINT(XØ,YØ-7): PAINT(XØ-4,YØ-13)
```

116

```
   CALL DRAWLINE(4,X0+5,Y0-12,14)
   CALL DRAWLINE(4,X0-7,Y0-12,6)
   CALL DRAWLINE(4,X0+2,Y0-6,4)
   CALL DRAWPOINT(2,X0,Y0,2)
   CALL DRAWPOINT(2,X0,Y0,2)
   CALL DRAWPOINT(2,X0,Y0,2)
   CALL DRAWLINE(1,X0+7,Y0+6,9)
RETURN

SUB DRAWLINE(K,X.C,Y.C,T) STATIC
 COLOR K
 PSET(X.C,Y.C)
 FOR I=1 TO T
   READ X,Y
   LINE -STEP(X,Y)
 NEXT
END SUB

SUB DRAWPOINT(K,X.C,Y.C,T) STATIC
 COLOR K
 FOR I=1 TO T
   READ X,Y
   PSET(X.C+X,Y.C+Y)
 NEXT
END SUB

BUNNY2:
 X0=246: Y0=107
 REM SHIRT
   CALL DRAWLINE(4,X0,Y0,73)
   PAINT(X0+4,Y0): PAINT(X0-13,Y0-6)
   PAINT(X0-6,Y0-4)
   CALL DRAWPOINT(2,X0,Y0,4)
 REM PANTS
   CALL DRAWLINE(7,X0+2,Y0+3,42)
   PAINT(X0+6,Y0+5)
   CALL DRAWPOINT(2,X0,Y0,5)
 REM FEET
   CALL DRAWLINE(5,X0+12,Y0+12,13)
   CALL DRAWLINE(5,X0-7,Y0+6,29)
   PAINT(X0-12,Y0+7)
   CALL DRAWPOINT(2,X0,Y0,5)
 REM HANDS
   CALL DRAWLINE(5,X0+17,Y0-8,36)
   PAINT(X0+25,Y0-13)
   CALL DRAWLINE(5,X0-17,Y0-8,28)
   PAINT(X0-25,Y0-11)
 REM HEAD
   CALL DRAWLINE(5,X0-1,Y0-3,51)
```

```
   PAINT(XØ+3,YØ-6)
  REM NOSE
   CALL DRAWLINE(4,XØ-2,YØ-8,6)
  REM MOUTH
   CALL DRAWLINE(2,XØ+1,YØ-5,6)
  REM EYE (& EYEBALL)
   CALL DRAWLINE(3,XØ+4,YØ-8,3)
   CALL DRAWLINE(2,XØ+2,YØ-8,1)
  REM EARS
   CALL DRAWLINE(4,XØ+9,YØ-11,5)
   CALL DRAWLINE(4,XØ+3,YØ-11,5)
  REM TAIL
   CALL DRAWLINE(1,XØ+11,YØ+4,4)
RETURN

PIGLET1:
  REM BOTTOM
   XØ=246: YØ=56
   CALL DRAWLINE(4,XØ,YØ,70)
   PAINT(XØ-6,YØ+3)
   CALL DRAWPOINT(2,XØ,YØ,13)
  REM TAIL
   CALL DRAWPOINT(1,XØ-21,YØ+3,14)
  REM VEST
   CALL DRAWLINE(7,XØ,YØ-1,53)
   PAINT(XØ+4,YØ-2)
   CALL DRAWPOINT(2,XØ,YØ,4)
  REM ARMS
   CALL DRAWLINE(4,XØ+7,YØ-1,18)
   PAINT(XØ+11,YØ-2)
   CALL DRAWLINE(4,XØ+22,YØ-4,7)
   CALL DRAWPOINT(2,XØ,YØ,4)
   CALL DRAWPOINT(2,XØ,YØ,2)
  REM HEAD
   CALL DRAWLINE(4,XØ,YØ-8,49)
   PAINT(XØ+8,YØ-11): PAINT(XØ-3,YØ-11)
   CALL DRAWLINE(5,XØ+17,YØ-8,9)
   CALL DRAWPOINT(2,XØ+17,YØ-8,14)
RETURN

PIGLET2:
  XØ=380: YØ=107
  REM BOTTOM
   CALL DRAWLINE(4,XØ,YØ+2,84)
   PAINT(XØ,YØ+5): PAINT(XØ+13,YØ+4)
   CALL DRAWPOINT(2,XØ,YØ,13)
  REM TAIL
   CALL DRAWPOINT(1,XØ-20,YØ+6,14)
  REM VEST
```

```
   CALL DRAWLINE(7,XØ,YØ+1,45)
   PAINT(XØ+4,YØ-1)
   CALL DRAWPOINT(2,XØ,YØ,5)
  REM ARMS
   CALL DRAWLINE(4,XØ+2,YØ-1,15)
   PAINT(XØ+6,YØ-2)
   CALL DRAWLINE(4,XØ+13,YØ-6,11)
   CALL DRAWPOINT(2,XØ,YØ,4)
  REM HEAD
   CALL DRAWLINE(4,XØ-2,YØ-4,57)
   PAINT(XØ-4,YØ-8): PAINT(XØ-18,YØ-7)
   CALL DRAWPOINT(2,XØ,YØ,9)
  REM SNOOT
   CALL DRAWLINE(5,XØ+1,YØ-9,8)
   PAINT(XØ+4,YØ-9)
   CALL DRAWPOINT(2,XØ,YØ,4)
 RETURN

GETSHAPES:
 GET(345,33)-(415,73),SHAPE(INDEX(1))
 GET(211,33)-(281,73),SHAPE(INDEX(2))
 GET(211,87)-(281,127),SHAPE(INDEX(3))
 GET(345,87)-(415,127),SHAPE(INDEX(4))
 RETURN

HEADING:
 COLOR 1,Ø
 LOCATE 17,24:PRINT "Please use menus,"
 LOCATE 19,23:PRINT "Click mouse to play"
 GOSUB CLICKIT
 RETURN

OPTIONS:
 ID = MENU(Ø): ITEM = MENU(1)
 ON ID GOSUB MENU1, MENU2, MENU3, GOODBYE
 ITEM = Ø
 RETURN

MENU1:
 MENU 1,RULES,1: MENU 1,ITEM,2
 RULES = ITEM
 RETURN

MENU2:
 MENU 2,DIFF.GAME,1: MENU 2,ITEM,2
 DIFF.GAME = ITEM
 RETURN
```

```
MENU3:
 MENU 3,FMOVE,1: MENU 3,ITEM,2
 FMOVE = ITEM
RETURN

GOODBYE:
 WINDOW CLOSE 2: WINDOW 1: MENU RESET
 SCREEN CLOSE 1
 IF ITEM = 2 THEN RUN "GAMES"
 IF ITEM = 3 THEN SYSTEM
 COLOR 1,0: CLS
 PRINT "Bye-Bye"
 STOP
RETURN

CLICKIT:
 S$ = ""
 WHILE MOUSE(0) = 0 AND S$ = ""
  S$ = INKEY$
 WEND
  X = MOUSE(1)
  Y = MOUSE(2)
 WHILE MOUSE(0)<> 0: WEND: REM RESET
RETURN

PLAY:
 IF RULES = 1 THEN GOSUB RULES
 GOSUB DRAWBOARD
 GOSUB RECORD
 WHILE GAME = 0 AND N <> 9
  ON PLAYER GOSUB AMIGA, HUMAN
  GOSUB MAKEMOVE
  GOSUB CHECK.FOR.END
  PLAYER = 3 - PLAYER
 WEND
 GOSUB GAMEOVER
RETURN

RULES:
 CLS
 PRINT
 PRINT "    I'm the Bunny.  And you're the";
 PRINT " Piglet.  Try to get"
 PRINT
 PRINT " three in a row before I do."
 LOCATE 20,26:PRINT "Click Mouse";
 GOSUB CLICKIT
RETURN
```

```
DRAWBOARD:
 CLS
 X1=128: X2=500: Y1=5: Y2=161
 LINE(X1,Y1)-(X2,Y2),3,BF
 REM GRID
  FOR I=1 TO 2
   LINE(I*124+126,Y1)-(I*124+130,Y2),1,BF
   LINE(X1,I*52+4)-(X2,I*52+6),1,BF
  NEXT
RETURN

RECORD:
 REM VACANT = 0: BUNNY = 1: PIGLET = 2
 FOR I=1 TO 49
  IF R(I) <> -9 THEN R(I) = 0
 NEXT
 DIFFICULTY = DIFF.GAME: MENU 2,0,0
 PLAYER = FMOVE: MENU 3,0,0
 GAME = 0
 N = 0: REM NUMBER OF MOVES
RETURN

AMIGA:
 MOVE = 0: HPTS = -999
 LOCATE 20,28: PRINT " My turn ... ";
 FOR I=17 TO 33
  IF R(I) = 0 THEN
   GOSUB RANKSQUARE
   IF PTS = HPTS AND RND > .8 THEN MOVE = I
   IF PTS > HPTS THEN HPTS = PTS: MOVE = I
  END IF
 NEXT I
 GOSUB CONVERT
RETURN

CONVERT:
 R = INT((MOVE-1)/7) + 1: C = MOVE - (R-1)*7
 R = R-2: C = C-2
RETURN

RANKSQUARE:
 PTS = -999
 FOR J=1 TO 2
  SCORE = -J
  GOSUB SCORE
  IF SCORE > PTS THEN PTS = SCORE
 NEXT J
RETURN
```

```
SCORE:
 FOR D=1 TO 4
  T=Ø: K=Ø: DLT = DR(D)
  REM FIRST HALF
   SQ = I
   FOR L=1 TO 2
    SQ = SQ + DLT
    IF R(SQ) = J OR R(SQ) = Ø THEN K = K+1
    IF R(SQ) = J THEN T = T+1
   NEXT L
  REM SECOND HALF
   SQ = I
   FOR L=1 TO 2
    SQ = SQ - DLT
    IF R(SQ) = J OR R(SQ) = Ø THEN K = K+1
    IF R(SQ) = J THEN T = T+1
   NEXT L
  REM RANK
   S1 = -(T=2)*1ØØØ:            REM 3-IN-ROW
   S2 = -(T=1 AND K=2)*1ØØ: REM 2-ON-A-ROW, BLANK
   S2 = -(DIFFICULTY = 2)*S2
   SCORE = SCORE + S1 + S2
 NEXT D
 REM CORNER SQUARE
  S3 = -(I=17 OR I=19 OR I=31 OR I=33)*125
  S3 = -(DIFFICULTY = 2)*S3
  SCORE = SCORE + S3
RETURN

HUMAN:
 SOUND 9ØØ,2
 LOCATE 2Ø,28: PRINT "Your turn ...";
 GOSUB CLICKIT
 R = INT( (Y-5)/52 ) + 1
 C = INT( (X-128)/124 ) + 1
 IF R<1 OR R>3 OR C<1 OR C>3 THEN HUMAN
 MOVE = (R+1)*7 + C+2
 IF R(MOVE) <> Ø THEN HUMAN
RETURN

MAKEMOVE:
 GOSUB FLASH
 R(MOVE) = PLAYER
 N = N + 1
RETURN

FLASH:
 X = FNX(C)
 Y = FNY(R)
```

122

```
   FOR FLASH = 1 TO 3
     GOSUB GURGLE
     PUT(X,Y),SHAPE(INDEX(PLAYER+2)),PSET
     FOR PAUSE=1 TO 1000: NEXT PAUSE
     PUT(X,Y),SHAPE(INDEX(PLAYER)),PSET
     FOR PAUSE=1 TO 1000: NEXT PAUSE
   NEXT FLASH
 RETURN

 GURGLE:
  FREQ = 300
  FOR G=1 TO 3
   FREQ = 500-FREQ
   SOUND FREQ,1,50
  NEXT G
 RETURN

 CHECK.FOR.END:
  SQUARE(3) = MOVE
  FOR D=1 TO 4
   T=0: DLT = DR(D)
   REM FIRST HALF
    SQ = MOVE
    FOR L=1 TO 2
     SQ = SQ + DLT
     IF R(SQ) = PLAYER THEN T=T+1: SQUARE(T) = SQ
    NEXT L
   REM SECOND HALF
    SQ = MOVE
    FOR L=1 TO 2
     SQ = SQ - DLT
     IF R(SQ) = PLAYER THEN T=T+1: SQUARE(T) = SQ
    NEXT L
   IF T = 2 THEN GAME = PLAYER: D = 4
  NEXT D
 RETURN

 GAMEOVER:
  LOCATE 5,54: PRINT "Winner:"
  LOCATE 6,54: PRINT W$(GAME)
  LOCATE 20,28: PRINT SPACE$(13);
  MENU 2,0,1: MENU 3,0,1
  IF GAME <> 0 THEN GOSUB VICTORY.DANCE
 RETURN

 VICTORY.DANCE:
  REM SORT
   FOR I=1 TO 2
    FOR J=1 TO 2
```

```
     IF SQUARE(J+1) < SQUARE(J) THEN
       SWAP SQUARE(J+1),SQUARE(J)
     END IF
    NEXT J,I
  REM DANCE
   PLAYER = GAME
   FOR I=1 TO 3
    MOVE = SQUARE(I): GOSUB CONVERT
    GOSUB FLASH
    PUT(X,Y),SHAPE(INDEX(PLAYER+2)),PSET
   NEXT I
RETURN

DECIDE:
 BUTTON = Ø
 GOSUB DRAWBUTTON
 GOSUB PUSHBUTTON
 COLOR 1,Ø
RETURN

DRAWBUTTON:
 LINE (337,167)-(433,181),1,BF
 FOR I=1 TO 2
  CIRCLE (XB(I),YB(I)),12,8-I
  PAINT (XB(I),YB(I)),8-I
  COLOR 1,8-I
  LOCATE 20: PRINT PTAB(XB(I)-4);LT$(I);
 NEXT I
RETURN

PUSHBUTTON:
 SOUND 44Ø,2
 GOSUB CLICKIT
 S$ = UCASE$(S$)
 IF S$ = "Y" THEN BUTTON = 1
 IF S$ = "N" THEN BUTTON = 2
 FOR I=1 TO 2
  XD = ABS(X-XB(I)): YD = ABS(Y-YB(I))
  IF XD<13 AND YD<7 THEN BUTTON = I: I=2
 NEXT
 IF BUTTON = Ø THEN PUSHBUTTON
RETURN

REM BUNNY1
 DATA Ø,-1,2,Ø,Ø,-1,1,Ø,Ø,-1,4,Ø,Ø,1,2,Ø,Ø,1,2,Ø
 DATA Ø,1,3,Ø,Ø,1,3,Ø,Ø,1,1,Ø,Ø,1,-2,Ø,Ø,1,-4,Ø
 DATA Ø,-1,-2,Ø,Ø,-1,-1,Ø,Ø,-1,-1,Ø,Ø,-1,-3,Ø,Ø,3
 DATA 1,Ø,Ø,1,1,Ø,Ø,2,-5,Ø,Ø,1,-11,Ø,Ø,-1,-4,Ø
 DATA Ø,-1,1,Ø,Ø,-1,2,Ø,Ø,-1,1,Ø,Ø,-1,-3,Ø,Ø,1
```

```
DATA -2,0,0,1,-5,0,0,-1,-3,0,0,-1,3,0,0,-1,3,0
DATA 0,-1,4,0,0,-1,4,0,0,-1,2,0,0,-1,3,0,0,-1
DATA 1,0,4,0,0,0,2,-1,4,-2,-3,-1,-5,-2,-9,2
DATA -8,1,-8,0,-13,3,-13,2,-14,2
DATA 1,0,0,1,2,0,0,1,1,0,0,1,1,0,0,2,-1,0,0,1
DATA -2,0,0,1,-6,0,0,-1,-3,0,0,1,-6,0,0,-1,-4,0
DATA 0,-1,-1,0,0,-1,-1,0,0,-1,1,0,0,-1,1,0,0,-1
DATA 1,0,0,-1,0,1,13,0,0,-1,2,0,0,13,0,12,0,11
DATA -1,10,-2,9,14,0,0,1,4,0,0,1,3,0,-1,0,0,1
DATA -2,0,0,1,-9,0,0,-1,-8,0,0,-1,-5,0,0,-1,-3,0
DATA 7,0,26,18,25,17,24,17,28,17,27,16
DATA -3,0,0,1,-5,0,0,1,-8,0,0,1,-10,0,0,-1,-2,0
DATA 1,0,0,-1,2,0,0,-1,7,0,0,-1,11,0,0,1,6,0
DATA -27,17,-26,16,-25,16,2,0,0,1,3,0,0,-1,1,0
DATA -3,0,0,-1,2,0,-1,0,0,-1,-3,0,0,-1,-1,0
DATA 2,0,-3,0,0,1,-2,0,0,1,-2,0,1,0,0,1,2,0,0,1
DATA 3,0,0,-1,2,0,-2,0,0,-1,-3,0,0,-1,2,0
DATA 1,0,0,-1,1,0,0,-1,3,0,0,-1,3,0,0,-1,3,0
DATA 0,-1,1,0,0,-1,-1,0,0,-1,-2,0,0,-1,-2,0,0,-1
DATA -1,0,0,-2,1,0,0,-1,2,0,0,-1,1,0,0,-2,-1,0
DATA 0,-1,-1,0,0,1,-2,0,0,1,-2,0,0,1,-2,0,0,3
DATA -2,0,0,-1,-3,0,0,-1,-4,0,0,1,-4,0,0,1,-3,0
DATA 0,1,-3,0,1,0,0,1,7,0,0,-1,3,0,0,-1,3,0,0,2
DATA -1,0,0,1,-1,0,0,1,-1,0,0,1,-1,0,1,0,0,1,2,0
DATA 0,1,3,0,0,1,1,0,2,0,0,-2,1,0,0,-1,2,0,0,-1
DATA 1,0,0,-1,0,1,-2,0,0,1,-2,0,0,1,-1,0,0,1
DATA -3,0,0,1,-4,0,2,0,0,-1,1,0
DATA 1,0,0,-1,2,0,-5,0,2,-4,3,-4
DATA 7,-9,6,-9,-1,-9,0,-9,2,0,0,1,2,0,0,2,-1,0
DATA 0,-1,-1,0,0,-1,-2,0
```

REM BUNNY2

```
DATA 0,-2,3,0,0,-1,2,0,0,-1,2,0,0,-1,1,0,0,-1,2,0
DATA 0,-1,2,0,0,-1,2,0,0,-1,5,0,0,1,1,0,0,1,-2,0
DATA 0,1,-3,0,0,1,-3,0,0,1,-2,0,0,1,-1,0,0,3,1,0
DATA 0,1,1,0,0,2,-1,0,0,-1,-9,0,0,1,-2,0,0,-1
DATA -1,0,0,-1,-3,0,0,-2,1,0,0,-2,-3,0,0,-1,-3,0
DATA 0,-1,-3,0,0,1,-1,0,0,-1,-3,0,0,-1,-1,0,2,0
DATA 0,-1,1,0,0,-1,1,0,0,1,3,0,0,1,2,0,0,1,4,0
DATA 0,1,2,0,0,1,1,0,0,1,1,0,-14,-5,-13,-6,12,-5
DATA 11,-6,7,0,0,1,1,0,0,1,1,0,0,1,3,0,0,1,3,0
DATA 0,1,1,0,0,1,1,0,0,1,-1,0,0,1,-8,0,0,-1,-1,0
DATA 0,-2,-3,0,0,-1,-6,0,0,-1,-3,0,0,3,-2,0,0,-1
DATA -1,0,0,-3,-4,0,0,-1,-1,0,1,0,0,-1,2,0,0,-1
DATA 4,0,0,1,2,0,0,1,4,0,0,4,1,5,2,6,-3,5,-2,6
DATA 9,0,0,1,3,0,0,1,2,0,0,1,-4,0,0,-1,-2,0,0,-1
DATA -4,0,0,-1,-2,0,0,3,1,0,0,1,-1,0,0,1,-2,0
DATA 0,-1,-2,0,0,-1,-2,0,0,-1,-2,0,0,-1,-2,0
DATA 0,-1,-1,0,0,-1,-1,0,0,-1,-1,0,1,0,0,-1,4,0
```

```
DATA 0,1,2,0,0,1,2,0,0,1,3,0,25,15,-18,4,-17,3
DATA -9,6,-9,7
DATA 1,0,0,-1,-1,0,2,0,0,-1,-1,0,2,0,0,-1,2,0
DATA 0,-1,4,0,0,1,2,0,-2,0,0,-1,1,0,0,-1,2,0
DATA 0,1,2,0,-2,0,0,-2,3,0,-6,0,0,-1,-3,0,0,-1
DATA -1,0,1,0,0,2,-1,0,0,1,-1,0,0,1,-1,0,0,1
DATA -2,0,0,-1,-2,0,0,-1,-2,0,0,-2,1,0,0,-1,1,0
DATA -1,0,0,1,-4,0,0,1,-5,0,2,0,0,2,-2,0,0,1
DATA -1,0,1,0,0,-1,2,0,0,1,1,0,0,-1,2,0,0,-1,3,0
DATA 3,0,0,-1,2,0,0,-1,2,0,0,-1,1,0,0,-1,2,0
DATA 0,-3,2,0,0,-1,2,0,0,-1,1,0,0,-1,1,0,0,-1
DATA -2,0,0,1,-3,0,0,1,-2,0,0,1,-1,0,0,1,-2,0
DATA 0,-1,-1,0,0,-1,-2,0,0,-1,-2,0,0,-1,-2,0
DATA 0,1,1,0,0,1,2,0,0,2,-1,0,0,1,-1,0,0,2,-4,0
DATA 0,1,1,0,0,1,1,0,0,1,2,0,-1,0,0,-1,-2,0,0,1
DATA -1,0,3,0,-1,0,0,-1,-3,0,1,0,0,1
DATA 1,0,1,0,0,-1,-1,0,1,0,2,0,0,-1,1,0,0,-1,1,0
DATA -1,0,0,-1,-1,0,0,-1,-1,0,4,0,0,1,1,0,-4,0
```

REM PIGLET1
```
DATA 2,0,0,1,3,0,0,1,2,0,0,2,3,0,0,-1,4,0,0,-1
DATA 0,1,1,0,-2,0,0,1,-2,0,0,2,2,0,0,1,-2,0,0,1
DATA -1,0,0,3,1,0,-4,0,0,-1,-2,0,1,0,0,-4,-7,0
DATA 0,1,-2,0,0,1,-2,0,0,1,-2,0,0,1,-3,0,0,2,1,0
DATA 0,1,-3,0,0,-1,-1,0,0,-1,-2,0,1,0,0,-1,1,0
DATA 0,-3,-2,0,0,-1,-2,0,0,-1,-2,0,0,-1,-1,0
DATA 0,-3,1,0,0,-1,1,0,0,-1,3,0,0,-1,5,0,0,-1
DATA 2,0,0,2,6,0,0,1,2,0,-2,2,-1,3,0,4,0,5,-1,6
DATA -1,7,-11,14,-10,14,8,6,9,5,10,5,11,12
DATA 10,12,0,0,-1,0,-2,0,-3,0,-4,0,-5,-1,-6,-1
DATA -7,-1,-8,-1,-9,-2,-7,-2,-6,-3,-5,-3,-4,-2
DATA 3,0,0,1,3,0,0,1,2,0,0,2,1,0,0,-1,4,0,0,-1
DATA 2,0,0,1,1,0,0,1,1,0,0,-1,1,0,0,-1,1,0,0,-1
DATA 1,0,0,-1,1,0,0,-4,-1,0,0,-1,-1,0,0,-1,-2,0
DATA 0,1,1,0,0,3,-2,0,0,-1,-1,0,0,-1,-6,0,0,-1
DATA -6,0,0,-1,-4,0,0,1,-1,0,0,1,-2,0,0,1,-2,0
DATA 0,1,-2,0,0,1,-2,0,9,0,0,1,14,2,16,1,18,-2
DATA 18,-3,0,-1,-1,0,0,-1,3,0,0,-1,4,0,0,1,2,0
DATA 0,2,3,0,0,1,2,0,0,1,-2,0,0,-1,-4,0,0,-1
DATA -6,0,0,-2,1,0,0,1,5,0,0,1,2,0,-8,0
DATA 20,1,21,1,29,-4,30,-4,16,-2,15,-3,1,0,0,-3
DATA -2,0,0,1,-1,0,0,1,-2,0,0,1,-1,0,0,-2,-2,0
DATA 0,-1,-1,0,2,0,0,-1,4,0,0,-1,2,0,0,-1,2,0
DATA 0,-1,12,0,0,-1,6,0,0,1,1,0,0,1,-1,0,0,1
DATA -1,0,0,-1,-3,0,0,2,1,0,0,2,2,0,0,1,-2,0
DATA 0,1,-1,0,0,3,1,0,-1,0,0,-1,-6,0,0,-1,-6,0
DATA 0,-1,-3,0,-3,0,0,-1,-2,0,1,0,0,-1,5,0,0,1
DATA 1,0,-4,0,-3,-1,-2,-1,0,-1,1,-1,-12,-3
DATA -11,-3,-6,-4,-5,-4,-10,0,-9,1,-8,1,-7,1
DATA -6,1,-16,-3
```

```
REM PIGLET2
 DATA 4,Ø,Ø,1,4,Ø,Ø,1,3,Ø,Ø,-1,3,Ø,Ø,-1,Ø,1,3,Ø
 DATA -1,Ø,Ø,1,-2,Ø,Ø,1,-2,Ø,Ø,1,-1,Ø,Ø,2,2,Ø,Ø,1
 DATA 2,Ø,Ø,1,3,Ø,Ø,1,2,Ø,Ø,1,2,Ø,Ø,1,1,Ø,-2,Ø
 DATA Ø,-1,-4,Ø,Ø,-1,-8,Ø,Ø,-1,-4,Ø,Ø,-1,-5,Ø,Ø,1
 DATA -2,Ø,Ø,1,-2,Ø,Ø,1,-2,Ø,Ø,1,-1,Ø,Ø,2,1,Ø,Ø,1
 DATA 1,Ø,-2,Ø,Ø,-1,-2,Ø,Ø,-1,-1,Ø,Ø,-3,-1,Ø
 DATA Ø,-1,-2,Ø,Ø,-1,-2,Ø,Ø,-1,-1,Ø,Ø,-1,-1,Ø
 DATA Ø,-1,-1,Ø,1,Ø,Ø,-1,1,Ø,Ø,-1,1,Ø,Ø,-1,2,Ø
 DATA Ø,-1,1,Ø,Ø,-1,1,Ø,Ø,3,2,Ø,Ø,-1,4,Ø,Ø,-1
 DATA 5,Ø,-5,17,-6,17,-7,17,24,13,25,13,-2,7,-1,8
 DATA -1,9,-1,1Ø,6,9,7,8,8,8,9,7
 DATA Ø,Ø,-1,Ø,-2,Ø,-3,Ø,-4,Ø,-5,-1,-6,-1,-7,-1
 DATA -8,-1,-9,-2,-7,-2,-6,-3,-5,-3,-4,-2
 DATA -6,Ø,Ø,1,-4,Ø,Ø,1,-2,Ø,1,Ø,Ø,-2,1,Ø,Ø,-1
 DATA 1,Ø,Ø,-4,1,Ø,Ø,1,7,Ø,Ø,-1,1Ø,Ø,Ø,-2,-2,Ø
 DATA Ø,-1,-1,Ø,2,Ø,Ø,1,4,Ø,Ø,1,2,Ø,Ø,1,1,Ø,Ø,1
 DATA 1,Ø,Ø,1,1,Ø,Ø,2,1,Ø,Ø,2,-3,Ø,Ø,-1,-2,Ø,Ø,1
 DATA -3,Ø,Ø,1,-1,Ø,Ø,-1,-4,Ø,Ø,-1,-5,Ø,14,1,15,Ø
 DATA 15,-1,14,-2,13,-3
 DATA Ø,-1,2,Ø,Ø,-1,2,Ø,Ø,-1,2,Ø,Ø,-1,3,Ø,Ø,1
 DATA -1,Ø,Ø,3,-2,Ø,Ø,1,-5,Ø,Ø,-1,2,Ø,Ø,1,1,Ø
 DATA Ø,-1,2,Ø,Ø,-1,1,Ø,Ø,-1,-2,Ø,Ø,1,-2,Ø
 DATA 1Ø,-6,11,-6,18,-9,19,-9
 DATA -5,Ø,Ø,-1,-3,Ø,Ø,-1,-1,Ø,Ø,-1,-2,Ø,Ø,-1
 DATA -2,Ø,Ø,1,-1,Ø,Ø,1,-1,Ø,Ø,1,-1,Ø,Ø,1,-2,Ø
 DATA Ø,1,Ø,-2,-1,Ø,Ø,-1,-1,Ø,Ø,-1,-1,Ø,3,Ø,Ø,-1
 DATA 4,Ø,Ø,-2,1,Ø,Ø,-1,3,Ø,Ø,-1,4,Ø,Ø,-1,2,Ø
 DATA Ø,-1,1,Ø,Ø,-1,1,Ø,Ø,-1,1,Ø,Ø,1,4,Ø,-1,Ø,Ø,1
 DATA -3,Ø,Ø,2,3,Ø,Ø,1,2,Ø,Ø,4,3,Ø,Ø,1,1,Ø,Ø,1
 DATA 1,Ø,-9,Ø,-9,-8,-8,-8,-4,-1Ø,-3,-1Ø,-3,-7
 DATA -2,-6,-1,-6,Ø,-6,-13,-8
 DATA 2,Ø,Ø,-1,3,Ø,Ø,1,1,Ø,-1,Ø,Ø,1,-4,Ø,3,-8
 DATA 4,-8,5,-9,6,-9
```

CHAPTER 3

Stop, Look, and Learn

CHAPTER 3

Stop, Look, and Learn

Text by John J. Flynn

Learning doesn't have to be hard. With the Amiga it can be easy, as these educational and entertaining programs illustrate. In fact, using them is almost like playing a game. And while there's no pressure to get a right answer, you'll be pleasantly rewarded if you do.

The first four programs deal with some basic operations in math: how to count, how to add and subtract, how to multiply, and how to do fractions. The fifth helps people of all ages learn a foreign language. Here's a quick look at the programs in this chapter.

Crazy Critters. Horses, ducks, witches, bunnies, monkeys, and kittens help a child learn to count to 20 in this delightful game. Age group: preschoolers to first grade.

Let's Add and Subtract. The computer checks the student's skills in adding and subtracting integers. Numbers are drawn large for easy viewing. There's an easy level and a difficult one. Age group: first grade through mid-elementary school.

Let's Multiply. Youngsters get help with their basic times tables. There's also an option to multiply numbers up to 1000, so older kids will like it, too. Age group: second grade and on. Adults can use the more difficult problems to sharpen rusty skills.

Fun with Fractions. Fractions don't have to be frustrating. With this program, students are taught not just to add fractions, but to find common denominators as well. Age group: third grade and up.

Foreign Language Flash Cards. A handy program that allows students to create their own vocabulary lists. Students are then tested on the words and their meanings. Age group: first grade and up.

With these programs kids of every age can make learning both fun and rewarding at the same time.

Stop, Look, and Learn Menu Driver

Save using the filename **LEARNING**

```
REM STOP, LOOK, AND LEARN
  GOSUB INITIALIZE
  GOSUB MAIN.MENU
  RUN TITLE.SHORT$(PICK)
END

INITIALIZE:
  GOSUB SETSCREEN
  GOSUB KEYVALUES
  GOSUB SETMENUS
  GOSUB SETCOLORS
  GOSUB SHAPES
RETURN

SETSCREEN:
  SCREEN 1,640,200,3,2
  WINDOW 2,"Stop, Look, and Learn",,0,1
RETURN

KEYVALUES:
  DEFINT A-Z
  N = 5
  DIM TITLE.LONG$(N),TITLE.SHORT$(N),DISCS(250)
  DISC.I(1) = 1: DISC.I(2) = 125
  READ CHAPTER$
  FOR I=1 TO N
    READ TITLE.LONG$(I),TITLE.SHORT$(I)
  NEXT
RETURN

SETMENUS:
  FOR I=2 TO 4
    MENU I,0,0,""
  NEXT
  MENU 1,0,1,"STOP"
  MENU 1,1,1," Go to BASIC"
  MENU 1,2,1," Go to System"
  MENU ON
  ON MENU GOSUB GOODBYE
RETURN

GOODBYE:
  WINDOW CLOSE 2: WINDOW 1: MENU RESET
  SCREEN CLOSE 1
  ITEM = MENU(1)
  IF ITEM = 2 THEN SYSTEM
```

```
   CLS
   PRINT "Bye-Bye"
   STOP
RETURN

SETCOLORS:
  REM TAN, GREEN, & RED
    PALETTE 4,.95,.7,.53
    PALETTE 5,.14,.43,0
    PALETTE 6,.93,.2,0
RETURN

SHAPES:
 X=313: Y=80
 LINE(X-12,Y-8)-(X+12,Y+8),4,BF
 FOR I=1 TO 2
  K = 7-I
  CIRCLE(X,Y),12,K: PAINT(X,Y),K
  GET(X-12,Y-8)-(X+12,Y+8),DISCS(DISC.I(I))
 NEXT
RETURN

MAIN.MENU:
 CLS
 RTN$ = "OFF": PICK = 1
 S$ = CHAPTER$: L = LEN(S$)
 LINE(313-10*L/2-15,15)-(313+10*L/2+15,27),1,B
 PAINT(313,20),6,1
 COLOR 1,6: LOCATE 3: PRINT PTAB(313-10*L/2)S$
 LINE(135,35)-(495,130),2,B: PAINT(313,80),4,2
 COLOR 2,4
 FOR I=1 TO N
  IF I = PICK THEN INX = 2 ELSE INX = 1
  CALL DRAW.CIRCLE(I,INX)
  LOCATE I*2+4,21: PRINT TITLE.LONG$(I)
 NEXT
 LINE(263,141)-(360,153),2,B: PAINT(313,145),3,2
 COLOR 2,3
 LOCATE 17: PRINT PTAB(282)"Return"
 COLOR 1,0
 LOCATE 19,11: PRINT "Click Mouse on Choice,";
 PRINT " then Click on Return"
 GOSUB CHOOSE
RETURN

SUB DRAW.CIRCLE(R,INX) STATIC
 SHARED DISCS(),DISC.I()
 Y = 18*R+22
 PUT(162,Y),DISCS(DISC.I(INX)),PSET
END SUB
```

133

```
CHOOSE:
 GOSUB GURGLE
 GOSUB CLICKIT
 IF S$ = "" THEN GOSUB LOCATION
 IF ASC(S$+" ") <> 13 AND RTN$ = "OFF" THEN
  GOTO CHOOSE
 END IF
RETURN

GURGLE:
 FREQ = 300
 FOR G=1 TO 5
  FREQ = 500 - FREQ
  SOUND FREQ,1,50
 NEXT
RETURN

CLICKIT:
 S$ = ""
 WHILE MOUSE(0) = 0 AND S$ = ""
  S$ = INKEY$
 WEND
 X = MOUSE(1)
 Y = MOUSE(2)
 WHILE MOUSE(0)<> 0: WEND: REM RESET
RETURN

LOCATION:
 IF X>263 AND X<360 AND Y>141 AND Y<153 THEN
  RTN$ = "ON"
 ELSE
  P = INT((Y-39)/18) + 1
  IF X>155 AND X<195 AND P>0 AND P<= N THEN
   CALL DRAW.CIRCLE(PICK,1)
   CALL DRAW.CIRCLE(P,2)
   PICK = P
  END IF
 END IF
RETURN

REM PROGRAMS
 DATA "Stop, Look, and Learn"
 DATA Crazy Critters, CRITTERS
 DATA Let's Add and Subtract, ADD
 DATA Let's Multiply, MULTIPLY
 DATA Fun with Fractions, FRACTIONS
 DATA Foreign Language Flash Cards, CARDS
```

Crazy Critters

This introductory program helps preschoolers and first graders learn how to count. It's easy to use, and its high-resolution graphics makes counting fun.

The program displays a random number of critters on the screen—to a total of 20, depending on the limit you've selected with a pull-down menu.

Six creatures are available: horses, ducks, witches, bunnies, monkeys, and kittens. The child counts the number of times the particular character appears and enters the value into the Amiga. The computer plays "Alouette" when the entry is right. When the entry is incorrect, the Amiga displays the correct number of critters.

"Crazy Critters" introduces the concept of counting. For beginners, limit the total number of characters shown to five. Then gradually increase this value as your child gains proficiency. The colorful creatures keep youngsters' attention and give them something easy and identifiable to tally.

After the rudiments of counting are mastered, the young student can move on to the next program, "Let's Add and Subtract."

Program 3-1. Crazy Critters
Save using the filename **CRITTERS**

```
REM CRAZY CRITTERS
  GOSUB INITIALIZE
PLAYGAME:
  GOSUB PLAY
PLAYAGAIN:
  CLS: LOCATE 10,21: PRINT "Play Again ? ";
  GOSUB DECIDE
  IF BUTTON = 1 THEN PLAYGAME
  GOSUB GOODBYE
END

INITIALIZE:
  GOSUB SETSCREEN
  GOSUB KEYVALUES
  GOSUB ALOUETTE
  GOSUB SETMENUS
  GOSUB SETCOLORS
  GOSUB DRAWSHAPES
  GOSUB HEADING
RETURN
```

```
SETSCREEN:
 SCREEN 1,640,200,3,2
 WINDOW 2,"Crazy Critters",,0,1
RETURN

KEYVALUES:
 DEFINT A-Z
 RANDOMIZE TIMER
 DIM SHAPE(2081),BANNER(500),X(20),Y(20)
 DIM TIMBRE2(255),TIMBRE3(255)
 DIM F(58),L(58)
 REM SHAPE INDICES
  FOR I=1 TO 8
    INDEX(I) = 1 + (I-1)*260
  NEXT
 REM BUTTON HOLES & LETTERS
  XB(1)=364: YB(1)=84
  XB(2)=406: YB(2)=84
  LT$(1) = "Y": LT$(2) = "N"
 REM NAMES
  DATA horses, ducks, witches, bunnies
  DATA monkeys, kittens, critters
  FOR I=1 TO 7
   READ NM$(I)
  NEXT
RETURN

ALOUETTE:
 LOCATE 10,25: PRINT "One moment ..."
 DATA 196,4,220,8,247,4,247,4,220,8,196,8,220,8
 DATA 247,8,196,4,147,4,196,4,220,8,247,4,247,4
 DATA 220,8,196,8,220,8,247,8,196,2,294,8,330,8
 DATA 294,8,262,8,247,8,220,8,196,4,294,8,294,8
 DATA 294,4,147,8,147,8,147,4,294,8,294,8,294,4
 DATA 147,8,147,8,147,4,0,36
 M! = 6.2838/256
 FOR I=0 TO 255
  TIMBRE2(I) = 48*SIN(2*I*M!)
  TIMBRE3(I) = 48*SIN(3*I*M!)
 NEXT
 WAVE 2,TIMBRE2: WAVE 3,TIMBRE3
 FOR I=1 TO 39
  READ F(I),L: L(I) = 18/L
 NEXT
 FOR I=1 TO 19
  F(I+39) = F(I)
  L(I+39) = L(I)
 NEXT
 REM NOTE GROUPS
```

```
   DATA 19,38,58
   FOR I=1 TO 3: READ NOTE.GROUP(I): NEXT
RETURN

SETMENUS:
 DATA 2, Rules, Yes, No
 DATA 4, Count, Up to  5 Critters
 DATA Up to 10 Critters, Up to 15 Critters
 DATA Up to 20 Critters
 DATA 7, Critters, Horses, Ducks, Witches
 DATA Bunnies, Monkeys, Kittens, Mixed
 DATA 3, Stop, Go to BASIC
 DATA Go to Learning Menu, Go to System
 FOR I=1 TO 4
  READ NUMBER
  FOR J=0 TO NUMBER
   READ TITLE$
   IF J<>0 THEN TITLE$ = SPACE$(3) + TITLE$
   STATUS = 1
    IF I<>4 AND J=1 THEN STATUS = 2
   MENU I,J,STATUS,TITLE$
 NEXT J,I
 RULES = 1: GAME = 1: CRITTER = 1
RETURN

SETCOLORS:
 REM PINK, BROWN, RED, GRAY
  PALETTE 4,1,.51,.64
  PALETTE 5,.82,.37,.07
  PALETTE 6,.93,.2,0
  PALETTE 7,.73,.83,.73
RETURN

DRAWSHAPES:
 CLS
 MENU ON
 ON MENU GOSUB OPTIONS
 GOSUB HORSE
 GOSUB DUCK1
 GOSUB WITCH
 GOSUB BUNNY
 GOSUB MONKEY
 GOSUB KITTEN
 GOSUB DUCK2
 GOSUB BANNER
 GOSUB GETSHAPES
RETURN
```

```
HORSE:
 X0=106: Y0=76
 CALL DRAWLINE(1,X0,Y0,151)
 PAINT (X0,Y0+3)
 CALL DRAWPOINT(0,X0,Y0,4)
RETURN

SUB DRAWLINE(K,X.C,Y.C,T) STATIC
 COLOR K
 PSET(X.C,Y.C)
 FOR I=1 TO T
  READ X,Y
  LINE -STEP(X,Y)
 NEXT
END SUB

SUB DRAWPOINT(K,X.C,Y.C,T) STATIC
 COLOR K
 FOR I=1 TO T
  READ X,Y
  PSET(X.C+X,Y.C+Y)
 NEXT
END SUB

DUCK1:
 X0=183: Y0=80
 CALL DRAWLINE(3,X0,Y0,73)
 PAINT (X0-9,Y0+4)
 PAINT (X0+17,Y0+4)
 CALL DRAWPOINT(2,X0,Y0,12)
 REM BILL
  COLOR 1
  PSET(X0+23,Y0+5)
  LINE -STEP(0,1): LINE -STEP(4,0)
RETURN

WITCH:
 REM DRESS/SHOES
  X0=263
  CALL DRAWLINE(2,X0,Y0,59)
  PAINT (X0+2,Y0+4)
  PAINT (X0-3,Y0-2)
 REM HAIR
  CALL DRAWPOINT(2,X0,Y0-6,7)
 REM BROOM
  LINE(X0-15,Y0+8)-(X0+30,Y0-5)
  CALL DRAWLINE(2,X0-15,Y0+8,9)
 REM CAPE
  CALL DRAWLINE(6,X0+4,Y0-5,26)
```

```
   PAINT (X0-12,Y0-3)
 REM HAT
  CALL DRAWLINE(6,X0+1,Y0-7,10)
 REM FACE
  CALL DRAWLINE(4,X0+4,Y0-6,8)
 REM ARMS
  CALL DRAWLINE(4,X0+11,Y0-1,3)
RETURN

BUNNY:
 X0=343
 CALL DRAWLINE(4,X0,Y0,80)
 PAINT (X0,Y0+3)
 CALL DRAWPOINT(2,X0,Y0,41)
RETURN

MONKEY:
 X0=423
 CALL DRAWLINE(5,X0,Y0,36)
 CALL DRAWLINE(5,X0,Y0,68)
 PAINT (X0+3,Y0+2)
 CALL DRAWLINE(5,X0+18,Y0+4,8)
 CALL DRAWPOINT(0,X0,Y0,10)
 CALL DRAWPOINT(2,X0,Y0,6)
RETURN

KITTEN:
 X0=503
 CALL DRAWLINE(7,X0,Y0,140)
 PAINT(X0,Y0-3)
 CALL DRAWPOINT(2,X0,Y0,16)
 CALL DRAWPOINT(6,X0,Y0,4)
RETURN

DUCK2:
 X0=350: Y0=40
 CALL DRAWLINE(3,X0,Y0,49)
 PAINT(X0-7,Y0-1): PAINT(X0+15,Y0-2)
 CALL DRAWPOINT(2,X0,Y0,5)
 CALL DRAWLINE(1,X0+22,Y0-2,2)
RETURN

BANNER:
 X0=280: Y0=40
 CALL DRAWLINE(6,X0,Y0,46)
 PAINT(X0+1,Y0+1)
 CALL DRAWLINE(6,X0+16,Y0-2,5)
 REM "Nice !"
  CALL DRAWLINE(1,X0-31,Y0-4,17)
```

```
   CALL DRAWLINE(1,XØ-19,YØ-3,1)
   CALL DRAWLINE(1,XØ-19,YØ-1,5)
   CALL DRAWLINE(1,XØ-6,YØ+1,11)
   CALL DRAWLINE(1,XØ,YØ-1,11)
   CALL DRAWLINE(1,XØ+11,YØ-5,3)
   CALL DRAWLINE(1,XØ+11,YØ+1,1)
RETURN

GETSHAPES:
 FOR I=1 TO 6
  X1 = 80*I-7: X2 = 80*I+53
  GET(X1,7Ø)-(X2,9Ø),SHAPE(INDEX(I))
 NEXT
 REM DUCK2 & BLANK, BANNER & BLANK
  GET(319,3Ø)-(379,5Ø),SHAPE(INDEX(7))
  GET(419,3Ø)-(479,5Ø),SHAPE(INDEX(8))
  GET(24Ø,34)-(318,47),BANNER(1)
  GET(1ØØ,34)-(178,47),BANNER(25Ø)
RETURN

HEADING:
 COLOR 1,Ø
 LOCATE 13,25:PRINT "Crazy Critters"
 LOCATE 17,24:PRINT "Please use menus,"
 LOCATE 19,23:PRINT "Click mouse to play"
 GOSUB CLICKIT
RETURN

OPTIONS:
 ID = MENU(Ø): ITEM = MENU(1)
 ON ID GOSUB MENU1,MENU2,MENU3,GOODBYE
 ITEM = Ø
RETURN

MENU1:
 MENU 1,RULES,1: MENU 1,ITEM,2
 RULES = ITEM
RETURN

MENU2:
 MENU 2,GAME,1: MENU 2,ITEM,2
 GAME = ITEM
RETURN

MENU3:
 MENU 3,CRITTER,1: MENU 3,ITEM,2
 CRITTER = ITEM
RETURN
```

```
GOODBYE:
 WINDOW CLOSE 2: WINDOW 1: MENU RESET
 SCREEN CLOSE 1
 IF ITEM = 2 THEN RUN "LEARNING"
 IF ITEM = 3 THEN SYSTEM
 COLOR 1,Ø: CLS
 PRINT "Bye-Bye"
 STOP
RETURN

CLICKIT:
 S$ = ""
 WHILE MOUSE(Ø) = Ø AND S$ = ""
  S$ = INKEY$
 WEND
  X = MOUSE(1)
  Y = MOUSE(2)
 WHILE MOUSE(Ø)<> Ø: WEND: REM RESET
RETURN

PLAY:
 IF RULES = 1 THEN GOSUB RULES
 CNT = Ø: GROUP = Ø
 FOR Q=1 TO 3
  GOSUB GET.VALUES
  GOSUB DRAW.CRITTERS
  GOSUB GUESS
  GOSUB EVALUATE
 NEXT Q
 IF CNT = 3 THEN GOSUB FLY
RETURN

RULES:
 CLS
 PRINT
 PRINT "   I'm going to draw a random";
 PRINT " number of crazy critters."
 PRINT
 PRINT " Count how many there are, and enter";
 PRINT " your guess."
 PRINT
 PRINT "   I'll give you three problems per";
 PRINT " game, and you'll enjoy"
 PRINT " a nice surprise if you count";
 PRINT " perfectly."
 LOCATE 2Ø,26:PRINT "Click Mouse";
 GOSUB CLICKIT
RETURN
```

```
GET.VALUES:
 N = INT(RND*5*GAME) + 1
 IF N = 1 THEN N = 2
 REM NUMBER OF ROWS
  NR = INT( (N-1)/5 ) + 1
 REM Y-COORDINATES
  FOR I=1 TO N
   R = INT((I-1)/5)+1
   IF NR = 1 THEN Y(I) = 80
   IF NR = 2 THEN Y(I) = 55*R - 10
   IF NR = 3 THEN Y(I) = 40*R - 10
   IF NR = 4 THEN Y(I) = 30*R - 5
  NEXT I
 REM X-COORDINATES
  FOR I=1 TO N
   RW = INT((I-1)/5)+1
   CL = I - (RW-1)*5
   X(I) = 90*CL + 43
  NEXT I
 REM CENTER LAST ROW
  E = NR*5 - 4
  FOR I=1 TO CL
   IF CL = 1 THEN X(E+I-1) = 313
   IF CL = 2 THEN X(E+I-1) = 90*I+178
   IF CL = 3 THEN X(E+I-1) = 90*I+133
   IF CL = 4 THEN X(E+I-1) = 90*I+88
  NEXT I
RETURN

DRAW.CRITTERS:
 CLS
 FOR I=1 TO N
  V = CRITTER
  IF CRITTER = 7 THEN V = INT(RND*6) + 1
  PUT(X(I)-35,Y(I)-20),SHAPE(INDEX(V)),PSET
 NEXT I
RETURN

GUESS:
 GOSUB GURGLE
 LOCATE 16,18
 PRINT "How many ";NM$(CRITTER);" are there";
 INPUT " ? ",S$
 GUESS = VAL(S$)
RETURN

EVALUATE:
 ON -(GUESS = N)+1 GOSUB WRONG, RIGHT
 LOCATE 20,26: PRINT "Press any key";
```

```
   GOSUB CLICKIT
RETURN

WRONG:
  SOUND 400,3: SOUND 300,3: SOUND 200,3
  LOCATE 18,18: PRINT "Sorry, there are";N;
  PRINT NM$(CRITTER);"."
RETURN

RIGHT:
  LOCATE 18,27: PRINT "Very Good !"
  GOSUB MUSIC
  CNT = CNT+1
RETURN

MUSIC:
  GROUP = GROUP + 1
  FIRST = NOTE.GROUP(GROUP-1) + 1
  LAST  = NOTE.GROUP(GROUP)
  FOR I = FIRST TO LAST
    SOUND WAIT
    FOR J=2 TO 3
      SOUND F(I),L(I),125,J
      SOUND 0,.5,,J
    NEXT J
    SOUND RESUME
  NEXT I
RETURN

GURGLE:
  FREQ = 300
  FOR G=1 TO 5
    FREQ = 500-FREQ
    SOUND FREQ,1,50
  NEXT G
RETURN

FLY:
  CLS
  DUCK = 2: YD(2)=81: YD(7) = 74
  LOCATE 18,22: PRINT "You got all 3 right !"
  FOR X=80 TO 610 STEP 5
    PUT(X,70),SHAPE(INDEX(DUCK)),PSET
    PUT(X-76,YD(DUCK)),BANNER(1),PSET
    FOR PAUSE=1 TO 500: NEXT PAUSE
    PUT(X,70),SHAPE(INDEX(8)),PSET
    PUT(X-76,YD(DUCK)),BANNER(250),PSET
    DUCK = 9-DUCK
  NEXT X
RETURN
```

```
DECIDE:
 BUTTON = Ø
 GOSUB DRAWBUTTON
 GOSUB PUSHBUTTON
 COLOR 1,Ø
RETURN

DRAWBUTTON:
 LINE (337,77)-(433,91),1,BF
 FOR I=1 TO 2
   CIRCLE (XB(I),YB(I)),12,I*3
   PAINT (XB(I),YB(I)),I*3
   COLOR 1,I*3
   LOCATE 1Ø: PRINT PTAB(XB(I)-4);LT$(I);
 NEXT I
RETURN

PUSHBUTTON:
 SOUND 44Ø,2
 GOSUB CLICKIT
 S$ = UCASE$(S$)
 IF S$ = "Y" THEN BUTTON = 1
 IF S$ = "N" THEN BUTTON = 2
 FOR I=1 TO 2
   XD = ABS(X-XB(I)): YD = ABS(Y-YB(I))
   IF XD<13 AND YD<7 THEN BUTTON = I: I=2
 NEXT
 IF BUTTON = Ø THEN PUSHBUTTON
RETURN

REM HORSE
 DATA -1Ø,Ø,Ø,-1,-9,Ø,Ø,1,-4,Ø,Ø,1,-1,Ø,Ø,1,-2,Ø
 DATA Ø,-1,-3,Ø,Ø,1,-2,Ø,Ø,2,1,Ø,Ø,3,-3,Ø,Ø,1
 DATA 1,Ø,Ø,-1,2,Ø,Ø,-1,1,Ø,Ø,-1,1,Ø,Ø,-1,-1,Ø
 DATA Ø,-2,4,Ø,Ø,2,1,Ø,Ø,1,2,Ø,Ø,3,-1,Ø,Ø,1
 DATA -3,Ø,Ø,5,3,Ø,-1,Ø,Ø,-4,2,Ø,Ø,-1,2,Ø,Ø,-1
 DATA 3,Ø,Ø,-1,3,Ø,Ø,2,-1,Ø,Ø,2,3,Ø,Ø,1,4,Ø,Ø,1
 DATA 2,Ø,Ø,1,3,Ø,-2,Ø,Ø,-1,-2,Ø,Ø,-1,-2,Ø,Ø,-1
 DATA -2,Ø,Ø,-2,1,Ø,Ø,-1,1,Ø,Ø,-1,1,Ø,Ø,-1,1,Ø
 DATA Ø,-1,2,Ø,Ø,1,1Ø,Ø,Ø,2,-1,Ø,Ø,4,-1,Ø,Ø,1
 DATA -1,Ø,1,Ø,Ø,1,4,Ø,-2,Ø,Ø,-4,1,Ø,Ø,-1,1,Ø
 DATA Ø,-1,1,Ø,Ø,-1,2,Ø,Ø,-2,3,Ø,Ø,1,3,Ø,Ø,1
 DATA 1,Ø,Ø,1,-1,Ø,Ø,1,-1,Ø,Ø,1,-2,Ø,Ø,1,1,Ø
 DATA Ø,-1,2,Ø,Ø,-1,1,Ø,Ø,-1,1,Ø,Ø,-1,1,Ø,Ø,-1
 DATA -1,Ø,Ø,-1,-3,Ø,Ø,-2,1,Ø,Ø,-1,-1,Ø,Ø,-3
 DATA 2,Ø,Ø,2,1,Ø,Ø,1,2,Ø,Ø,-1,1,Ø,Ø,-1,2,Ø
 DATA Ø,-3,-1,Ø,Ø,-1,-2,Ø,Ø,-1,-8,Ø,Ø,1,-4,Ø
 DATA Ø,1,-3,Ø,Ø,1,-1,Ø,Ø,1,-1,Ø,Ø,1,-3,Ø
 DATA -2Ø,6,-19,7,2Ø,-2,21,-2
```

```
REM DUCK #1
 DATA 3,0,-1,0,0,2,-1,0,0,2,3,0,0,1,7,0,0,-1
 DATA 2,0,0,-1,7,0,0,1,1,0,0,1,1,0,-2,0
 DATA 0,1,-5,0,0,-1,-5,0,0,1,-4,0,0,1,-4,0
 DATA 0,1,-13,0,0,-1,-6,0,0,-1,-5,0,0,-1
 DATA -4,0,9,0,0,-1,2,0,0,-2,1,0,0,-1,1,0,0,-1
 DATA 1,0,0,-2,-1,0,0,-1,-1,0,0,-2,-1,0,0,-2
 DATA 1,0,0,-1,1,0,0,1,2,0,0,1,2,0,0,1,2,0,0,1
 DATA 1,0,0,1,1,0,0,1,2,0,0,-2,2,0,0,1,1,0
 DATA 0,1,1,0,0,1,1,0,0,1
 DATA -4,-1,-3,0,-3,1,-2,2,-2,3,-1,4,1,5,2,6
 DATA 1,7,0,7,18,4,19,4

REM WITCH
 DATA 0,1,2,0,1,0,10,0,0,3,-2,0,0,1,-2,0,0,1
 DATA -2,0,0,1,-2,0,0,1,-1,0,0,-1,-2,0,0,2,0,-1
 DATA -1,0,0,-1,-6,0,1,0,0,-1,2,0,0,-1,2,0,0,-2
 DATA -4,0,0,-1,-1,0,0,-1,1,0,0,-3,1,0,0,-1,1,0
 DATA 0,-1,2,0,0,-1,8,0,0,1,1,0,0,1,1,0,0,1,2,0
 DATA -3,0,0,1,-1,0,0,1,0,-1,-2,0,0,-2,-2,0,0,1
 DATA -1,0,0,1,-2,0,0,1
 DATA -1,0,1,0,2,0,3,0,3,-1,4,-1,5,-1
 DATA -2,0,0,1,-4,0,0,1,-5,0,9,0,0,-1,2,0,0,-1
 DATA -6,0,0,-1,-7,0,0,1,-7,0,0,1,-4,0,0,1,-9,0
 DATA 1,0,0,1,11,0,0,1,3,0,0,1,3,0,0,-1,1,0
 DATA 0,-1,1,0,0,-1,2,0,0,-1,2,0,0,-1,3,0
 DATA 1,0,0,-1,8,0,-3,0,0,-1,-3,0,0,-1,-2,0
 DATA 1,0,0,1
 DATA 3,0,0,1,1,0,0,-1,2,0,-2,0,0,-1,-1,0
 DATA 1,0,1,0,0,1

REM BUNNY
 DATA 0,-1,3,0,0,-1,8,0,0,1,4,0,0,1,3,0,0,1,1,0
 DATA 0,1,1,0,0,3,3,0,0,1,1,0,0,1,-1,0,0,1,-12,0
 DATA 0,1,-16,0,1,0,0,-2,-2,0,0,1,-3,0,1,0,0,-1
 DATA 2,0,0,-2,-1,0,0,-1,-3,0,0,-1,-1,0,0,-1
 DATA -1,0,0,-1,-7,0,0,-1,-1,0,0,-1,-1,0,1,0
 DATA 0,-1,2,0,0,-1,2,0,0,-2,-1,0,0,-1,-1,0,0,-2
 DATA -1,0,1,0,0,-1,1,0,0,1,3,0,0,1,1,0,0,3,4,0
 DATA 0,-2,1,0,0,-1,4,0,0,-1,2,0,0,2,-1,0,0,1
 DATA -2,0,0,1,-1,0,0,2,2,0,0,1,4,0,-15,-5
 DATA -14,-5,-15,-6,-14,-6,-15,-7,-8,-4,-8,-5
 DATA -7,-6,-6,-6,-15,-1,-14,-1,-13,-1,-14,-2
 DATA -13,-2,-11,1,-10,1,-9,0,-8,0,-8,8,-3,9
 DATA -2,7,-1,6,4,8,3,8,2,8,1,7,0,6,0,5,0,4,2,3
 DATA 4,2,8,2,9,2,10,2,12,3,17,6,18,5,19,5
 DATA -19,1,-18,1,-17,1
```

145

```
REM MONKEY
  DATA -4,0,0,1,-1,0,0,1,-1,0,0,5,-3,0,0,1,-10,0
  DATA 0,-1,-4,0,0,-1,-2,0,0,-1,-2,0,0,-1,-1,0
  DATA 0,-4,1,0,0,-1,1,0,0,-1,5,0,0,2,-3,0,3,0
  DATA 0,-1,1,0,-1,0,0,-1,-5,0,0,1,-2,0,0,1,-1,0
  DATA 0,3,-2,0,0,-1,3,0,0,-1,3,0,0,-1,4,0,0,-2
  DATA 2,0,0,-1,1,0,0,-1,4,0,0,1,2,0,0,2,-1,0,0,2
  DATA -2,0,0,-1,-3,0,0,2,1,0,0,2,1,0,0,1,3,0,0,-1
  DATA 2,0,0,-1,2,0,0,-1,3,0,0,-1,3,0,0,1,1,0,-6,0
  DATA 0,1,-2,0,0,1,-2,0,0,3,-1,0,0,-1,-3,0,0,-1
  DATA -2,0,0,-1,-4,0,0,2,4,0,0,1,-2,0,0,1,-2,0
  DATA 0,1,-4,0,0,1,6,0,-2,0,0,1,-8,0,1,0,0,-2
  DATA -2,0,0,1,-3,0,1,0,0,1,2,0,0,2,0,-1,2,0,0,1
  DATA 1,0,0,5,2,4,3,3,4,3,3,6,5,5,8,4,7,0,8,1
  DATA 16,3,12,-5,13,-5,15,-5,16,-5,15,-3,9,-5

REM KITTEN
  DATA 0,1,3,0,0,-1,2,0,0,1,2,0,0,2,1,0,0,3,-2,0
  DATA 0,1,-2,0,0,1,-3,0,5,0,0,-1,2,0,0,-1,2,0
  DATA 0,-1,3,0,-1,0,0,-3,2,0,0,1,1,0,0,1,1,0,0,2
  DATA -1,0,0,1,-1,0,0,1,-3,0,4,0,0,-1,1,0,0,-1
  DATA 2,0,0,-1,1,0,0,-1,1,0,-1,0,0,-1,-1,0,0,-1
  DATA -1,0,0,-4,1,0,0,-2,6,0,0,1,2,0,0,1,2,0,0,4
  DATA -1,0,0,1,1,0,0,2,2,0,-1,0,0,-3,1,0,0,-1,1,0
  DATA 0,-2,-1,0,0,-1,-1,0,0,-1,-2,0,0,-1,-4,0
  DATA 0,-1,-3,0,0,-1,-3,0,0,-1,-3,0,0,-1,-5,0
  DATA 0,-1,-7,0,0,1,-6,0,0,1,-2,0,0,1,-2,0,0,1
  DATA -6,0,0,-1,-1,0,0,-1,0,1,-7,0,0,1,-5,0,0,-1
  DATA 0,1,1,0,0,2,1,0,0,1,1,0,0,1,2,0,0,1,1,0
  DATA 0,1,1,0,0,1,2,0,0,1,2,0,0,1,1,0,0,2,1,0,0,3
  DATA -2,0,3,0,0,-1,1,0,0,-3,2,0,0,3,3,0,-1,0
  DATA 0,-3,1,0,0,-1,1,0,0,-1,2,0,0,-1,3,0,-2,0
  DATA -10,3,-11,4,-11,5,13,2,14,1
  DATA 16,0,5,0,6,-1,5,-2,-17,-1,-16,-1,-15,-1
  DATA -12,-2,-11,-3,-11,-4,-12,-5,-21,-3,-20,-3
  DATA -16,-4,-15,-4

REM DUCK #2
  DATA 5,0,0,-1,2,0,0,-1,5,0,0,1,7,0,0,-1,2,0
  DATA -1,0,0,-1,-3,0,0,-1,-5,0,0,1,-4,0,0,1,-5,0
  DATA 0,-1,-5,0,0,-1,-10,0,0,1,-5,0,0,1,-11,0
  DATA 2,0,0,1,6,0,0,1,3,0,0,2,-2,0,0,1,-3,0
  DATA 0,1,-4,0,0,1,-1,0,10,0,0,-1,5,0,0,-1,4,0
  DATA 0,-1,3,0,0,-1,4,0,0,-1,15,-3,16,-3,1,0
  DATA -16,0,-15,-1,0,1,5,0
```

```
REM BANNER
 DATA 0,-3,1,0,0,-1,5,0,0,-1,4,0,0,-1,6,0,0,-1
 DATA 0,6,1,0,0,2,1,0,0,1,1,0,-2,0,0,1,-3,0,0,1
 DATA -4,0,0,1,-8,0,0,1,-11,0,0,-1,-8,0,0,-1
 DATA -6,0,0,-1,-13,0,1,0,0,-2,1,0,0,-3,-1,0
 DATA 0,-4,-1,0,13,0,0,1,5,0,0,1,6,0,0,1,10,0
 DATA 0,-1,3,0,4,0,0,-1,7,0,0,1,14,0
 DATA 0,6,1,0,0,-6,1,0,0,1,1,0,0,1,1,0,0,1,1,0
 DATA 0,1,1,0,0,2,1,0,0,-6,-1,0,0,3,1,0,0,4
 DATA -1,0,3,0,-1,0,0,-4,-1,0,0,-1,-4,0,0,3,-1,0
 DATA 0,-2,1,0,0,3,4,0,0,-1,1,0
 DATA 5,0,0,1,1,0,0,1,-6,0,0,-1,-1,0,0,2,1,0,0,1
 DATA 5,0,0,4,1,0,0,-4,1,0
```

Let's Add and Subtract

This addition and subtraction game is a bit more advanced than Crazy Critters. Instead of counting images and entering the number of creatures, the child is challenged with some easy additions and subtractions using integers.

Since young children may have difficulty in carrying over numbers from one column to the next, this program gives them the option of selecting either simple problems without carrying or more complex ones with carrying.

When entering an answer, the child should enter the digit in the right-hand column first, just as in school with pencil and paper. In the example 7 + 3, for instance, 0 is keyed in first, followed by 1.

The Amiga rewards a right answer with a dancing bunny and a few notes from a lively Bach minuet. And for four right answers in a row, it produces something really special.

Finally, the pull-down menus are used to select number size, addition or subtraction, and place-carrying on or off.

Program 3-2. Let's Add and Subtract
Save using the filename **ADD**

```
REM LET'S ADD & SUBTRACT
 CLEAR ,37000&
 GOSUB INITIALIZE
PLAYGAME:
 GOSUB PLAY
PLAYAGAIN:
 CLS: LOCATE 10,21: PRINT "Play Again ? ";
 GOSUB DECIDE
 IF BUTTON = 1 THEN PLAYGAME
 GOSUB GOODBYE
END

INITIALIZE:
 GOSUB SETSCREEN
 GOSUB KEYVALUES
 GOSUB BACH.MINUET
 GOSUB SETMENUS
 GOSUB SETCOLORS
 GOSUB DRAWSHAPES
 GOSUB HEADING
RETURN
```

```
SETSCREEN:
 SCREEN 1,640,200,3,2
 WINDOW 2,"Let's Add and Subtract",,0,1
RETURN

KEYVALUES:
 DEFINT A-Z
 RANDOMIZE TIMER
 K = 4: REM PROBLEMS IN A SET
 DIM NUMBERS(4181),DUCK(781),BANNER(500)
 DIM BUNNY(1250),SIGNS(400),DISC(250)
 DIM TIMBRE2(255),TIMBRE3(255)
 DIM F(127),L(127),INDEX(11)
 REM DIGIT INDICES
  FOR I=1 TO 11
   INDEX(I) = 1 + (I-1)*380
  NEXT
 REM DUCK INDICES
  FOR I=1 TO 3
   DUCK.INDEX(I) = 1 + (I-1)*260
  NEXT
 REM BUTTON HOLES & LETTERS
  XB(1)=364: YB(1)=84
  XB(2)=406: YB(2)=84
  LT$(1) = "Y": LT$(2) = "N"
RETURN

BACH.MINUET:
 DATA 294,4,196,8,220,8,247,8,262,8,294,4,196,4
 DATA 196,4,330,4,262,8,294,8,330,8,370,8,392,4
 DATA 196,4,196,4,262,4,294,8,262,8,247,8,220,8
 DATA 247,4,262,8,247,8,220,8,196,8,185,4,196,8
 DATA 220,8,247,8,196,8,247,4,220,2,294,4,196,8
 DATA 220,8,247,8,262,8,294,4,196,4,196,4,330,4
 DATA 262,8,294,8,330,8,370,8,392,4,196,4,196,4
 DATA 262,4,294,8,262,8,247,8,220,8,247,4,262,8
 DATA 247,8,220,8,196,8,220,4,247,8,220,8,196,8
 DATA 185,8,196,2,494,4,392,8,440,8,494,8,392,8
 DATA 440,4,294,8,330,8,370,8,294,8,392,4,330,8
 DATA 370,8,392,8,294,8,277,4,247,8,277,8,220,4
 DATA 220,8,247,8,277,8,294,8,330,8,370,8,392,4
 DATA 370,4,330,4,370,4,220,4,277,4,294,2,294,4
 DATA 196,8,185,8,196,4,330,4,196,8,185,8,196,4
 DATA 294,4,262,4,247,4,220,8,196,8,185,8,196,8
 DATA 220,4,147,8,165,8,185,8,196,8,220,8,247,8
 DATA 262,4,247,4,220,4,247,8,294,8,196,4,185,4
 DATA 196,2
 LOCATE 10,25: PRINT "One moment ..."
 M! = 6.2838/256
```

149

```
 FOR I=Ø TO 255
   TIMBRE2(I) = 48*SIN(2*I*M↓)
   TIMBRE3(I) = 48*SIN(3*I*M↓)
 NEXT
 WAVE 2,TIMBRE2: WAVE 3,TIMBRE3
 FOR I=1 TO 127
   READ F(I),L: L(I) = 18/L
 NEXT
 REM NOTE GROUPS
   DATA 33, 65, 97, 127
   FOR I=1 TO 4: READ NOTE.GROUP(I): NEXT
RETURN

SETMENUS:
 DATA 2, Rules, Yes, No
 DATA 2, Problem, Without Place Carrying
 DATA With Place Carrying
 DATA 5, Number Sizes, Up to 9, Up to 20
 DATA Up to 50, Up to 100, Up to 1000
 DATA 2, Operation, Addition, Subtraction
 DATA 3, Stop, Go to BASIC
 DATA Go to Learning Menu, Go to System
 FOR I=1 TO 5
   READ V
   FOR J=Ø TO V
     READ TITLE$
     IF J<>Ø THEN TITLE$ = SPACE$(3) + TITLE$
     STATUS = 1
       IF I<>5 AND J=1 THEN STATUS = 2
     MENU I,J,STATUS,TITLE$
 NEXT J,I
 RULES = 1: CARRY = 1: SIZE = 1: OPERATION = 1
RETURN

SETCOLORS:
 REM PINK, FLESH, RED, BLUE
   PALETTE 4,1,.51,.64
   PALETTE 5,1,.87,.73
   PALETTE 6,.93,.2,0
   PALETTE 7,.4,.6,1
RETURN

DRAWSHAPES:
 CLS
 MENU ON
 ON MENU GOSUB OPTIONS
 FOR Z=1 TO 11
   ON Z GOSUB BK,NØ,N1,N2,N3,N4,N5,N6,N7,N8,N9
```

```
   GOSUB GET.IT
  NEXT Z
  GOSUB SIGNS.CIRCLE
  GOSUB DUCK1
  GOSUB DUCK2
  GOSUB BANNER
  GOSUB BUNNY1
  GOSUB BUNNY2
 RETURN

 BK:
  XØ=313: YØ=8Ø
  X1=286: X2=34Ø: Y1=65: Y2=95
  GOSUB GET.IT
 RETURN

 GET.IT:
  GET(X1,Y1)-(X2,Y2),NUMBERS(INDEX(Z))
  PUT(X1,Y1),NUMBERS(1),PSET: REM ERASE
 RETURN

 NØ:
  CALL DRAWLINE(3,XØ+26,YØ-11,8)
  CALL DRAWLINE(3,XØ+15,YØ-8,8)
  PAINT(XØ+2Ø,YØ)
 RETURN

 SUB DRAWLINE(K,X.C,Y.C,T) STATIC
  COLOR K
  PSET(X.C,Y.C)
  FOR I=1 TO T
   READ X,Y
   LINE -STEP(X,Y)
  NEXT
 END SUB

 SUB DRAWPOINT(K,X.C,Y.C,T) STATIC
  COLOR K
  FOR I=1 TO T
   READ X,Y
   PSET(X.C+X,Y.C+Y)
  NEXT
 END SUB

 N1:
  CALL DRAWLINE(3,XØ+5,YØ-15,11)
  PAINT (XØ+1,YØ+1)
 RETURN
```

151

```
N2:
 CALL DRAWLINE(3,X0+16,Y0+2,19)
 PAINT(X0+1,Y0+1)
RETURN

N3:
 CALL DRAWLINE(3,X0+12,Y0-3,20)
 PAINT(X0+4,Y0-1)
RETURN

N4:
 CALL DRAWLINE(3,X0-1,Y0,14)
 PAINT(X0+2,Y0)
RETURN

N5:
 CALL DRAWLINE(3,X0-16,Y0-4,20)
 PAINT(X0,Y0-2)
RETURN

N6:
 CALL DRAWLINE(3,X0-12,Y0+2,8)
 CALL DRAWLINE(3,X0-16,Y0-2,13)
 PAINT(X0+2,Y0)
RETURN

N7:
 CALL DRAWLINE(3,X0-27,Y0-15,11)
 PAINT(X0,Y0)
RETURN

N8:
 CALL DRAWLINE(3,X0-10,Y0+2,8)
 CALL DRAWLINE(3,X0-10,Y0-11,8)
 CALL DRAWLINE(3,X0-19,Y0-15,14)
 PAINT(X0,Y0)
RETURN

N9:
 CALL DRAWLINE(3,X0-12,Y0-11,8)
 CALL DRAWLINE(3,X0-19,Y0-15,12)
 PAINT(X0,Y0)
RETURN

SIGNS.CIRCLE:
 REM -
  LINE(293,78)-(333,82),1,BF
  GET(293,71)-(333,89),SIGNS(200)
 REM +
```

```
   LINE(307,71)-(319,89),1,BF
   GET(293,71)-(333,89),SIGNS(1)
   PUT(X1,Y1),NUMBERS(1),PSET
 REM CIRCLE
   CIRCLE(X0,Y0),12,6: PAINT(X0,Y0),6
   GET(X0-12,Y0-8)-(X0+12,Y0+8),DISC
   PUT(X1,Y1),NUMBERS(1),PSET
RETURN

DUCK1:
 X0=350: Y0=40
 CALL DRAWLINE(3,X0,Y0,73)
 PAINT (X0-9,Y0+4)
 PAINT (X0+17,Y0+4)
 CALL DRAWPOINT(2,X0,Y0,12)
 REM BILL
   COLOR 1
   PSET(X0+23,Y0+5)
   LINE -STEP(0,1): LINE -STEP(4,0)
 GET(319,30)-(379,50),DUCK(1)
 LINE(319,30)-(379,50),0,BF
RETURN

DUCK2:
 CALL DRAWLINE(3,X0,Y0,49)
 PAINT(X0-7,Y0-1): PAINT(X0+15,Y0-2)
 CALL DRAWPOINT(2,X0,Y0,5)
 CALL DRAWLINE(1,X0+22,Y0-2,2)
 GET(319,30)-(379,50),DUCK(261)
 GET(419,30)-(479,50),DUCK(521): REM BLANK
RETURN

BANNER:
 X0=280: Y0=40
 CALL DRAWLINE(6,X0,Y0,46)
 PAINT(X0+1,Y0+1)
 CALL DRAWLINE(6,X0+16,Y0-2,5)
 REM "Nice !"
   CALL DRAWLINE(1,X0-31,Y0-4,17)
   CALL DRAWLINE(1,X0-19,Y0-3,1)
   CALL DRAWLINE(1,X0-19,Y0-1,5)
   CALL DRAWLINE(1,X0-6,Y0+1,11)
   CALL DRAWLINE(1,X0,Y0-1,11)
   CALL DRAWLINE(1,X0+11,Y0-5,3)
   CALL DRAWLINE(1,X0+11,Y0+1,1)
 GET(240,34)-(318,47),BANNER(1)
 GET(100,34)-(178,47),BANNER(250)
RETURN
```

```
BUNNY1:
 REM SHIRT
  X0=313: Y0=80
  CALL DRAWLINE(4,X0,Y0,67)
  PAINT(X0,Y0+3): PAINT(X0+12,Y0+1)
  CALL DRAWPOINT(2,X0,Y0,11)
 REM PANTS
  CALL DRAWLINE(7,X0+6,Y0+7,34)
  PAINT(X0,Y0+10)
  CALL DRAWPOINT(2,X0,Y0,5)
 REM FEET
  CALL DRAWLINE(5,X0+8,Y0+14,17)
  PAINT(X0+11,Y0+16)
  CALL DRAWPOINT(2,X0,Y0,5)
  CALL DRAWLINE(5,X0-1,Y0+15,18)
  PAINT(X0-16,Y0+15)
  CALL DRAWPOINT(2,X0,Y0,3)
 REM HANDS
  CALL DRAWLINE(5,X0+16,Y0+6,14)
  CALL DRAWLINE(5,X0-19,Y0+4,17)
 REM FACE
  CALL DRAWLINE(5,X0,Y0-2,70)
  PAINT(X0,Y0-7): PAINT(X0-4,Y0-13)
  CALL DRAWLINE(4,X0+5,Y0-12,14)
  CALL DRAWLINE(4,X0-7,Y0-12,6)
  CALL DRAWLINE(4,X0+2,Y0-6,4)
  CALL DRAWPOINT(2,X0,Y0,2)
  CALL DRAWPOINT(2,X0,Y0,2)
  CALL DRAWPOINT(2,X0,Y0,2)
  CALL DRAWLINE(1,X0+7,Y0+6,9)
  GET(278,60)-(348,100),BUNNY(1)
  LINE(278,60)-(348,100),0,BF
RETURN

BUNNY2:
 REM SHIRT
  CALL DRAWLINE(4,X0,Y0,73)
  PAINT(X0+4,Y0): PAINT(X0-13,Y0-6)
  PAINT(X0-6,Y0-4)
  CALL DRAWPOINT(2,X0,Y0,4)
 REM PANTS
  CALL DRAWLINE(7,X0+2,Y0+3,42)
  PAINT(X0+6,Y0+5)
  CALL DRAWPOINT(2,X0,Y0,5)
 REM FEET
  CALL DRAWLINE(5,X0+12,Y0+12,13)
  CALL DRAWLINE(5,X0-7,Y0+6,29)
  PAINT(X0-12,Y0+7)
  CALL DRAWPOINT(2,X0,Y0,5)
```

```
 REM HANDS
  CALL DRAWLINE(5,XØ+17,YØ-8,36)
  PAINT(XØ+25,YØ-13)
  CALL DRAWLINE(5,XØ-17,YØ-8,28)
  PAINT(XØ-25,YØ-11)
 REM HEAD
  CALL DRAWLINE(5,XØ-1,YØ-3,51)
  PAINT(XØ+3,YØ-6)
  CALL DRAWLINE(4,XØ-2,YØ-8,6)
  CALL DRAWLINE(2,XØ+1,YØ-5,6)
  CALL DRAWLINE(3,XØ+4,YØ-8,3)
  CALL DRAWLINE(2,XØ+2,YØ-8,1)
  CALL DRAWLINE(4,XØ+9,YØ-11,5)
  CALL DRAWLINE(4,XØ+3,YØ-11,5)
  CALL DRAWLINE(1,XØ+11,YØ+4,4)
  GET(278,6Ø)-(348,1ØØ),BUNNY(625)
RETURN

HEADING:
 COLOR 1,Ø
 LOCATE 13,21:PRINT "Let's Add and Subtract"
 LOCATE 17,24:PRINT "Please use menus,"
 LOCATE 19,23:PRINT "Click mouse to play"
 GOSUB CLICKIT
RETURN

OPTIONS:
 ID = MENU(Ø): ITEM = MENU(1)
 ON ID GOSUB MENU1,MENU2,MENU3,MENU4,GOODBYE
 ITEM = Ø
RETURN

MENU1:
 MENU 1,RULES,1: MENU 1,ITEM,2
 RULES = ITEM
RETURN

MENU2:
 MENU 2,CARRY,1: MENU 2,ITEM,2
 CARRY = ITEM
RETURN

MENU3:
 MENU 3,SIZE,1: MENU 3,ITEM,2
 SIZE = ITEM
RETURN
```

```
MENU4:
 MENU 4,OPERATION,1: MENU 4,ITEM,2
 OPERATION = ITEM
RETURN

GOODBYE:
 WINDOW CLOSE 2: WINDOW 1: MENU RESET
 SCREEN CLOSE 1
 IF ITEM = 2 THEN RUN "LEARNING"
 IF ITEM = 3 THEN SYSTEM
 COLOR 1,Ø: CLS
 PRINT "Bye-Bye"
 STOP
RETURN

CLICKIT:
 S$ = ""
 WHILE MOUSE(Ø) = Ø AND S$ = ""
  S$ = INKEY$
 WEND
  X = MOUSE(1)
  Y = MOUSE(2)
 WHILE MOUSE(Ø)<> Ø: WEND: REM RESET
RETURN

PLAY:
 IF RULES = 1 THEN GOSUB RULES
 CNT = Ø: GROUP = Ø
 FOR Q=1 TO K
  GOSUB GET.VALUES
  GOSUB PROBLEM
  GOSUB GUESS
  GOSUB EVALUATE
 NEXT Q
 IF CNT = K THEN GOSUB FLY
RETURN

RULES:
 CLS
 PRINT
 PRINT "    I'll make up some nice addition and";
 PRINT " subtraction problems"
 PRINT " for you."
 PRINT
 PRINT " Please enter your answers just as";
 PRINT " you derive them: from"
 PRINT " right to left."
 LOCATE 9: PRINT " In the problem";TAB(22);
 PRINT ", for example, first enter the Ø and"
```

```
      LOCATE 8,19: PRINT "7"
      LOCATE 9,18: PRINT "+3"
      LINE(170,79)-(190,79),3
      LOCATE 10,18: PRINT "10"
      LOCATE 11,1: PRINT " then the 1."
     PRINT: PRINT
     PRINT "   I'll give you";K;"problems per";
     PRINT " game, and you'll enjoy a"
     PRINT " nice surprise if you tally";
     PRINT " perfectly."
     LOCATE 20,26:PRINT "Click Mouse";
     GOSUB CLICKIT
   RETURN

   GET.VALUES:
    CLS
    LOCATE 10,25: PRINT "One moment ..."
    REM HIGHEST NUMBER
     HN = 9
     IF SIZE = 2 THEN HN = 20
     IF SIZE = 3 THEN HN = 50
     IF SIZE = 4 THEN HN = 100
     IF SIZE = 5 THEN HN = 1000
    SEARCH$ = "ON"
    WHILE SEARCH$ = "ON"
     FOR I=1 TO 2
      N(I) = INT(RND*HN) + 1
     NEXT I
     SEARCH$ = "OFF"
     IF N(2) > N(1) THEN SWAP N(2),N(1)
     GOSUB DIGITS
     REM CHECK FOR PLACE CARRYING
      IF CARRY = 1 THEN
       PC$ = "OFF"
       ON OPERATION GOSUB PC.ADD, PC.SUB
       IF PC$ = "ON" THEN SEARCH$ = "ON"
      END IF
     WEND
     REM ANSWER
      IF OPERATION = 1 THEN
       AW = N(1) + N(2)
      ELSE
       AW = N(1) - N(2)
      END IF
   RETURN

   DIGITS:
    FOR I=1 TO 2
     S$ = MID$( STR$(N(I)),2 ): L(I) = LEN(S$)
```

157

```
  S$ = RIGHT$("000" + S$,4)
  FOR J=1 TO 4
   D(I,J) = VAL( MID$(S$,5-J,1) )
 NEXT J,I
RETURN

PC.ADD:
 FOR J=1 TO 4
  IF D(1,J) + D(2,J) > 9 THEN PC$ = "ON"
 NEXT J
RETURN

PC.SUB:
 FOR J=1 TO 4
  IF D(1,J) - D(2,J) < 0 THEN PC$ = "ON"
 NEXT J
RETURN

PROBLEM:
 LOCATE 10,25: PRINT SPACE$(14)
 FOR I=1 TO 2
  X = 350: Y = 35*I - 15
  FOR J=1 TO L(I)
   D = D(I,J)
   PUT(X,Y),NUMBERS(INDEX(D+2)),PSET
   X = X - 70
 NEXT J,I
 S = OPERATION
 PUT(X+6,Y+6),SIGNS(199*S-198),PSET
 LINE(348-L(1)*70,Y+35)-(404,Y+40),1,BF
RETURN

GUESS:
 GOSUB GURGLE
 X = 350: Y = 100: GUESS$ = "ON"
 LOCATE 17,11
 PRINT "Please enter your answer, then";
 PRINT " Hit Return."
 G$ = ""
 WHILE GUESS$ = "ON"
  PUT(X+23,Y+7),DISC,PSET
  GOSUB ENTER.DIGIT
  IF GUESS$ = "ON" THEN
   PUT(X,Y),NUMBERS(INDEX(INX)),PSET
   G$ = RIGHT$(STR$(DIGIT),1) + G$
   X = X-70
  END IF
 WEND
 PUT(X,Y),NUMBERS(1),PSET
RETURN
```

```
GURGLE:
 FREQ = 300
 FOR G=1 TO 5
  FREQ = 500-FREQ
  SOUND FREQ,1,50
 NEXT G
RETURN

ENTER.DIGIT:
 S$ = ""
 WHILE S$ = ""
  S$ = INKEY$
 WEND
 A = ASC(S$)
 IF A = 13 THEN GUESS$ = "OFF"
 IF A=8 OR A=30 THEN
  IF G$ = "" THEN SOUND 900,2
  IF G$ <> "" THEN GOSUB MOVE.RIGHT
  GOTO ENTER.DIGIT
 END IF
 IF A <> 13 AND (A < 48 OR A > 57) THEN
  SOUND 900,2
  GOTO ENTER.DIGIT
 END IF
 DIGIT = A - 48
 INX = DIGIT + 2
RETURN

MOVE.RIGHT:
 G$ = MID$(G$,2)
 PUT(X,Y),NUMBERS(1),PSET
 X = X+70
 PUT(X,Y),NUMBERS(1),PSET
 PUT(X+23,Y+7),DISC,PSET
RETURN

EVALUATE:
 LOCATE 17,11: PRINT SPACE$(42)
 GUESS = VAL(G$)
 ON -(GUESS = AW)+1 GOSUB WRONG, RIGHT
 LOCATE 20,26: PRINT "Press any key";
 GOSUB CLICKIT
RETURN

WRONG:
 SOUND 400,3: SOUND 300,3: SOUND 200,3
 LOCATE 17,21:
 PRINT "Sorry, the answer is";AW;CHR$(8);"."
RETURN
```

```
RIGHT:
 LOCATE 17,27: PRINT "Very Good !"
 X=475: Y=50
 PUT(X,Y),BUNNY(1),PSET
 GOSUB MUSIC
 GOSUB DANCE
 CNT = CNT+1
RETURN

MUSIC:
 GROUP = GROUP + 1
 IF GROUP = K+1 THEN GROUP = 1
 FIRST = NOTE.GROUP(GROUP-1) + 1
 LAST  = NOTE.GROUP(GROUP)
 FOR I = FIRST TO LAST
   SOUND WAIT
   FOR J=2 TO 3
     SOUND F(I),L(I),125,J
     SOUND 0,.5,,J
   NEXT J
   SOUND RESUME
 NEXT I
RETURN

DANCE:
 V = 1
 FOR FLASH = 1 TO 9
   PUT(X,Y),BUNNY(V),PSET
   FOR PAUSE=1 TO 1000: NEXT PAUSE
   V = 626-V
 NEXT FLASH
RETURN

FLY:
 CLS
 V = 1: YD(1) = 81: YD(2) = 74
 LOCATE 18,22: PRINT "You got all";K;"right !"
 FOR X=80 TO 610 STEP 5
   PUT(X,70),DUCK(DUCK.INDEX(V)),PSET
   PUT(X-76,YD(V)),BANNER(1),PSET
   FOR PAUSE=1 TO 500: NEXT PAUSE
   PUT(X,70),DUCK(DUCK.INDEX(3)),PSET
   PUT(X-76,YD(V)),BANNER(250),PSET
   V = 3-V
 NEXT X
RETURN

DECIDE:
 BUTTON = 0
```

```
   GOSUB DRAWBUTTON
   GOSUB PUSHBUTTON
   COLOR 1,Ø
RETURN

DRAWBUTTON:
 LINE (337,77)-(433,91),1,BF
 FOR I=1 TO 2
   CIRCLE (XB(I),YB(I)),12,I*3
   PAINT (XB(I),YB(I)),I*3
   COLOR 1,I*3
   LOCATE 1Ø: PRINT PTAB(XB(I)-4);LT$(I);
 NEXT I
RETURN

PUSHBUTTON:
 SOUND 44Ø,2
 GOSUB CLICKIT
 S$ = UCASE$(S$)
 IF S$ = "Y" THEN BUTTON = 1
 IF S$ = "N" THEN BUTTON = 2
 FOR I=1 TO 2
   XD = ABS(X-XB(I)): YD = ABS(Y-YB(I))
   IF XD<13 AND YD<7 THEN BUTTON = I: I=2
 NEXT
 IF BUTTON = Ø THEN PUSHBUTTON
RETURN

REM ZERO
 DATA Ø,22,-8,4,-37,Ø,-8,-4,Ø,-22,8,-4,37,Ø,8,4
 DATA Ø,16,-6,3,-19,Ø,-6,-3,Ø,-16,6,-3,19,Ø,6,3

REM ONE
 DATA Ø,26,9,Ø,Ø,4,-29,Ø,Ø,-4,9,Ø,Ø,-21,-7,Ø
 DATA Ø,-2,7,-3,11,Ø

REM TWO
 DATA -26,Ø,-6,3,Ø,6,42,Ø,Ø,4,-53,Ø,Ø,-11,12,-6
 DATA 30,Ø,Ø,-9,-29,Ø,-8,4,-5,Ø,Ø,-4,8,-4,37,Ø
 DATA 8,4,Ø,8,-10,5

REM THREE
 DATA 14,7,Ø,7,-8,4,-37,Ø,-8,-4,Ø,-3,9,Ø,4,3
 DATA 23,Ø,6,-4,Ø,-1,-6,-4,-14,Ø,Ø,-4,18,-9
 DATA -40,Ø,Ø,-4,53,Ø,Ø,5,-14,7

REM FOUR
 DATA Ø,15,11,Ø,Ø,-13,16,Ø,Ø,-4,-16,Ø,Ø,-13
 DATA -11,Ø,Ø,13,-15,Ø,Ø,-13,-11,Ø,Ø,17,26,Ø
```

161

```
REM FIVE
 DATA 32,0,10,5,0,9,-10,5,-35,0,-8,-4,0,-3,9,0
 DATA 4,3,25,0,4,-2,0,-7,-4,-2,-30,0,-8,-4
 DATA 0,-11,53,0,0,4,-42,0,0,7

REM SIX
 DATA 23,0,4,2,0,5,-4,2,-23,0,-4,-2,0,-5,4,-2
 DATA 34,0,8,4,0,9,-8,4,-37,0,-8,-4,0,-17,18,-9
 DATA 35,0,0,4,-28,0,-14,7,0,2

REM SEVEN
 DATA 53,0,0,5,-1,0,-34,17,1,0,0,8,-11,0,0,-10
 DATA 32,-16,-40,0,0,-4

REM EIGHT
 DATA 19,0,6,3,0,3,-6,3,-19,0,-6,-3,0,-3,6,-3
 DATA 19,0,6,3,0,3,-6,3,-19,0,-6,-3,0,-3,6,-3
 DATA 37,0,8,4,0,7,-8,4,8,4,0,7,-8,4,-37,0
 DATA -8,-4,0,-7,8,-4,-8,-4,0,-7,8,-4

REM NINE
 DATA 23,0,4,2,0,5,-4,2,-23,0,-4,-2,0,-5,4,-2
 DATA 37,0,8,4,0,15,-22,11,-31,0,0,-4,26,0
 DATA 16,-9,-34,0,-8,-4,0,-9,8,-4

REM DUCK #1
 DATA 3,0,-1,0,0,2,-1,0,0,2,3,0,0,1,7,0,0,-1
 DATA 2,0,0,-1,7,0,0,1,1,0,0,1,1,0,-2,0
 DATA 0,1,-5,0,0,-1,-5,0,0,1,-4,0,0,1,-4,0
 DATA 0,1,-13,0,0,-1,-6,0,0,-1,-5,0,0,-1
 DATA -4,0,9,0,0,-1,2,0,0,-2,1,0,0,-1,1,0,0,-1
 DATA 1,0,0,-2,-1,0,0,-1,-1,0,0,-2,-1,0,0,-2
 DATA 1,0,0,-1,1,0,0,1,2,0,0,1,2,0,0,1,2,0,0,1
 DATA 1,0,0,1,1,0,0,1,2,0,0,-2,2,0,0,1,1,0
 DATA 0,1,1,0,0,1,1,0,0,1
 DATA -4,-1,-3,0,-3,1,-2,2,-2,3,-1,4,1,5,2,6
 DATA 1,7,0,7,18,4,19,4

REM DUCK #2
 DATA 5,0,0,-1,2,0,0,-1,5,0,0,1,7,0,0,-1,2,0
 DATA -1,0,0,-1,-3,0,0,-1,-5,0,0,1,-4,0,0,1,-5,0
 DATA 0,-1,-5,0,0,-1,-10,0,0,1,-5,0,0,1,-11,0
 DATA 2,0,0,1,6,0,0,1,3,0,0,2,-2,0,0,1,-3,0
 DATA 0,1,-4,0,0,1,-1,0,10,0,0,-1,5,0,0,-1,4,0
 DATA 0,-1,3,0,0,-1,4,0,0,-1,15,-3,16,-3,1,0
 DATA -16,0,-15,-1,0,1,5,0
```

```
REM BANNER
 DATA 0,-3,1,0,0,-1,5,0,0,-1,4,0,0,-1,6,0,0,-1
 DATA 0,6,1,0,0,2,1,0,0,1,1,0,-2,0,0,1,-3,0,0,1
 DATA -4,0,0,1,-8,0,0,1,-11,0,0,-1,-8,0,0,-1
 DATA -6,0,0,-1,-13,0,1,0,0,-2,1,0,0,-3,-1,0
 DATA 0,-4,-1,0,13,0,0,1,5,0,0,1,6,0,0,1,10,0
 DATA 0,-1,3,0,4,0,0,-1,7,0,0,1,14,0
 DATA 0,6,1,0,0,-6,1,0,0,1,1,0,0,1,1,0,0,1,1,0
 DATA 0,1,1,0,0,2,1,0,0,-6,-1,0,0,3,1,0,0,4
 DATA -1,0,3,0,-1,0,0,-4,-1,0,0,-1,-4,0,0,3,-1,0
 DATA 0,-2,1,0,0,3,4,0,0,-1,1,0
 DATA 5,0,0,1,1,0,0,1,-6,0,0,-1,-1,0,0,2,1,0,0,1
 DATA 5,0,0,4,1,0,0,-4,1,0

REM BUNNY1
 DATA 0,-1,2,0,0,-1,1,0,0,-1,4,0,0,1,2,0,0,1,2,0
 DATA 0,1,3,0,0,1,3,0,0,1,1,0,0,1,-2,0,0,1,-4,0
 DATA 0,-1,-2,0,0,-1,-1,0,0,-1,-1,0,0,-1,-3,0,0,3
 DATA 1,0,0,1,1,0,0,2,-5,0,0,1,-11,0,0,-1,-4,0
 DATA 0,-1,1,0,0,-1,2,0,0,-1,1,0,0,-1,-3,0,0,1
 DATA -2,0,0,1,-5,0,0,-1,-3,0,0,-1,3,0,0,-1,3,0
 DATA 0,-1,4,0,0,-1,4,0,0,-1,2,0,0,-1,3,0,0,-1
 DATA 1,0,4,0,0,0,2,-1,4,-2,-3,-1,-5,-2,-9,2
 DATA -8,1,-8,0,-13,3,-13,2,-14,2
 DATA 1,0,0,1,2,0,0,1,1,0,0,1,1,0,0,2,-1,0,0,1
 DATA -2,0,0,1,-6,0,0,-1,-3,0,0,1,-6,0,0,-1,-4,0
 DATA 0,-1,-1,0,0,-1,-1,0,0,-1,1,0,0,-1,1,0,0,-1
 DATA 1,0,0,-1,0,1,13,0,0,-1,2,0,0,13,0,12,0,11
 DATA -1,10,-2,9,14,0,0,1,4,0,0,1,3,0,-1,0,0,1
 DATA -2,0,0,1,-9,0,0,-1,-8,0,0,-1,-5,0,0,-1,-3,0
 DATA 7,0,26,18,25,17,24,17,28,17,27,16
 DATA -3,0,0,1,-5,0,0,1,-8,0,0,1,-10,0,0,-1,-2,0
 DATA 1,0,0,-1,2,0,0,-1,7,0,0,-1,11,0,0,1,6,0
 DATA -27,17,-26,16,-25,16,2,0,0,1,3,0,0,-1,1,0
 DATA -3,0,0,-1,2,0,-1,0,0,-1,-3,0,0,-1,-1,0
 DATA 2,0,-3,0,0,1,-2,0,0,1,-2,0,1,0,0,1,2,0,0,1
 DATA 3,0,0,-1,2,0,-2,0,0,-1,-3,0,0,-1,2,0
 DATA 1,0,0,-1,1,0,0,-1,3,0,0,-1,3,0,0,-1,3,0
 DATA 0,-1,1,0,0,-1,-1,0,0,-1,-2,0,0,-1,-2,0,0,-1
 DATA -1,0,0,-2,1,0,0,-1,2,0,0,-1,1,0,0,-2,-1,0
 DATA 0,-1,-1,0,0,1,-2,0,0,1,-2,0,0,1,-2,0,0,3
 DATA -2,0,0,-1,-3,0,0,-1,-4,0,0,1,-4,0,0,1,-3,0
 DATA 0,1,-3,0,1,0,0,1,7,0,0,-1,3,0,0,-1,3,0,0,2
 DATA -1,0,0,1,-1,0,0,1,-1,0,0,1,-1,0,1,0,0,1,2,0
 DATA 0,1,3,0,0,1,1,0,2,0,0,-2,1,0,0,-1,2,0,0,-1
 DATA 1,0,0,-1,0,1,-2,0,0,1,-2,0,0,1,-1,0,0,1
 DATA -3,0,0,1,-4,0,2,0,0,-1,1,0
 DATA 1,0,0,-1,2,0,-5,0,2,-4,3,-4
 DATA 7,-9,6,-9,-1,-9,0,-9,2,0,0,1,2,0,0,2,-1,0
 DATA 0,-1,-1,0,0,-1,-2,0
```

```
REM BUNNY2
 DATA 0,-2,3,0,0,-1,2,0,0,-1,2,0,0,-1,1,0,0,-1,2,0
 DATA 0,-1,2,0,0,-1,2,0,0,-1,5,0,0,1,1,0,0,1,-2,0
 DATA 0,1,-3,0,0,1,-3,0,0,1,-2,0,0,1,-1,0,0,3,1,0
 DATA 0,1,1,0,0,2,-1,0,0,-1,-9,0,0,1,-2,0,0,-1
 DATA -1,0,0,-1,-3,0,0,-2,1,0,0,-2,-3,0,0,-1,-3,0
 DATA 0,-1,-3,0,0,1,-1,0,0,-1,-3,0,0,-1,-1,0,2,0
 DATA 0,-1,1,0,0,-1,1,0,0,1,3,0,0,1,2,0,0,1,4,0
 DATA 0,1,2,0,0,1,1,0,0,1,1,0,-14,-5,-13,-6,12,-5
 DATA 11,-6,7,0,0,1,1,0,0,1,1,0,0,1,3,0,0,1,3,0
 DATA 0,1,1,0,0,1,1,0,0,1,-1,0,0,1,-8,0,0,-1,-1,0
 DATA 0,-2,-3,0,0,-1,-6,0,0,-1,-3,0,0,3,-2,0,0,-1
 DATA -1,0,0,-3,-4,0,0,-1,-1,0,1,0,0,-1,2,0,0,-1
 DATA 4,0,0,1,2,0,0,1,4,0,0,4,1,5,2,6,-3,5,-2,6
 DATA 9,0,0,1,3,0,0,1,2,0,0,1,-4,0,0,-1,-2,0,0,-1
 DATA -4,0,0,-1,-2,0,0,3,1,0,0,1,-1,0,0,1,-2,0
 DATA 0,-1,-2,0,0,-1,-2,0,0,-1,-2,0,0,-1,-2,0
 DATA 0,-1,-1,0,0,-1,-1,0,0,-1,-1,0,1,0,0,-1,4,0
 DATA 0,1,2,0,0,1,2,0,0,1,3,0,25,15,-18,4,-17,3
 DATA -9,6,-9,7
 DATA 1,0,0,-1,-1,0,2,0,0,-1,-1,0,2,0,0,-1,2,0
 DATA 0,-1,4,0,0,1,2,0,-2,0,0,-1,1,0,0,-1,2,0
 DATA 0,1,2,0,-2,0,0,-2,3,0,-6,0,0,-1,-3,0,0,-1
 DATA -1,0,1,0,0,2,-1,0,0,1,-1,0,0,1,-1,0,0,1
 DATA -2,0,0,-1,-2,0,0,-1,-2,0,0,-2,1,0,0,-1,1,0
 DATA -1,0,0,1,-4,0,0,1,-5,0,2,0,0,2,-2,0,0,1
 DATA -1,0,1,0,0,-1,2,0,0,1,1,0,0,-1,2,0,0,-1,3,0
 DATA 3,0,0,-1,2,0,0,-1,2,0,0,-1,1,0,0,-1,2,0
 DATA 0,-3,2,0,0,-1,2,0,0,-1,1,0,0,-1,1,0,0,-1
 DATA -2,0,0,1,-3,0,0,1,-2,0,0,1,-1,0,0,1,-2,0
 DATA 0,-1,-1,0,0,-1,-2,0,0,-1,-2,0,0,-1,-2,0
 DATA 0,1,1,0,0,1,2,0,0,2,-1,0,0,1,-1,0,0,2,-4,0
 DATA 0,1,1,0,0,1,1,0,0,1,2,0,-1,0,0,-1,-2,0,0,1
 DATA -1,0,3,0,-1,0,0,-1,-3,0,1,0,0,1
 DATA 1,0,1,0,0,-1,-1,0,1,0,2,0,0,-1,1,0,0,-1,1,0
 DATA -1,0,0,-1,-1,0,0,-1,-1,0,4,0,0,1,1,0,-4,0
```

Let's Multiply

Many people have trouble with multiplication tables when they are first learning to multiply. Since practice is the best method for both learning and understanding how to multiply, this program will be of value in gaining this important basic skill.

As in the previous program, all answers should be entered just as they are derived. For example, the result for 4 X 3 = ? would be 12. First enter the 2 and then the 1.

Students can practice almost any integer problem they like. Acceptable values for the first multiplier range from 1 to 9, but the second multiplier can be up to 1000 (the pull-down menus are used to make selections). Youngsters can thus practice the easier low numbers and then advance to more complicated problems as they gain experience.

Program 3-3. Let's Multiply
Save using the filename **MULTIPLY**

```
REM LET'S MULTIPLY
 CLEAR ,37000&
 GOSUB INITIALIZE
PLAYGAME:
 GOSUB PLAY
PLAYAGAIN:
 CLS: LOCATE 10,21: PRINT "Play Again ? ";
 GOSUB DECIDE
 IF BUTTON = 1 THEN PLAYGAME
 GOSUB GOODBYE
END

INITIALIZE:
 GOSUB SETSCREEN
 GOSUB KEYVALUES
 GOSUB BACH.MINUET
 GOSUB SETMENUS
 GOSUB SETCOLORS
 GOSUB DRAWSHAPES
 GOSUB HEADING
RETURN

SETSCREEN:
 SCREEN 1,640,200,3,2
 WINDOW 2,"Let's Multiply",,0,1
RETURN
```

```
KEYVALUES:
 DEFINT A-Z
 RANDOMIZE TIMER
 K = 4: REM PROBLEMS IN A SET
 DIM NUMBERS(4181),DUCK(781),BANNER(500)
 DIM BUNNY(1250),SIGN(200),DISC(250)
 DIM TIMBRE2(255),TIMBRE3(255)
 DIM F(127),L(127),INDEX(11)
 REM DIGIT INDICES
  FOR I=1 TO 11
   INDEX(I) = 1 + (I-1)*380
  NEXT
 REM DUCK INDICES
  FOR I=1 TO 3
   DUCK.INDEX(I) = 1 + (I-1)*260
  NEXT
 REM BUTTON HOLES & LETTERS
  XB(1)=364: YB(1)=84
  XB(2)=406: YB(2)=84
  LT$(1) = "Y": LT$(2) = "N"
RETURN

BACH.MINUET:
 DATA 294,4,196,8,220,8,247,8,262,8,294,4,196,4
 DATA 196,4,330,4,262,8,294,8,330,8,370,8,392,4
 DATA 196,4,196,4,262,4,294,8,262,8,247,8,220,8
 DATA 247,4,262,8,247,8,220,8,196,8,185,4,196,8
 DATA 220,8,247,8,196,8,247,4,220,2,294,4,196,8
 DATA 220,8,247,8,262,8,294,4,196,4,196,4,330,4
 DATA 262,8,294,8,330,8,370,8,392,4,196,4,196,4
 DATA 262,4,294,8,262,8,247,8,220,8,247,4,262,8
 DATA 247,8,220,8,196,8,220,4,247,8,220,8,196,8
 DATA 185,8,196,2,494,4,392,8,440,8,494,8,392,8
 DATA 440,4,294,8,330,8,370,8,294,8,392,4,330,8
 DATA 370,8,392,8,294,8,277,4,247,8,277,8,220,4
 DATA 220,8,247,8,277,8,294,8,330,8,370,8,392,4
 DATA 370,4,330,4,370,4,220,4,277,4,294,2,294,4
 DATA 196,8,185,8,196,4,330,4,196,8,185,8,196,4
 DATA 294,4,262,4,247,4,220,8,196,8,185,8,196,8
 DATA 220,4,147,8,165,8,185,8,196,8,220,8,247,8
 DATA 262,4,247,4,220,4,247,8,294,8,196,4,185,4
 DATA 196,2
 LOCATE 10,25: PRINT "One moment ..."
 M! = 6.2838/256
 FOR I=0 TO 255
  TIMBRE2(I) = 48*SIN(2*I*M!)
  TIMBRE3(I) = 48*SIN(3*I*M!)
 NEXT
 WAVE 2,TIMBRE2: WAVE 3,TIMBRE3
```

```
 FOR I=1 TO 127
   READ F(I),L: L(I) = 18/L
 NEXT
 REM NOTE GROUPS
   DATA 33, 65, 97, 127
   FOR I=1 TO 4: READ NOTE.GROUP(I): NEXT
RETURN

SETMENUS:
 DATA 2, Rules, Yes, No
 DATA 1, Practice, With Number 1
 DATA 5, Size of Other Number, Up to 9, Up to 20
 DATA Up to 50, Up to 100, Up to 1000
 DATA 3, Stop, Go to BASIC
 DATA Go to Learning Menu, Go to System
 FOR I=1 TO 4
   READ V
   FOR J=0 TO V
     READ TITLE$
     IF J<>0 THEN TITLE$ = SPACE$(3) + TITLE$
     STATUS = 1
       IF I<>4 AND J=1 THEN STATUS = 2
     MENU I,J,STATUS,TITLE$
   NEXT J,I
 FOR I=2 TO 9
   MENU 2,I,1,SPACE$(3)+"With Number"+STR$(I)
 NEXT
 RULES = 1: PRACTICE = 1: SIZE = 1
RETURN

SETCOLORS:
 REM PINK, FLESH, RED, BLUE
   PALETTE 4,1,.51,.64
   PALETTE 5,1,.87,.73
   PALETTE 6,.93,.2,0
   PALETTE 7,.4,.6,1
RETURN

DRAWSHAPES:
 CLS
 MENU ON
 ON MENU GOSUB OPTIONS
 FOR Z=1 TO 11
   ON Z GOSUB BK,N0,N1,N2,N3,N4,N5,N6,N7,N8,N9
   GOSUB GET.IT
 NEXT Z
 GOSUB SIGN.CIRCLE
 GOSUB DUCK1
 GOSUB DUCK2
```

```
     GOSUB BANNER
     GOSUB BUNNY1
     GOSUB BUNNY2
    RETURN

    BK:
     X0=313: Y0=80
     X1=286: X2=340: Y1=65: Y2=95
     GOSUB GET.IT
    RETURN

    GET.IT:
     GET(X1,Y1)-(X2,Y2),NUMBERS(INDEX(Z))
     PUT(X1,Y1),NUMBERS(1),PSET: REM ERASE
    RETURN

    N0:
     CALL DRAWLINE(3,X0+26,Y0-11,8)
     CALL DRAWLINE(3,X0+15,Y0-8,8)
     PAINT(X0+20,Y0)
    RETURN

    SUB DRAWLINE(K,X.C,Y.C,T) STATIC
     COLOR K
     PSET(X.C,Y.C)
     FOR I=1 TO T
      READ X,Y
      LINE -STEP(X,Y)
     NEXT
    END SUB

    SUB DRAWPOINT(K,X.C,Y.C,T) STATIC
     COLOR K
     FOR I=1 TO T
      READ X,Y
      PSET(X.C+X,Y.C+Y)
     NEXT
    END SUB

    N1:
     CALL DRAWLINE(3,X0+5,Y0-15,11)
     PAINT (X0+1,Y0+1)
    RETURN

    N2:
     CALL DRAWLINE(3,X0+16,Y0+2,19)
     PAINT(X0+1,Y0+1)
    RETURN
```

```
N3:
 CALL DRAWLINE(3,X0+12,Y0-3,20)
 PAINT(X0+4,Y0-1)
RETURN

N4:
 CALL DRAWLINE(3,X0-1,Y0,14)
 PAINT(X0+2,Y0)
RETURN

N5:
 CALL DRAWLINE(3,X0-16,Y0-4,20)
 PAINT(X0,Y0-2)
RETURN

N6:
 CALL DRAWLINE(3,X0-12,Y0+2,8)
 CALL DRAWLINE(3,X0-16,Y0-2,13)
 PAINT(X0+2,Y0)
RETURN

N7:
 CALL DRAWLINE(3,X0-27,Y0-15,11)
 PAINT(X0,Y0)
RETURN

N8:
 CALL DRAWLINE(3,X0-10,Y0+2,8)
 CALL DRAWLINE(3,X0-10,Y0-11,8)
 CALL DRAWLINE(3,X0-19,Y0-15,14)
 PAINT(X0,Y0)
RETURN

N9:
 CALL DRAWLINE(3,X0-12,Y0-11,8)
 CALL DRAWLINE(3,X0-19,Y0-15,12)
 PAINT(X0,Y0)
RETURN

SIGN.CIRCLE:
 REM X SIGN
  CALL DRAWLINE(3,X0-12,Y0-10,6)
  PAINT(X0,Y0)
  CALL DRAWLINE(3,X0+12,Y0-10,6)
  PAINT(X0-10,Y0+5): PAINT(X0+10,Y0-5)
  GET(290,70)-(336,90),SIGN
  PUT(X1,Y1),NUMBERS(1),PSET
 REM CIRCLE
  CIRCLE(X0,Y0),12,6: PAINT(X0,Y0),6
```

```
  GET(X0-12,Y0-8)-(X0+12,Y0+8),DISC
  PUT(X1,Y1),NUMBERS(1),PSET
RETURN

DUCK1:
 X0=350: Y0=40
 CALL DRAWLINE(3,X0,Y0,73)
 PAINT (X0-9,Y0+4)
 PAINT (X0+17,Y0+4)
 CALL DRAWPOINT(2,X0,Y0,12)
 REM BILL
  COLOR 1
  PSET(X0+23,Y0+5)
  LINE -STEP(0,1): LINE -STEP(4,0)
 GET(319,30)-(379,50),DUCK(1)
 LINE(319,30)-(379,50),0,BF
RETURN

DUCK2:
 CALL DRAWLINE(3,X0,Y0,49)
 PAINT(X0-7,Y0-1): PAINT(X0+15,Y0-2)
 CALL DRAWPOINT(2,X0,Y0,5)
 CALL DRAWLINE(1,X0+22,Y0-2,2)
 GET(319,30)-(379,50),DUCK(261)
 GET(419,30)-(479,50),DUCK(521): REM BLANK
RETURN

BANNER:
 X0=280: Y0=40
 CALL DRAWLINE(6,X0,Y0,46)
 PAINT(X0+1,Y0+1)
 CALL DRAWLINE(6,X0+16,Y0-2,5)
 REM "Nice !"
  CALL DRAWLINE(1,X0-31,Y0-4,17)
  CALL DRAWLINE(1,X0-19,Y0-3,1)
  CALL DRAWLINE(1,X0-19,Y0-1,5)
  CALL DRAWLINE(1,X0-6,Y0+1,11)
  CALL DRAWLINE(1,X0,Y0-1,11)
  CALL DRAWLINE(1,X0+11,Y0-5,3)
  CALL DRAWLINE(1,X0+11,Y0+1,1)
 GET(240,34)-(318,47),BANNER(1)
 GET(100,34)-(178,47),BANNER(250)
RETURN

BUNNY1:
 REM SHIRT
  X0=313: Y0=80
  CALL DRAWLINE(4,X0,Y0,67)
  PAINT(X0,Y0+3): PAINT(X0+12,Y0+1)
```

170

```
   CALL DRAWPOINT(2,XØ,YØ,11)
 REM PANTS
  CALL DRAWLINE(7,XØ+6,YØ+7,34)
  PAINT(XØ,YØ+1Ø)
  CALL DRAWPOINT(2,XØ,YØ,5)
 REM FEET
  CALL DRAWLINE(5,XØ+8,YØ+14,17)
  PAINT(XØ+11,YØ+16)
  CALL DRAWPOINT(2,XØ,YØ,5)
  CALL DRAWLINE(5,XØ-1,YØ+15,18)
  PAINT(XØ-16,YØ+15)
  CALL DRAWPOINT(2,XØ,YØ,3)
 REM HANDS
  CALL DRAWLINE(5,XØ+16,YØ+6,14)
  CALL DRAWLINE(5,XØ-19,YØ+4,17)
 REM FACE
  CALL DRAWLINE(5,XØ,YØ-2,7Ø)
  PAINT(XØ,YØ-7): PAINT(XØ-4,YØ-13)
  CALL DRAWLINE(4,XØ+5,YØ-12,14)
  CALL DRAWLINE(4,XØ-7,YØ-12,6)
  CALL DRAWLINE(4,XØ+2,YØ-6,4)
  CALL DRAWPOINT(2,XØ,YØ,2)
  CALL DRAWPOINT(2,XØ,YØ,2)
  CALL DRAWPOINT(2,XØ,YØ,2)
  CALL DRAWLINE(1,XØ+7,YØ+6,9)
  GET(278,6Ø)-(348,1ØØ),BUNNY(1)
  LINE(278,6Ø)-(348,1ØØ),Ø,BF
RETURN

BUNNY2:
 REM SHIRT
  CALL DRAWLINE(4,XØ,YØ,73)
  PAINT(XØ+4,YØ): PAINT(XØ-13,YØ-6)
  PAINT(XØ-6,YØ-4)
  CALL DRAWPOINT(2,XØ,YØ,4)
 REM PANTS
  CALL DRAWLINE(7,XØ+2,YØ+3,42)
  PAINT(XØ+6,YØ+5)
  CALL DRAWPOINT(2,XØ,YØ,5)
 REM FEET
  CALL DRAWLINE(5,XØ+12,YØ+12,13)
  CALL DRAWLINE(5,XØ-7,YØ+6,29)
  PAINT(XØ-12,YØ+7)
  CALL DRAWPOINT(2,XØ,YØ,5)
 REM HANDS
  CALL DRAWLINE(5,XØ+17,YØ-8,36)
  PAINT(XØ+25,YØ-13)
  CALL DRAWLINE(5,XØ-17,YØ-8,28)
  PAINT(XØ-25,YØ-11)
```

```
  REM HEAD
   CALL DRAWLINE(5,XØ-1,YØ-3,51)
   PAINT(XØ+3,YØ-6)
   CALL DRAWLINE(4,XØ-2,YØ-8,6)
   CALL DRAWLINE(2,XØ+1,YØ-5,6)
   CALL DRAWLINE(3,XØ+4,YØ-8,3)
   CALL DRAWLINE(2,XØ+2,YØ-8,1)
   CALL DRAWLINE(4,XØ+9,YØ-11,5)
   CALL DRAWLINE(4,XØ+3,YØ-11,5)
   CALL DRAWLINE(1,XØ+11,YØ+4,4)
   GET(278,6Ø)-(348,1ØØ),BUNNY(625)
 RETURN

 HEADING:
  COLOR 1,Ø
  LOCATE 13,25:PRINT "Let's Multiply"
  LOCATE 17,24:PRINT "Please use menus,"
  LOCATE 19,23:PRINT "Click mouse to play"
  GOSUB CLICKIT
 RETURN

 OPTIONS:
  ID = MENU(Ø): ITEM = MENU(1)
  ON ID GOSUB MENU1,MENU2,MENU3,GOODBYE
  ITEM = Ø
 RETURN

 MENU1:
  MENU 1,RULES,1: MENU 1,ITEM,2
  RULES = ITEM
 RETURN

 MENU2:
  MENU 2,PRACTICE,1: MENU 2,ITEM,2
  PRACTICE = ITEM
 RETURN

 MENU3:
  MENU 3,SIZE,1: MENU 3,ITEM,2
  SIZE = ITEM
 RETURN

 GOODBYE:
  WINDOW CLOSE 2: WINDOW 1: MENU RESET
  SCREEN CLOSE 1
  IF ITEM = 2 THEN RUN "LEARNING"
  IF ITEM = 3 THEN SYSTEM
  COLOR 1,Ø: CLS
  PRINT "Bye-Bye"
```

```
  STOP
RETURN

CLICKIT:
 S$ = ""
 WHILE MOUSE(Ø) = Ø AND S$ = ""
  S$ = INKEY$
 WEND
  X = MOUSE(1)
  Y = MOUSE(2)
 WHILE MOUSE(Ø)<> Ø: WEND: REM RESET
RETURN

PLAY:
 IF RULES = 1 THEN GOSUB RULES
 CNT = Ø: GROUP = Ø
 FOR Q=1 TO K
  GOSUB GET.VALUES
  GOSUB PROBLEM
  GOSUB GUESS
  GOSUB EVALUATE
 NEXT Q
 IF CNT = K THEN GOSUB FLY
RETURN

RULES:
 CLS
 PRINT
 PRINT "   Let's learn to multiply with Bunny";
 PRINT " Rabitt."
 PRINT
 PRINT " Please enter your answers just as";
 PRINT " you derive them: from"
 PRINT " right to left."
 LOCATE 9: PRINT " In the problem";TAB(22);
 PRINT ", for example, first enter the 1 and"
 LOCATE 8,19: PRINT "7"
 LOCATE 9,18: PRINT "x3"
 LINE(17Ø,79)-(19Ø,79),3
 LOCATE 1Ø,18: PRINT "21"
 LOCATE 11,1: PRINT " then the 2."
 PRINT: PRINT
 PRINT "   I'll give you";K;"problems per";
 PRINT " game, and you'll enjoy a"
 PRINT " nice surprise if you multiply";
 PRINT " perfectly."
 LOCATE 2Ø,26:PRINT "Click Mouse";
 GOSUB CLICKIT
RETURN
```

```
GET.VALUES:
 CLS
 LOCATE 10,25: PRINT "One moment ..."
 N(2) = PRACTICE: REM PRACTICE NUMBER
 REM HIGHEST OTHER NUMBER
  HN = 9
  IF SIZE = 2 THEN HN = 20
  IF SIZE = 3 THEN HN = 50
  IF SIZE = 4 THEN HN = 100
  IF SIZE = 5 THEN HN = 1000
  N(1) = INT(RND*HN) + 1
  GOSUB DIGITS
 REM ANSWER
  AW = N(1)*N(2)
RETURN

DIGITS:
 FOR I=1 TO 2
  S$ = MID$( STR$(N(I)),2 ): L(I) = LEN(S$)
  S$ = RIGHT$("000" + S$,4)
  FOR J=1 TO 4
   D(I,J) = VAL( MID$(S$,5-J,1) )
 NEXT J,I
RETURN

PROBLEM:
 LOCATE 10,25: PRINT SPACE$(14)
 FOR I=1 TO 2
  X = 350: Y = 35*I - 15
  FOR J=1 TO L(I)
   D = D(I,J)
   PUT(X,Y),NUMBERS(INDEX(D+2)),PSET
   X = X - 70
 NEXT J,I
 PUT(X+6,Y+6),SIGN,PSET
 LINE(348-L(1)*70,Y+35)-(404,Y+40),1,BF
RETURN

GUESS:
 GOSUB GURGLE
 X = 350: Y = 100: GUESS$ = "ON"
 LOCATE 17,11
 PRINT "Please enter your answer, then";
 PRINT " Hit Return."
 G$ = ""
 WHILE GUESS$ = "ON"
  PUT(X+23,Y+7),DISC,PSET
  GOSUB ENTER.DIGIT
  IF GUESS$ = "ON" THEN
```

```
      PUT(X,Y),NUMBERS(INDEX(INX)),PSET
      G$ = RIGHT$(STR$(DIGIT),1) + G$
      X = X-7Ø
    END IF
  WEND
  PUT(X,Y),NUMBERS(1),PSET
RETURN

GURGLE:
  FREQ = 3ØØ
  FOR G=1 TO 5
    FREQ = 5ØØ-FREQ
    SOUND FREQ,1,5Ø
  NEXT G
RETURN

ENTER.DIGIT:
  S$ = ""
  WHILE S$ = ""
    S$ = INKEY$
  WEND
  A = ASC(S$)
  IF A = 13 THEN GUESS$ = "OFF"
  IF A=8 OR A=3Ø THEN
    IF G$ = "" THEN SOUND 9ØØ,2
    IF G$ <> "" THEN GOSUB MOVE.RIGHT
    GOTO ENTER.DIGIT
  END IF
  IF A <> 13 AND (A < 48 OR A > 57) THEN
    SOUND 9ØØ,2
    GOTO ENTER.DIGIT
  END IF
  DIGIT = A - 48
  INX = DIGIT + 2
RETURN

MOVE.RIGHT:
  G$ = MID$(G$,2)
  PUT(X,Y),NUMBERS(1),PSET
  X = X+7Ø
  PUT(X,Y),NUMBERS(1),PSET
  PUT(X+23,Y+7),DISC,PSET
RETURN

EVALUATE:
  LOCATE 17,11: PRINT SPACE$(42)
  GUESS = VAL(G$)
  ON -(GUESS = AW)+1 GOSUB WRONG, RIGHT
  LOCATE 2Ø,26: PRINT "Press any key";
```

```
  GOSUB CLICKIT
RETURN

WRONG:
  SOUND 400,3: SOUND 300,3: SOUND 200,3
  LOCATE 17,21:
  PRINT "Sorry, the answer is";AW;CHR$(8);"."
RETURN

RIGHT:
  LOCATE 17,27: PRINT "Very Good !"
  X=475: Y=50
  PUT(X,Y),BUNNY(1),PSET
  GOSUB MUSIC
  GOSUB DANCE
  CNT = CNT+1
RETURN

MUSIC:
  GROUP = GROUP + 1
  IF GROUP = K+1 THEN GROUP = 1
  FIRST = NOTE.GROUP(GROUP-1) + 1
  LAST  = NOTE.GROUP(GROUP)
  FOR I = FIRST TO LAST
    SOUND WAIT
    FOR J=2 TO 3
      SOUND F(I),L(I),125,J
      SOUND 0,.5,,J
    NEXT J
    SOUND RESUME
  NEXT I
RETURN

DANCE:
  V = 1
  FOR FLASH = 1 TO 9
    PUT(X,Y),BUNNY(V),PSET
    FOR PAUSE=1 TO 1000: NEXT PAUSE
    V = 626-V
  NEXT FLASH
RETURN

FLY:
  CLS
  V = 1: YD(1) = 81: YD(2) = 74
  LOCATE 18,22: PRINT "You got all";K;"right !"
  FOR X=80 TO 610 STEP 5
    PUT(X,70),DUCK(DUCK.INDEX(V)),PSET
    PUT(X-76,YD(V)),BANNER(1),PSET
```

```
    FOR PAUSE=1 TO 500: NEXT PAUSE
    PUT(X,70),DUCK(DUCK.INDEX(3)),PSET
    PUT(X-76,YD(V)),BANNER(250),PSET
    V = 3-V
  NEXT X
RETURN

DECIDE:
 BUTTON = 0
 GOSUB DRAWBUTTON
 GOSUB PUSHBUTTON
 COLOR 1,0
RETURN

DRAWBUTTON:
 LINE (337,77)-(433,91),1,BF
 FOR I=1 TO 2
   CIRCLE (XB(I),YB(I)),12,I*3
   PAINT (XB(I),YB(I)),I*3
   COLOR 1,I*3
   LOCATE 10: PRINT PTAB(XB(I)-4);LT$(I);
 NEXT I
RETURN

PUSHBUTTON:
 SOUND 440,2
 GOSUB CLICKIT
 S$ = UCASE$(S$)
 IF S$ = "Y" THEN BUTTON = 1
 IF S$ = "N" THEN BUTTON = 2
 FOR I=1 TO 2
   XD = ABS(X-XB(I)): YD = ABS(Y-YB(I))
   IF XD<13 AND YD<7 THEN BUTTON = I: I=2
 NEXT
 IF BUTTON = 0 THEN PUSHBUTTON
RETURN

REM ZERO
 DATA 0,22,-8,4,-37,0,-8,-4,0,-22,8,-4,37,0,8,4
 DATA 0,16,-6,3,-19,0,-6,-3,0,-16,6,-3,19,0,6,3

REM ONE
 DATA 0,26,9,0,0,4,-29,0,0,-4,9,0,0,-21,-7,0
 DATA 0,-2,7,-3,11,0

REM TWO
 DATA -26,0,-6,3,0,6,42,0,0,4,-53,0,0,-11,12,-6
 DATA 30,0,0,-9,-29,0,-8,4,-5,0,0,-4,8,-4,37,0
 DATA 8,4,0,8,-10,5
```

```
REM THREE
 DATA 14,7,0,7,-8,4,-37,0,-8,-4,0,-3,9,0,4,3
 DATA 23,0,6,-4,0,-1,-6,-4,-14,0,0,-4,18,-9
 DATA -40,0,0,-4,53,0,0,5,-14,7

REM FOUR
 DATA 0,15,11,0,0,-13,16,0,0,-4,-16,0,0,-13
 DATA -11,0,0,13,-15,0,0,-13,-11,0,0,17,26,0

REM FIVE
 DATA 32,0,10,5,0,9,-10,5,-35,0,-8,-4,0,-3,9,0
 DATA 4,3,25,0,4,-2,0,-7,-4,-2,-30,0,-8,-4
 DATA 0,-11,53,0,0,4,-42,0,0,7

REM SIX
 DATA 23,0,4,2,0,5,-4,2,-23,0,-4,-2,0,-5,4,-2
 DATA 34,0,8,4,0,9,-8,4,-37,0,-8,-4,0,-17,18,-9
 DATA 35,0,0,4,-28,0,-14,7,0,2

REM SEVEN
 DATA 53,0,0,5,-1,0,-34,17,1,0,0,8,-11,0,0,-10
 DATA 32,-16,-40,0,0,-4

REM EIGHT
 DATA 19,0,6,3,0,3,-6,3,-19,0,-6,-3,0,-3,6,-3
 DATA 19,0,6,3,0,3,-6,3,-19,0,-6,-3,0,-3,6,-3
 DATA 37,0,8,4,0,7,-8,4,8,4,0,7,-8,4,-37,0
 DATA -8,-4,0,-7,8,-4,-8,-4,0,-7,8,-4

REM NINE
 DATA 23,0,4,2,0,5,-4,2,-23,0,-4,-2,0,-5,4,-2
 DATA 37,0,8,4,0,15,-22,11,-31,0,0,-4,26,0
 DATA 16,-9,-34,0,-8,-4,0,-9,8,-4

REM X SIGN
 DATA 34,17,0,3,-11,0,-34,-17,0,-3,11,0
 DATA -34,17,0,3,11,0,34,-17,0,-3,-11,0

REM DUCK #1
 DATA 3,0,-1,0,0,2,-1,0,0,2,3,0,0,1,7,0,0,-1
 DATA 2,0,0,-1,7,0,0,1,1,0,0,1,1,0,-2,0
 DATA 0,1,-5,0,0,-1,-5,0,0,1,-4,0,0,1,-4,0
 DATA 0,1,-13,0,0,-1,-6,0,0,-1,-5,0,0,-1
 DATA -4,0,9,0,0,-1,2,0,0,-2,1,0,0,-1,1,0,0,-1
 DATA 1,0,0,-2,-1,0,0,-1,-1,0,0,-2,-1,0,0,-2
 DATA 1,0,0,-1,1,0,0,1,2,0,0,1,2,0,0,1,2,0,0,1
 DATA 1,0,0,1,1,0,0,1,2,0,0,-2,2,0,0,1,1,0
 DATA 0,1,1,0,0,1,1,0,0,1
 DATA -4,-1,-3,0,-3,1,-2,2,-2,3,-1,4,1,5,2,6
 DATA 1,7,0,7,18,4,19,4
```

```
REM DUCK #2
 DATA 5,0,0,-1,2,0,0,-1,5,0,0,1,7,0,0,-1,2,0
 DATA -1,0,0,-1,-3,0,0,-1,-5,0,0,1,-4,0,0,1,-5,0
 DATA 0,-1,-5,0,0,-1,-10,0,0,1,-5,0,0,1,-11,0
 DATA 2,0,0,1,6,0,0,1,3,0,0,2,-2,0,0,1,-3,0
 DATA 0,1,-4,0,0,1,-1,0,10,0,0,-1,5,0,0,-1,4,0
 DATA 0,-1,3,0,0,-1,4,0,0,-1,15,-3,16,-3,1,0
 DATA -16,0,-15,-1,0,1,5,0

REM BANNER
 DATA 0,-3,1,0,0,-1,5,0,0,-1,4,0,0,-1,6,0,0,-1
 DATA 0,6,1,0,0,2,1,0,0,1,1,0,-2,0,0,1,-3,0,0,1
 DATA -4,0,0,1,-8,0,0,1,-11,0,0,-1,-8,0,0,-1
 DATA -6,0,0,-1,-13,0,1,0,0,-2,1,0,0,-3,-1,0
 DATA 0,-4,-1,0,13,0,0,1,5,0,0,1,6,0,0,1,10,0
 DATA 0,-1,3,0,4,0,0,-1,7,0,0,1,14,0
 DATA 0,6,1,0,0,-6,1,0,0,1,1,0,0,1,1,0,0,1,1,0
 DATA 0,1,1,0,0,2,1,0,0,-6,-1,0,0,3,1,0,0,4
 DATA -1,0,3,0,-1,0,0,-4,-1,0,0,-1,-4,0,0,3,-1,0
 DATA 0,-2,1,0,0,3,4,0,0,-1,1,0
 DATA 5,0,0,1,1,0,0,1,-6,0,0,-1,-1,0,0,2,1,0,0,1
 DATA 5,0,0,4,1,0,0,-4,1,0

REM BUNNY1
 DATA 0,-1,2,0,0,-1,1,0,0,-1,4,0,0,1,2,0,0,1,2,0
 DATA 0,1,3,0,0,1,3,0,0,1,1,0,0,1,-2,0,0,1,-4,0
 DATA 0,-1,-2,0,0,-1,-1,0,0,-1,-1,0,0,-1,-3,0,0,3
 DATA 1,0,0,1,1,0,0,2,-5,0,0,1,-11,0,0,-1,-4,0
 DATA 0,-1,1,0,0,-1,2,0,0,-1,1,0,0,-1,-3,0,0,1
 DATA -2,0,0,1,-5,0,0,-1,-3,0,0,-1,3,0,0,-1,3,0
 DATA 0,-1,4,0,0,-1,4,0,0,-1,2,0,0,-1,3,0,0,-1
 DATA 1,0,4,0,0,0,2,-1,4,-2,-3,-1,-5,-2,-9,2
 DATA -8,1,-8,0,-13,3,-13,2,-14,2
 DATA 1,0,0,1,2,0,0,1,1,0,0,1,1,0,0,2,-1,0,0,1
 DATA -2,0,0,1,-6,0,0,-1,-3,0,0,1,-6,0,0,-1,-4,0
 DATA 0,-1,-1,0,0,-1,-1,0,0,-1,1,0,0,-1,1,0,0,-1
 DATA 1,0,0,-1,0,1,13,0,0,-1,2,0,0,13,0,12,0,11
 DATA -1,10,-2,9,14,0,0,1,4,0,0,1,3,0,-1,0,0,1
 DATA -2,0,0,1,-9,0,0,-1,-8,0,0,-1,-5,0,0,-1,-3,0
 DATA 7,0,26,18,25,17,24,17,28,17,27,16
 DATA -3,0,0,1,-5,0,0,1,-8,0,0,1,-10,0,0,-1,-2,0
 DATA 1,0,0,-1,2,0,0,-1,7,0,0,-1,11,0,0,1,6,0
 DATA -27,17,-26,16,-25,16,2,0,0,1,3,0,0,-1,1,0
 DATA -3,0,0,-1,2,0,-1,0,0,-1,-3,0,0,-1,-1,0
 DATA 2,0,-3,0,0,1,-2,0,0,1,-2,0,1,0,0,1,2,0,0,1
 DATA 3,0,0,-1,2,0,-2,0,0,-1,-3,0,0,-1,2,0
 DATA 1,0,0,-1,1,0,0,-1,3,0,0,-1,3,0,0,-1,3,0
 DATA 0,-1,1,0,0,-1,-1,0,0,-1,-2,0,0,-1,-2,0,0,-1
 DATA -1,0,0,-2,1,0,0,-1,2,0,0,-1,1,0,0,-2,-1,0
```

179

```
DATA 0,-1,-1,0,0,1,-2,0,0,1,-2,0,0,1,-2,0,0,3
DATA -2,0,0,-1,-3,0,0,-1,-4,0,0,1,-4,0,0,1,-3,0
DATA 0,1,-3,0,1,0,0,1,7,0,0,-1,3,0,0,-1,3,0,0,2
DATA -1,0,0,1,-1,0,0,1,-1,0,0,1,-1,0,1,0,0,1,2,0
DATA 0,1,3,0,0,1,1,0,2,0,0,-2,1,0,0,-1,2,0,0,-1
DATA 1,0,0,-1,0,1,-2,0,0,1,-2,0,0,1,-1,0,0,1
DATA -3,0,0,1,-4,0,2,0,0,-1,1,0
DATA 1,0,0,-1,2,0,-5,0,2,-4,3,-4
DATA 7,-9,6,-9,-1,-9,0,-9,2,0,0,1,2,0,0,2,-1,0
DATA 0,-1,-1,0,0,-1,-2,0

REM BUNNY2
DATA 0,-2,3,0,0,-1,2,0,0,-1,2,0,0,-1,1,0,0,-1,2,0
DATA 0,-1,2,0,0,-1,2,0,0,-1,5,0,0,1,1,0,0,1,-2,0
DATA 0,1,-3,0,0,1,-3,0,0,1,-2,0,0,1,-1,0,0,3,1,0
DATA 0,1,1,0,0,2,-1,0,0,-1,-9,0,0,1,-2,0,0,-1
DATA -1,0,0,-1,-3,0,0,-2,1,0,0,-2,-3,0,0,-1,-3,0
DATA 0,-1,-3,0,0,1,-1,0,0,-1,-3,0,0,-1,-1,0,2,0
DATA 0,-1,1,0,0,-1,1,0,0,1,3,0,0,1,2,0,0,1,4,0
DATA 0,1,2,0,0,1,1,0,0,1,1,0,-14,-5,-13,-6,12,-5
DATA 11,-6,7,0,0,1,1,0,0,1,1,0,0,1,3,0,0,1,3,0
DATA 0,1,1,0,0,1,1,0,0,1,-1,0,0,1,-8,0,0,-1,-1,0
DATA 0,-2,-3,0,-1,-6,0,0,-1,-3,0,0,3,-2,0,0,-1
DATA -1,0,0,-3,-4,0,0,-1,-1,0,1,0,0,-1,2,0,0,-1
DATA 4,0,0,1,2,0,0,1,4,0,0,4,1,5,2,6,-3,5,-2,6
DATA 9,0,0,1,3,0,0,1,2,0,0,1,-4,0,0,-1,-2,0,0,-1
DATA -4,0,0,-1,-2,0,0,3,1,0,0,1,-1,0,0,1,-2,0
DATA 0,-1,-2,0,0,-1,-2,0,0,-1,-2,0,0,-1,-2,0
DATA 0,-1,-1,0,0,-1,-1,0,0,-1,-1,0,1,0,0,-1,4,0
DATA 0,1,2,0,0,1,2,0,0,1,3,0,25,15,-18,4,-17,3
DATA -9,6,-9,7
DATA 1,0,0,-1,-1,0,2,0,0,-1,-1,0,2,0,0,-1,2,0
DATA 0,-1,4,0,0,1,2,0,-2,0,0,-1,1,0,0,-1,2,0
DATA 0,1,2,0,-2,0,0,-2,3,0,-6,0,0,-1,-3,0,0,-1
DATA -1,0,1,0,0,2,-1,0,0,1,-1,0,0,1,-1,0,0,1
DATA -2,0,0,-1,-2,0,0,-1,-2,0,0,-2,1,0,0,-1,1,0
DATA -1,0,0,1,-4,0,0,1,-5,0,2,0,0,2,-2,0,0,1
DATA -1,0,1,0,0,-1,2,0,0,1,1,0,0,-1,2,0,0,-1,3,0
DATA 3,0,0,-1,2,0,0,-1,2,0,0,-1,1,0,0,-1,2,0
DATA 0,-3,2,0,0,-1,2,0,0,-1,1,0,0,-1,1,0,0,-1
DATA -2,0,0,1,-3,0,0,1,-2,0,0,1,-1,0,0,1,-2,0
DATA 0,-1,-1,0,0,-1,-2,0,0,-1,-2,0,0,-1,-2,0
DATA 0,1,1,0,0,1,2,0,0,2,-1,0,0,1,-1,0,0,2,-4,0
DATA 0,1,1,0,0,1,1,0,0,1,2,0,-1,0,0,-1,-2,0,0,1
DATA -1,0,3,0,-1,0,0,-1,-3,0,1,0,0,1
DATA 1,0,1,0,0,-1,-1,0,1,0,2,0,0,-1,1,0,0,-1,1,0
DATA -1,0,0,-1,-1,0,0,-1,-1,0,4,0,0,1,1,0,-4,0
```

Fun with Fractions

Fractions are always tougher than they look. How can two fractions like 1/4 and 5/9 possibly be added together? Well, with a little practice and patience, students will quickly find that the above problem is much easier than it looks.

"Fun with Fractions" has two levels of difficulty. The easy level makes the bottom number (denominator) in both fractions the same value. To solve the problem, only the two top numbers (the numerators) must be added together. If the problem was, for example, 1/4 + 2/4 = ?, the answer would be 3/4. Again, only the two top numbers have to be added together. The denominator stays the same.

The more difficult level has different values for the two denominators. Since these numbers are not the same, they cannot be added together without some adjustment. For instance, suppose the problem was 1/3 + 1/2 = ?. To solve this, we will have to find some kind of relationship between the two values, some kind of *common denominator*.

The best approach is to multiply each fraction by 1, but with a little twist. First, multiply 1/3 by 2/2, which is the same as multiplying by 1 since 2 divided by 2 equals 1. The new fraction is 2/6. Now, multiply 1/2 by 3/3, and the result is 3/6.

Our original equation 1/3 + 1/2 = ? has now become 2/6 + 3/6 = ?, which quickly yields the desired result of 5/6. The key to solving an equation with different denominators, then, is to multiply each fraction by 1, using the denominator of the other fraction divided by itself.

Program 3-4. Fun with Fractions
Save using the filename **FRACTIONS**

```
REM FUN WITH FRACTIONS
  CLEAR ,35000&
  GOSUB INITIALIZE
PLAYGAME:
  GOSUB PLAY
PLAYAGAIN:
  CLS: LOCATE 10,21: PRINT "Play Again ? ";
  GOSUB DECIDE
  IF BUTTON = 1 THEN PLAYGAME
  GOSUB GOODBYE
END
```

```
INITIALIZE:
  GOSUB SETSCREEN
  GOSUB KEYVALUES
  GOSUB DIXIE
  GOSUB SETMENUS
  GOSUB SETCOLORS
  GOSUB DRAWSHAPES
  GOSUB HEADING
RETURN

SETSCREEN:
  SCREEN 1,640,200,3,2
  WINDOW 2,"Fun with Fractions",,0,1
RETURN

KEYVALUES:
  DEFINT B-F,H-Z
  RANDOMIZE TIMER
  K = 5: REM PROBLEMS IN A SET
  DIM NUMBERS(4181),DUCK(781),LITTLE.X(50)
  DIM PIGLET(1250),SIGNS(400),CURSOR(75)
  DIM TIMBRE(255)
  DIM F(113),L(113),INDEX(11)
  T$(1) = "Numerator": T$(2) = "Denominator"
  REM DIGIT INDICES
    FOR I=1 TO 11
      INDEX(I) = 1 + (I-1)*380
    NEXT
  REM DUCK INDICES
    FOR I=1 TO 3
      DUCK.INDEX(I) = 1 + (I-1)*260
    NEXT
  REM BUTTON HOLES & LETTERS
    XB(1)=364: YB(1)=84
    XB(2)=406: YB(2)=84
    LT$(1) = "Y": LT$(2) = "N"
RETURN

DIXIE:
  DATA 196,1,165,1,131,2,131,2,131,1,147,1,165,1
  DATA 175,1,196,2,196,2,196,2,165,2,220,2,220,2
  DATA 220,2,196,2,220,2,196,2,220,1,247,1,262,1
  DATA 294,1,330,6,262,1,196,1,262,6,196,1,165,1
  DATA 196,6,147,1,165,1,131,4,196,1,165,1,131,2
  DATA 131,2,131,1,147,1,165,1,175,1,196,2,196,2
  DATA 196,2,165,2,220,2,220,2,220,2,196,2,220,2
  DATA 196,2,220,1,247,1,262,1,294,1,330,6,262,1
  DATA 196,1,262,6,196,1,165,1,196,6,147,1,165,1
  DATA 131,4,196,1,196,1,262,2,330,2,294,2,262,2
  DATA 220,2,262,4,220,2,294,6,220,2,294,6,196,2
```

182

```
DATA 262,2,330,2,294,2,262,2,220,2,247,2,262,2
DATA 220,2,196,2,165,2,262,2,165,2,165,2,147,4
DATA 165,2,131,6,165,2,147,6,220,2,196,2,165,2
DATA 262,2,330,2,294,2,262,4,165,2,131,6,165,2
DATA 146,6,220,2,196,2,165,2,330,3,262,2,294,2
DATA 262,4
LOCATE 10,25: PRINT "One moment ..."
M! = 6.2838/256
FOR I=0 TO 255
  TIMBRE(I) = 48*SIN(2*I*M!)
NEXT
WAVE 2,TIMBRE: WAVE 3,TIMBRE
FOR I=1 TO 113
  READ F(I),L(I)
NEXT
REM NOTE GROUPS
  DATA 32,64,91,102,113
  FOR I=1 TO 5: READ NOTE.GROUP(I): NEXT
RETURN

SETMENUS:
  DATA 2, Rules, Yes, No
  DATA 2, Version, With Common Denominator
  DATA Without Common Denominator
  DATA 2, Operation, Addition, Subtraction
  DATA 3, Stop, Go to BASIC
  DATA Go to Learning Menu, Go to System
  FOR I=1 TO 4
   READ V
   FOR J=0 TO V
    READ TITLE$
    IF J<>0 THEN TITLE$ = SPACE$(3) + TITLE$
    STATUS = 1
     IF I<>4 AND J=1 THEN STATUS = 2
    MENU I,J,STATUS,TITLE$
  NEXT J,I
  RULES = 1: VERSION = 1: OPERATION = 1
RETURN

SETCOLORS:
  REM PINK, FLESH, RED, BLUE
   PALETTE 4,1,.51,.64
   PALETTE 5,1,.87,.73
   PALETTE 6,.93,.2,0
   PALETTE 7,.4,.6,1
RETURN

DRAWSHAPES:
 CLS
```

183

```
      MENU ON
      ON MENU GOSUB OPTIONS
      FOR Z=1 TO 11
        ON Z GOSUB BK,NØ,N1,N2,N3,N4,N5,N6,N7,N8,N9
        GOSUB GET.IT
      NEXT Z
      GOSUB LITTLE.X
      GOSUB SIGNS.CURSOR
      GOSUB DUCK1
      GOSUB DUCK2
      GOSUB PIGLET1
      GOSUB PIGLET2
RETURN

BK:
  XØ=313: YØ=80
  X1=286: X2=340: Y1=65: Y2=95
  GOSUB GET.IT
RETURN

GET.IT:
  GET(X1,Y1)-(X2,Y2),NUMBERS(INDEX(Z))
  PUT(X1,Y1),NUMBERS(1),PSET: REM ERASE
RETURN

NØ:
  CALL DRAWLINE(3,XØ+26,YØ-11,8)
  CALL DRAWLINE(3,XØ+15,YØ-8,8)
  PAINT(XØ+20,YØ)
RETURN

SUB DRAWLINE(K,X.C,Y.C,T) STATIC
  COLOR K
  PSET(X.C,Y.C)
  FOR I=1 TO T
    READ X,Y
    LINE -STEP(X,Y)
  NEXT
END SUB

SUB DRAWPOINT(K,X.C,Y.C,T) STATIC
  COLOR K
  FOR I=1 TO T
    READ X,Y
    PSET(X.C+X,Y.C+Y)
  NEXT
END SUB
```

```
N1:
  CALL DRAWLINE(3,X0+5,Y0-15,11)
  PAINT (X0+1,Y0+1)
RETURN

N2:
  CALL DRAWLINE(3,X0+16,Y0+2,19)
  PAINT(X0+1,Y0+1)
RETURN

N3:
  CALL DRAWLINE(3,X0+12,Y0-3,20)
  PAINT(X0+4,Y0-1)
RETURN

N4:
  CALL DRAWLINE(3,X0-1,Y0,14)
  PAINT(X0+2,Y0)
RETURN

N5:
  CALL DRAWLINE(3,X0-16,Y0-4,20)
  PAINT(X0,Y0-2)
RETURN

N6:
  CALL DRAWLINE(3,X0-12,Y0+2,8)
  CALL DRAWLINE(3,X0-16,Y0-2,13)
  PAINT(X0+2,Y0)
RETURN

N7:
  CALL DRAWLINE(3,X0-27,Y0-15,11)
  PAINT(X0,Y0)
RETURN

N8:
  CALL DRAWLINE(3,X0-10,Y0+2,8)
  CALL DRAWLINE(3,X0-10,Y0-11,8)
  CALL DRAWLINE(3,X0-19,Y0-15,14)
  PAINT(X0,Y0)
RETURN

N9:
  CALL DRAWLINE(3,X0-12,Y0-11,8)
  CALL DRAWLINE(3,X0-19,Y0-15,12)
  PAINT(X0,Y0)
RETURN
```

```
LITTLE.X:
 CALL DRAWLINE(2,X0-3,Y0-3,3)
 CALL DRAWLINE(2,X0+3,Y0-3,3)
 GET(X0-3,Y0-3)-(X0+4,Y0+3),LITTLE.X
 PUT(X1,Y1),NUMBERS(1),PSET
RETURN

SIGNS.CURSOR:
 REM -
  LINE(293,78)-(333,82),1,BF
  GET(293,71)-(333,89),SIGNS(200)
 REM +
  LINE(307,71)-(319,89),1,BF
  GET(293,71)-(333,89),SIGNS(1)
  PUT(X1,Y1),NUMBERS(1),PSET
 REM CURSOR
  LINE(X0-6,Y0-8)-(X0+6,Y0+8),6,BF
  GET(X0-6,Y0-8)-(X0+6,Y0+8),CURSOR
  PUT(X1,Y1),NUMBERS(1),PSET
RETURN

DUCK1:
 X0=350: Y0=40
 CALL DRAWLINE(3,X0,Y0,73)
 PAINT (X0-9,Y0+4)
 PAINT (X0+17,Y0+4)
 CALL DRAWPOINT(2,X0,Y0,12)
 REM BILL
  COLOR 1
  PSET(X0+23,Y0+5)
  LINE -STEP(0,1): LINE -STEP(4,0)
 GET(319,30)-(379,50),DUCK(1)
 LINE(319,30)-(379,50),0,BF
RETURN

DUCK2:
 CALL DRAWLINE(3,X0,Y0,49)
 PAINT(X0-7,Y0-1): PAINT(X0+15,Y0-2)
 CALL DRAWPOINT(2,X0,Y0,5)
 CALL DRAWLINE(1,X0+22,Y0-2,2)
 GET(319,30)-(379,50),DUCK(261)
 LINE(319,30)-(379,50),0,BF
 GET(319,30)-(379,50),DUCK(521): REM BLANK
RETURN

PIGLET1:
 REM BOTTOM
  X0=313: Y0=80
  CALL DRAWLINE(4,X0,Y0,70)
```

```
      PAINT(XØ-6,YØ+3)
      CALL DRAWPOINT(2,XØ,YØ,13)
   REM TAIL
      CALL DRAWPOINT(1,XØ-21,YØ+3,14)
   REM VEST
      CALL DRAWLINE(7,XØ,YØ-1,53)
      PAINT(XØ+4,YØ-2)
      CALL DRAWPOINT(2,XØ,YØ,4)
   REM ARMS
      CALL DRAWLINE(4,XØ+7,YØ-1,18)
      PAINT(XØ+11,YØ-2)
      CALL DRAWLINE(4,XØ+22,YØ-4,7)
      CALL DRAWPOINT(2,XØ,YØ,4)
      CALL DRAWPOINT(2,XØ,YØ,2)
   REM HEAD
      CALL DRAWLINE(4,XØ,YØ-8,49)
      PAINT(XØ+8,YØ-11): PAINT(XØ-3,YØ-11)
      CALL DRAWLINE(5,XØ+17,YØ-8,9)
      CALL DRAWPOINT(2,XØ+17,YØ-8,14)
      GET(278,6Ø)-(348,1ØØ),PIGLET(1)
      LINE(278,6Ø)-(348,1ØØ),Ø,BF
RETURN

PIGLET2:
   REM BOTTOM
      CALL DRAWLINE(4,XØ,YØ+2,84)
      PAINT(XØ,YØ+5): PAINT(XØ+13,YØ+4)
      CALL DRAWPOINT(2,XØ,YØ,13)
   REM TAIL
      CALL DRAWPOINT(1,XØ-2Ø,YØ+6,14)
   REM VEST
      CALL DRAWLINE(7,XØ,YØ+1,45)
      PAINT(XØ+4,YØ-1)
      CALL DRAWPOINT(2,XØ,YØ,5)
   REM ARMS
      CALL DRAWLINE(4,XØ+2,YØ-1,15)
      PAINT(XØ+6,YØ-2)
      CALL DRAWLINE(4,XØ+13,YØ-6,11)
      CALL DRAWPOINT(2,XØ,YØ,4)
   REM HEAD
      CALL DRAWLINE(4,XØ-2,YØ-4,57)
      PAINT(XØ-4,YØ-8): PAINT(XØ-18,YØ-7)
      CALL DRAWPOINT(2,XØ,YØ,9)
   REM SNOOT
      CALL DRAWLINE(5,XØ+1,YØ-9,8)
      PAINT(XØ+4,YØ-9)
      CALL DRAWPOINT(2,XØ,YØ,4)
      GET(278,6Ø)-(348,1ØØ),PIGLET(625)
RETURN
```

```
HEADING:
 COLOR 1,Ø
 LOCATE 13,23:PRINT "Fun with Fractions"
 LOCATE 17,24:PRINT "Please use menus,"
 LOCATE 19,23:PRINT "Click mouse to play"
 GOSUB CLICKIT
RETURN

OPTIONS:
 ID = MENU(Ø): ITEM = MENU(1)
 ON ID GOSUB MENU1,MENU2,MENU3,GOODBYE
 ITEM = Ø
RETURN

MENU1:
 MENU 1,RULES,1: MENU 1,ITEM,2
 RULES = ITEM
RETURN

MENU2:
 MENU 2,VERSION,1: MENU 2,ITEM,2
 VERSION = ITEM
RETURN

MENU3:
 MENU 3,OPERATION,1: MENU 3,ITEM,2
 OPERATION = ITEM
RETURN

GOODBYE:
 WINDOW CLOSE 2: WINDOW 1: MENU RESET
 SCREEN CLOSE 1
 IF ITEM = 2 THEN RUN "LEARNING"
 IF ITEM = 3 THEN SYSTEM
 COLOR 1,Ø: CLS
 PRINT "Bye-Bye"
 STOP
RETURN

CLICKIT:
 S$ = ""
 WHILE MOUSE(Ø) = Ø AND S$ = ""
  S$ = INKEY$
 WEND
  X = MOUSE(1)
  Y = MOUSE(2)
 WHILE MOUSE(Ø)<> Ø: WEND: REM RESET
RETURN
```

```
PLAY:
 IF RULES = 1 THEN GOSUB RULES
 CNT = Ø: GROUP = Ø
 FOR Q=1 TO K
  GOSUB GET.VALUES
  GOSUB PROBLEM
  IF VERSION = 2 THEN GOSUB RATIO
  GOSUB GUESS
  GOSUB EVALUATE
 NEXT Q
 IF CNT = K THEN GOSUB FLY
RETURN

RULES:
 CLS
 PRINT
 PRINT "    Let's learn to add and subtract";
 PRINT " fractions with Little"
 PRINT " Piglet."
 PRINT
 PRINT " Two versions of the game are";
 PRINT " available: one where the"
 PRINT " fractions have a common denominator,";
 PRINT " and the other where"
 PRINT " they don't.";
 PRINT: PRINT
 PRINT "    I'll give you";K;"problems per";
 PRINT " game, and you'll enjoy a"
 PRINT " nice surprise if you tally";
 PRINT " perfectly."
 LOCATE 20,26:PRINT "Click Mouse";
 GOSUB CLICKIT
RETURN

GET.VALUES:
 CLS
 LOCATE 10,25: PRINT "One moment ..."
 SEARCH$ = "ON"
 WHILE SEARCH$ = "ON"
  FOR I=1 TO 2
   N(I) = INT(RND*8) + 1
   D(I) = INT(RND*8) + 1
  NEXT I
  IF VERSION = 1 THEN D(2) = D(1)
  IF NOT( VERSION = 2 AND D(1) = D(2) ) THEN
   SEARCH$ = "OFF"
  END IF
 WEND
 IF N(2)/D(2) > N(1)/D(1) THEN
```

```
     SWAP N(2),N(1): SWAP D(2),D(1)
   END IF
   REM ANSWER
    IF OPERATION=1 THEN SIGN = 1 ELSE SIGN = -1
    IF VERSION = 1 THEN
     AW(1) = N(1) + SIGN*N(2)
     AW(2) = D(1)
    ELSE
     AW(1) = N(1)*D(2) + SIGN*N(2)*D(1)
     AW(2) = D(1)*D(2)
    END IF
    IF AW(1) > 99 THEN GET.VALUES
    AW = AW(1)/AW(2)
RETURN

PROBLEM:
 CLS
 FOR I=1 TO 2
  X = 210*I - 160
  PUT(X,35),NUMBERS(INDEX(N(I)+2)),PSET
  PUT(X,79),NUMBERS(INDEX(D(I)+2)),PSET
  LINE(X,70)-(X+54,74),1,BF
 NEXT I
 REM SIGN
  S = OPERATION
  X1 = 161: X2 = 383
  IF VERSION = 2 THEN X1 = 209: X2 = 420
  PUT(X1,63),SIGNS(199*S-198),PSET
 REM =
  LINE(X2,65)-(X2+25,69),1,BF
  LINE(X2,75)-(X2+25,79),1,BF
 REM BAR FOR ANSWER
  LINE(465,70)-(585,74),1,BF
RETURN

RATIO:
 LOCATE 17,15
 PRINT "Please enter a ratio to multiply by."
 FOR I=1 TO 2
  X = 210*I-82
  PUT(X-15,69),LITTLE.X,PSET
  LINE(X,30)-(X+72,114),2,BF
  LINE(X+4,32)-(X+68,112),0,BF
  LINE(X+9,70)-(X+63,74),2,BF
  PUT(X+31,40),CURSOR,PSET
  LOCATE 19,28: PRINT "Ratio: ?": GOSUB GURGLE
  R(I) = 0
  WHILE R(I) < 1
   S$ = INKEY$
```

190

```
    R(I) = VAL(S$)
   WEND
   PUT(X+9,35),NUMBERS(INDEX(R(I)+2)),PSET
   PUT(X+9,79),NUMBERS(INDEX(R(I)+2)),PSET
  NEXT I
  GOSUB CLEAR.LINES
  REM CHECK ENTRY
   IF D(1)*R(1) <> D(2)*R(2) THEN
    GOSUB NOT.COMMON
    GOTO RATIO
   END IF
 RETURN

GURGLE:
 FREQ = 300
 FOR G=1 TO 5
  FREQ = 500-FREQ
  SOUND FREQ,1,50
 NEXT G
RETURN

CLEAR.LINES:
 LOCATE 17,11: PRINT SPACE$(47)
 LOCATE 19,26: PRINT SPACE$(13)
RETURN

NOT.COMMON:
 SOUND 400,3: SOUND 300,3: SOUND 200,3
 LOCATE 17,16:
 PRINT "WARNING: No common denominator !"
 LOCATE 19,26: PRINT "Press any key"
 GOSUB CLICKIT
 GOSUB CLEAR.LINES
RETURN

GUESS:
 FOR I=1 TO 2
  GOSUB GURGLE
  LOCATE 17,11
  PRINT "Please enter your ";T$(I);", then";
  PRINT " Hit Return."
  X = 465: Y = 44*I - 9
  G$ = "": GUESS$ = "ON"
  WHILE GUESS$ = "ON"
   PUT(X,Y+7),CURSOR,PSET
   GOSUB ENTER.DIGIT
   IF GUESS$ = "ON" THEN
    PUT(X,Y),NUMBERS(INDEX(INX)),PSET
    G$ = G$ + RIGHT$(STR$(DIGIT),1)
```

191

```
     X = X+67
    END IF
   WEND
   PUT(X,Y),NUMBERS(1),PSET
   G(I) = VAL(G$)
 NEXT I
RETURN

ENTER.DIGIT:
 S$ = ""
 WHILE S$ = ""
  S$ = INKEY$
 WEND
 A = ASC(S$)
 IF A = 13 THEN GUESS$ = "OFF"
 IF A=8 OR A=31 THEN
  IF G$ = "" THEN SOUND 900,2
  IF G$ <> "" THEN GOSUB MOVE.LEFT
  GOTO ENTER.DIGIT
 END IF
 IF A <> 13 AND (A < 48 OR A > 57) THEN
  SOUND 900,2
  GOTO ENTER.DIGIT
 END IF
 DIGIT = A - 48
 INX = DIGIT + 2
RETURN

MOVE.LEFT:
 G$ = LEFT$(G$,LEN(G$)-1)
 PUT(X,Y),NUMBERS(1),PSET
 X = X-67
 PUT(X,Y),NUMBERS(1),PSET
 PUT(X,Y+7),CURSOR,PSET
RETURN

EVALUATE:
 GOSUB CLEAR.LINES
 GUESS = 0
 IF G(2) <> 0 THEN GUESS = G(1)/G(2)
 ON -(ABS(GUESS-AW)<.0001)+1 GOSUB WRONG,RIGHT
 LOCATE 20,26: PRINT "Press any key";
 GOSUB CLICKIT
RETURN

WRONG:
 SOUND 400,3: SOUND 300,3: SOUND 200,3
 LOCATE 17,21:
 PRINT "Sorry, the answer is";AW(1);CHR$(8);
```

```
 PRINT "/";MID$(STR$(AW(2)),2);"."
RETURN

RIGHT:
 LOCATE 20,27: PRINT "Very Good !";
 X=280: Y=122
 PUT(X,Y),PIGLET(1),PSET
 GOSUB MUSIC
 GOSUB DANCE
 CNT = CNT+1
RETURN

MUSIC:
 GROUP = GROUP + 1
 IF GROUP = K+1 THEN GROUP = 1
 FIRST = NOTE.GROUP(GROUP-1) + 1
 LAST  = NOTE.GROUP(GROUP)
 FOR I = FIRST TO LAST
   SOUND WAIT
   FOR J=2 TO 3
     SOUND F(I),L(I),125,J
     SOUND 0,.5,,J
   NEXT J
   SOUND RESUME
 NEXT I
RETURN

DANCE:
 V = 1
 FOR FLASH = 1 TO 9
   PUT(X,Y),PIGLET(V),PSET
   FOR PAUSE=1 TO 1000: NEXT PAUSE
   V = 626-V
 NEXT FLASH
RETURN

FLY:
 CLS
 V = 1
 LOCATE 20,22: PRINT "You got all";K;"right !";
 Y(0) = 70
 FOR I=1 TO 10
   DELTA = 10*I
   IF I/2 <> INT(I/2) THEN DELTA = -10*I
   Y(I) = 70 + DELTA
 NEXT
 FOR X=60 TO 750 STEP 5
   FOR J=0 TO K-1
    XD = INT( (J+1)/2 )*70
```

193

```
    PUT(X-XD,Y(J)),DUCK(DUCK.INDEX(V)),PSET
   NEXT J
   FOR PAUSE=1 TO 150: NEXT PAUSE
   FOR J=0 TO K-1
    XD = INT( (J+1)/2 )*70
    PUT(X-XD,Y(J)),DUCK(DUCK.INDEX(3)),PSET
   NEXT J
   V = 3-V
  NEXT X
RETURN

DECIDE:
 BUTTON = 0
 GOSUB DRAWBUTTON
 GOSUB PUSHBUTTON
 COLOR 1,0
RETURN

DRAWBUTTON:
 LINE (337,77)-(433,91),1,BF
 FOR I=1 TO 2
   CIRCLE (XB(I),YB(I)),12,I*3
   PAINT (XB(I),YB(I)),I*3
   COLOR 1,I*3
   LOCATE 10: PRINT PTAB(XB(I)-4);LT$(I);
 NEXT I
RETURN

PUSHBUTTON:
 SOUND 440,2
 GOSUB CLICKIT
 S$ = UCASE$(S$)
 IF S$ = "Y" THEN BUTTON = 1
 IF S$ = "N" THEN BUTTON = 2
 FOR I=1 TO 2
   XD = ABS(X-XB(I)): YD = ABS(Y-YB(I))
   IF XD<13 AND YD<7 THEN BUTTON = I: I=2
 NEXT
 IF BUTTON = 0 THEN PUSHBUTTON
RETURN

REM ZERO
 DATA 0,22,-8,4,-37,0,-8,-4,0,-22,8,-4,37,0,8,4
 DATA 0,16,-6,3,-19,0,-6,-3,0,-16,6,-3,19,0,6,3

REM ONE
 DATA 0,26,9,0,0,4,-29,0,0,-4,9,0,0,-21,-7,0
 DATA 0,-2,7,-3,11,0
```

```
REM TWO
 DATA -26,0,-6,3,0,6,42,0,0,4,-53,0,0,-11,12,-6
 DATA 30,0,0,-9,-29,0,-8,4,-5,0,0,-4,8,-4,37,0
 DATA 8,4,0,8,-10,5

REM THREE
 DATA 14,7,0,7,-8,4,-37,0,-8,-4,0,-3,9,0,4,3
 DATA 23,0,6,-4,0,-1,-6,-4,-14,0,0,-4,18,-9
 DATA -40,0,0,-4,53,0,0,5,-14,7

REM FOUR
 DATA 0,15,11,0,0,-13,16,0,0,-4,-16,0,0,-13
 DATA -11,0,0,13,-15,0,0,-13,-11,0,0,17,26,0

REM FIVE
 DATA 32,0,10,5,0,9,-10,5,-35,0,-8,-4,0,-3,9,0
 DATA 4,3,25,0,4,-2,0,-7,-4,-2,-30,0,-8,-4
 DATA 0,-11,53,0,0,4,-42,0,0,7

REM SIX
 DATA 23,0,4,2,0,5,-4,2,-23,0,-4,-2,0,-5,4,-2
 DATA 34,0,8,4,0,9,-8,4,-37,0,-8,-4,0,-17,18,-9
 DATA 35,0,0,4,-28,0,-14,7,0,2

REM SEVEN
 DATA 53,0,0,5,-1,0,-34,17,1,0,0,8,-11,0,0,-10
 DATA 32,-16,-40,0,0,-4

REM EIGHT
 DATA 19,0,6,3,0,3,-6,3,-19,0,-6,-3,0,-3,6,-3
 DATA 19,0,6,3,0,3,-6,3,-19,0,-6,-3,0,-3,6,-3
 DATA 37,0,8,4,0,7,-8,4,8,4,0,7,-8,4,-37,0
 DATA -8,-4,0,-7,8,-4,-8,-4,0,-7,8,-4

REM NINE
 DATA 23,0,4,2,0,5,-4,2,-23,0,-4,-2,0,-5,4,-2
 DATA 37,0,8,4,0,15,-22,11,-31,0,0,-4,26,0
 DATA 16,-9,-34,0,-8,-4,0,-9,8,-4

REM LITTLE.X
 DATA 6,6,1,0,-6,-6,-6,6,1,0,6,-6

REM DUCK #1
 DATA 3,0,-1,0,0,2,-1,0,0,2,3,0,0,1,7,0,0,-1
 DATA 2,0,0,-1,7,0,0,1,1,0,0,1,1,0,-2,0
 DATA 0,1,-5,0,0,-1,-5,0,0,1,-4,0,0,1,-4,0
 DATA 0,1,-13,0,0,-1,-6,0,0,-1,-5,0,0,-1
 DATA -4,0,9,0,0,-1,2,0,0,-2,1,0,0,-1,1,0,0,-1
 DATA 1,0,0,-2,-1,0,0,-1,-1,0,0,-2,-1,0,0,-2
```

195

```
    DATA 1,0,0,-1,1,0,0,1,2,0,0,1,2,0,0,1,2,0,0,1
    DATA 1,0,0,1,1,0,0,1,2,0,0,-2,2,0,0,1,1,0
    DATA 0,1,1,0,0,1,1,0,0,1
    DATA -4,-1,-3,0,-3,1,-2,2,-2,3,-1,4,1,5,2,6
    DATA 1,7,0,7,18,4,19,4

REM DUCK #2
    DATA 5,0,0,-1,2,0,0,-1,5,0,0,1,7,0,0,-1,2,0
    DATA -1,0,0,-1,-3,0,0,-1,-5,0,0,1,-4,0,0,1,-5,0
    DATA 0,-1,-5,0,0,-1,-10,0,0,1,-5,0,0,1,-11,0
    DATA 2,0,0,1,6,0,0,1,3,0,0,2,-2,0,0,1,-3,0
    DATA 0,1,-4,0,0,1,-1,0,10,0,0,-1,5,0,0,-1,4,0
    DATA 0,-1,3,0,0,-1,4,0,0,-1,15,-3,16,-3,1,0
    DATA -16,0,-15,-1,0,1,5,0

REM PIGLET1
    DATA 2,0,0,1,3,0,0,1,2,0,0,2,3,0,0,-1,4,0,0,-1
    DATA 0,1,1,0,-2,0,0,1,-2,0,0,2,2,0,0,1,-2,0,0,1
    DATA -1,0,0,3,1,0,-4,0,0,-1,-2,0,1,0,0,-4,-7,0
    DATA 0,1,-2,0,0,1,-2,0,0,1,-2,0,0,1,-3,0,0,2,1,0
    DATA 0,1,-3,0,0,-1,-1,0,0,-1,-2,0,1,0,0,-1,1,0
    DATA 0,-3,-2,0,0,-1,-2,0,0,-1,-2,0,0,-1,-1,0
    DATA 0,-3,1,0,0,-1,1,0,0,-1,3,0,0,-1,5,0,0,-1
    DATA 2,0,0,2,6,0,0,1,2,0,-2,2,-1,3,0,4,0,5,-1,6
    DATA -1,7,-11,14,-10,14,8,6,9,5,10,5,11,12
    DATA 10,12,0,0,-1,0,-2,0,-3,0,-4,0,-5,-1,-6,-1
    DATA -7,-1,-8,-1,-9,-2,-7,-2,-6,-3,-5,-3,-4,-2
    DATA 3,0,0,1,3,0,0,1,2,0,0,2,1,0,0,-1,4,0,0,-1
    DATA 2,0,0,1,1,0,0,1,1,0,0,-1,1,0,0,-1,1,0,0,-1
    DATA 1,0,0,-1,1,0,0,-4,-1,0,0,-1,-1,0,0,-1,-2,0
    DATA 0,1,1,0,0,3,-2,0,0,-1,-1,0,0,-1,-6,0,0,-1
    DATA -6,0,0,-1,-4,0,0,1,-1,0,0,1,-2,0,0,1,-2,0
    DATA 0,1,-2,0,0,1,-2,0,9,0,0,1,14,2,16,1,18,-2
    DATA 18,-3,0,-1,-1,0,0,-1,3,0,0,-1,4,0,0,1,2,0
    DATA 0,2,3,0,0,1,2,0,0,1,-2,0,0,-1,-4,0,0,-1
    DATA -6,0,0,-2,1,0,0,1,5,0,0,1,2,0,-8,0
    DATA 20,1,21,1,29,-4,30,-4,16,-2,15,-3,1,0,0,-3
    DATA -2,0,0,1,-1,0,0,1,-2,0,0,1,-1,0,0,-2,-2,0
    DATA 0,-1,-1,0,2,0,0,-1,4,0,0,-1,2,0,0,-1,2,0
    DATA 0,-1,12,0,0,-1,6,0,0,1,1,0,0,1,-1,0,0,1
    DATA -1,0,0,-1,-3,0,0,2,1,0,0,2,2,0,0,1,-2,0
    DATA 0,1,-1,0,0,3,1,0,-1,0,0,-1,-6,0,0,-1,-6,0
    DATA 0,-1,-3,0,-3,0,0,-1,-2,0,1,0,0,-1,5,0,0,1
    DATA 1,0,-4,0,-3,-1,-2,-1,0,-1,1,-1,-12,-3
    DATA -11,-3,-6,-4,-5,-4,-10,0,-9,1,-8,1,-7,1
    DATA -6,1,-16,-3
```

```
REM PIGLET2
 DATA 4,0,0,1,4,0,0,1,3,0,0,-1,3,0,0,-1,0,1,3,0
 DATA -1,0,0,1,-2,0,0,1,-2,0,0,1,-1,0,0,2,2,0,0,1
 DATA 2,0,0,1,3,0,0,1,2,0,0,1,2,0,0,1,1,0,-2,0
 DATA 0,-1,-4,0,0,-1,-8,0,0,-1,-4,0,0,-1,-5,0,0,1
 DATA -2,0,0,1,-2,0,0,1,-2,0,0,1,-1,0,0,2,1,0,0,1
 DATA 1,0,-2,0,0,-1,-2,0,0,-1,-1,0,0,-3,-1,0
 DATA 0,-1,-2,0,0,-1,-2,0,0,-1,-1,0,0,-1,-1,0
 DATA 0,-1,-1,0,1,0,0,-1,1,0,0,-1,1,0,0,-1,2,0
 DATA 0,-1,1,0,0,-1,1,0,0,3,2,0,0,-1,4,0,0,-1
 DATA 5,0,-5,17,-6,17,-7,17,24,13,25,13,-2,7,-1,8
 DATA -1,9,-1,10,6,9,7,8,8,8,9,7
 DATA 0,0,-1,0,-2,0,-3,0,-4,0,-5,-1,-6,-1,-7,-1
 DATA -8,-1,-9,-2,-7,-2,-6,-3,-5,-3,-4,-2
 DATA -6,0,0,1,-4,0,0,1,-2,0,1,0,0,-2,1,0,0,-1
 DATA 1,0,0,-4,1,0,0,1,7,0,0,-1,10,0,0,-2,-2,0
 DATA 0,-1,-1,0,2,0,0,1,4,0,0,1,2,0,0,1,1,0,0,1
 DATA 1,0,0,1,1,0,0,2,1,0,0,2,-3,0,0,-1,-2,0,0,1
 DATA -3,0,0,1,-1,0,0,-1,-4,0,0,-1,-5,0,14,1,15,0
 DATA 15,-1,14,-2,13,-3
 DATA 0,-1,2,0,0,-1,2,0,0,-1,2,0,0,-1,3,0,0,1
 DATA -1,0,0,3,-2,0,0,1,-5,0,0,-1,2,0,0,1,1,0
 DATA 0,-1,2,0,0,-1,1,0,0,-1,-2,0,0,1,-2,0
 DATA 10,-6,11,-6,18,-9,19,-9
 DATA -5,0,0,-1,-3,0,0,-1,-1,0,0,-1,-2,0,0,-1
 DATA -2,0,0,1,-1,0,0,1,-1,0,0,1,-1,0,0,1,-2,0
 DATA 0,1,0,-2,-1,0,0,-1,-1,0,0,-1,-1,0,3,0,0,-1
 DATA 4,0,0,-2,1,0,0,-1,3,0,0,-1,4,0,0,-1,2,0
 DATA 0,-1,1,0,0,-1,1,0,0,-1,1,0,0,1,4,0,-1,0,0,1
 DATA -3,0,0,2,3,0,0,1,2,0,0,4,3,0,0,1,1,0,0,1
 DATA 1,0,-9,0,-9,-8,-8,-8,-4,-10,-3,-10,-3,-7
 DATA -2,-6,-1,-6,0,-6,-13,-8
 DATA 2,0,0,-1,3,0,0,1,1,0,-1,0,0,1,-4,0,3,-8
 DATA 4,-8,5,-9,6,-9
```

Foreign Language Flash Cards

Now your Amiga can teach a foreign language. "Foreign Language Flash Cards" displays a word in either English or the language being practiced, and the student types in its meaning in the other language. For example, if you were studying French and the computer flashed *la maison*, you would type in its English meaning, *the house*.

You must prepare and type in your own lists of words. You can get simple vocabulary words from any of the elementary language texts. When you create lists, you'll enter both the English and the foreign meaning. This program uses the word *Spanish* throughout, but when entering the program, you can change it to the language you're studying. If you've purchased the *Amiga Applications* disk, simply change the appropriate DATA statement in the KEYVALUES subroutine near the beginning of the listing.

When you practice a list, you have the option of viewing either the English version of the word or the foreign version. Either way, the computer will keep track of the number of right and wrong answers, which allows you to grade yourself and measure your progress.

Students will find this program especially helpful. Say you have a test soon, and you have to know a specified list of vocabulary words. Well, type them in along with their English equivalents and let the flash cards drill you until you know your words inside and out. And since you can save your old lists, you'll always be able to refresh your memory for the final exam.

Travelers can benefit by practicing common words that will help them in everyday situations abroad. Many of these words can be found in pocket dictionaries and phrase books available in many bookstores. You'll get a lot more enjoyment traveling if you try to speak the native tongue and don't assume that everyone around the world speaks English.

Foreign Language Flash Cards also creates a catalog of all the word lists that you generate. This saves you the trouble of remembering names like NOUNS2 or VERBS3. The catalog is accessed each time you run the program.

Program 3-5. Foreign Language Flash Cards
Save using the filename **CARDS**

```
REM FOREIGN LANGUAGE FLASH CARDS
 GOSUB INITIALIZE
 GOSUB PLAY
 GOSUB GOODBYE
END
```

```
INITIALIZE:
 GOSUB SETSCREEN
 GOSUB KEYVALUES
 GOSUB SETMENUS
 GOSUB SETCOLORS
 GOSUB GET.CIRCLE
 GOSUB HEADING
 GOSUB CATALOG
RETURN

SETSCREEN:
 SCREEN 1,640,200,3,2
 HEADING$ = "Foreign Language Flash Cards"
 WINDOW 2,HEADING$,,0,1
RETURN

KEYVALUES:
 DEFINT A-J,L-Z
 RANDOMIZE TIMER
REM MAX WORDS PER FILE, MAX FILES
 DATA 200, 100
 READ MWORDS, MFILES
 DIM R(MWORDS),WORDS$(MWORDS,2),FILE$(MFILES)
 DIM SHAPE(250)
REM SHAPE INDICES
 DATA 1,125
 READ INDEX(1), INDEX(2)
REM LANGUAGES
 DATA English, Spanish
 FOR I=1 TO 2
  READ L$
  LG$(I) = LEFT$(L$,15)
 NEXT
REM TYPES OF TRANSLATION
 TR$(1) = LG$(1) + " to " + LG$(2)
 TR$(2) = LG$(2) + " to " + LG$(1)
REM BUTTON VALUES
 XB(1) = 292: XB(2) = 334
 LT$(1) = "Y": LT$(2) = "N"
REM MENU CHOICES
 DATA Practice your words
 DATA Create a new word list
 DATA Delete an old word list, View file names
 DATA Exit
 FOR I=1 TO 5
  READ PICK$(I)
 NEXT
 PICK = 1
 MESSAGE$ = ""
RETURN
```

```
SETMENUS:
 DATA 2, Instructions, Yes, No
 DATA 4, Card Color, Brown, Pink, White, Blue
 DATA 2, Translation, T1, T2
 DATA 3, Stop, Go to BASIC
 DATA Go to Learning Menu, Go to System
 FOR I=1 TO 4
  READ NUMBER
  FOR J=0 TO NUMBER
   READ TITLE$
   IF I=3 AND J<>0 THEN TITLE$ = TR$(J)
   IF J<>0 THEN TITLE$ = SPACE$(3) + TITLE$
    STATUS = 1
    IF I <> 4 AND J = 1 THEN STATUS = 2
   MENU I,J,STATUS,TITLE$
 NEXT J,I
 RULES = 1: CARD = 1: TYPE = 1
RETURN

SETCOLORS:
 REM BROWN, PINK, WHITE, BLUE
  DATA .8,.6,.53, 1,.51,.64, 1,1,1, .4,.6,1
  FOR I=1 TO 4
   FOR J=1 TO 3
    READ KOLOR(I,J)
  NEXT J,I
 REM BROWN, GREEN, & RED
  PALETTE 4,.8,.6,.53
  PALETTE 5,.14,.43,0
  PALETTE 6,.93,.2,0
RETURN

GET.CIRCLE:
 X0=313: Y0=80
 FOR I=1 TO 2
  K = I*5-4
  CIRCLE(X0,Y0),12,K: PAINT(X0,Y0),K
  GET(X0-12,Y0-8)-(X0+12,Y0+8),SHAPE(INDEX(I))
 NEXT
RETURN

HEADING:
 MENU ON
 ON MENU GOSUB OPTIONS
 CLS
 COLOR 3,0: LOCATE 18,30:PRINT "then"
 COLOR 1,0
 LOCATE 10,18: PRINT HEADING$
 LOCATE 17,24:PRINT "Please use menus,"
```

```
  LOCATE 19,23:PRINT "Click mouse to play"
  GOSUB CLICKIT
RETURN

OPTIONS:
 ID = MENU(Ø): ITEM = MENU(1)
 ON ID GOSUB MENU1,MENU2,MENU3,GOODBYE
 ITEM = Ø
RETURN

MENU1:
 MENU 1,RULES,1: MENU 1,ITEM,2
 RULES = ITEM
RETURN

MENU2:
 K1 = KOLOR(ITEM,1): K2 = KOLOR(ITEM,2)
 K3 = KOLOR(ITEM,3)
 PALETTE 4,K1,K2,K3
 MENU 2,CARD,1: MENU 2,ITEM,2
 CARD = ITEM
RETURN

MENU3:
 MENU 3,TYPE,1: MENU 3,ITEM,2
 TYPE = ITEM
RETURN

GOODBYE:
 WINDOW CLOSE 2: WINDOW 1: MENU RESET
 SCREEN CLOSE 1
 IF ITEM = 2 THEN RUN "LEARNING"
 IF ITEM = 3 THEN SYSTEM
 COLOR 1,Ø: CLS
 PRINT "Au Revoir, Adios, Bye-Bye"
 STOP
RETURN

CATALOG:
 CLS
 LOCATE 5,16
 PRINT "Do you have word lists on disk ?"
 ROW = 7: GOSUB DECIDE
 NFILES = Ø
 IF BUTTON = 1 THEN
  OPEN "I",#1,"WORDCAT"
  INPUT #1,NFILES
  FOR I=1 TO NFILES
   INPUT #1,FILE$(I)
```

```
   NEXT
   CLOSE
  END IF
 RETURN

 DECIDE:
  BUTTON = Ø
  GOSUB DRAWBUTTON
  GOSUB PUSHBUTTON
  COLOR 1,Ø
 RETURN

 DRAWBUTTON:
  YØ = 9*ROW-13
  YB=YØ+7
  LINE (265,YØ)-(361,YØ+14),1,BF
  FOR I=1 TO 2
   CIRCLE (XB(I),YB),12,4+I
   PAINT (XB(I),YB),4+I
   COLOR 1,4+I
   LOCATE ROW: PRINT PTAB(XB(I)-4);LT$(I);
  NEXT I
 RETURN

 PUSHBUTTON:
  SOUND 44Ø,2
  GOSUB CLICKIT
  S$ = UCASE$(S$)
  IF S$ = "Y" THEN BUTTON = 1
  IF S$ = "N" THEN BUTTON = 2
  FOR I=1 TO 2
   XD = ABS(X-XB(I)): YD = ABS(Y-YB)
   IF XD<13 AND YD<7 THEN BUTTON = I: I=2
  NEXT
  IF BUTTON = Ø THEN PUSHBUTTON
 RETURN

 CLICKIT:
  S$ = ""
  WHILE MOUSE(Ø) = Ø AND S$ = ""
   S$ = INKEY$
  WEND
   X = MOUSE(1)
   Y = MOUSE(2)
  WHILE MOUSE(Ø)<> Ø: WEND: REM RESET
 RETURN

 PLAY:
  IF RULES = 1 THEN GOSUB RULES
```

```
 GOSUB MAIN.MENU
 ON PICK GOSUB PRACTICE,CREATE,STRIKE,VIEW
 IF PICK <> 5 THEN PLAY
RETURN

RULES:
 CLS
 PRINT
 PRINT "    Practice your words with ";HEADING$;"."
 PRINT
 PRINT "    You can create a new list of words,";
 PRINT " play with an old"
 PRINT " one, and delete files."
 PRINT
 PRINT "    When you save a list of words to";
 PRINT " disk, I'll add the"
 PRINT " file's name to a permanent catalog."
 PRINT
 PRINT "    This will spare you the trouble of";
 PRINT " remembering names"
 PRINT " like NOUNS2 or VERBS3."
 LOCATE 20,27:PRINT "Click Mouse";
 GOSUB CLICKIT
 ITEM = 2: GOSUB MENU1: REM TURN OFF RULES
RETURN

MAIN.MENU:
 CLS
 LOCATE 2,3: PRINT MESSAGE$
 LOCATE 5,23: PRINT "Would you like to"
 FOR I=1 TO 5
  IF I = PICK THEN INX = 2 ELSE INX = 1
  CALL DRAW.CIRCLE(I,INX)
  LOCATE I*2+5,25: PRINT PICK$(I)
 NEXT
 LOCATE 20,13: PRINT "Click Mouse on Choice,";
 PRINT " then Hit Return";
 GOSUB CHOOSE
 IF NFILES = Ø THEN
  IF PICK=1 OR PICK=3 OR PICK=4 THEN
   MESSAGE$ = "There aren't any lists on file."
   GOTO MAIN.MENU
  END IF
 END IF
 MESSAGE$ = ""
RETURN

SUB DRAW.CIRCLE(R,INX) STATIC
 SHARED SHAPE(),INDEX()
```

```
  Y = 18*R+31
  PUT(2Ø2,Y),SHAPE(INDEX(INX)),PSET
END SUB

CHOOSE:
 GOSUB GURGLE
 GOSUB CLICKIT
 IF S$ = "" THEN GOSUB LOCATION: GOTO CHOOSE
 IF ASC(S$) <> 13 THEN CHOOSE
RETURN

LOCATION:
 V = INT((Y-48)/18) + 1
 IF X>195 AND X<235 AND V>Ø AND V<6 THEN
  CALL DRAW.CIRCLE(PICK,1)
  CALL DRAW.CIRCLE(V,2)
  PICK = V
 END IF
RETURN

GURGLE:
 FREQ = 3ØØ
 FOR G=1 TO 5
  FREQ = 5ØØ-FREQ
  SOUND FREQ,1,5Ø
 NEXT G
RETURN

PRACTICE:
 CLS
 LOCATE 3,25: PRINT "PRACTICE SESSION"
 GOSUB FILENAME
 IF DUP$ = "NO" THEN
  MESSAGE$ = FILE$ + " doesn't exist."
 END IF
 IF DUP$ = "YES" THEN
  GOSUB READ.WORDS
  GOSUB SHUFFLE.WORDS
  GOSUB PAINT.SCREEN
  MENU 3,Ø,Ø
  GOSUB DRILL
  MENU 3,Ø,1
 END IF
RETURN

FILENAME:
 FILE$ = ""
 WHILE FILE$ = ""
  LOCATE 8,3: INPUT "File Name ";FILE$
```

```
   WEND
   REM CHECK EXISTENCE
    DUP$ = "NO"
    IF NFILES <> Ø THEN
     FOR I=1 TO NFILES
      IF FILE$ = FILE$(I) THEN DUP$="YES": SPOT=I
     NEXT
    END IF
RETURN

READ.WORDS:
 LOCATE 10,26: PRINT "Reading Words"
 OPEN "I",#1,FILE$
 INPUT #1,N
 FOR I=1 TO N
  INPUT #1,WORDS$(I,1),WORDS$(I,2)
 NEXT
 CLOSE
RETURN

SHUFFLE.WORDS:
 LOCATE 10,25: PRINT "Shuffling Words"
 FOR I=1 TO N: R(I)=Ø: NEXT
 FOR I=1 TO N
  LOOK$ = "ON"
  WHILE LOOK$ = "ON"
   V = 1+INT(N*RND)
   IF R(V) = Ø THEN LOOK$ = "OFF"
  WEND
  R(V) = I
 NEXT
RETURN

PAINT.SCREEN:
 CLS
 LOCATE 2,25: PRINT "PRACTICE SESSION"
 LOCATE 3,4: PRINT "FILE: ";FILE$
 LOCATE 4,3: PRINT "WORDS: ";N
 LINE (20,43)-(116,53),6,BF
 COLOR 1,6: LOCATE 6,4: PRINT "Word No."
 LINE(425,43)-(556,53),6,BF
 LOCATE 6,44: PRINT "Number Right"
 COLOR 2,4
 FOR I=1 TO 2
  LINE(20,27*I+41)-(174,27*I+55),4,BF
 NEXT
 LOCATE 9,18-LEN(LG$(TYPE)): PRINT LG$(TYPE)
 LOCATE 12,18-LEN(LG$(3-TYPE)): PRINT LG$(3-TYPE)
RETURN
```

```
DRILL:
  R$(Ø) = "Sorry ...": R$(1) = "Good !"
  NRIGHT = Ø
  FOR I=1 TO N
    GOSUB GURGLE
    COLOR 1,Ø
    LOCATE 6,13: PRINT I
    LOCATE 9,2Ø: PRINT SPACE$(4Ø)
    LOCATE 12,2Ø: PRINT SPACE$(4Ø)
    LOCATE 9,2Ø: PRINT WORDS$(R(I),TYPE)
    LOCATE 12,2Ø: INPUT "",W$
    GOSUB RESULT
  NEXT
RETURN

RESULT:
  V = -( W$ = WORDS$(R(I),3-TYPE) )
  LOCATE 15,32-LEN(R$(V))/2: PRINT R$(V)
  IF V = Ø THEN
    SOUND 4ØØ,3: SOUND 3ØØ,3
    LINE(95,142)-(174,152),6,BF
    LOCATE 17,11: COLOR 1,6: PRINT "MEANING";
    COLOR 1,Ø
    LOCATE 17,2Ø: PRINT WORDS$(R(I),3-TYPE)
  END IF
  IF V = 1 THEN
    NRIGHT = NRIGHT + 1
    LOCATE 6,57: PRINT NRIGHT
  END IF
  LOCATE 2Ø,26: PRINT "Press any key";
  GOSUB CLICKIT
  LOCATE 15,27: PRINT SPACE$(1Ø)
  LINE(95,142)-(174,152),Ø,BF
  LOCATE 17,2Ø: PRINT SPACE$(4Ø)
  LOCATE 2Ø,26: PRINT SPACE$(13);
RETURN

CREATE:
  GOSUB NUMBER.OF.WORDS
  GOSUB ENTER.NAME
  IF CNT$ = "YES" THEN
    GOSUB ENTER.WORDS
    GOSUB SAVE.DATA
  END IF
RETURN

NUMBER.OF.WORDS:
  CLS
  LOCATE 3,2Ø: PRINT "CREATING A NEW WORD LIST"
```

```
A$ = "ASK"
WHILE A$ = "ASK"
 A$ = "OK"
 LOCATE 6,25: PRINT SPACE$(20)
 SOUND 900,2
 LOCATE 6,3: INPUT "Number of new words ";N$
 N = VAL(N$)
 IF N < 1 OR N > MWORDS THEN A$ = "ASK"
 IF N > MWORDS THEN
  LOCATE 17,18
  PRINT "Sorry, only";MWORDS;"are allowed."
  SOUND 900,2
 END IF
WEND
 LOCATE 17,18: PRINT SPACE$(28)
RETURN

ENTER.NAME:
 GOSUB FILENAME
 CNT$ = "YES"
 IF DUP$ = "YES" THEN
  LOCATE 10,3: PRINT FILE$;" already exists !"
  LOCATE 13,16
  PRINT "Would you like to write over it ?"
  ROW=15: GOSUB DECIDE
  IF BUTTON = 2 THEN CNT$ = "NO"
 END IF
RETURN


ENTER.WORDS:
 GOSUB FORMAT
 FOR Q=1 TO N
  GOSUB WORDS
 NEXT Q
RETURN

FORMAT:
 CLS
 PRINT
 PRINT TAB(5)"Please enter your ";LG$(1);
 PRINT " words and their"
 PRINT TAB(3)LG$(2);" equivalents."
 LINE (20,34)-(116,44),6,BF
 COLOR 1,6: LOCATE 5,4: PRINT "Word No."
 COLOR 2,4
 FOR I=1 TO 2
  LINE(20,27*I+32)-(174,27*I+46),4,BF
  LOCATE 3*I+5,18-LEN(LG$(I)): PRINT LG$(I)
```

207

```
  NEXT
 RETURN

 WORDS:
  COLOR 1,Ø: LOCATE 5,13: PRINT Q
  LOCATE 8,2Ø: PRINT SPACE$(4Ø)
  LOCATE 11,2Ø: PRINT SPACE$(4Ø)
  FOR J=1 TO 2
   W$ = ""
   WHILE W$ = ""
     LOCATE 3*J+5,2Ø: INPUT "", W$
   WEND
   WORDS$(Q,J) = LEFT$(W$,35)
  NEXT J
  LOCATE 17,28: PRINT "Changes ?"
  ROW = 15: GOSUB DECIDE
  LOCATE 17,28: PRINT SPACE$(9)
  LINE (265,YØ)-(361,YØ+14),Ø,BF
  IF BUTTON = 1 THEN WORDS
 RETURN

 SAVE.DATA:
  IF DUP$ = "NO" THEN
   NFILES = NFILES + 1
   FILE$(NFILES) = FILE$
  END IF
  GOSUB SAVE.WORDS
  GOSUB UPDATE.CAT
  MESSAGE$ = FILE$ + " is saved."
 RETURN

 SAVE.WORDS:
  CLS
  LOCATE 1Ø,26: PRINT "Saving Words"
  OPEN "O",#1,FILE$
  WRITE #1,N
  FOR I=1 TO N
   WRITE #1,WORDS$(I,1),WORDS$(I,2)
  NEXT
  CLOSE
 RETURN

 UPDATE.CAT:
  OPEN "O",#1,"WORDCAT"
  WRITE #1,NFILES
  FOR I=1 TO NFILES
   WRITE #1,FILE$(I)
  NEXT
  CLOSE
 RETURN
```

```
STRIKE:
 CLS
 LOCATE 3,25: PRINT "DELETING A FILE"
 GOSUB FILENAME
 IF DUP$ = "NO" THEN
  MESSAGE$ = FILE$ + " doesn't exist."
 END IF
 IF DUP$ = "YES" THEN
  GOSUB KILL.IT
  IF NFILES > Ø THEN GOSUB UPDATE.CAT
  IF NFILES = Ø THEN
   KILL "WORDCAT": KILL "WORDCAT.INFO"
   S$ = "You no longer have any word"
   MESSAGE$ = S$ + " lists on disk."
  END IF
 END IF
RETURN

KILL.IT:
 IF SPOT <> NFILES THEN
  FOR I = SPOT+1 TO NFILES
   FILE$(I-1) = FILE$(I)
  NEXT
 END IF
 NFILES = NFILES - 1
 KILL FILE$: KILL FILE$+".INFO"
 MESSAGE$ = FILE$ + " is deleted."
RETURN

VIEW:
 FOR I=1 TO NFILES STEP 15
  CLS
  LOCATE 2,23: PRINT "WORD LISTS ON DISK:"
  PRINT
  FOR J = I TO I+14
   IF J <= NFILES THEN
    L = LEN(FILE$(J))
    PRINT TAB(32-L/2);FILE$(J)
   END IF
  NEXT J
  LOCATE 20,26: PRINT "Click Mouse";
  GOSUB CLICKIT
 NEXT I
RETURN
```

CHAPTER 4

Household Helpers

CHAPTER 4

Household Helpers

Computers have a reputation for being the perfect devices for doing calculations. In scientific disciplines, computers forecast the weather, explore the structure of atomic particles, and compute satellite orbits. In the business world, they calculate our bank balances, bill our charge cards, and review our tax returns.

Computers have a place in the home, too. Computing the return on an IRA is a good example. Another is performing "what-if" drills in determining how much to borrow for that new home or car. Put your personal computer to work helping you out around the house. Here are short descriptions of the programs:

IRA Planner. Calculate what your Individual Retirement Account (IRA) will be worth at maturity, in both today's dollars and in dollars adjusted for inflation.

Loan Payments. Compute the monthly, quarterly, or yearly payment on a car or home loan, as well as the total payment over the life of the loan.

Multifunction Calculator. Use the mouse or keyboard to perform the basic operations of addition, subtraction, multiplication, division, and exponentiation. Use of parentheses is allowed, so you can compute fairly complex formulas as well.

Paycheck Analysis. Use this handy program to verify the accuracy of your paycheck, to project future take-home pay when that raise comes through, and even to tally a payroll.

Household Helpers Menu Driver
Save using the filename **HELPERS**

```
REM HOUSEHOLD HELPERS
 GOSUB INITIALIZE
 GOSUB MAIN.MENU
 RUN TITLE.SHORT$(PICK)
END

INITIALIZE:
 GOSUB SETSCREEN
 GOSUB KEYVALUES
```

```
     GOSUB  SETMENUS
     GOSUB  SETCOLORS
     GOSUB  SHAPES
   RETURN

   SETSCREEN:
    SCREEN  1,640,200,3,2
    WINDOW  2,"Household Helpers",,0,1
   RETURN

   KEYVALUES:
    DEFINT A-Z
    N = 4
    DIM TITLE.LONG$(N),TITLE.SHORT$(N),DISCS(250)
    DISC.I(1) = 1: DISC.I(2) = 125
    READ CHAPTER$
    FOR I=1 TO N
      READ TITLE.LONG$(I),TITLE.SHORT$(I)
    NEXT
   RETURN

   SETMENUS:
    FOR I=2 TO 4
      MENU I,0,0,""
    NEXT
    MENU 1,0,1,"STOP"
    MENU 1,1,1," Go to BASIC"
    MENU 1,2,1," Go to System"
    MENU ON
    ON MENU GOSUB GOODBYE
   RETURN

   GOODBYE:
    WINDOW CLOSE 2: WINDOW 1: MENU RESET
    SCREEN CLOSE 1
    ITEM = MENU(1)
    IF ITEM = 2 THEN SYSTEM
    CLS
    PRINT "Bye-Bye"
    STOP
   RETURN

   SETCOLORS:
    REM TAN, GREEN, & RED
      PALETTE 4,.95,.7,.53
      PALETTE 5,.14,.43,0
      PALETTE 6,.93,.2,0
   RETURN
```

```
SHAPES:
 X=313: Y=80
 LINE(X-12,Y-8)-(X+12,Y+8),4,BF
 FOR I=1 TO 2
  K = 7-I
  CIRCLE(X,Y),12,K: PAINT(X,Y),K
  GET(X-12,Y-8)-(X+12,Y+8),DISCS(DISC.I(I))
 NEXT
RETURN

MAIN.MENU:
 CLS
 RTN$ = "OFF": PICK = 1
 S$ = CHAPTER$: L = LEN(S$)
 LINE(313-10*L/2-15,15)-(313+10*L/2+15,27),1,B
 PAINT(313,20),6,1
 COLOR 1,6: LOCATE 3: PRINT PTAB(313-10*L/2)S$
 LINE(135,35)-(495,130),2,B: PAINT(313,80),4,2
 COLOR 2,4
 FOR I=1 TO N
  IF I = PICK THEN INX = 2 ELSE INX = 1
  CALL DRAW.CIRCLE(I,INX)
  LOCATE I*2+4,21: PRINT TITLE.LONG$(I)
 NEXT
 LINE(263,141)-(360,153),2,B: PAINT(313,145),3,2
 COLOR 2,3
 LOCATE 17: PRINT PTAB(282)"Return"
 COLOR 1,0
 LOCATE 19,11: PRINT "Click Mouse on Choice,";
 PRINT " then Click on Return"
 GOSUB CHOOSE
RETURN

SUB DRAW.CIRCLE(R,INX) STATIC
 SHARED DISCS(),DISC.I()
 Y = 18*R+22
 PUT(162,Y),DISCS(DISC.I(INX)),PSET
END SUB

CHOOSE:
 GOSUB GURGLE
 GOSUB CLICKIT
 IF S$ = "" THEN GOSUB LOCATION
 IF ASC(S$+" ") <> 13 AND RTN$ = "OFF" THEN
  GOTO CHOOSE
 END IF
RETURN
```

```
GURGLE:
  FREQ = 300
  FOR G=1 TO 5
   FREQ = 500 - FREQ
   SOUND FREQ,1,50
  NEXT
RETURN

CLICKIT:
  S$ = ""
  WHILE MOUSE(0) = 0 AND S$ = ""
   S$ = INKEY$
  WEND
   X = MOUSE(1)
   Y = MOUSE(2)
  WHILE MOUSE(0)<> 0: WEND: REM RESET
RETURN

LOCATION:
  IF X>263 AND X<360 AND Y>141 AND Y<153 THEN
   RTN$ = "ON"
  ELSE
   P = INT((Y-39)/18) + 1
   IF X>155 AND X<195 AND P>0 AND P<= N THEN
    CALL DRAW.CIRCLE(PICK,1)
    CALL DRAW.CIRCLE(P,2)
    PICK = P
   END IF
  END IF
RETURN

REM PROGRAMS
 DATA Household Helpers
 DATA IRA Planner, IRA
 DATA Loan Payments, LOAN
 DATA Multi-Function Calculator, CALCULATOR
 DATA Paycheck Analysis, PAYCHECK
```

IRA Planner

Individual Retirement Accounts are extremely popular. Not only are they a way to save for retirement, but funds in IRAs are not taxed until they're withdrawn. Also, you can deduct the money placed in an IRA from your federal tax.

You actually reap double benefits from IRAs—you get a tax deduction now and savings for later. If you're in a high tax bracket, IRAs are especially attractive. Since you assume you'll be making less money when you retire, you'll be taxed at a lower rate when you do withdraw the money. For many people, IRAs are a good idea.

There is a catch, however. You can't withdraw money from your IRAs before age 59½ without suffering a stiff penalty. You must also begin to withdraw the money before age 70½. And, though IRAs may make many of us millionaires in 35 or 40 years if interest rates are high, inflation may mercilessly erode the buying power of those future dollars.

"IRA Planner" will ask you to enter the interest and inflation rates that you think will prevail, on average, over the life of your IRA. The figures you enter, of course, will only be estimates. There's no way you can gaze into the future. If you could, you probably wouldn't need an IRA. It's best to plot your IRA contributions several times, using different interest and inflation rates. That way, you can get a better idea of what will happen to your money in several different conditions.

Once you've entered your data, the Amiga presents the kind of report similar to that in Figure 4-1. The important figures are near the bottom of the screen.

Current dollars. This is the amount you'd actually see listed in your IRA account after the number of years you specified for contributing have passed.

Constant dollars. This is the amount of money you'll end up with, adjusted for inflation. In other words, this is how much your IRA will be worth in terms of today's dollar value.

Use a pull-down menu to select age 59 or 70 for the life of your IRA. Remember, however, that the program doesn't tell you to invest in an IRA, or even when. Those decisions are up to you.

Figure 4-1. IRA Payoff Through Age 70

```
              Your Age = 33 years
              IRA Span = 37 years

         Interest Rate = 12.00 %
        Inflation Rate = 5.00 %

    PAYMENTS
                Annual = $ 2,000.00
                 Total = $ 74,000.00

    IRA PAYOFF
        Current-Dollar = $ 1,217,661.07
       Constant-Dollar = $ 200,226.87
```

Program 4-1. IRA Planner
Save using the filename **IRA**

```
REM IRA
 GOSUB INITIALIZE
COMPUTE:
 GOSUB RUN.IRA
COMPUTE.AGAIN:
 LOCATE 20,18: PRINT "Compute again ?";
 GOSUB DECIDE
 IF BUTTON = 1 THEN COMPUTE
 GOSUB GOODBYE
END

INITIALIZE:
 GOSUB SETSCREEN
 GOSUB KEYVALUES
 GOSUB SETMENUS
 GOSUB SETCOLORS
 GOSUB HEADING
RETURN

SETSCREEN:
 SCREEN 1,640,200,3,2
 HEADING$ = "Individual Retirement Account"
 WINDOW 2,HEADING$,,0,1
RETURN

KEYVALUES:
 DEFINT A-Z: DEFDBL D,K,R,V
 REM BUTTON VALUES
```

```
   XB(1) = 362: XB(2) = 404: YB = 174
   LT$(1) = "Y": LT$(2) = "N"
  REM RATES
   DATA Interest, Inflation
   READ RATE$(1), RATE$(2)
  REM MATURITIES
   DATA 59,70
   FOR I=1 TO 2
    READ MATURITY(I)
   NEXT
RETURN

SETMENUS:
 DATA 2, Instructions, Yes, No
 DATA 2, Compute IRA, Through age 59
 DATA Through age 70
 DATA 3, Stop, Go to BASIC
 DATA Go to Helpers Menu, Go to System
 FOR I=1 TO 3
  READ NUMBER
  FOR J=0 TO NUMBER
   READ TITLE$
   IF J<>0 THEN TITLE$ = SPACE$(3) + TITLE$
    STATUS = 1
    IF I <> 3 AND J = 1 THEN STATUS = 2
   MENU I,J,STATUS,TITLE$
 NEXT J,I
 MENU 4,0,0,""
 INSTRUCTIONS = 1: TYPE = 1
RETURN

SETCOLORS:
 REM GREEN, & RED
  PALETTE 5,.14,.43,0
  PALETTE 6,.93,.2,0
RETURN

HEADING:
 MENU ON
 ON MENU GOSUB OPTIONS
 CLS
 COLOR 3,0: LOCATE 18,30:PRINT "then"
 COLOR 1,0
 LOCATE 10,18: PRINT HEADING$
 LOCATE 17,24:PRINT "Please use menus,"
 LOCATE 19,21:PRINT "Click mouse to compute"
 GOSUB CLICKIT
RETURN
```

```
OPTIONS:
 ID = MENU(Ø): ITEM = MENU(1)
 ON ID GOSUB MENU1,MENU2,GOODBYE
 ITEM = Ø
RETURN

MENU1:
 MENU 1,INSTRUCTIONS,1: MENU 1,ITEM,2
 INSTRUCTIONS = ITEM
RETURN

MENU2:
 MENU 2,TYPE,1: MENU 2,ITEM,2
 TYPE = ITEM
RETURN

GOODBYE:
 WINDOW CLOSE 2: WINDOW 1: MENU RESET
 SCREEN CLOSE 1
 IF ITEM = 2 THEN RUN "HELPERS"
 IF ITEM = 3 THEN SYSTEM
 COLOR 1,Ø: CLS
 PRINT "Bye-Bye"
 STOP
RETURN

CLICKIT:
 S$ = ""
 WHILE MOUSE(Ø) = Ø AND S$ = ""
  S$ = INKEY$
 WEND
  X = MOUSE(1)
  Y = MOUSE(2)
 WHILE MOUSE(Ø)<> Ø: WEND: REM RESET
RETURN

RUN.IRA:
 IF INSTRUCTIONS = 1 THEN GOSUB INSTRUCTIONS
 GOSUB CURRENT.AGE
 MENU 2,Ø,Ø
 GOSUB YEARLY.DEPOSIT
 FOR I=1 TO 2
  GOSUB RATES
 NEXT
 GOSUB CALCULATE
 GOSUB RESULTS
 MENU 2,Ø,1
RETURN
```

```
INSTRUCTIONS:
 CLS
 PRINT
 PRINT "   This program computes the value of";
 PRINT " your IRA at age 59"
 PRINT " and 70.
 PRINT
 PRINT " Age 59 is the earliest that you can";
 PRINT " start withdrawing"
 PRINT " funds without penalty."
 PRINT
 PRINT " Age 70 is the latest that you can";
 PRINT " delay withdrawing."
 LOCATE 20,27:PRINT "Click Mouse";
 GOSUB CLICKIT
 ITEM = 2: GOSUB MENU1: REM TURN OFF INSTRUCTIONS
RETURN

GURGLE:
 FREQ = 300
 FOR G=1 TO 5
  FREQ = 500-FREQ
  SOUND FREQ,1,50
 NEXT G
RETURN

CURRENT.AGE:
 CLS
 LOCATE 2,3: PRINT "Pardon my asking, but";
 PRINT " how old are you"
 AGE = 0
 WHILE NOT (AGE > 0 AND AGE <= 125)
  LOCATE 2,42: PRINT SPACE$(10)
  GOSUB GURGLE
  LOCATE 2,40: INPUT " ";A$
  AGE = VAL(A$)
  IF AGE <= 0 OR AGE > 125 THEN
   LOCATE 19,22: PRINT "Who are you kidding !"
  END IF
 WEND
 MATURITY = MATURITY(TYPE)
 LOCATE 19,22: PRINT SPACE$(21)
 IF AGE >= MATURITY THEN
  GOSUB WARNING
  GOTO CURRENT.AGE
 END IF
RETURN
```

```
WARNING:
 SOUND 400,3: SOUND 300,2: SOUND 200,2
 LOCATE 5,3: PRINT "Sorry:  Your IRA matures";
 PRINT " at age";MATURITY;"!"
 LOCATE 19,26: PRINT "Click Mouse"
 GOSUB CLICKIT
RETURN

YEARLY.DEPOSIT:
 CLS
 DEPOSIT = 0
 WHILE DEPOSIT <= 0
  LOCATE 2,3: PRINT "Please enter the amount";
  PRINT " of money that you'd like to"
  PRINT " deposit in your IRA each year."
  LOCATE 5,14: PRINT SPACE$(30)
  GOSUB GURGLE
  LOCATE 5,2
  INPUT "Deposit = ";D$
  DEPOSIT = VAL(D$)
 WEND
RETURN

RATES:
 CLS
 LOCATE 2,3: PRINT "Please enter the ";RATE$(I);
 PRINT " Rate that you expect will"
 PRINT " prevail, on average, over the life";
 PRINT " of your IRA."
 PRINT
 PRINT " For example, enter 7 for 7%, 10 for";
 PRINT " 10 %, and so on."
 LOCATE 7,11-LEN( RATE$(I) )
 PRINT RATE$(I);" Rate"
 RATE(I) = 0
 WHILE RATE(I) <= 0
  GOSUB GURGLE
  LOCATE 7,21: PRINT SPACE$(30)
  LOCATE 7,17: INPUT "= ";R$
  RATE(I) = VAL(R$)
 WEND
RETURN

CALCULATE:
 REM YEARS UNTIL MATURITY
 N = MATURITY - AGE
 REM CURRENT-DOLLAR VALUES
 VALUE = 0
 FOR I=1 TO N
```

```
    V = DEPOSIT*(1+RATE(1)/100)^(N-I+1)
    VALUE = VALUE + V
   NEXT
 REM DEFLATE
  DEFLATOR = (1+RATE(2)/100)^N
  KVALUE = VALUE/DEFLATOR
RETURN

RESULTS:
 CLS
 LOCATE 2,21: PRINT "IRA PAYOFF THROUGH AGE";
 PRINT MATURITY
 F1$ = "## years"
 F2$ = "##.## %"
 F3$ = "= $$#,#########.##"
 GOSUB DATA.INPUT
 GOSUB DATA.OUTPUT
RETURN

DATA.INPUT:
 LINE(15,25)-(105,35),3,BF
 LINE(15,43)-(105,53),3,BF
 COLOR 2,3
 LOCATE 4,3: PRINT "Your Age"
 LOCATE 6,3: PRINT "IRA Span"
 COLOR 1,0
 LOCATE 4,12: PRINT USING F1$;AGE
 LOCATE 6,12: PRINT USING F1$;N
 LINE(365,25)-(512,35),3,BF
 LINE(365,43)-(512,53),3,BF
 COLOR 2,3
 LOCATE 4,39: PRINT "Interest Rate"
 LOCATE 6,38: PRINT "Inflation Rate"
 COLOR 1,0
 LOCATE 4,53: PRINT USING F2$;RATE(1)
 LOCATE 6,53: PRINT USING F2$;RATE(2)
RETURN

DATA.OUTPUT:
 LINE(86,70)-(235,80),6,BF
 LINE(86,88)-(235,98),6,BF
 COLOR 1,6
 LOCATE 9,10: PRINT "Annual Payment"
 LOCATE 11,11: PRINT "Total Payment"
 COLOR 1,0
 LOCATE 9,25: PRINT USING F3$;DEPOSIT
 LOCATE 11,25: PRINT USING F3$;N*DEPOSIT
 LINE(15,115)-(235,125),5,BF
 LINE(15,133)-(235,143),5,BF
```

```
      COLOR 1,5
      LOCATE 14,4: PRINT "Current-Dollar Worth"
      LOCATE 16,3: PRINT "Constant-Dollar Worth"
      COLOR 1,0
      LOCATE 14,25: PRINT USING F3$;VALUE;
      LOCATE 16,25: PRINT USING F3$;KVALUE;
      COLOR 3,0
      FOR I=14 TO 16 STEP 2
        LOCATE I,44: PRINT "(at maturity)"
      NEXT
      COLOR 1,0
    RETURN

    DECIDE:
      BUTTON = 0
      GOSUB DRAWBUTTON
      GOSUB PUSHBUTTON
      COLOR 1,0
    RETURN

    DRAWBUTTON:
      LINE (335,167)-(431,181),1,BF
      FOR I=1 TO 2
        CIRCLE (XB(I),YB),12,4+I
        PAINT (XB(I),YB),4+I
        COLOR 1,4+I
        LOCATE 20: PRINT PTAB(XB(I)-4);LT$(I);
      NEXT I
    RETURN

    PUSHBUTTON:
      SOUND 440,2
      GOSUB CLICKIT
      S$ = UCASE$(S$)
      IF S$ = "Y" THEN BUTTON = 1
      IF S$ = "N" THEN BUTTON = 2
      FOR I=1 TO 2
        XD = ABS(X-XB(I)): YD = ABS(Y-YB)
        IF XD<13 AND YD<7 THEN BUTTON = I: I=2
      NEXT
      IF BUTTON = 0 THEN PUSHBUTTON
    RETURN
```

Loan Payments

When you're buying a house or car, there is an array of decisions that must be made, not the least of which is knowing just what you can afford. With "Loan Payments" you can see what payments will be on different amounts of money borrowed.

By using Loan Payments you can play some invaluable what-if games like shortening your mortgage from 30 to 20 years to view the impact on cost. On a moderately priced house, this could save you a bundle of money over the life of your loan. But, remember, the Amiga just does the computing; the deciding is up to you.

By way of example, suppose you're borrowing $50,000 at 12.5 percent interest, with payments paid monthly over a 30-year period. After entering this data (use a pull-down menu to choose frequency of payment), Loan Payments tells you that your constant monthly bill is roughly $534. Total payments over the life of the loan are $192,106, with $50,000 paid to principal and $142,106 paid to interest.

Now, the power of the Amiga comes into play. Loan data information is displayed on the left of the screen, and loan payments on the right. To make changes to any of your input values, simply click the mouse on the item of your choice. Then enter the new value, and watch as the Amiga ripples along the right side, displaying updated output.

When you're through making changes, the Amiga will display the details of each loan payment (Figure 4-2).

Figure 4-2. Division of Monthly Payments

Year:Month	Paid to Principal	Paid to Interest
1:1	$ 12.80	$520.83
1:2	12.93	520.70
1:3	13.06	520.57
.		
.		
.		
30:12	$528.13	$ 5.50

Program 4-2. Loan Payments
Save using the filename **LOAN**

```
REM LOAN PAYMENT
 GOSUB INITIALIZE
COMPUTE:
 GOSUB RUN.LOAN
 LOCATE 18,25: PRINT "Compute Again ?"
 GOSUB DECIDE
 IF BUTTON = 1 THEN COMPUTE
 GOSUB GOODBYE
END

INITIALIZE:
 GOSUB SETSCREEN
 GOSUB KEYVALUES
 GOSUB SETMENUS
 GOSUB SETCOLORS
 GOSUB HEADING
RETURN

SETSCREEN:
 SCREEN 1,640,200,3,2
 WINDOW 2,"Loan Payments",,0,1
RETURN

KEYVALUES:
 DEFINT A-Z: DEFSNG L,P,R,T,X
 REM BUTTON VALUES
  XB(1) = 292: XB(2) = 334: YB = 174
  LT$(1) = "Y": LT$(2) = "N"
 REM LOAN TITLES & ROWS FOR LEFT BOX
  DATA Amount,5, "  Years",10, "  Months",12
  DATA Interest Rate,15
  FOR I=1 TO 4
   READ NM$(I), ROW.LEFT(I)
  NEXT
 REM ROWS FOR RIGHT BOX
  DATA 5,7,9,13
  FOR I=1 TO 4
   READ ROW.RIGHT(I)
  NEXT
 REM PRINT-FORMATS
  F$(1) = "$$##,#####.##"
  F$(2) = "       ###    "
  F$(3) = "        %##.##"
 REM FORMATS FOR LEFT BOX
  DATA 1,2,2,3
  FOR I=1 TO 4
```

```
      READ F(I)
    NEXT
  REM PAYMENT PERIOD
    DATA Year,1, Quarter,4, Month,12
    FOR I=1 TO 3
      READ FREQ$(I), FREQ(I)
    NEXT
  FIRST.RUN$ = "ON"
RETURN

SETMENUS:
  DATA 2, Instructions, Yes, No
  DATA 3, Compute Loan
  DATA For yearly payments, For quarterly payments
  DATA For monthly payments
  DATA 3, Stop, Go to BASIC
  DATA Go to Helpers Menu, Go to System
  FOR I=1 TO 3
    READ NUMBER
    FOR J=0 TO NUMBER
      READ TITLE$
      IF J<>0 THEN TITLE$ = SPACE$(3) + TITLE$
      STATUS = 1
      IF I <> 3 AND J = 1 THEN STATUS = 2
      MENU I,J,STATUS,TITLE$
  NEXT J,I
  MENU 4,0,0,""
  INSTRUCTIONS = 1: TYPE = 1
RETURN

SETCOLORS:
  REM BROWN, GREEN, & RED
    PALETTE 4,.8,.6,.53
    PALETTE 5,.14,.43,0
    PALETTE 6,.93,.2,0
RETURN

HEADING:
  MENU ON
  ON MENU GOSUB OPTIONS
  CLS
  COLOR 3,0: LOCATE 18,30:PRINT "then"
  COLOR 1,0
  LOCATE 10: PRINT PTAB(247)"Loan Payments"
  LOCATE 17,24:PRINT "Please use menus,"
  LOCATE 19,21:PRINT "Click mouse to compute"
  GOSUB CLICKIT
RETURN
```

```
OPTIONS:
 ID = MENU(Ø): ITEM = MENU(1)
 ON ID GOSUB MENU1,MENU2,GOODBYE
 ITEM = Ø
RETURN

MENU1:
 MENU 1,INSTRUCTIONS,1: MENU 1,ITEM,2
 INSTRUCTIONS = ITEM
RETURN

MENU2:
 MENU 2,TYPE,1: MENU 2,ITEM,2
 TYPE = ITEM
RETURN

GOODBYE:
 WINDOW CLOSE 2: WINDOW 1: MENU RESET
 SCREEN CLOSE 1
 IF ITEM = 2 THEN RUN "HELPERS"
 IF ITEM = 3 THEN SYSTEM
 COLOR 1,Ø: CLS
 PRINT "Bye-Bye"
 STOP
RETURN

CLICKIT:
 S$ = ""
 WHILE MOUSE(Ø) = Ø AND S$ = ""
  S$ = INKEY$
 WEND
  X = MOUSE(1)
  Y = MOUSE(2)
 WHILE MOUSE(Ø)<> Ø: WEND: REM RESET
RETURN

RUN.LOAN:
 VARIABLE = 1
 IF INSTRUCTIONS = 1 THEN GOSUB INSTRUCTIONS
 IF FIRST.RUN$ = "ON" THEN GOSUB ENTER.DATA
 GOSUB COMPUTE.PAYMENT
 GOSUB PAINT.SCREEN
 GOSUB SHOW.SUMMARY
 GOSUB ASK.TO.CHANGE
 GOSUB PAYMENTS.PER.PERIOD
RETURN

INSTRUCTIONS:
 CLS
```

```
PRINT
PRINT "    This program computes annual,";
PRINT " quarterly, and monthly"
PRINT " payments on a loan."
PRINT
PRINT "    In the display that follows, basic";
PRINT " loan values are on"
PRINT " the left.  Change these to play";
PRINT " what-if games like tallying"
PRINT " the dollar impact of an";
PRINT " increase in interest rates."
PRINT
PRINT "    Total loan payments are on the";
PRINT " right, including the amount"
PRINT " you pay to principal and to interest."
LOCATE 20,27:PRINT "Click Mouse";
GOSUB CLICKIT
ITEM = 2: GOSUB MENU1: REM TURN OFF INSTRUCTIONS
RETURN

ENTER.DATA:
 GOSUB AMOUNT
 GOSUB LENGTH
 GOSUB INTEREST.RATE
 FIRST.RUN$ = "OFF"
RETURN

AMOUNT:
 CLS
 PRINT
 PRINT "  Please enter the amount of money";
 PRINT " that you'd like to borrow."
 X(1) = Ø
 WHILE X(1) <= Ø
  LOCATE 4,12: PRINT SPACE$(2Ø)
  GOSUB GURGLE
  LOCATE 4,3: INPUT "Amount ";S$
  X(1) = VAL(S$)
 WEND
RETURN

LENGTH:
 LOCATE 7,3: PRINT "Please enter the length of";
 PRINT " your loan in years and months."
 X(2) = -9: REM YEARS
 WHILE X(2) < Ø
  LOCATE 9,13: PRINT SPACE$(2Ø)
  GOSUB GURGLE
  LOCATE 9,4: INPUT "Years = ";S$
```

```
   X(2) = INT(VAL(S$))
  WEND
  X(3) = -9: REM MONTHS
  WHILE X(3) < Ø
   LOCATE 1Ø,13: PRINT SPACE$(2Ø)
   GOSUB GURGLE
   LOCATE 1Ø,3: INPUT "Months = ";S$
   X,3) = INT(VAL(S$))
  WEND
  IF X(2) + X(3) = Ø THEN LENGTH
RETURN

INTEREST.RATE:
  LOCATE 13,3: PRINT "Please enter the interest";
  PRINT " rate on your loan.  For example,"
  PRINT "   enter 7 for 7%, 1Ø for 1Ø%, and so on."
  X(4) = Ø
  WHILE X(4) <= Ø
   GOSUB GURGLE
   LOCATE 16,12: PRINT SPACE$(2Ø)
   LOCATE 16,3: INPUT "Rate = ";S$
   X(4) = VAL(S$)
  WEND
RETURN

COMPUTE.PAYMENT:
  FREQ = FREQ(TYPE): REM PAYMENTS PER YEAR
  FREQ$ = FREQ$(TYPE)
  REM TOTAL YEARS
   TYEARS = X(2) + X(3)/12
  REM TOTAL NUMBER OF PAYMENTS
   N = TYEARS*FREQ
  REM INTEREST RATE PER PERIOD
   R = (X(4)/1ØØ)/FREQ
  REM PAYMENT PER PERIOD
   REM NUMERATOR
    P1 = X(1)*R*(1+R)^N
   REM DENOMINATOR
    P2 = (1+R)^N - 1
   P(4) = P1/P2
  REM TOTAL PAYMENT
   P(1) = N*P(4)
  REM PRINCIPAL & INTEREST
   P(2) = X(1)
   P(3) = P(1) - P(2)
RETURN

PAINT.SCREEN:
  CLS
```

```
     LINE(10,4)-(306,143),4,BF
     LINE(324,4)-(620,143),1,BF
     REM LEFT BOX
      COLOR 2,4
      LOCATE 2,11: PRINT "LOAN VALUES"
      FOR I=1 TO 4
       LOCATE ROW.LEFT(I),3: PRINT NM$(I);
       PRINT TAB(17) USING F$(F(I));X(I)
      NEXT
      LOCATE 8,3: PRINT "Length"
     REM RIGHT BOX
      COLOR 0,1
      LOCATE 2,42: PRINT "LOAN PAYMENTS"
      LOCATE 5,35: PRINT "Total"
      LINE(355,52)-(452,62),5,BF
      COLOR 1,5
      LOCATE 7,37: PRINT "Principal"
      LINE(355,70)-(452,80),6,BF
      COLOR 1,6
      LOCATE 9,37: PRINT "Interest"
      COLOR 0,1
      LOCATE 12,35: PRINT "Payment"
      LOCATE 13,35: PRINT "Per"
     RETURN

     SHOW.SUMMARY:
      COLOR 0,1
      LOCATE 3,39: PRINT SPACE$(18)
      S$ = "("+FREQ$+"ly Basis)": L = LEN(S$)
      LOCATE 3: PRINT PTAB(475-10*L/2);S$
      LOCATE 13,39: PRINT FREQ$;SPACE$(2)
      FOR I=1 TO 4
       LOCATE ROW.RIGHT(I),49
       PRINT USING F$(1);P(I)
      NEXT
     RETURN

     ASK.TO.CHANGE:
      COLOR 1,0
      LOCATE 18,28: PRINT "Changes ?"
      GOSUB DECIDE
      LOCATE 18,28: PRINT SPACE$(9)
      IF BUTTON = 1 THEN
       CALL HIGHLIGHT(VARIABLE,3)
       COLOR 1,0
       LINE(265,167)-(361,181),0,BF
       LOCATE 19,13: PRINT "Click Mouse on Choice,";
       PRINT " then Hit Return"
       GOSUB CHOOSE
```

```
      GOTO ASK.TO.CHANGE
    END IF
  RETURN

  SUB HIGHLIGHT(V,KOLOR) STATIC
    SHARED NM$(), ROW.LEFT()
    R = ROW.LEFT(V)
    L = LEN(NM$(V))
    XØ = 15: X1 = L*1Ø + 25
    YØ = 9*R - 11: Y1 = YØ + 1Ø
    LINE(XØ,YØ)-(X1,Y1),KOLOR,BF
    COLOR KOLOR-2,KOLOR
    LOCATE R,3: PRINT NM$(V)
  END SUB

  CHOOSE:
    GOSUB GURGLE
    GOSUB CLICKIT
    IF S$ = "" THEN GOSUB LOCATION: GOTO CHOOSE
    IF ASC(S$) <> 13 THEN CHOOSE
    GOSUB CHANGE
  RETURN

  GURGLE:
    FREQ = 3ØØ
    FOR G=1 TO 5
      FREQ = 5ØØ-FREQ
      SOUND FREQ,1,5Ø
    NEXT G
  RETURN

  LOCATION:
    R = INT(Y/9) + 1
    I=Ø: V=Ø
    WHILE V=Ø AND I <= 4
      I = I + 1
      IF ROW.LEFT(I) = R THEN V = I
    WEND
    IF X>14 AND X<175 AND V <> Ø THEN
      CALL HIGHLIGHT(VARIABLE,4)
      CALL HIGHLIGHT(V,3)
      VARIABLE = V
    END IF
  RETURN

  DECIDE:
    BUTTON = Ø
    GOSUB DRAWBUTTON
    GOSUB PUSHBUTTON
```

```
  COLOR 1,Ø
RETURN

DRAWBUTTON:
 LINE (265,167)-(361,181),1,BF
 FOR I=1 TO 2
  CIRCLE (XB(I),YB),12,4+I
  PAINT (XB(I),YB),4+I
  COLOR 1,4+I
  LOCATE 20: PRINT PTAB(XB(I)-4);LT$(I);
 NEXT I
RETURN

PUSHBUTTON:
 SOUND 44Ø,2
 GOSUB CLICKIT
 S$ = UCASE$(S$)
 IF S$ = "Y" THEN BUTTON = 1
 IF S$ = "N" THEN BUTTON = 2
 FOR I=1 TO 2
  XD = ABS(X-XB(I)): YD = ABS(Y-YB)
  IF XD<13 AND YD<7 THEN BUTTON = I: I=2
 NEXT
 IF BUTTON = Ø THEN PUSHBUTTON
RETURN

CHANGE:
 ROW = ROW.LEFT(VARIABLE)
 COLOR 1,Ø
 LOCATE 19,13: PRINT SPACE$(38);
 LOCATE 19,26: LINE INPUT; "New Value ? ";S$
 IF VARIABLE = 2 OR VARIABLE = 3 THEN
  X(VARIABLE) = INT(VAL(S$))
 ELSE
  X(VARIABLE) = VAL(S$)
 END IF
 LOCATE 19,26: PRINT SPACE$(3Ø);
 COLOR 4
 COLOR 2,4: LOCATE ROW,17
 PRINT USING F$(F(VARIABLE));X(VARIABLE)
 GOSUB COMPUTE.PAYMENT
 GOSUB SHOW.SUMMARY
RETURN

PAYMENTS.PER.PERIOD:
 LOCATE 18,14: PRINT "Would you like to see";
 PRINT " each payment ?"
 GOSUB DECIDE
 LOCATE 18,14: PRINT SPACE$(36)
```

```
      IF BUTTON = 1 THEN
        GOSUB SHOW.DETAILS
        GOSUB PAINT.SCREEN
        GOSUB SHOW.SUMMARY
        COLOR 1,0
      END IF
    RETURN

    SHOW.DETAILS:
      LOAN = X(1)
      YR=1: QT=1: MT=1
      TITLE$ = FREQ$ + "ly" + " Payment Equals: $"
      TITLE$ = TITLE$ + STR$(INT(P(4)*100+.5)/100)
      IF FREQ = 1 THEN PERIOD$ = "Year"
      IF FREQ = 4 THEN PERIOD$ = "Year:Quarter"
      IF FREQ =12 THEN PERIOD$ = "Year:Month"
      FOR I=1 TO N STEP 12
        GOSUB LABEL
        GOSUB BODY
      NEXT I
    RETURN

    LABEL:
      CLS
      LOCATE 2,32-LEN(TITLE$)/2: PRINT TITLE$
      L = LEN(PERIOD$)
      LINE(90-10*L/2,34)-(110+10*L/2,44),3,BF
      COLOR 2,3
      LOCATE 5,11-L/2: PRINT PERIOD$
      LINE(230,24)-(340,44),5,BF
      COLOR 1,5
      LOCATE 4,25: PRINT "Paid to"
      LOCATE 5,25: PRINT "Principal"
      LINE(430,24)-(530,44),6,BF
      COLOR 1,6
      LOCATE 4,45: PRINT "Paid to"
      LOCATE 5,45: PRINT "Interest"
    RETURN

    BODY:
      COLOR 1,0
      ROW = 7
      FOR J = I TO I+11
        IF J <= N THEN
          PTI = R*LOAN     : REM PAID TO INTEREST
          PTP = P(4) - PTI: REM PAID TO PRINCIPAL
          IF FREQ = 1 THEN GOSUB YEAR
          IF FREQ = 4 THEN GOSUB QUARTER
          IF FREQ =12 THEN GOSUB MONTH
```

```
     ROW = ROW + 1
     LOAN = LOAN - PTP
    END IF
  NEXT J
  LOCATE 20,26: PRINT "Press any key";
  GOSUB CLICKIT
RETURN

YEAR:
 LOCATE ROW,10: PRINT USING "##";YR;
 PRINT TAB(21) USING F$(1);PTP;
 PRINT TAB(40) USING F$(1);PTI
 YR = YR + 1
RETURN

QUARTER:
 LOCATE ROW,9: PRINT USING "##:#";YR,QT;
 PRINT TAB(21) USING F$(1);PTP;
 PRINT TAB(40) USING F$(1);PTI
 IF QT = 4 THEN
  YR = YR + 1
  QT = 1
 ELSE
  QT = QT + 1
 END IF
RETURN

MONTH:
 LOCATE ROW,8
 IF MT <= 9 THEN
  PRINT USING "##:#";YR,MT;
 ELSE
  PRINT USING "##:##";YR,MT;
 END IF
 PRINT TAB(21) USING F$(1);PTP;
 PRINT TAB(40) USING F$(1);PTI
 IF MT = 12 THEN
  YR = YR + 1
  MT = 1
 ELSE
  MT = MT + 1
 END IF
RETURN
```

Multifunction Calculator

"Multifunction Calculator" (Figure 4-3) helps you evaluate simple arithmetic expressions and highly complex formulas. Enter digits and symbols into the calculator with either the keyboard or the mouse.

You can add, subtract, multiply, divide, and raise numbers to a power. Plus, you can use parentheses for more complex operations. The calculator handles simple operations like $2 + 3$ and complex expressions like $(7-3)*(2^3+1)/(17.9+5)$.

Three special calculator keys to remember are

> C to Clear the display
> M to access Memory
> R to Return (execute an operation)

If you're entering an expression, for example, and want to erase everything you've entered, press the C on the keyboard or click the mouse on the Clear key on the screen. Your display window will clear and only the vertical cursor bar will remain. To delete just the last character entered, use the left arrow.

Try pressing M after clearing the display. The Amiga will retrieve from memory the result of your last calculation and will display it using as many decimal places as you've selected from the pull-down menu.

If you try to perform an illegal mathematical operation, don't worry. The Amiga will let you know what the problem is, such as division by zero. You can then clear the display and enter a new expression.

The calculator evaluates expressions just as Amiga BASIC does. Namely, it computes from left to right according to the following precedence of operations: exponentiation, multiplication and division, addition and subtraction. Use parentheses if you need to change this ordering.

Figure 4-3. Multifunction Calculator

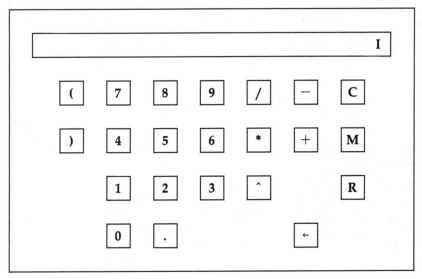

Program 4-3. Multifunction Calculator
Save using the filename **CALCULATOR**

```
REM MULTI-FUNCTION CALCULATOR
 GOSUB INITIALIZE
 IF INSTRUCTIONS = 1 THEN GOSUB INSTRUCTIONS
 GOSUB DRAW.CALCULATOR
 GOSUB OPERATE
END

INITIALIZE:
 GOSUB SETSCREEN
 GOSUB KEYVALUES
 GOSUB SETMENUS
 GOSUB SETCOLORS
 GOSUB HEADING
RETURN

SETSCREEN:
 SCREEN 1,640,200,3,2
 WINDOW 2,"Multi-Function Calculator",,0,1
RETURN

KEYVALUES:
 DEFINT A-J,L-Z: DEFDBL Q,V
 RANDOMIZE TIMER
```

237

```
   DIM B(28),F(28),S(28),V(25),SYM(25)
   GOSUB KEY.SYMBOLS
   GOSUB KEY.POINTS
   GOSUB ERROR.CODES
   GOSUB LEGAL.VALUES
RETURN

KEY.SYMBOLS:
 REM SYMBOLS; FOREGROUND & BACKGROUND COLORS
 REM D = DUMMY (NO KEY)
  DATA (,2,3, 7,1,2, 8,1,2, 9,1,2
  DATA /,2,3, -,2,3, C,1,5
  DATA ),2,3, 4,1,2, 5,1,2, 6,1,2
  DATA *,2,3, +,2,3, M,1,5
  DATA D,Ø,Ø, 1,1,2, 2,1,2, 3,1,2
  DATA ^,2,3, D,Ø,Ø, R,1,5
  DATA D,Ø,Ø, Ø,1,2, .,1,2, D,Ø,Ø
  DATA D,Ø,Ø, -,1,6, D,Ø,Ø
  FOR I=1 TO 4
   FOR J=1 TO 7
    CNT = (I-1)*7 + J
    READ C$,F(CNT),B(CNT)
    S(CNT) = ASC(C$)
   NEXT J,I
RETURN

KEY.POINTS:
 REM BORDER
  DATA -5,3,Ø,6,5,3,13,Ø,5,-3,Ø,-6,-5,-3
  FOR I=1 TO 7
   READ KEY.BX(I),KEY.BY(I)
  NEXT
 REM CENTER
  DATA -4,2,Ø,6,4,2,13,Ø,4,-2,Ø,-6,-4,-2
  FOR I=1 TO 7
   READ KEY.CX(I), KEY.CY(I)
  NEXT
RETURN

ERROR.CODES:
  DATA Parentheses, Division by Zero, Syntax
  DATA Exponentiation
  FOR I=1 TO 4
   READ ERROR.CODE$(I)
  NEXT
RETURN

LEGAL.VALUES:
 REM TO THE LEFT OF (
```

```
   DATA 32,40,42,43,45,47,94
   FOR I=1 TO 7
    READ LEFT(I)
   NEXT
  REM TO THE RIGHT OF )
   DATA 32,41,42,43,45,47,94
   FOR I=1 TO 7
    READ RIGHT(I)
   NEXT
RETURN

SETMENUS:
 DATA 2, Instructions, Yes, No
 DATA 5, Calculator, Brown, Blue, Green
 DATA Gray, Random
 DATA 7, Decimals, 0 Places, 1 Place, 2 Places
 DATA 3 Places, 4 Places, 5 Places, 6 Places
 DATA 3, Stop, Go to BASIC
 DATA Go to Helpers Menu, Go to System
 FOR I=1 TO 4
  READ NUMBER
  FOR J=0 TO NUMBER
   READ TITLE$
   IF J<>0 THEN TITLE$ = SPACE$(3) + TITLE$
   STATUS = 1
   IF I < 3 AND J=1 THEN STATUS = 2
   IF I = 3 AND J=3 THEN STATUS = 2
   MENU I,J,STATUS,TITLE$
 NEXT J,I
 INSTRUCTIONS = 1: DP = 2: CAL.COLOR = 1
RETURN

SETCOLORS:
 REM BROWN, BLUE, GREEN, GRAY
  DATA .8,.6,.53, .36,.57,1
  DATA .26,.59,.47, .58,.52,.6
  FOR I=1 TO 4
   FOR J=1 TO 3
    READ KOLOR(I,J)
  NEXT J,I
 REM BROWN, GREEN, & RED
  PALETTE 4,.8,.6,.53
  PALETTE 5,0,.39,.19
  PALETTE 6,.93,.2,0
RETURN

HEADING:
 MENU ON
 ON MENU GOSUB OPTIONS
```

239

```
   CLS
   COLOR 3,0: LOCATE 18,30:PRINT "then"
   COLOR 1,0
   LOCATE 10,20: PRINT "Multi-Function Calculator"
   LOCATE 17,24:PRINT "Please use menus,"
   LOCATE 19,21:PRINT "Click mouse to compute"
   GOSUB CLICKIT
RETURN

OPTIONS:
  ID = MENU(0): ITEM = MENU(1)
  ON ID GOSUB MENU1,MENU2,MENU3,GOODBYE
  ITEM = 0
RETURN

MENU1:
  MENU 1,INSTRUCTIONS,1: MENU 1,ITEM,2
  INSTRUCTIONS = ITEM
RETURN

MENU2:
  K1 = KOLOR(ITEM,1): K2 = KOLOR(ITEM,2)
  K3 = KOLOR(ITEM,3)
  IF ITEM=5 THEN K1=RND: K2=RND: K3=RND
  PALETTE 4,K1,K2,K3
  MENU 2,CAL.COLOR,1: MENU 2,ITEM,2
  CAL.COLOR = ITEM
RETURN

MENU3:
  MENU 3,DP+1,1: MENU 3,ITEM,2
  DP = ITEM-1
RETURN

GOODBYE:
  WINDOW CLOSE 2: WINDOW 1: MENU RESET
  SCREEN CLOSE 1
  IF ITEM = 2 THEN RUN "HELPERS"
  IF ITEM = 3 THEN SYSTEM
  COLOR 1,0: CLS
  PRINT "Bye-Bye"
  STOP
RETURN

CLICKIT:
  S$ = ""
  WHILE MOUSE(0) = 0 AND S$ = ""
   S$ = INKEY$
  WEND
```

```
    X = MOUSE(1)
    Y = MOUSE(2)
   WHILE MOUSE(Ø)<> Ø: WEND: REM RESET
  RETURN

  INSTRUCTIONS:
   CLS
   PRINT
   PRINT "    Multi-Function Calculator helps you";
   PRINT " evaluate simple"
   PRINT " arithmetic expressions and highly";
   PRINT " complex formulas."
   PRINT
   PRINT "    Enter digits and symbols into the";
   PRINT " calculator with either"
   PRINT " the keyboard or mouse."
   PRINT
   PRINT "    You can add, subtract, multiply,";
   PRINT " divide, and raise numbers"
   PRINT " to a power.  And you can use";
   PRINT " parentheses."
   PRINT
   PRINT "    Three special calculator keys to";
   PRINT " remember are:"
   PRINT
   PRINT TAB(15)"C  to Clear the display"
   PRINT TAB(15)"M  to access Memory"
   PRINT TAB(15)"R  to Return (execute an";
   PRINT " operation)"
   LOCATE 2Ø,27:PRINT "Click Mouse";
   GOSUB CLICKIT
  RETURN

  DRAW.CALCULATOR:
   CLS
   LINE(93,15)-(533,115),4,BF
   LINE(93,15)-(533,115),2,B
   LINE(113,25)-(513,35),Ø,BF: REM DISPLAY
   LINE(112,24)-(514,36),2,B
   REM DRAW SYMBOLS
    FOR I=1 TO 4
     FOR J=1 TO 7
       Y = 18*I + 25
       X = 4Ø*J + 145
       CNT = (I-1)*7 + J
       IF S(CNT) <> 68 THEN GOSUB DRAW.KEY
    NEXT J,I
   REM DRAW ARROW
    COLOR 1,6
```

241

```
   LINE(391,100)-STEP(-4,2)
   LINE -STEP(4,2): LINE -STEP(0,-4)
   PAINT(389,102)
   LINE(387,102)-(401,102)
   S(27) = 31: S(21) = 13
 REM SET INITIAL VALUE
   COLOR 1,0
   E$ = "": L = 0: VALUE = 0
   LOCATE 4,51: PRINT CHR$(124)
 RETURN

DRAW.KEY:
 REM BORDER
   COLOR 0
   AREA (X+3,Y-1)
   FOR L=1 TO 7
    AREA STEP(KEY.BX(L),KEY.BY(L))
   NEXT L
   AREAFILL
 REM CENTER
   COLOR B(CNT)
   AREA (X+3,Y)
   FOR L=1 TO 7
    AREA STEP(KEY.CX(L),KEY.CY(L))
   NEXT L
   AREAFILL
   COLOR F(CNT),B(CNT)
   LOCATE I*2+4,J*4+16: PRINT CHR$(S(CNT))
 RETURN

OPERATE:
 GOSUB GET.INPUT
 IF L > 0 THEN GOSUB EVALUATE
 GOTO OPERATE
RETURN

GET.INPUT:
 GOSUB CLICKIT
 KEY$ = "BAD"
 IF S$ = "" THEN
  GOSUB MOUSE.ENTRY
 ELSE
  GOSUB KEYBOARD
 END IF
 REM CHECK FOR MAX LENGTH
  IF L = 39 THEN
   IF A<>13 AND A<>31 AND A<>67 THEN KEY$="BAD"
  END IF
 REM NO EXPRESSION
```

242

```
   IF L = Ø AND A = 31 THEN KEY$ = "BAD"
 REM MEMORY ACCESS
   IF L <> Ø AND A = 77 THEN KEY$ = "BAD"
 IF KEY$ = "BAD" THEN
   SOUND 9ØØ,2
   GOTO GET.INPUT
 END IF
 IF A=31 THEN GOSUB BACKSPACE
 IF A=67 THEN GOSUB CLEAR.DISPLAY
 IF A=77 THEN GOSUB MEMORY
 IF NOT (A=13 OR A=31 OR A=67 OR A=77) THEN
   GOSUB DISPLAY
 END IF
 IF A <> 13 THEN GET.INPUT
RETURN

MOUSE.ENTRY:
 ROW = INT((Y-4Ø)/18) + 1
 COL = INT((X-175)/4Ø) + 1
 IF ROW>Ø AND ROW<5 AND COL>Ø AND COL<8 THEN
   KEY$ = "OK"
 END IF
 IF KEY$ = "OK" THEN
   KEY = (ROW-1)*7+COL
   IF S(KEY)=68 THEN KEY$ = "BAD"
   A = S(KEY)
 END IF
RETURN

KEYBOARD:
 A = ASC(UCASE$(S$))
 IF A=8 OR A=127 THEN A=31: REM BACKSPACE
 IF A=82 THEN A=13: REM RETURN
 REM VALIDITY
   IF A <> 44 AND A>39 AND A<58 THEN KEY$ = "OK"
   IF A=13 OR A=31 OR A=67 THEN KEY$ = "OK"
   IF A=77 OR A=94 THEN KEY$ = "OK"
RETURN

BACKSPACE:
 E$ = LEFT$(E$,L-1)
 LOCATE 4,52-L: PRINT " "+E$
 L = L-1
 IF L=Ø THEN LOCATE 4,51: PRINT CHR$(124)
RETURN

CLEAR.DISPLAY:
 E$ = ""
 LOCATE 4,52-L: PRINT SPACE$(L)
```

```
  L = Ø
  LOCATE 4,51: PRINT CHR$(124)
RETURN

MEMORY:
  V = INT(VALUE*1Ø^DP+.5)/1Ø^DP
  E$ = STR$(V)
  IF V >= Ø THEN E$ = MID$(E$,2)
  L = LEN(E$)
  LOCATE 4,52-L: PRINT E$
RETURN

DISPLAY:
  E$ = E$ + CHR$(A)
  L = L+1
  LOCATE 4,52-L: PRINT E$
RETURN

EVALUATE:
  GOOF = Ø
  EXPRESSION$ = E$
  LOCATE 4,13: PRINT SPACE$(39)
  LOCATE 4,27: PRINT "Calculating"
  GOSUB GURGLE
  GOSUB STRIKE.PARENTHESES
  IF GOOF = Ø THEN GOSUB CALCULATE
  LOCATE 4,27: PRINT SPACE$(11)
  IF GOOF = Ø THEN GOSUB MEMORY ELSE GOSUB GOOF
RETURN

GURGLE:
  FREQ = 3ØØ
  FOR G=1 TO 5
   FREQ = 5ØØ-FREQ
   SOUND FREQ,1,5Ø
  NEXT G
RETURN

STRIKE.PARENTHESES:
  PL=Ø: PR=Ø
  FOR I=1 TO L
   C$ = MID$(E$,I,1): A = ASC(C$)
   IF A=4Ø THEN PL = I
   IF A=41 THEN PR = I: I=L
  NEXT
  IF PR-PL = 1 THEN GOOF = 1
  IF PL=Ø AND PR>Ø THEN GOOF = 1
  IF PR=Ø AND PL>Ø THEN GOOF = 1
  IF GOOF = Ø AND PR <> Ø THEN
```

```
      GOSUB REMOVE
      GOTO STRIKE.PARENTHESES
    END IF
  RETURN

REMOVE:
  LF$ = MID$(E$,1,PL-1)
  MD$ = MID$(E$,PL+1,PR-PL-1)
  RT$ = MID$(E$,PR+1,L-PR)
  REM CHECK LEFT OF (
    LK = ASC(RIGHT$(" " + LF$,1))
    GOOF=3: J=1
    WHILE GOOF = 3 AND J <= 7
      IF LK = LEFT(J) THEN GOOF = Ø
      J = J+1
    WEND
  REM CHECK RIGHT OF )
    RK = ASC(LEFT$(RT$ + " ",1))
    GOOF=3: J=1
    WHILE GOOF = 3 AND J <= 7
      IF RK = RIGHT(J) THEN GOOF = Ø
      J = J+1
    WEND
  REM CONTINUE
    IF GOOF = Ø THEN
      E$ = MD$: GOSUB CALCULATE
      S$ = STR$(VALUE)
      IF VALUE >=Ø THEN S$ = MID$(S$,2)
      E$ = LF$ + S$ + RT$
      L = LEN(E$)
    END IF
  RETURN

CALCULATE:
  E$ = E$ + CHR$(32): T=Ø: P=Ø: SG=1
  GOSUB TAKE.APART
  IF GOOF = Ø THEN
    IF T > 1 THEN GOSUB TALLY
    IF GOOF = Ø THEN VALUE = V(T)
  END IF
  IF SYM(T) <> 32 THEN GOOF = 3
  RETURN

TAKE.APART:
  P = P+1
  C$ = MID$(E$,P,1): A=ASC(C$)
  REM + OR -
    IF A=43 OR A=45 THEN
      IF A = 45 THEN SG = - SG
```

245

```
     NM$ = "OFF"
      GOTO TAKE.APART
    END IF
  REM DIGIT OR DECIMAL
    IF A=46 OR (A>47 AND A<58) THEN
      GOSUB NUMBER
    ELSE
      IF A <> 32 THEN GOOF = 3
    END IF
  REM CONTINUE
    IF GOOF = Ø AND A <> 32 THEN
      SG=1: GOTO TAKE.APART
    END IF
  IF NM$ = "OFF" THEN GOOF = 3
RETURN

NUMBER:
  N$ = C$
  DEC$ = "OFF": DGT$ = "OFF"
  IF A=46 THEN DEC$ = "ON"
  IF A>47 AND A<58 THEN DGT$ = "ON"
LOOP:
  REM GET NUMBER
    P = P+1
    C$ = MID$(E$,P,1): A=ASC(C$)
    IF A=46 AND DEC$ = "ON" THEN GOOF = 3
    IF A=46 THEN DEC$ = "ON"
    IF A>47 AND A<58 THEN DGT$ = "ON"
    IF GOOF=Ø AND A=46 OR (A>47 AND A<58) THEN
      N$ = N$ + C$
      GOTO LOOP
    END IF
  REM CHECK FOR DIGIT
    IF DGT$ = "OFF" THEN GOOF = 3
  REM STORE NUMBER
    IF GOOF = Ø THEN
      T = T+1
      V(T) = SG*VAL(N$)
      SYM(T) = A
      NM$ = "ON"
    END IF
RETURN

TALLY:
  GOSUB EXPONENTIATION
  IF GOOF = Ø THEN GOSUB MULT.DIV
  IF GOOF = Ø THEN GOSUB ADD.SUB
RETURN
```

```
EXPONENTIATION:
 FOR I=1 TO T-1
  IF SYM(I) = 94 THEN
   IF V(I) < 0 AND V(I+1) < 1 THEN GOOF = 4
   IF GOOF = 0 THEN
    V(I+1) = V(I)^V(I+1)
    SYM(I) = -9
   END IF
  END IF
 NEXT
RETURN

MULT.DIV:
 FOR I=1 TO T-1
  S = SYM(I)
  IF S = 42 OR S = 47 THEN
   Q = V(I)
   FOR J = I+1 TO T
    IF SYM(J) <> -9 THEN GOSUB MD: J = T
   NEXT J
  END IF
 NEXT I
RETURN

MD:
 IF S = 42 THEN V(J)=Q*V(J): SYM(I) = -9
 IF S = 47 AND V(J) = 0 THEN GOOF = 2
 IF S = 47 AND GOOF = 0 THEN
 V(J) = Q/V(J)
 SYM(I) = -9
 END IF
RETURN

ADD.SUB:
 FOR I=1 TO T-1
  S = SYM(I)
  IF S = 43 OR S = 45 THEN
   Q = V(I)
   FOR J = I+1 TO T
    IF SYM(J) <> - 9 THEN
     IF S = 43 THEN V(J) = Q + V(J)
     IF S = 45 THEN V(J) = Q - V(J)
     SYM(I) = -9
     J = T
    END IF
   NEXT J
  END IF
 NEXT I
RETURN
```

```
GOOF:
 COLOR 1,6
 LINE(95,124)-(155,134),6,BF
 LOCATE 15,11: PRINT "Error"
 COLOR 1,Ø
 E$ = EXPRESSION$: L = LEN(E$)
 LOCATE 4,52-L: PRINT E$
 LOCATE 15,17: PRINT ERROR.CODE$(GOOF)
 LOCATE 19,26: PRINT "Press any key"
 GOSUB CLICKIT
 LINE(95,124)-(155,134),Ø,BF
 LOCATE 15,17: PRINT SPACE$(16)
 LOCATE 19,26: PRINT SPACE$(13)
RETURN
```

Paycheck Analysis

With "Paycheck Analysis" you can verify that your paycheck has been calculated correctly. Furthermore, you can use the program to project future take-home pay when that raise comes through and even to tally a payroll.

Before you use Payroll Analysis, you'll probably want to customize it a bit. As it's listed, the program calculates withholding for a single person. If you're in another classification, such as married filing jointly or married filing separately, you need to change some of the program lines. And the rates are likely to change from year to year.

Nevertheless, all you need is a copy of the tax rate schedules, which you can obtain from the Internal Revenue Service. Ask for Schedule X. You will also need information on your state taxes. Then insert the new data in the STATE.TAX and FEDERAL.TAX subroutines at the very end of the program. These lines compute taxes using the formula

A + B* (Y — C)

The variable Y is your annual income, or weekly pay times 52; A, B, and C are from the tax tables. For example, your federal tax would be

$251.3 + .14 * (Y — $ $4580)

if Y is between $4,580 and $6,750. In this case, then, A = 251.3, B = 14, and C = 4580. To change the rates, place the new information in the lines using the same format.

Current state tax rates are from Virginia. The same formula as the federal withholding is used. You can replace these lines with ones that match your own state's tax rates.

As soon as you've made these customizations, you can check your paycheck. The display shows such things as weekly hours, hourly wage, insurance, and retirement fund. The last item, FICA, stands for the Federal Insurance Contributions Act, or Social Security. Presently, 7.15 percent of your paycheck is deducted for this, for up to $42,000 of annual income. If Congress changes these figures, make sure you alter the program appropriately.

To enter your own figures, simply click the mouse on the item of your choice. Then key in the new number. The Amiga will show updated figures on the right side of the screen.

You can compute paychecks for the following periods: one week, two weeks, four weeks, and one year. By using a pull-down menu, you can perform weekly and yearly analyses without having to enter your basic data more than once.

Program 4-4. Paycheck Analysis
Save using the filename **PAYCHECK**

```
REM PAYCHECK ANALYSIS
  GOSUB INITIALIZE
ANALYZE:
  GOSUB DO.PAY
  LOCATE 20,11: PRINT "Compute Again ?";
  GOSUB DECIDE
  IF BUTTON = 1 THEN ANALYZE
  GOSUB GOODBYE
END

INITIALIZE:
  GOSUB SETSCREEN
  GOSUB KEYVALUES
  GOSUB BASE.PAY
  GOSUB SETMENUS
  GOSUB SETCOLORS
  GOSUB HEADING
RETURN

SETSCREEN:
  SCREEN 1,640,200,3,2
  WINDOW 2,"Paycheck Analysis",,0,1
RETURN

KEYVALUES:
  DEFINT A-Z: DEFSNG M,P,T,X,Y
  DIM NM$(20),X(20),F(20)
  DEF FNTAX(X1,X2,X3) = X1 + X2/100*(Y-X3)
  REM BUTTON VALUES
  XB(1) = 292: XB(2) = 334: YB = 174
  LT$(1) = "Y": LT$(2) = "N"
  REM NUMBER OF ITEMS
  DATA 9
  READ N
  REM PRINT-FORMATS
  F$(1) = "$$######.##"
  F$(2) = "     ###.##"
  F$(3) = "    %##.##"
  F$(4) = "$$##,#####.##"
  REM FORMATS FOR LEFT BOX
  DATA 2,1,2,1,2,1,1,1,3
  FOR I=1 TO N
    READ F(I)
```

```
     NEXT
   REM PAY PERIODS
     DATA One Week,1, Two Weeks,2, Four Weeks,4
     DATA 52 Weeks, 52
     FOR I=1 TO 4
       READ PERIOD$(I), PERIOD(I)
     NEXT
   REM ROWS FOR RIGHT BOX (PAY RESULTS)
     DATA 5,8,10,12,16,18
     FOR I=1 TO 6
       READ ROW(I)
     NEXT
RETURN

BASE.PAY:
 DATA Weekly Hours, 40
 DATA Hourly Wage, 10
 DATA Overtime Hours, 0
 DATA Overtime Wage, 15
 DATA Fed. Exemptions, 1
 DATA Insurance, 15
 DATA Charity, 10
 DATA Retirement Fund, 50
 DATA F.I.C.A, 7.15
 FOR I=1 TO N
   READ NM$(I),X(I)
 NEXT
RETURN

SETMENUS:
 DATA 2, Instructions, Yes, No
 DATA 4, Compute Paycheck
 DATA For one week (5 days), For two weeks
 DATA For four weeks, For 52 weeks
 DATA 3, Stop, Go to BASIC
 DATA Go to Helpers Menu, Go to System
 FOR I=1 TO 3
  READ NUMBER
  FOR J=0 TO NUMBER
    READ TITLE$
    IF J<>0 THEN TITLE$ = SPACE$(3) + TITLE$
    STATUS = 1
    IF I <> 3 AND J = 1 THEN STATUS = 2
    MENU I,J,STATUS,TITLE$
 NEXT J,I
 MENU 4,0,0,""
 INSTRUCTIONS = 1: LENGTH = 1
RETURN
```

```
SETCOLORS:
 REM BROWN, GREEN, & RED
  PALETTE 4,.8,.6,.53
  PALETTE 5,.14,.43,0
  PALETTE 6,.93,.2,0
RETURN

HEADING:
 MENU ON
 ON MENU GOSUB OPTIONS
 CLS
 COLOR 3,0: LOCATE 18,30:PRINT "then"
 COLOR 1,0
 LOCATE 10: PRINT PTAB(224)"Paycheck Analysis"
 LOCATE 17,24:PRINT "Please use menus,"
 LOCATE 19,21:PRINT "Click mouse to compute"
 GOSUB CLICKIT
RETURN

OPTIONS:
 ID = MENU(0): ITEM = MENU(1)
 ON ID GOSUB MENU1,MENU2,GOODBYE
 ITEM = 0
RETURN

MENU1:
 MENU 1,INSTRUCTIONS,1: MENU 1,ITEM,2
 INSTRUCTIONS = ITEM
RETURN

MENU2:
 MENU 2,LENGTH,1: MENU 2,ITEM,2
 LENGTH = ITEM
RETURN

GOODBYE:
 WINDOW CLOSE 2: WINDOW 1: MENU RESET
 SCREEN CLOSE 1
 IF ITEM = 2 THEN RUN "HELPERS"
 IF ITEM = 3 THEN SYSTEM
 COLOR 1,0: CLS
 PRINT "Bye-Bye"
 STOP
RETURN

CLICKIT:
 S$ = ""
 WHILE MOUSE(0) = 0 AND S$ = ""
  S$ = INKEY$
```

```
    WEND
     X = MOUSE(1)
     Y = MOUSE(2)
     WHILE MOUSE(0)<> 0: WEND: REM RESET
    RETURN

   DO.PAY:
    ACCOUNT = 1
    IF INSTRUCTIONS = 1 THEN GOSUB INSTRUCTIONS
    GOSUB COMPUTE.PAY
    GOSUB PAINT.SCREEN
    GOSUB SHOW.PAY
    GOSUB ASK.TO.CHANGE
   RETURN

   INSTRUCTIONS:
    CLS
    PRINT
    PRINT "     This program computes a paycheck."
    PRINT
    PRINT "     It shows how much of your base pay";
    PRINT " goes to Federal and"
    PRINT " State taxes, and how much to Social";
    PRINT " Security."
    PRINT
    PRINT "     Use the program to verify the";
    PRINT " accuracy of your paycheck,"
    PRINT " to project future take-home pay when";
    PRINT " that raise comes"
    PRINT " through, and even to tally a payroll."
    PRINT
    PRINT "     In the display that follows,";
    PRINT " paycheck underpinnings are"
    PRINT " on the left; these are always weekly";
    PRINT " figures."
    PRINT
    PRINT "     Paycheck results are on the right,";
    PRINT " and these can be"
    PRINT " for 1, 2, 4, or 52 weeks."
    LOCATE 20,27:PRINT "Click Mouse";
    GOSUB CLICKIT
    ITEM = 2: GOSUB MENU1: REM TURN OFF INSTRUCTIONS
   RETURN

   COMPUTE.PAY:
    P(1) = X(1)*X(2) + X(3)*X(4): REM GROSS
    REM FEDERAL TAXES
     REM TAXABLE INCOME PER WEEK
      Y = P(1) - (1040/52)*X(5)
```

```
    GOSUB FEDERAL.TAX
    P(2) = TAX/52
 REM FICA; MX = MAX WEEKLY SALARY
   MX = 42000&/52
   IF P(1) > MX THEN
    P(3) = MX*X(9)/100
   ELSE
    P(3) = P(1)*X(9)/100
   END IF
 REM STATE OF VIRGINIA TAXES
   REM TAXABLE INCOME PER WEEK
    Y = P(1) - (600/52)*X(5)
    GOSUB STATE.TAX
    P(4) = TAX/52
 REM OTHER DEDUCTIONS
   P(5) = X(6) + X(7) + X(8)
 REM TAKE-HOME PAY
   P(6) = P(1) - P(2) - P(3) - P(4) - P(5)
 REM ADJUST FOR PAY PERIOD
   FOR I=1 TO 6
    P(I) = P(I)*PERIOD(LENGTH)
   NEXT
RETURN

PAINT.SCREEN:
 CLS
 LINE(10,4)-(306,163),4,BF
 LINE(324,4)-(620,163),1,BF
 REM LEFT BOX (RAW DATA)
   COLOR 2,4
   FOR I=1 TO 9
    LOCATE I*2,3: PRINT NM$(I);
    PRINT TAB(19) USING F$(F(I));X(I)
   NEXT
 REM RIGHT BOX
   COLOR 0,1
   LOCATE 2,42: PRINT "TAKE-HOME PAY"
   LOCATE 5,35: PRINT "Gross Pay"
   COLOR 6
   LOCATE 8,35: PRINT "Federal Taxes"
   LOCATE 10,35: PRINT "F.I.C.A"
   LOCATE 12,35: PRINT "State Taxes"
   COLOR 0
   LOCATE 15,35: PRINT "Other"
   LOCATE 16,35: PRINT "Deductions"
   LINE(335,151)-(474,161),5,BF
   COLOR 1,5
   LOCATE 18,35: PRINT "Take-Home Pay"
RETURN
```

```
SHOW.PAY:
 COLOR Ø,1
 LOCATE 3,4Ø: PRINT SPACE$(15)
 S$ = "("+PERIOD$(LENGTH)+")": L = LEN(S$)
 LOCATE 3: PRINT PTAB (475-1Ø*L/2);S$
 FOR I=1 TO 6
  LOCATE ROW(I),49: PRINT USING F$(4);P(I)
 NEXT
RETURN

ASK.TO.CHANGE:
 COLOR 1,Ø
 LOCATE 2Ø,17: PRINT "Changes ?";
 GOSUB DECIDE
 IF BUTTON = 1 THEN
  CALL HIGHLIGHT(ACCOUNT,3)
  COLOR 1,Ø
  LINE(265,167)-(361,181),Ø,BF
  LOCATE 2Ø,17: PRINT SPACE$(9);
  LOCATE 2Ø,13: PRINT "Click Mouse on Choice,";
  PRINT " then Hit Return";
  GOSUB CHOOSE
  GOTO ASK.TO.CHANGE
 END IF
RETURN

SUB HIGHLIGHT(ACNT,KOLOR) STATIC
 SHARED NM$()
 L = LEN(NM$(ACNT))
 XØ = 15: X1 = L*1Ø + 25
 YØ = 18*ACNT - 11: Y1 = YØ + 1Ø
 LINE(XØ,YØ)-(X1,Y1),KOLOR,BF
 COLOR KOLOR-2,KOLOR
 LOCATE ACNT*2,3: PRINT NM$(ACNT)
END SUB

CHOOSE:
 GOSUB GURGLE
 GOSUB CLICKIT
 IF S$ = "" THEN GOSUB LOCATION: GOTO CHOOSE
 IF ASC(S$) <> 13 THEN CHOOSE
 GOSUB CHANGE
RETURN

GURGLE:
 FREQ = 3ØØ
 FOR G=1 TO 5
  FREQ = 5ØØ-FREQ
  SOUND FREQ,1,5Ø
```

```
 NEXT G
RETURN

LOCATION:
 V = INT((Y-3)/18) + 1
 IF X>14 AND X<175 AND V>Ø AND V<1Ø THEN
  CALL HIGHLIGHT(ACCOUNT,4)
  CALL HIGHLIGHT(V,3)
  ACCOUNT = V
 END IF
RETURN

DECIDE:
 BUTTON = Ø
 GOSUB DRAWBUTTON
 GOSUB PUSHBUTTON
 COLOR 1,Ø
RETURN

DRAWBUTTON:
 LINE (265,167)-(361,181),1,BF
 FOR I=1 TO 2
  CIRCLE (XB(I),YB),12,4+I
  PAINT (XB(I),YB),4+I
  COLOR 1,4+I
  LOCATE 2Ø: PRINT PTAB(XB(I)-4);LT$(I);
 NEXT I
RETURN

PUSHBUTTON:
 SOUND 44Ø,2
 GOSUB CLICKIT
 S$ = UCASE$(S$)
 IF S$ = "Y" THEN BUTTON = 1
 IF S$ = "N" THEN BUTTON = 2
 FOR I=1 TO 2
  XD = ABS(X-XB(I)): YD = ABS(Y-YB)
  IF XD<13 AND YD<7 THEN BUTTON = I: I=2
 NEXT
 IF BUTTON = Ø THEN PUSHBUTTON
RETURN

CHANGE:
 ROW = 2*ACCOUNT
 COLOR 1,Ø
 LOCATE 2Ø,13: PRINT SPACE$(38);
 LOCATE 2Ø,26: LINE INPUT; "New Value ? ";S$
 X(ACCOUNT) = VAL(S$)
 LOCATE 2Ø,26: PRINT SPACE$(3Ø);
```

```
    COLOR 4
    COLOR 2,4: LOCATE ROW,19
    PRINT USING F$(F(ACCOUNT));X(ACCOUNT)
    GOSUB COMPUTE.PAY
    GOSUB SHOW.PAY
RETURN

STATE.TAX:
 Y = Y*52
 TAX = FNTAX(0,2,0)
 IF Y > 3000 THEN TAX = FNTAX(60,3,3000)
 IF Y > 5000 THEN TAX = FNTAX(120,5,5000)
 IF Y > 12000 THEN TAX = FNTAX(470,5.75,12000)
RETURN

FEDERAL.TAX:
 Y = Y*52
 TAX = FNTAX(0,0,0)
 IF Y > 2390 THEN TAX = FNTAX(0,11,2390)
 IF Y > 3540 THEN TAX = FNTAX(126.5,12,3540)
 IF Y > 4580 THEN TAX = FNTAX(251.3,14,4580)
 IF Y > 6760 THEN TAX = FNTAX(556.5,15,6760)
 IF Y > 8850 THEN TAX = FNTAX(870,16,8850)
 IF Y > 11240 THEN TAX = FNTAX(1252.4,18,11240)
 IF Y > 13430 THEN TAX = FNTAX(1646.6,20,13430)
 IF Y > 15610 THEN TAX = FNTAX(2082.6,23,15610)
 IF Y > 18940 THEN TAX = FNTAX(2848.5,26,18940)
 IF Y > 24460 THEN TAX = FNTAX(4283.7,30,24460)
 IF Y > 29970 THEN TAX = FNTAX(5936.7,34,29970)
 IF Y > 35490& THEN TAX = FNTAX(7813.5,38,35490&)
 IF Y > 43190& THEN TAX = FNTAX(10739.5,42,43190&)
 IF Y > 57550& THEN TAX = FNTAX(16770.7,48,57550&)
 IF Y > 85130& THEN TAX = FNTAX(30009.1,50,85130&)
RETURN
```

CHAPTER 5

Business and Finance

CHAPTER 5

Business and Finance

This chapter presents a series of programs designed to help manage finances. The programs can be used by corporate planners, small-company executives, and budding entrepreneurs to better manage their financial resources. Indeed, since scarcity of goods and services is a problem faced by all, you may want to use some of these routines to help manage your personal finances, too. Here are the four programs:

Electronic Spreadsheet. This program turns your Amiga into a one-page worksheet that's easy to use, yet highly capable. With it, you can create a screenful of numbers, labels, and formulas to represent a problem you're trying to solve or a situation you're trying to track. When you tally the sheet, the Amiga computes values for the formulas and nicely formats the results to your specification. You can save your spreadsheet on disk, and you can dump reports to a printer.

Least-Squares Forecasting. For centuries, many have tried to peer into the future. Soothsayers, oracles, palm readers, and even economists try to foretell what will be. You can join this elite group of mystics by using this program to forecast the future value of a variable through the use of simple linear regression analysis.

Future Worth. Questions about buying or leasing or return on investments often involve determining the future value of money. This program assists with this type of analysis.

Computer Cash Register. Turn your Amiga into a fast-working and easy-to-use cash register with this program. It automatically figures sales tax and even tallies the receipts at the end of the day.

Business and Finance Menu Driver
Save using the filename **FINANCE**

```
REM BUSINESS AND FINANCE
  GOSUB INITIALIZE
  GOSUB MAIN.MENU
  RUN TITLE.SHORT$(PICK)
END

INITIALIZE:
  GOSUB SETSCREEN
  GOSUB KEYVALUES
  GOSUB SETMENUS
  GOSUB SETCOLORS
  GOSUB SHAPES
RETURN

SETSCREEN:
  SCREEN 1,640,200,3,2
  WINDOW 2,"Business and Finance",,0,1
RETURN

KEYVALUES:
  DEFINT A-Z
  N = 4
  DIM TITLE.LONG$(N),TITLE.SHORT$(N),DISCS(250)
  DISC.I(1) = 1: DISC.I(2) = 125
  READ CHAPTER$
  FOR I=1 TO N
    READ TITLE.LONG$(I),TITLE.SHORT$(I)
  NEXT
RETURN

SETMENUS:
  FOR I=2 TO 4
    MENU I,0,0,""
  NEXT
  MENU 1,0,1,"STOP"
  MENU 1,1,1," Go to BASIC"
  MENU 1,2,1," Go to System"
  MENU ON
  ON MENU GOSUB GOODBYE
RETURN

GOODBYE:
  WINDOW CLOSE 2: WINDOW 1: MENU RESET
  SCREEN CLOSE 1
  ITEM = MENU(1)
  IF ITEM = 2 THEN SYSTEM
```

```
  CLS
  PRINT "Bye-Bye"
  STOP
RETURN

SETCOLORS:
 REM TAN, GREEN, & RED
   PALETTE 4,.95,.7,.53
   PALETTE 5,.14,.43,0
   PALETTE 6,.93,.2,0
RETURN

SHAPES:
 X=313: Y=80
 LINE(X-12,Y-8)-(X+12,Y+8),4,BF
 FOR I=1 TO 2
   K = 7-I
   CIRCLE(X,Y),12,K: PAINT(X,Y),K
   GET(X-12,Y-8)-(X+12,Y+8),DISCS(DISC.I(I))
 NEXT
RETURN

MAIN.MENU:
 CLS
 RTN$ = "OFF": PICK = 1
 S$ = CHAPTER$: L = LEN(S$)
 LINE(313-10*L/2-15,15)-(313+10*L/2+15,27),1,B
 PAINT(313,20),6,1
 COLOR 1,6: LOCATE 3: PRINT PTAB(313-10*L/2)S$
 LINE(135,35)-(495,130),2,B: PAINT(313,80),4,2
 COLOR 2,4
 FOR I=1 TO N
  IF I = PICK THEN INX = 2 ELSE INX = 1
  CALL DRAW.CIRCLE(I,INX)
  LOCATE I*2+4,21: PRINT TITLE.LONG$(I)
 NEXT
 LINE(263,141)-(360,153),2,B: PAINT(313,145),3,2
 COLOR 2,3
 LOCATE 17: PRINT PTAB(282)"Return"
 COLOR 1,0
 LOCATE 19,11: PRINT "Click Mouse on Choice,";
 PRINT " then Click on Return"
 GOSUB CHOOSE
RETURN

SUB DRAW.CIRCLE(R,INX) STATIC
 SHARED DISCS(),DISC.I()
 Y = 18*R+22
 PUT(162,Y),DISCS(DISC.I(INX)),PSET
END SUB
```

```
CHOOSE:
 GOSUB GURGLE
 GOSUB CLICKIT
 IF S$ = "" THEN GOSUB LOCATION
 IF ASC(S$+" ") <> 13 AND RTN$ = "OFF" THEN
  GOTO CHOOSE
 END IF
RETURN

GURGLE:
 FREQ = 300
 FOR G=1 TO 5
  FREQ = 500 - FREQ
  SOUND FREQ,1,50
 NEXT
RETURN

CLICKIT:
 S$ = ""
 WHILE MOUSE(0) = 0 AND S$ = ""
  S$ = INKEY$
 WEND
  X = MOUSE(1)
  Y = MOUSE(2)
 WHILE MOUSE(0)<> 0: WEND: REM RESET
RETURN

LOCATION:
 IF X>263 AND X<360 AND Y>141 AND Y<153 THEN
  RTN$ = "ON"
 ELSE
  P = INT((Y-39)/18) + 1
  IF X>155 AND X<195 AND P>0 AND P<= N THEN
   CALL DRAW.CIRCLE(PICK,1)
   CALL DRAW.CIRCLE(P,2)
   PICK = P
  END IF
 END IF
RETURN

REM PROGRAMS
 DATA Business and Finance
 DATA Electronic Spreadsheet, SPREADSHEET
 DATA Least-Squares Forecasting, LSF
 DATA Future Worth, WORTH
 DATA Amiga Cash Register, REGISTER
```

Electronic Spreadsheet

Spreadsheets are programs that manipulate rows and columns of numbers. They can be used for applications ranging from simple record keeping to sophisticated modeling and forecasting.

This program turns your Amiga into a one-page electronic spreadsheet. With it, you can create a screenful of numbers, labels, and formulas to represent a problem you're trying to solve or a situation you're trying to track. Use it to keep track of utility bills, to compute simple statistics, and to tally bowling averages, to name just a few of an almost endless string of possible applications.

When you tally the spreadsheet, the Amiga computes values for the formulas and nicely formats the results to your specification. You can save your spreadsheet on disk, and you can dump reports to a printer.

Spreadsheet Labels

The best way to learn how to use the spreadsheet is to run it. Many of its statements are self-explanatory, and after a few minutes of experimenting, you'll know most of the tricks.

Suppose, then, that we purchase an Individual Retirement Account (IRA) for $2,000, paying 10 percent interest per annum. We want to know what our investment will be worth in 25 years.

To find out, we invoke the *Make a new spreadsheet* option in the main menu of the program. The Amiga paints row numbers and column headings on the screen and positions the long cursor, or bar, in the upper left corner (Figure 5-1). Notice that columns are denoted by letters and rows by numbers. The intersections of columns and rows are called *cells*, with A1 denoting column A and row 1.

Let's type in a title for our spreadsheet, say, "IRA Account." That's right, first enter an *I*, then an *R*, and so on. As soon as you press a letter, the Amiga knows that you're producing a label, or a string of up to nine characters.

After keying in *IRA Accou*, hit the rightward arrow. Cell A1 now holds the label, and the cursor moves to cell B1. Now type *nt* followed by seven blank spaces. The spaces are to make sure that the *nt* is left-justified in the cell.

That's all there is to creating spreadsheet labels. Move the cursor anywhere you want by using the arrows or mouse, and then type in your letters.

Now it's your turn. Try producing the labels in Figure 5-2. If you hit a wrong letter, press the BACKSPACE or DELete key to erase it. And press ES-Cape to delete the entire contents of a cell.

Figure 5-1. Spreadsheet Setup

```
FILE: Example                                        ESC: Erase Cell
=====A======B======C======D======E======F====
  1
  2    [         ]
  3
  4
  5
  .
  .
  .
 14
```

Figure 5-2. Spreadsheet Example

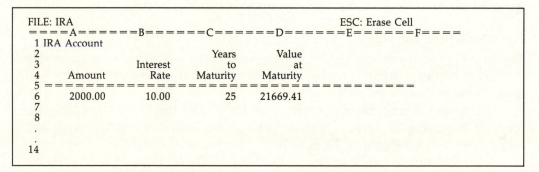

```
FILE: IRA                                            ESC: Erase Cell
====A======B======C======D======E======F====
 1 IRA Account
 2                          Years     Value
 3             Interest      to        at
 4    Amount     Rate     Maturity  Maturity
 5 ==========================================
 6    2000.00   10.00        25     21669.41
 7
 8
 .
 .
14
```

Entering Values

With the labels entered, let's now tackle values, or numbers. To enter 2000 under the column heading "Amount," for example, first move the cursor to cell A6 (the column is always written first and the row second). Next, enter the four digits: 2, 0, 0, and 0. As soon as you hit the 2, the Amiga realizes that your entry is a value instead of a label or formula. The spreadsheet allows 15 digits for a number at the bottom of the screen, including spaces for a decimal point and a minus sign. Only the nine leftmost characters will be displayed in the cell, however.

Now, enter 10% for the interest rate on the IRA account and 25 years for time to maturity.

Spreadsheet Formulas

Without computational capability, an electronic spreadsheet is little better than an accountant's pile of paper generated a decade ago. That's why the Amiga lets us use formulas to calculate key values.

The worth of our IRA investment at maturity, for example, is $2000*1.10^25. That is, a 10 percent interest rate (1.10 in index form) compounded annually gives a multiplier of $1.10^25 after a quarter century. This figure times our principal, $2,000, is the desired answer.

To have the spreadsheet calculate this value, first move the cursor to cell D6. Next, hit one of the Function keys, labeled F1 to F10. This tells the Amiga that you're entering a formula. Now, key in

A6*(1+B6/100)^C6

Believe it or not, this expression represents the future worth of our $2,000. When the Amiga tallies the spreadsheet, the values 2000, 10, and 25 are substituted for cells A6, B6, and C6 in the formula. The rest is just pure arithmetic.

In general, the Amiga allows formulas with up to 35 characters, 9 of which are displayed in a cell. It evaluates formulas just as in the "Calculator" program of the last chapter.

Tallying the Spreadsheet

With labels, values, and formulas entered for our IRA computation, we now ask the Amiga to tally our spreadsheet. Give the go-ahead by using a pull-down menu.

The Amiga quickly works its way through the sheet. Beginning in the upper left corner, it shimmies down column A, rows 1 to 14. It skips over cells that are blank and cells that are labels. When it finds a value, it formats the number to however many decimal places you've chosen, also using a pull-down menu. And when it encounters a formula, it evaluates the expression and likewise formats the result.

After dispensing with column A, the Amiga tackles columns B, C, and so on, through the end of the sheet. We'll see nicely formatted numbers when it's finished. The formula in cell D6, by the way, yields a value of $21,669.42 for the worth of our IRA at maturity.

Printing Reports

After the Amiga tallies your sheet, you might want a nicely formatted hardcopy record. The program produces two reports: spreadsheet formulas and calculated values. The former is a handy reference, and the latter is identical to screen output.

A word of warning. It's always a good idea to tally your spreadsheet just before printing a report. This is because the Amiga relies on the latest set of values that it has calculated. Hence, if you change your spreadsheet and omit the tally step, bizarre results are likely to occur.

Saving Data

To save your spreadsheet to disk, use the appropriate pull-down menu and then enter a commonsense filename, such as IRA. A nice feature of this program is that it creates a catalog of all the spreadsheet files that you generate. This saves you the trouble of remembering names like IRA1986 or IRA1987. The catalog is accessed each time you run the program, and the only thing you have to recall is whether you do in fact have any spreadsheets on disk.

Program 5-1. Electronic Spreadsheet
Save using the filename **SPREADSHEET**

```
REM ELECTRONIC SPREADSHEET
 CLEAR ,30000
 GOSUB INITIALIZE
 GOSUB PLAY
 GOSUB GOODBYE
END

INITIALIZE:
 GOSUB SETSCREEN
 GOSUB KEYVALUES
 GOSUB SETMENUS
 GOSUB SETCOLORS
 GOSUB SHAPES
 GOSUB HEADING
 GOSUB RULES
 GOSUB TURN.ON.PRINTER
 GOSUB CATALOG
RETURN

SETSCREEN:
 SCREEN 1,640,200,3,2
 HEADING$ = "Electronic Spreadsheet"
 WINDOW 2,HEADING$,,0,1
RETURN

KEYVALUES:
 RANDOMIZE TIMER
 DEFINT A-Z: DEFDBL K,Q,V
 DIM DISC(250),BAR(450),FILE$(50)
 DIM K(14,6),S(14,6),D$(14,6),V(30),SYM(30)
 REM SHAPE INDICES
```

```
   DISC.I(1) = 1: DISC.I(2) = 125
   BAR.I(1) = 1 : BAR.I(2) = 225
 REM BUTTON VALUES
   XB(1) = 292: XB(2) = 334
   LT$(1) = "Y": LT$(2) = "N"
 GOSUB MAIN.MENU.CHOICES
 GOSUB PRINT.CHOICES
 GOSUB ERROR.CODES
 GOSUB SCREEN.DATA
 GOSUB LEGAL.VALUES
 PICK = 1
 MESSAGE$ = ""
 DASH.LINE$ = STRING$(57,"=")
RETURN

MAIN.MENU.CHOICES:
 DATA Load a spreadsheet
 DATA Make a new spreadsheet
 DATA Delete an old spreadsheet
 DATA View spreadsheet names
 FOR I=1 TO 4
   READ PICK$(I)
 NEXT
RETURN

PRINT.CHOICES:
 DATA Print formulas, Print calculated values
 DATA Return to spreadsheet
 FOR I=1 TO 3
   READ CHOICE$(I)
 NEXT
RETURN

ERROR.CODES:
 DATA Parentheses, Cell Code, Division by Zero
 DATA Syntax, Exponentiation
 FOR I=1 TO 5
   READ ERROR.CODE$(I)
 NEXT
RETURN

SCREEN.DATA:
 REM COLUMN HEADING
   CH$ = ""
   FOR I=1 TO 6
     CH$ = CH$ + "====" + CHR$(64+I) + "===="
   NEXT
 REM COLORS FOR CELL
   DATA 2,3,1,0
```

```
   FOR I=1 TO 2
     READ C.F(I),C.B(I)
   NEXT
  REM ROW & COL DELTAS FOR ARROWS
   DATA -1,Ø,1,Ø,Ø,1,Ø,-1
   FOR I=1 TO 4
     READ RD(I),CD(I)
   NEXT
  REM FIELDS (LENGTH & NAME)
   DATA "Formula:",35, "  Value:",15
   DATA "  Label:",9
   FOR I=1 TO 3
     READ T$(I),LN(I)
   NEXT
  REM FORMATS
   F$(Ø) = "#########"
   F$(1) = "#######.#"
   F$(2) = "######.##"
RETURN

LEGAL.VALUES:
  REM TO THE LEFT OF (
   DATA 32,4Ø,42,43,45,47,94
   FOR I=1 TO 7
     READ LEFT(I)
   NEXT
  REM TO THE RIGHT OF )
   DATA 32,41,42,43,45,47,94
   FOR I=1 TO 7
     READ RIGHT(I)
   NEXT
RETURN

SETMENUS:
  DATA 5, Color, Yellow, Blue, Green, Violet
  DATA Random
  DATA 3, Decimals, Ø Places, 1 Place, 2 Places
  DATA 4, Actions, Tally the Spreadsheet
  DATA Print a Report, Save the Spreadsheet
  DATA Return to Main Menu
  DATA 3, Stop, Go to BASIC
  DATA Go to Finance Menu, Go to System
  FOR I=1 TO 4
   READ NUMBER
   FOR J=Ø TO NUMBER
    READ TITLE$
    IF J<>Ø THEN TITLE$ = SPACE$(3) + TITLE$
    STATUS = 1
    IF I=1 AND J=1 THEN STATUS = 2
```

```
    IF I=2 AND J=3 THEN STATUS = 2
   MENU I,J,STATUS,TITLE$
 NEXT J,I
 MENU 3,0,0
 KOLOR% = 1: DP = 2
RETURN

SETCOLORS:
 REM YELLOW, BLUE, GREEN, VIOLET
  DATA .95,.65,.19, .36,.57,1
  DATA .17,.73,.07, .95,.07,.93
  FOR I=1 TO 4
   FOR J=1 TO 3
    READ KOLOR(I,J)
  NEXT J,I
 REM YELLOW, GREEN, & RED
  PALETTE 4,.95,.65,.19
  PALETTE 5,.14,.43,0
  PALETTE 6,.93,.2,0
RETURN

SHAPES:
 REM DISCS
  X0=313: Y0=80
  FOR I=1 TO 2
   K% = I*5-4
   CIRCLE(X0,Y0),12,K%: PAINT(X0,Y0),K%
   GET(X0-12,Y0-8)-(X0+12,Y0+8),DISC(DISC.I(I))
  NEXT
  CLS
 REM BARS
  X1 = X0-45: X2 = X0+44: Y1 = Y0-4: Y2 = Y0+6
  FOR I=1 TO 2
   K% = 6-3*I
   LINE(X1,Y1)-(X2,Y2),K%,BF
   GET(X1,Y1)-(X2,Y2),BAR(BAR.I(I))
  NEXT
RETURN

HEADING:
 MENU ON
 ON MENU GOSUB OPTIONS
 CLS
 LINE (163,60)-(463,90),4,BF
 LINE (163,60)-(200,160),4,BF
 COLOR 2,4
 LOCATE 9,25: PRINT "Amiga Spreadsheet"
 COLOR 3,0: LOCATE 14,31:PRINT "then"
 COLOR 1,0
```

```
     LOCATE 13,25:PRINT "Please use menus,"
     LOCATE 15,23:PRINT "Click mouse to start"
     GOSUB CLICKIT
  RETURN

  OPTIONS:
   ID = MENU(0): ITEM = MENU(1)
   ON ID GOSUB MENU1,MENU2,MENU3,GOODBYE
   ITEM = 0
  RETURN

  MENU1:
   K1 = KOLOR(ITEM,1): K2 = KOLOR(ITEM,2)
   K3 = KOLOR(ITEM,3)
   IF ITEM=5 THEN K1=RND: K2=RND: K3=RND
   PALETTE 4,K1,K2,K3
   MENU 1,KOLOR%,1: MENU 1,ITEM,2
   KOLOR% = ITEM
  RETURN

  MENU2:
   MENU 2,DP+1,1: MENU 2,ITEM,2
   DP = ITEM-1
  RETURN

  MENU3:
   ACTION = ITEM
  RETURN

  GOODBYE:
   WINDOW CLOSE 2: WINDOW 1: MENU RESET
   SCREEN CLOSE 1
   IF ITEM = 2 THEN RUN "FINANCE"
   IF ITEM = 3 THEN SYSTEM
   COLOR 1,0: CLS
   PRINT "Bye-Bye"
   STOP
  RETURN

  RULES:
   CLS
   PRINT
   PRINT "    This little program turns your";
   PRINT " Amiga into a one-page"
   PRINT " electronic spreadsheet."
   PRINT
   PRINT "    Use the arrows or mouse to move the";
   PRINT " cursor (bar) from"
   PRINT " cell to cell."
```

```
  PRINT
  PRINT "    Enter numbers and labels simply";
  PRINT " by keying them in."
  PRINT " For formulas, hit one of the Function";
  PRINT " Keys (F1 to F1Ø)"
  PRINT " before entering your expression."
  PRINT
  PRINT "    When you save a spreadsheet to";
  PRINT " disk, I'll add the"
  PRINT " file's name to a permanent catalog."
  PRINT
  PRINT "    This will spare you the trouble of";
  PRINT " remembering names"
  PRINT " like SPREAD2 or SPREAD3."
  LOCATE 2Ø,27: PRINT "Click Mouse";
  GOSUB CLICKIT
RETURN

CLICKIT:
 S$ = "": ACTION = Ø
 WHILE MOUSE(Ø) = Ø AND S$ = "" AND ACTION = Ø
  S$ = INKEY$
 WEND
  X = MOUSE(1)
  Y = MOUSE(2)
 WHILE MOUSE(Ø)<> Ø: WEND: REM RESET
RETURN

TURN.ON.PRINTER:
 REM ASK TO TURN ON PRINTER
  CLS
  LOCATE 2,2Ø
  PRINT "Are you using a printer ?"
  ROW = 4: GOSUB DECIDE
 IF BUTTON = 2 THEN
  MENU 3,2,Ø
 ELSE
  LOCATE 7,12: PRINT "PLEASE:": PRINT
  PRINT TAB(14)"(1) Insert Workbench"
  PRINT TAB(14)"(2) Turn on your printer"
  PRINT TAB(14)"(3) Press any key"
  GOSUB CLICKIT
  LPRINT
  LOCATE 14,13: PRINT "FINALLY:": PRINT
  PRINT TAB(14)"(1) Re-insert your";
  PRINT " Applications Disk"
  PRINT TAB(14)"(2) Press any key"
  GOSUB CLICKIT
 END IF
RETURN
```

```
CATALOG:
 CLS
 LOCATE 5,15
 PRINT "Do you have spreadsheets on disk ?"
 ROW = 7: GOSUB DECIDE
 NFILES = Ø
 IF BUTTON = 1 THEN
  OPEN "I",#1,"SPREADCAT"
  INPUT #1,NFILES
  FOR I=1 TO NFILES
   INPUT #1,FILE$(I)
  NEXT
  CLOSE
 END IF
RETURN

DECIDE:
 BUTTON = Ø
 GOSUB DRAWBUTTON
 GOSUB PUSHBUTTON
 COLOR 1,Ø
RETURN

DRAWBUTTON:
 YØ = 9*ROW-13
 YB=YØ+7
 LINE (265,YØ)-(361,YØ+14),1,BF
 FOR I=1 TO 2
  CIRCLE (XB(I),YB),12,4+I
  PAINT (XB(I),YB),4+I
  COLOR 1,4+I
  LOCATE ROW: PRINT PTAB(XB(I)-4);LT$(I);
 NEXT I
RETURN

PUSHBUTTON:
 SOUND 44Ø,2
 GOSUB CLICKIT
 S$ = UCASE$(S$)
 IF S$ = "Y" THEN BUTTON = 1
 IF S$ = "N" THEN BUTTON = 2
 FOR I=1 TO 2
  XD = ABS(X-XB(I)): YD = ABS(Y-YB)
  IF XD<13 AND YD<7 THEN BUTTON = I: I=2
 NEXT
 IF BUTTON = Ø THEN PUSHBUTTON
RETURN
```

```
PLAY:
 GOSUB MAIN.MENU
 ON PICK GOSUB LOAD.SHEET,CREATE,PURGE,VIEW
 GOTO PLAY
RETURN

MAIN.MENU:
 CLS
 LOCATE 2,3: PRINT MESSAGE$
 LOCATE 5,23: PRINT "Would you like to"
 FOR I=1 TO 4
  IF I = PICK THEN INX = 2 ELSE INX = 1
  CALL DRAW.CIRCLE(I,INX)
  LOCATE I*2+5,25: PRINT PICK$(I)
 NEXT
 LOCATE 19,13: PRINT "Click Mouse on Choice,";
 PRINT " then Hit Return"
 GOSUB CHOOSE
 IF NFILES = 0 THEN
  IF PICK=1 OR PICK=3 OR PICK=4 THEN
   S$ = "There aren't any spreadsheets"
   MESSAGE$ = S$ + " on file."
   GOTO MAIN.MENU
  END IF
 END IF
 MESSAGE$ = ""
RETURN

SUB DRAW.CIRCLE(R,INX) STATIC
 SHARED DISC(),DISC.I()
 Y = 18*R+31
 PUT(202,Y),DISC(DISC.I(INX)),PSET
END SUB

CHOOSE:
 GOSUB GURGLE
 GOSUB CLICKIT
 IF S$ = "" THEN GOSUB LOCATION
 IF ASC(S$+" ") <> 13 THEN CHOOSE
RETURN

LOCATION:
 P = INT((Y-48)/18) + 1
 IF X>195 AND X<235 AND P>0 AND P<5 THEN
  CALL DRAW.CIRCLE(PICK,1)
  CALL DRAW.CIRCLE(P,2)
  PICK = P
 END IF
RETURN
```

275

```
GURGLE:
 FREQ = 300
 FOR G=1 TO 5
  FREQ = 500-FREQ
  SOUND FREQ,1,50
 NEXT G
RETURN

LOAD.SHEET:
 CLS
 LOCATE 3,25: PRINT "LOADING A FILE"
 GOSUB FILENAME
 IF DUP$ = "NO" THEN
  MESSAGE$ = FILE$ + " doesn't exist."
 END IF
 IF DUP$ = "YES" THEN
  GOSUB READ.CONTENTS
  GOSUB PAINT.SCREEN
  GOSUB SHOW.VALUES
  GOSUB RUN.SHEET
 END IF
RETURN

FILENAME:
 FILE$ = ""
 WHILE FILE$ = ""
  LOCATE 8,3: INPUT "File Name ";FILE$
 WEND
 REM CHECK EXISTENCE
  DUP$ = "NO"
  IF NFILES <> 0 THEN
   FOR I=1 TO NFILES
    IF FILE$ = FILE$(I) THEN DUP$="YES": SPOT=I
   NEXT
  END IF
RETURN

READ.CONTENTS:
 LOCATE 10,24: PRINT "Reading Contents"
 OPEN "I",#1,FILE$
 FOR R=1 TO 14
  FOR C=1 TO 6
   INPUT #1,S(R,C),D$(R,C)
 NEXT C,R
 CLOSE
RETURN

PAINT.SCREEN:
 CLS
```

```
 LOCATE 1,2: PRINT "File: ";FILE$;
 PRINT TAB(44)"ESC: Erase Cell"
 LINE(7,8)-(585,17),4,BF
 LINE(7,17)-(32,152),4,BF
 COLOR 2,4
 LOCATE 2,5: PRINT CH$
 FOR I=1 TO 14
  LOCATE 3+I,2: PRINT USING "##";I
 NEXT
 GOSUB BOTTOM
RETURN

BOTTOM:
 LINE(7,16Ø)-(5Ø,17Ø),6,BF
 COLOR 1,6: LOCATE 19,2: PRINT "Cell";
RETURN

SHOW.VALUES:
 FOR C=1 TO 6
  FOR R=1 TO 14
   INX = 1: GOSUB CURSOR
   INX = 2: GOSUB CURSOR
 NEXT R,C
RETURN

CURSOR:
 X = 9Ø*C - 5Ø
 Y = R*9 + 16
 PUT(X,Y),BAR(BAR.I(INX)),PSET
 COLOR C.F(INX),C.B(INX)
 S$ = LEFT$(D$(R,C),9)
 LOCATE R+3,9*C-LEN(S$)+5: PRINT S$
RETURN

CELL:
 COLOR 1,Ø
 LOCATE 19,7
 PRINT CHR$(64+C);MID$(STR$(R),2);SPACE$(5Ø)
 LOCATE 19,12
 T = S(R,C)
 IF T <> Ø THEN PRINT T$(T);" ";D$(R,C)
RETURN

RUN.SHEET:
 MENU 3,Ø,1
 R=1: C=1: INX=1: ACTION=Ø
 WHILE ACTION <> 4
  GOSUB CURSOR
  GOSUB CELL
```

```
     GOSUB GET.INPUT
     IF ACTION = 1 THEN GOSUB TALLY.SHEET
     IF ACTION = 2 THEN GOSUB WRITE.REPORT
     IF ACTION = 3 THEN GOSUB SAVE.SHEET
     IF ACTION = 5 THEN GOSUB RUB.OUT
     IF ACTION = 6 THEN GOSUB MOVE.BAR
     IF ACTION = 7 THEN GOSUB MAKE.ENTRY
    WEND
RETURN

GET.INPUT:
 GOSUB CLICKIT
 IF ACTION = Ø THEN
  IF S$="" THEN GOSUB MOUSEY ELSE GOSUB KEY.BD
 END IF
RETURN

MOUSEY:
 ROW = INT((Y-25)/9) + 1
 COL = INT((X-4Ø)/9Ø) + 1
 IF COL>Ø AND COL<7 AND ROW>Ø AND ROW<15 THEN
  ACTION = 6
 END IF
RETURN

KEY.BD:
 A = ASC(S$)
 REM MOVE CURSOR
  IF A>27 AND A<32 THEN
   V = A-27
   ACTION = 6
   ROW = R + RD(V)
   COL = C + CD(V)
   IF ROW=Ø OR ROW=15 OR COL=Ø OR COL=7 THEN
    ROW = R: COL = C
   END IF
  END IF
 REM ERASE
  IF A=27 THEN ACTION = 5
 REM FORMULA
  IF A>128 AND A<139 THEN
   ACTION = 7: TYPE = 1
  END IF
 REM NUMBER
  IF A=45 OR A=46 OR (A>47 AND A<58) THEN
   ACTION = 7: TYPE = 2
  END IF
 REM LABEL
  IF (A>31 AND A<43) OR (A>58 AND A<129) THEN
```

```
      ACTION = 7: TYPE = 3
   END IF
RETURN

RUB.OUT:
 S(R,C) = Ø: D$(R,C) = ""
RETURN

MOVE.BAR:
 INX=2: GOSUB CURSOR
 R = ROW: C = COL: INX=1
RETURN

MAKE.ENTRY:
 S$ = ""
 IF TYPE <> 1 THEN S$ = CHR$(A)
 LN = LN(TYPE)
 LOCATE 19,12: PRINT T$(TYPE);SPACE$(35)
 COLOR Ø,1: LOCATE 19,21: PRINT SPACE$(LN)
 LOCATE 19,21: PRINT S$;:L = LEN(S$)
 GOSUB KEY
 COLOR 1,Ø: LOCATE 19,12: PRINT SPACE$(45)
RETURN

KEY:
 C$ = "": ROW = R: COL = C
 WHILE C$ = "": C$ = INKEY$: WEND
 A = ASC(C$)
 IF A = 127 THEN A = 8
 REM ARROWS
  IF A>27 AND A<32 THEN
   GOSUB ARROWS
   IF M$ = "BAD" THEN GOTO KEY ELSE A = 13
  END IF
 REM CHECK FOR MAX LENGTH
  IF L = LN THEN
   IF A <> 13 AND A <> 8 THEN
    SOUND 9ØØ,2
    GOTO KEY
   END IF
  END IF
 REM BACKSPACE
  IF A = 8 THEN GOSUB BACKSPACE
 REM CHECK VALIDITY
  IF A <> 13 AND A <> 8 THEN
   CK$ = "BAD"
   ON TYPE GOSUB CK.FORMULA, CK.VALUE, CK.LABEL
   IF CK$ = "OK" THEN
    PRINT C$;
```

```
        S$ = S$ + C$
        L = L+1
      END IF
    END IF
  REM CONTINUE
    IF A <> 13 THEN KEY
  REM EXIT
    IF S$ <> "" THEN
      S(R,C) = TYPE: D$(R,C) = S$
    END IF
    INX = 2: GOSUB CURSOR
    R = ROW: C = COL: INX = 1
RETURN


ARROWS:
  M$ = "OK"
  V = A-27
  ROW = R+RD(V)
  COL = C+CD(V)
  IF ROW=0 OR ROW=15 OR COL=0 OR COL=7 THEN
    SOUND 900,2: M$ = "BAD"
    ROW = R: COL = C
  END IF
RETURN


BACKSPACE:
  IF L > 0 THEN
    PRINT CHR$(8);
    S$ = LEFT$(S$,L-1)
    L = L-1
  ELSE
    SOUND 900,2
  END IF
RETURN


CK.FORMULA:
  IF A > 96 THEN A = A-32: C$ = CHR$(A)
  IF A>39 AND A<58 AND A<>44 THEN CK$ = "OK"
  IF A=94 THEN CK$ = "OK"
  IF A>64 AND A<71 THEN CK$ = "OK"
RETURN


CK.VALUE:
  IF A=45 OR A=46 THEN CK$ = "OK"
  IF A>47 AND A<58 THEN CK$ = "OK"
RETURN


CK.LABEL:
  IF A > 31 THEN CK$ = "OK"
RETURN
```

```
TALLY.SHEET:
 INX = 2: GOSUB CURSOR
 GOOF = Ø
 GOSUB CLEAR.BOTTOM
 GOSUB TRANSFER.VALUES
 REM COMPUTE
  FOR C=1 TO 6
   FOR R=1 TO 14
    INX = 1: GOSUB CURSOR
    IF S(R,C) = 1 THEN GOSUB FORMULA
    IF S(R,C) = 2 THEN
     VALUE = VAL(D$(R,C))
     GOSUB DISPLAY.VALUE
    END IF
    IF GOOF > Ø THEN
     R.HOLD = R: C.HOLD = C
     R = 14: C = 6
    END IF
    IF GOOF=Ø AND S(R,C)=Ø OR S(R,C)=3 THEN
     INX = 2: GOSUB CURSOR
    END IF
   NEXT R,C
 REM CONTINUE
  COLOR 2
  LOCATE 2Ø,26: PRINT "Press any key";
  COLOR 1
  GOSUB CLICKIT
  GOSUB CLEAR.BOTTOM
  GOSUB BOTTOM
  R=1: C=1: INX = 1
  IF GOOF>Ø THEN R = R.HOLD: C = C.HOLD
RETURN

CLEAR.BOTTOM:
 COLOR 1,Ø
 LINE(7,16Ø)-(5Ø,17Ø),Ø,BF
 LOCATE 19,7: PRINT SPACE$(5Ø)
 LOCATE 2Ø,26: PRINT SPACE$(13);
RETURN

TRANSFER.VALUES:
 LOCATE 19,2Ø: PRINT "Tallying the Spreadsheet"
 FOR R=1 TO 14
  FOR C=1 TO 6
   K(R,C) = Ø
   IF S(R,C) = 2 THEN K(R,C) = VAL(D$(R,C))
 NEXT C,R
RETURN
```

281

```
FORMULA:
 GOOF = Ø
 E$ = D$(R,C): L = LEN(E$)
 GOSUB STRIKE.PARENTHESES
 IF GOOF = Ø THEN GOSUB CALCULATE
 IF GOOF = Ø THEN
  K(R,C) = VALUE
  GOSUB DISPLAY.VALUE
 ELSE
  GOSUB GOOF
 END IF
RETURN

STRIKE.PARENTHESES:
 PL=Ø: PR=Ø
 FOR I=1 TO L
  C$ = MID$(E$,I,1): A = ASC(C$)
  IF A=4Ø THEN PL = I
  IF A=41 THEN PR = I: I=L
 NEXT
 IF PR-PL = 1 THEN GOOF = 1
 IF PL=Ø AND PR>Ø THEN GOOF = 1
 IF PR=Ø AND PL>Ø THEN GOOF = 1
 IF GOOF = Ø AND PR <> Ø THEN
  GOSUB REMOVE
  GOTO STRIKE.PARENTHESES
 END IF
RETURN

REMOVE:
 LF$ = MID$(E$,1,PL-1)
 MD$ = MID$(E$,PL+1,PR-PL-1)
 RT$ = MID$(E$,PR+1,L-PR)
 REM CHECK LEFT OF (
  LK = ASC(RIGHT$(" " + LF$,1))
  GOOF=4: J=1
  WHILE GOOF = 4 AND J <= 7
   IF LK = LEFT(J) THEN GOOF = Ø
   J = J+1
  WEND
 REM CHECK RIGHT OF )
  RK = ASC(LEFT$(RT$ + " ",1))
  GOOF=4: J=1
  WHILE GOOF = 4 AND J <= 7
   IF RK = RIGHT(J) THEN GOOF = Ø
   J = J+1
  WEND
 REM CONTINUE
  IF GOOF = Ø THEN
```

```
    E$ = MD$: GOSUB CALCULATE
    S$ = STR$(VALUE)
    IF VALUE >=Ø THEN S$ = MID$(S$,2)
    E$ = LF$ + S$ + RT$
    L = LEN(E$)
  END IF
RETURN

CALCULATE:
 E$ = E$ + CHR$(32): T=Ø: P=Ø: SG=1
 GOSUB TAKE.APART
 IF GOOF = Ø THEN
  IF T > 1 THEN GOSUB TALLY
  IF GOOF = Ø THEN VALUE = V(T)
 END IF
 IF SYM(T) <> 32 THEN GOOF = 4
RETURN

TAKE.APART:
 P = P+1
 C$ = MID$(E$,P,1): A=ASC(C$)
 REM + OR -
  IF A=43 OR A=45 THEN
   IF A = 45 THEN SG = - SG
   NM$ = "OFF"
   GOTO TAKE.APART
  END IF
 REM CELL CODE
  IF A > 64 AND A < 71 THEN
   GOSUB CELL.CODE
   GOTO CONTINUE
  END IF
 REM DIGIT OR DECIMAL
  IF A = 46 OR (A > 47 AND A < 58) THEN
   GOSUB NUMBER
   GOTO CONTINUE
  END IF
 REM BAD CHARACTER
  IF A <> 32 THEN GOOF = 4
CONTINUE:
 IF GOOF = Ø AND A <> 32 THEN
  SG=1: GOTO TAKE.APART
 END IF
 IF NM$ = "OFF" THEN GOOF = 4
RETURN

CELL.CODE:
 ROW = VAL(MID$(E$,P+1,2)): COL = A-64
 IF ROW<1 OR ROW>14 THEN GOOF = 2
```

```
REM SYMBOL FOLLOWING CELL
  IF GOOF = Ø THEN
   P = P + 2 + -1*(ROW > 9)
   C$ = MID$(E$,P,1): A = ASC(C$)
   GOOF = 4
   IF A=32 OR A=42 OR A=43 THEN GOOF = Ø
   IF A=45 OR A=47 OR A=94 THEN GOOF = Ø
  END IF
 REM STORE VALUE
  IF GOOF = Ø THEN
   T = T+1
   V(T) = SG*K(ROW,COL)
   NM$ = "ON"
   SYM(T) = A
  END IF
RETURN

NUMBER:
 N$ = C$
 DEC$ = "OFF": DGT$ = "OFF"
 IF A=46 THEN DEC$ = "ON"
 IF A>47 AND A<58 THEN DGT$ = "ON"
LOOP:
 REM GET NUMBER
  P = P+1
  C$ = MID$(E$,P,1): A=ASC(C$)
  IF A=46 AND DEC$ = "ON" THEN GOOF = 4
  IF A=46 THEN DEC$ = "ON"
  IF A>47 AND A<58 THEN DGT$ = "ON"
  IF GOOF=Ø AND A=46 OR (A>47 AND A<58) THEN
   N$ = N$ + C$
   GOTO LOOP
  END IF
 REM CHECK FOR DIGIT
  IF DGT$ = "OFF" THEN GOOF = 4
 REM SYMBOL FOLLOWING NUMBER
  IF GOOF = Ø THEN
   GOOF = 4
   IF A=32 OR A=42 OR A=43 THEN GOOF = Ø
   IF A=45 OR A=47 OR A=94 THEN GOOF = Ø
  END IF
 REM STORE NUMBER
  IF GOOF = Ø THEN
   T = T+1
   V(T) = SG*VAL(N$)
   SYM(T) = A
   NM$ = "ON"
  END IF
RETURN
```

```
TALLY:
 GOSUB EXPONENTIATION
 IF GOOF = Ø THEN GOSUB MULT.DIV
 IF GOOF = Ø THEN GOSUB ADD.SUB
RETURN

EXPONENTIATION:
 FOR I=1 TO T-1
  IF SYM(I) = 94 THEN
   IF V(I) < Ø AND V(I+1) < 1 THEN GOOF = 5
   IF GOOF = Ø THEN
    V(I+1) = V(I)^V(I+1)
    SYM(I) = -9
   END IF
  END IF
 NEXT
RETURN

MULT.DIV:
 FOR I=1 TO T-1
  S = SYM(I)
  IF S = 42 OR S = 47 THEN
   Q = V(I)
   FOR J = I+1 TO T
    IF SYM(J) <> -9 THEN GOSUB MD: J = T
   NEXT J
  END IF
 NEXT I
RETURN

MD:
 IF S = 42 THEN V(J)=Q*V(J): SYM(I) = -9
 IF S = 47 AND V(J) = Ø THEN GOOF = 3
 IF S = 47 AND GOOF = Ø THEN
  V(J) = Q/V(J)
  SYM(I) = -9
 END IF
RETURN

ADD.SUB:
 FOR I=1 TO T-1
  S = SYM(I)
  IF S = 43 OR S = 45 THEN
   Q = V(I)
   FOR J = I+1 TO T
    IF SYM(J) <> - 9 THEN
     IF S = 43 THEN V(J) = Q + V(J)
     IF S = 45 THEN V(J) = Q - V(J)
     SYM(I) = -9
```

```
       J = T
     END IF
   NEXT J
  END IF
 NEXT I
RETURN

GOOF:
  SOUND 400,3: SOUND 300,3: SOUND 200,3
  GOSUB CLEAR.BOTTOM
  COLOR 1,6
  LINE(7,160)-(50,170),6,BF
  LOCATE 19,2: PRINT "Goof"
  COLOR 1,0: LOCATE 19,7: PRINT ERROR.CODE$(GOOF)
RETURN

DISPLAY.VALUE:
  PUT(X,Y),BAR(225),PSET: REM ERASE
  COLOR 1,0
  LOCATE R+3,9*C-4
  PRINT USING F$(DP);VALUE
RETURN

WRITE.REPORT:
  MENU 3,0,0
  R.HOLD = R: C.HOLD = C
  CHOICE = 1
  GOSUB SELECT.REPORT
  GOSUB PAINT.SCREEN
  GOSUB SHOW.VALUES
  INX = 1: R = R.HOLD: C = C.HOLD
  MENU 3,0,1
RETURN

SELECT.REPORT:
  COLOR 1,0
  CLS
  LOCATE 5,23: PRINT "Would you like to"
  FOR I=1 TO 3
   IF I = CHOICE THEN INX = 2 ELSE INX = 1
   CALL DRAW.CIRCLE(I,INX)
   LOCATE I*2+5,25: PRINT CHOICE$(I)
  NEXT
  LOCATE 14,13: PRINT "Click Mouse on Choice,";
  PRINT " then Hit Return"
  SELECT$ = "ON"
  WHILE SELECT$ = "ON"
   GOSUB GURGLE
   GOSUB CLICKIT
```

```
    IF S$ = "" THEN GOSUB POSITION
    IF ASC(S$ + " ") = 13 THEN
     ON CHOICE GOSUB PRINT.FORMULAS,PRINT.VALUES
     IF CHOICE = 3 THEN SELECT$ = "OFF"
    END IF
  WEND
RETURN

POSITION:
 P = INT((Y-48)/18) + 1
 IF X>195 AND X<235 AND P>0 AND P<4 THEN
  CALL DRAW.CIRCLE(CHOICE,1)
  CALL DRAW.CIRCLE(P,2)
  CHOICE = P
 END IF
RETURN

PRINT.FORMULAS:
 GOSUB SET.PRINTER
 LPRINT "Formulas (Column,Row):"
 LPRINT
 LPRINT DASH.LINE$
 FOR I=1 TO 6
  FOR J=1 TO 14
   IF S(J,I) = 1 THEN
    LPRINT "(";CHR$(64+I);
    LPRINT USING "##) ";J;
    LPRINT D$(J,I)
   END IF
 NEXT J,I
 LPRINT DASH.LINE$
 LPRINT: LPRINT: LPRINT
RETURN

SET.PRINTER:
 LOCATE 17,17
 PRINT "Press any key to begin printing"
 GOSUB CLICKIT
 LOCATE 17,17: PRINT SPACE$(31)
 LPRINT "File: ";FILE$
 LPRINT
RETURN

PRINT.VALUES:
 GOSUB SET.PRINTER
 LPRINT "Spreadsheet Calculations:"
 LPRINT
 LPRINT TAB(4)CH$
 FOR I=1 TO 14
```

```
      LPRINT USING "## ";I;
      FOR J=1 TO 6
       REM NUMBER; LABEL OR BLANK
         IF S(I,J)=1 OR S(I,J)=2 THEN
          LPRINT USING F$(DP);K(I,J);
         ELSE
          S$ = STRING$(9," ") + D$(I,J)
          LPRINT RIGHT$(S$,9);
         END IF
      NEXT J
      LPRINT
     NEXT I
     LPRINT DASH.LINE$
     LPRINT: LPRINT: LPRINT
   RETURN

   SAVE.SHEET:
    GOSUB CLEAR.BOTTOM
    IF DUP$ = "NO" THEN
     NFILES = NFILES + 1
     FILE$(NFILES) = FILE$
    END IF
    GOSUB SAVE.DATA
    GOSUB UPDATE.CAT
    LOCATE 19,26
    PRINT FILE$;" is saved.";SPACE$(5)
    LOCATE 20,26: PRINT "Press any key";
    GOSUB CLICKIT
    GOSUB CLEAR.BOTTOM
    GOSUB BOTTOM
   RETURN

   SAVE.DATA:
    LOCATE 19,26: PRINT "Saving Sheet"
    OPEN "O",#1,FILE$
    FOR I=1 TO 14
     FOR J=1 TO 6
       WRITE #1,S(I,J),D$(I,J)
    NEXT J,I
    CLOSE
   RETURN

   UPDATE.CAT:
    OPEN "O",#1,"SPREADCAT"
    WRITE #1,NFILES
    FOR I=1 TO NFILES
     WRITE #1,FILE$(I)
    NEXT
    CLOSE
   RETURN
```

```
CREATE:
 CLS
 LOCATE 3,19: PRINT "CREATING A NEW SPREADSHEET"
 GOSUB ENTER.NAME
 IF CNT$ = "YES" THEN
  GOSUB PAINT.SCREEN
  GOSUB INITIAL.VALUES
  GOSUB RUN.SHEET
 END IF
RETURN

ENTER.NAME:
 GOSUB FILENAME
 CNT$ = "YES"
 IF DUP$ = "YES" THEN
  LOCATE 10,3: PRINT FILE$;" already exists !"
  LOCATE 13,16
  PRINT "Would you like to write over it ?"
  ROW=15: GOSUB DECIDE
  IF BUTTON = 2 THEN CNT$ = "NO"
 END IF
RETURN

INITIAL.VALUES:
 FOR R=1 TO 14
  FOR C=1 TO 6
   K(R,C)=Ø: S(R,C)=Ø: D$(R,C)=""
 NEXT C,R
RETURN

PURGE:
 CLS
 LOCATE 3,25: PRINT "DELETING A FILE"
 GOSUB FILENAME
 IF DUP$ = "NO" THEN
  MESSAGE$ = FILE$ + " doesn't exist."
 END IF
 IF DUP$ = "YES" THEN
  GOSUB KILL.IT
  IF NFILES > Ø THEN GOSUB UPDATE.CAT
  IF NFILES = Ø THEN
   KILL "SPREADCAT": KILL "SPREADCAT.INFO"
   S$ = "You no longer have any spread"
   MESSAGE$ = S$ + "sheets on disk."
  END IF
 END IF
RETURN
```

```
KILL.IT:
  IF SPOT <> NFILES THEN
   FOR I = SPOT+1 TO NFILES
    FILE$(I-1) = FILE$(I)
   NEXT
  END IF
  NFILES = NFILES - 1
  KILL FILE$: KILL FILE$+".INFO"
  MESSAGE$ = FILE$ + " is deleted."
RETURN

VIEW:
  FOR I=1 TO NFILES STEP 15
   CLS
   LOCATE 2,22: PRINT "SPREADSHEETS ON DISK:"
   PRINT
   FOR J = I TO I+14
    IF J <= NFILES THEN
     L = LEN(FILE$(J))
     PRINT TAB(32-L/2);FILE$(J)
    END IF
   NEXT J
   LOCATE 19,26: PRINT "Press any key";
   GOSUB CLICKIT
  NEXT I
RETURN
```

Least-Squares Forecasting

For centuries, many have tried to peer into the future. Soothsayers, oracles, palm readers, bone throwers, and even economists try to foretell what will be. You can join this elite group of mystics by using your Amiga and "Least-Squares Forecasting."

Let's try some elementary forecasting and make a prediction about stock prices next year. First, we'll hypothesize that the stock market rises when interest rates fall, and that it falls when interest rates rise. We can test this supposition using the data of Table 5-1.

Standard and Poor's Index is called the dependent variable in our forecasting exercise, or the variable we want to explain or predict. The Treasury Bill rate is called the explanatory variable, or the term to do the explaining. These variables are usually denoted Y and X, respectively.

After keying our data into the Amiga, we're rewarded with the regression results of Figure 5-3. The coefficient is also called the slope of our line, and it measures the change in Y over the change in X. That is, the value of almost -7.9 means that if interest rates were to increase by 1 percentage point, stock prices would be expected to fall by almost 7.9 points. The inverse relationship between stock prices and interest rates holds, as suspected.

You can use estimates of the constant term and the coefficient to draw a trend line between Y and X, as Figure 5-4 shows.

R-squared, or the coefficient of determination, is the proportion of variation in Y (stock prices) explained by X (interest rates). The statistic ranges from 0 to 1. As Figure 5-5 shows, the higher the value, the better the regression line fits the data.

To forecast stock prices next year, enter a Treasury Bill rate that you think will prevail, say, 5 percent. The Amiga will respond with a point on the trend line (predicted Y) and with a 95 percent confidence interval:

Value of X   = 5
Predicted Y   = 181.696
Lower bound   = 123.853
Upper bound   = 239.540

In other words, you're forecasting a Standard & Poor's Index of roughly 182. And the 95 percent confidence interval means that you're 95 percent sure that the true Index will be covered by the range 124 to 240. This band, by the way, is computed under the strict assumption that the value of X, or the level of interest rates next year, is known with perfect certainty.

Finally, try forecasting some of your own business's figures, such as sales or production. You may be surprised at how accurate your estimates are.

Table 5-1. Stock Prices and Interest Rates

Year and Quarter	Standard and Poor's Index of 500 Leading Stocks	3-Month T-Bill Rate, %
82:1	114.2	12.8
82:2	114.2	12.4
82:3	113.8	9.3
82:4	136.7	7.9
83:1	147.7	8.1
83:2	162.7	8.4
83:3	165.5	9.1
83:4	165.7	8.8
84:1	160.4	9.2
84:2	155.8	9.8
84:3	160.5	10.3

Figure 5-3. Regression Results

Term	Estimated Value	t-Statistic
Constant	220.978	6.273
Coefficient	−7.856	−2.179

R-Squared = 0.345
F-Statistic = 4.747

Figure 5-4. Trend Line

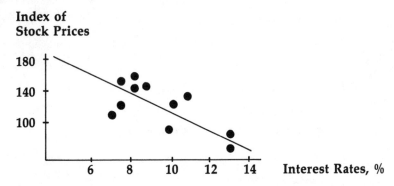

Figure 5-5. Goodness-of-Fit

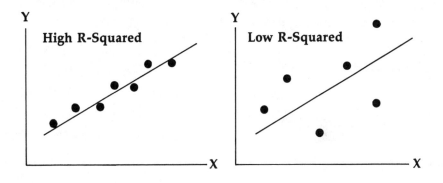

Program 5-2. Least-Squares Forecasting
Save using the filename **LSF**

```
REM LEAST-SQUARES FORECASTING
  GOSUB INITIALIZE
  GOSUB ENTER.DATA
CONTINUE:
  GOSUB EDIT.DATA
  GOSUB COMPUTE
  IF GOOF = Ø THEN
    GOSUB SHOW.RESULTS
    GOSUB FORECAST
  ELSE
    IF CNT$ = "YES" THEN CONTINUE
  END IF
```

```
 GOSUB GOODBYE
END

INITIALIZE:
 GOSUB SETSCREEN
 GOSUB KEYVALUES
 GOSUB SETMENUS
 GOSUB SETCOLORS
 GOSUB SHAPES
 GOSUB HEADING
 IF INSTRUCTIONS = 1 THEN GOSUB INSTRUCTIONS
RETURN

SETSCREEN:
 SCREEN 1,640,200,3,2
 WINDOW 2,"Least-Squares Forecasting",,0,1
RETURN

KEYVALUES:
 RANDOMIZE TIMER
 DEFINT A-Z: DEFDBL A,B,D-F,M,P,S
 REM make X DBL for VERY big or small raw data
  DEFSNG K,T,X
 REM MAXIMUM NUMBER OF OBSERVATIONS
  DATA 150
  READ NX
  OPTION BASE 1
  DIM X(NX,2),CIRCLE.SHAPE(150)
  V$(1) = "Y": V$(2) = "X"
 REM BUTTON VALUES
  XB(1) = 292: XB(2) = 334: YB = 165
  LT$(1) = "Y": LT$(2) = "N"
 REM SHAPE INDICES
  INDEX(1) = 1: INDEX(2) = 75
 REM VALUES IN APPROXIMATION FORMULA FOR t
  DATA 1.96, .60033, .9591, -.90259, .115
  READ T1, T2, T3, T4, T5
 REM ACTUAL t VALUES FOR V <= 3
  DATA 12.706, 4.303, 3.182
  FOR I=1 TO 3
   READ T.ACTUAL(I)
  NEXT
 REM FORMATS FOR OUTPUT
  FOR I=2 TO 8
   F$(I) = STRING$(18-I,"#")
   F$(I) = F$(I) + "." + STRING$(I,"#")
  NEXT
RETURN
```

```
SETMENUS:
 DATA 2, Instructions, Yes, No
 DATA 5, Color, Lt. Brown, Blue, Green, Gray
 DATA Random
 DATA 7, Decimals, 2 Places, 3 Places, 4 Places
 DATA 5 Places, 6 Places, 7 Places, 8 Places
 DATA 3, Stop, Go to BASIC
 DATA Go to Finance Menu, Go to System
 FOR I=1 TO 4
  READ NUMBER
  FOR J=Ø TO NUMBER
   READ TITLE$
   IF J<>Ø THEN TITLE$ = SPACE$(3) + TITLE$
   STATUS = 1
   IF I < 3 AND J = 1 THEN STATUS = 2
   IF I = 3 AND J = 2 THEN STATUS = 2
   MENU I,J,STATUS,TITLE$
 NEXT J,I
 INSTRUCTIONS = 1: KOLOR = 1: DP% = 3
 F$ = F$(DP%)
 F.SHORT$ = MID$(F$,5)
RETURN

SETCOLORS:
 REM BROWN, BLUE, GREEN, GRAY
  DATA .95,.7,.53, .36,.57,1
  DATA .22,.76,.68, .72,.7,.86
  FOR I=1 TO 4
   FOR J=1 TO 3
    READ KOLOR(I,J)
  NEXT J,I
 REM BROWN, GREEN, & RED
  PALETTE 4,.95,.7,.53
  PALETTE 5,.14,.43,Ø
  PALETTE 6,.93,.2,Ø
RETURN

SHAPES:
 X=313: Y=8Ø
 X1 = X-7: X2 = X+7: Y1 = Y-3: Y2 = Y+3
 LINE(X1,Y1)-(X2,Y2),4,BF
 CIRCLE(X,Y),7,2: PAINT(X,Y),6,2
 GET(X1,Y1)-(X2,Y2),CIRCLE.SHAPE(1)
 CIRCLE(X,Y),7,2: PAINT(X,Y),1,2
 GET(X1,Y1)-(X2,Y2),CIRCLE.SHAPE(75)
RETURN

HEADING:
 MENU ON
```

```
 ON MENU GOSUB OPTIONS
 CLS
 COLOR 3,Ø: LOCATE 18,30:PRINT "then"
 COLOR 1,Ø
 LOCATE 10,20: PRINT "Least-Squares Forecasting"
 LOCATE 17,24:PRINT "Please use menus,"
 LOCATE 19,21:PRINT "Click mouse to start"
 GOSUB CLICKIT
RETURN

OPTIONS:
 ID = MENU(Ø): ITEM = MENU(1)
 ON ID GOSUB MENU1,MENU2,MENU3,GOODBYE
 ITEM = Ø
RETURN

MENU1:
 MENU 1,INSTRUCTIONS,1: MENU 1,ITEM,2
 INSTRUCTIONS = ITEM
RETURN

MENU2:
 K1 = KOLOR(ITEM,1): K2 = KOLOR(ITEM,2)
 K3 = KOLOR(ITEM,3)
 IF ITEM=5 THEN K1=RND: K2=RND: K3=RND
 PALETTE 4,K1,K2,K3
 MENU 2,KOLOR,1: MENU 2,ITEM,2
 KOLOR = ITEM
RETURN

MENU3:
 MENU 3,DP%-1,1: MENU 3,ITEM,2
 DP% = ITEM + 1
 F$ = F$(DP%)
 F.SHORT$ = MID$(F$,5)
RETURN

GOODBYE:
 WINDOW CLOSE 2: WINDOW 1: MENU RESET
 SCREEN CLOSE 1
 IF ITEM = 2 THEN RUN "FINANCE"
 IF ITEM = 3 THEN SYSTEM
 COLOR 1,Ø: CLS
 PRINT "Bye-Bye"
 STOP
RETURN

CLICKIT:
 S$ = ""
```

```
WHILE MOUSE(Ø) = Ø AND S$ = ""
 S$ = INKEY$
WEND
 X = MOUSE(1)
 Y = MOUSE(2)
WHILE MOUSE(Ø)<> Ø: WEND: REM RESET
RETURN

INSTRUCTIONS:
 CLS
 PRINT
 PRINT "   This program estimates a simple";
 PRINT " linear regression"
 PRINT " equation.
 PRINT
 PRINT "   Future values of the dependent";
 PRINT " variable (Y) are predicted"
 PRINT " based on the value of X that you enter."
 PRINT
 PRINT "   A 95% confidence interval is";
 PRINT " generated for the forecast."
 LOCATE 20,27:PRINT "Click Mouse";
 GOSUB CLICKIT
RETURN

ENTER.DATA:
 REM Y
  CLS
  PRINT
  PRINT "    Please enter observations on the";
  PRINT " dependent variable, Y."
  PRINT " Hit RETURN when you're through."
  GOSUB ON.Y
 REM X
  GOSUB ON.X
RETURN

ON.Y:
 GOSUB GURGLE
 N = NX
 FOR J=1 TO NX
  LOCATE 5,14: PRINT SPACE$(3Ø)
  LOCATE 5,3: PRINT "Y(";J
  LOCATE 5,9: PRINT ")= ? ";
  INPUT "",X$
  IF X$ = "" THEN
   N = J-1
   J = NX
  ELSE
```

```
   X(J,1) = VAL(X$)
  END IF
 NEXT
 REM DEGREES OF FREEDOM
  V = N-2
  IF V < 1 THEN
   LOCATE 18,8: PRINT "At least 3 observations";
   PRINT " are needed !  Try again."
   GOTO ON.Y
  END IF
RETURN

ON.X:
 CLS
 GOSUB GURGLE
 PRINT
 PRINT "  Please enter data on the explanatory";
 PRINT " variable, X."
 FOR J=1 TO N
  LOCATE 4,14: PRINT SPACE$(30)
  LOCATE 4,3: PRINT "X(";J
  LOCATE 4,9: PRINT ")= ? ";
  INPUT "",X$
  X(J,2) = VAL(X$)
 NEXT
RETURN

GURGLE:
 FREQ = 300
 FOR G=1 TO 5
  FREQ = 500-FREQ
  SOUND FREQ,1,50
 NEXT G
RETURN

EDIT.DATA:
 FOR I=1 TO 2
  FOR J=1 TO N STEP 10
   GOSUB DISPLAY
   GOSUB CORRECT
 NEXT J,I
RETURN

DISPLAY:
 CLS
 LINE(200,7)-(430,17),1,BF
 COLOR 6,1
 LOCATE 2,22
 PRINT "These are values of " + V$(I)
```

```
  LINE (40,25)-(590,116),4,BF
  COLOR 2,4
  R = 0: HOLD.ROW = 0
  FOR L = J TO J+9
   IF L <= N THEN
    R = R+1
    CALL DRAW.IT(R,1)
    LOCATE R+3,10: PRINT V$(I);"(";MID$(STR$(L),2)
    LOCATE R+3,15: PRINT ")= ";X(L,I)
   END IF
  NEXT L
RETURN

SUB DRAW.IT(RW,INX) STATIC
 SHARED CIRCLE.SHAPE(),INDEX()
 Y = (RW+3)*9 - 9
 PUT(65,Y),CIRCLE.SHAPE(INDEX(INX)),PSET
END SUB

CORRECT:
 COLOR 1,0
 LOCATE 16,24: PRINT "To make changes,"
 LOCATE 17,13: PRINT "Click mouse on circle,";
 PRINT " then hit Return"
 GOSUB CHOOSE
 IF HOLD.ROW <> 0 THEN
  GOSUB CHANGE: GOTO CORRECT
 END IF
RETURN

CHOOSE:
 GOSUB GURGLE
 GOSUB CLICKIT
 IF S$ = "" THEN GOSUB LOCATION: GOTO CHOOSE
 IF ASC(S$) <> 13 THEN CHOOSE
RETURN

LOCATION:
 ROW = INT(Y/9) - 2
 IF ROW > 0 AND ROW <= R AND X>55 AND X<90 THEN
  IF HOLD.ROW <> 0 THEN
   CALL DRAW.IT(HOLD.ROW,1)
  END IF
  CALL DRAW.IT(ROW,2)
  HOLD.ROW = ROW
 END IF
RETURN
```

```
CHANGE:
 LOCATE 16,24: PRINT SPACE$(16)
 LOCATE 17,13: PRINT SPACE$(38)
 LINE(65,133)-(185,143),5,BF
 COLOR 1,5
 LOCATE 16,8: PRINT "New Value ?"
 COLOR 1,0
 LOCATE 16,21: INPUT "",V$
 X(J+HOLD.ROW-1,I) = VAL(V$)
 COLOR 2,4
 LOCATE HOLD.ROW+3,18: PRINT SPACE$(30)
 LOCATE HOLD.ROW+3,18: PRINT X(J+HOLD.ROW-1,I)
 CALL DRAW.IT(HOLD.ROW,1)
 HOLD.ROW = 0
 LINE(65,133)-(185,143),0,BF
 COLOR 1,0
 LOCATE 16,21: PRINT SPACE$(30)
RETURN

COMPUTE:
 GOOF = 0
 CLS
 LOCATE 10,26: PRINT "Computing ..."
 GOSUB KEYSUMS
 IF GOOF = 0 THEN GOSUB EQUATION
 IF GOOF = 0 THEN GOSUB ANOVA
 IF GOOF = 0 THEN
  GOSUB TSTATISTIC
  GOSUB XTERMS
 ELSE
  GOSUB GOOF
 END IF
RETURN

KEYSUMS:
 SX=0: SY=0: SQ.X=0: SQ.Y=0: PROD=0
 FOR I=1 TO N
  SX   = SX   + X(I,2)
  SY   = SY   + X(I,1)
  SQ.X = SQ.X + X(I,2)^2
  SQ.Y = SQ.Y + X(I,1)^2
  PROD = PROD + X(I,1)*X(I,2)
 NEXT
 DMT = N*SQ.X - SX*SX
 IF DMT = 0 THEN GOOF = 1
RETURN

EQUATION:
 B = (N*PROD - SX*SY)/DMT
```

```
 A = (SY - B*SX)/N
RETURN

ANOVA:
 REM SUMS OF SQUARES
  SS.TOTAL = SQ.Y - SY*SY/N
  SS.REGRN = B*(PROD - SX*SY/N)
  SS.RESDL = SS.TOTAL - SS.REGRN
 REM ERROR VARIANCE
  EV = SS.RESDL/V
  IF EV = Ø THEN GOOF = 1
 REM STANDARD ERRORS OF ESTIMATES OF A & B
  SB = SQR(N*EV/DMT)
  SA = SQR(EV*SQ.X/DMT)
RETURN

TSTATISTIC:
 IF V <= 3 THEN
  T = T.ACTUAL(V)
 ELSE
  T.NUMERATOR   = T1*V + T2 + T3/V
  T.DENOMINATOR = V + T4 + T5/V
  T = T.NUMERATOR/T.DENOMINATOR
 END IF
RETURN

XTERMS:
 REM X-BAR
  SUM = Ø
  FOR I=1 TO N
   SUM = SUM + X(I,2)
  NEXT
  MEAN = SUM/N
 REM SUM OF SQUARED DEVIATIONS
  SD = SQ.X - SX*SX/N
RETURN

GOOF:
 CLS
 LINE(82,79)-(15Ø,89),6,BF
 COLOR 1,6
 LOCATE 1Ø,1Ø: PRINT "Sorry:"
 COLOR 1,Ø
 LOCATE 1Ø,17: PRINT "I can't estimate";
 PRINT " a regression equation"
 LOCATE 11,17: PRINT "with the data you've";
 PRINT " entered."
 LOCATE 17,28: PRINT "Continue ?"
 GOSUB GURGLE
```

```
 GOSUB DECIDE
 CNT$ = "NO"
 IF BUTTON% = 1 THEN CNT$ = "YES"
RETURN

SHOW.RESULTS:
 GOSUB PAINT.SCREEN
 GOSUB SHOW.EQUATION
 GOSUB SHOW.ANOVA
RETURN

PAINT.SCREEN:
 CLS
 LINE(35,3)-(595,120),4,BF
 COLOR 2,4
 LOCATE 2,23: PRINT "REGRESSION RESULTS"
 COLOR 1,6
 LINE(65,34)-(115,44),6,BF
 LOCATE 5,8: PRINT "Term"
 LINE(215,34)-(375,44),6,BF
 LOCATE 5,23: PRINT "Estimated Value"
 LINE(455,34)-(575,44),6,BF
 LOCATE 5,47: PRINT "t-Statistic"
RETURN

SHOW.EQUATION:
 COLOR 2,4
 LOCATE 7,6: PRINT "Constant";
 PRINT TAB(19) USING F$; A;
 PRINT TAB(39) USING F$; A/SA
 LOCATE 8,6: PRINT "Coefficient";
 PRINT TAB(19) USING F$; B;
 PRINT TAB(39) USING F$; B/SB
RETURN

SHOW.ANOVA:
 LOCATE 11,6: PRINT "R-Squared   =";
 PRINT USING F.SHORT$;SS.REGRN/SS.TOTAL
 LOCATE 13,6: PRINT "F-Statistic =";
 PRINT USING F.SHORT$;SS.REGRN/EV
RETURN

DECIDE:
 BUTTON% = 0
 GOSUB DRAWBUTTON
 GOSUB PUSHBUTTON
 COLOR 1,0
RETURN
```

```
DRAWBUTTON:
 LINE (265,158)-(361,172),1,BF
 FOR I=1 TO 2
  CIRCLE (XB(I),YB),12,4+I
  PAINT (XB(I),YB),4+I
  COLOR 1,4+I
  LOCATE 19: PRINT PTAB(XB(I)-4);LT$(I);
 NEXT I
RETURN

PUSHBUTTON:
 SOUND 440,2
 GOSUB CLICKIT
 S$ = UCASE$(S$)
 IF S$ = "Y" THEN BUTTON% = 1
 IF S$ = "N" THEN BUTTON% = 2
 FOR I=1 TO 2
  XD = ABS(X-XB(I)): YD = ABS(Y-YB)
  IF XD<13 AND YD<7 THEN BUTTON% = I: I=2
 NEXT
 IF BUTTON% = 0 THEN PUSHBUTTON
RETURN

FORECAST:
 GOSUB ASK.TO.FORECAST
 IF BUTTON% = 1 THEN GOSUB LABEL.SCREEN
 WHILE BUTTON% = 1
  GOSUB PREDICT
  GOSUB ASK.TO.FORECAST
 WEND
RETURN

ASK.TO.FORECAST:
 COLOR 1,0
 LOCATE 16,17
 PRINT "Would you like to forecast Y ?"
 GOSUB DECIDE
RETURN

LABEL.SCREEN:
 CLS
 LINE(35,3)-(595,120),4,BF
 COLOR 2,4
 LOCATE 2,21: PRINT "LEAST-SQUARES FORECASTS"
 LOCATE 3,20: PRINT "(95% Confidence Interval)"
 COLOR 1,5
 LINE(45,43)-(175,53),5,BF
 LOCATE 6,6: PRINT " Value of X"
 COLOR 1,6
```

```
    LINE(45,70)-(175,80),6,BF
    LOCATE 9,6: PRINT "Predicted Y"
    COLOR 2,4
    LOCATE 11,7: PRINT "Lower Bound ="
    LOCATE 12,7: PRINT "Upper Bound ="
RETURN

PREDICT:
    LINE (265,158)-(361,172),0,BF
    COLOR 1,0
    LOCATE 16,17: PRINT SPACE$(30)
    LOCATE 16,6: PRINT "Value of X ? ";
    GOSUB GURGLE
    INPUT "",X$
    XV = VAL(X$)
    P = A + B*XV
    LOCATE 16,6: PRINT SPACE$(45)
    COLOR 2,4
    LOCATE 6,20: PRINT USING F.SHORT$;XV
    LOCATE 9,20: PRINT USING F.SHORT$;P
    GOSUB INTERVAL
RETURN

INTERVAL:
    REM FORECAST VARIANCE
     FV = EV*(1 + 1/N + (XV-MEAN)^2/SD)
    REM INTERVAL
     LOCATE 11,20
     PRINT USING F.SHORT$;P - T*SQR(FV)
     LOCATE 12,20
     PRINT USING F.SHORT$;P + T*SQR(FV)
RETURN
```

Future Worth

Program 5-3, "Future Worth," computes the future value of an investment. The investment might be for yourself or for a business. We'll illustrate both cases.

First, suppose you buy a money-market certificate from the local Savings and Loan for $5,000. It pays 9 percent per annum and matures in ten years. If you enter this data into the Amiga, you'll see that your certificate will be worth $12,298 at maturity, assuming that interest is compounded continuously. To change the compounding to annually, quarterly, or daily, use the pull-down menu.

Second, suppose you now buy some prime commercial real estate for $10,000. You expect it to appreciate in value 15 percent each year, and you'd like to hold onto it for five years. The Amiga computes that your land will be worth $20,114 in half a decade, given yearly compounding of interest.

On the other hand, however, perhaps your acreage will grow in value at only 10 percent per year. But, then again, maybe a 20 percent per annum figure is within the realm of possibility. When you're faced with this kind of uncertainty, the power of the Amiga can help. Instead of reentering all of your data, simply click the mouse on the item you want to change, like the rate of interest, and then enter in a new number. For interest rates of 10 to 20 percent, you'll discover that the spread of plausible future worths of your land is roughly $16,000 to $25,000.

Program 5-3. Future Worth
Save using the filename **WORTH**

```
REM FUTURE WORTH
 GOSUB INITIALIZE
COMPUTE:
 GOSUB FUTURE.WORTH
 LOCATE 18,25: PRINT "Compute Again ?"
 GOSUB DECIDE
 IF BUTTON = 1 THEN COMPUTE
 GOSUB GOODBYE
END

INITIALIZE:
 GOSUB SETSCREEN
 GOSUB KEYVALUES
 GOSUB SETMENUS
 GOSUB SETCOLORS
```

```
 GOSUB HEADING
RETURN


SETSCREEN:
 SCREEN 1,640,200,3,2
 WINDOW 2,"Future Worth",,0,1
RETURN


KEYVALUES:
 DEFINT A-Z: DEFSNG E,T,X,Y
 REM EFFECTIVE INTEREST RATE
  DEF FN EFFRT(V) = ( 1 + (X(4)/100)/V )^V
 REM BUTTON VALUES
  XB(1) = 292: XB(2) = 334: YB = 174
  LT$(1) = "Y": LT$(2) = "N"
 REM TITLES & ROWS FOR LEFT BOX
  DATA Amount,5, "  Years",10, "  Months",12
  DATA Interest Rate,15
  FOR I=1 TO 4
   READ NM$(I), ROW.LEFT(I)
  NEXT
 REM ROWS FOR RIGHT BOX
  DATA 6,8,10,14
  FOR I=1 TO 4
   READ ROW.RIGHT(I)
  NEXT
 REM PRINT-FORMATS
  F$(1) = "$$##,#####.##"
  F$(2) = "        ###      "
  F$(3) = "          %##.##"
 REM FORMATS FOR LEFT & RIGHT BOXES
  DATA 1,2,2,3
  DATA 1,1,1,3
  FOR I=1 TO 4: READ F.LEFT(I) : NEXT
  FOR I=1 TO 4: READ F.RIGHT(I): NEXT
 REM FREQUENCIES OF INTEREST COMPOUNDING
  DATA Annual, Quarterly, Daily, Continuous
  FOR I=1 TO 4
   READ S$
   FREQ$(I) = "(" + S$ + " Compounding)"
  NEXT
 FIRST.RUN$ = "ON"
RETURN


SETMENUS:
 DATA 2, Instructions, Yes, No
 DATA 4, Interest Compounding, Annual
 DATA Quarterly, Daily, Continuously
 DATA 3, Stop, Go to BASIC
```

```
 DATA Go to Finance Menu, Go to System
 FOR I=1 TO 3
  READ NUMBER
  FOR J=0 TO NUMBER
   READ TITLE$
   IF J<>0 THEN TITLE$ = SPACE$(3) + TITLE$
   STATUS = 1
   IF I <> 3 AND J = 1 THEN STATUS = 2
   MENU I,J,STATUS,TITLE$
 NEXT J,I
 MENU 4,0,0,""
 INSTRUCTIONS = 1: TYPE = 1
RETURN

SETCOLORS:
 REM BROWN, GREEN, & RED
  PALETTE 4,.8,.6,.53
  PALETTE 5,.14,.43,0
  PALETTE 6,.93,.2,0
RETURN

HEADING:
 MENU ON
 ON MENU GOSUB OPTIONS
 CLS
 COLOR 3,0: LOCATE 18,30:PRINT "then"
 COLOR 1,0
 LOCATE 10: PRINT PTAB(247)"Future Worth"
 LOCATE 17,24:PRINT "Please use menus,"
 LOCATE 19,21:PRINT "Click mouse to start"
 GOSUB CLICKIT
RETURN

OPTIONS:
 ID = MENU(0): ITEM = MENU(1)
 ON ID GOSUB MENU1,MENU2,GOODBYE
 ITEM = 0
RETURN

MENU1:
 MENU 1,INSTRUCTIONS,1: MENU 1,ITEM,2
 INSTRUCTIONS = ITEM
RETURN

MENU2:
 MENU 2,TYPE,1: MENU 2,ITEM,2
 TYPE = ITEM
RETURN
```

```
GOODBYE:
 WINDOW CLOSE 2: WINDOW 1: MENU RESET
 SCREEN CLOSE 1
 IF ITEM = 2 THEN RUN "FINANCE"
 IF ITEM = 3 THEN SYSTEM
 COLOR 1,0: CLS
 PRINT "Bye-Bye"
 STOP
RETURN

CLICKIT:
 S$ = ""
 WHILE MOUSE(0) = 0 AND S$ = ""
  S$ = INKEY$
 WEND
  X = MOUSE(1)
  Y = MOUSE(2)
 WHILE MOUSE(0)<> 0: WEND: REM RESET
RETURN

FUTURE.WORTH:
 VARIABLE = 1
 IF INSTRUCTIONS = 1 THEN GOSUB INSTRUCTIONS
 IF FIRST.RUN$ = "ON" THEN GOSUB ENTER.DATA
 GOSUB COMPUTE.FW
 GOSUB PAINT.SCREEN
 GOSUB SHOW.SUMMARY
 GOSUB ASK.TO.CHANGE
RETURN

INSTRUCTIONS:
 CLS
 PRINT
 PRINT "    This program computes how much";
 PRINT " an investment will be"
 PRINT " worth in the future."
 PRINT
 PRINT "    In the display that follows, basic";
 PRINT " investment values are"
 PRINT " on the left.  Change these to play";
 PRINT " what-if games like"
 PRINT " tallying the dollar impact of holding";
 PRINT " a security for an"
 PRINT " extra year."
 PRINT
 PRINT "    The future worth of your investment";
 PRINT " is on the right."
 LOCATE 20,27:PRINT "Click Mouse";
 GOSUB CLICKIT
```

```
   ITEM = 2: GOSUB MENU1: REM TURN OFF INSTRUCTIONS
RETURN

ENTER.DATA:
 GOSUB AMOUNT
 GOSUB LENGTH
 GOSUB INTEREST.RATE
 FIRST.RUN$ = "OFF"
RETURN

AMOUNT:
 CLS
 PRINT
 PRINT "  Please enter the amount of money";
 PRINT " that you'd like to invest."
 X(1) = 0
 WHILE X(1) <= 0
  LOCATE 4,12: PRINT SPACE$(20)
  GOSUB GURGLE
  LOCATE 4,3: INPUT "Amount ";S$
  X(1) = VAL(S$)
 WEND
RETURN

LENGTH:
 LOCATE 7,3: PRINT "Please enter the length of";
 PRINT " your investment in years and"
 PRINT "  months."
 X(2) = -9: REM YEARS
 WHILE X(2) < 0
  LOCATE 10,13: PRINT SPACE$(20)
  GOSUB GURGLE
  LOCATE 10,4: INPUT "Years = ";S$
  X(2) = INT(VAL(S$))
 WEND
 X(3) = -9: REM MONTHS
 WHILE X(3) < 0
  LOCATE 11,13: PRINT SPACE$(20)
  GOSUB GURGLE
  LOCATE 11,3: INPUT "Months = ";S$
  X(3) = INT(VAL(S$))
 WEND
 IF X(2) + X(3) = 0 THEN LENGTH
RETURN

INTEREST.RATE:
 LOCATE 14,3: PRINT "Please enter the interest";
 PRINT " rate on your investment.  For"
 PRINT "  example, enter 7 for 7%, 10 for 10%,";
```

```
 PRINT " and so on."
 X(4) = 0
 WHILE X(4) <= 0
   GOSUB GURGLE
   LOCATE 17,12: PRINT SPACE$(20)
   LOCATE 17,3: INPUT "Rate = ";S$
   X(4) = VAL(S$)
 WEND
RETURN

COMPUTE.FW:
 REM EFFECTIVE INTEREST RATE
  IF TYPE = 1 THEN EFF.RATE = FN EFFRT(1)
  IF TYPE = 2 THEN EFF.RATE = FN EFFRT(4)
  IF TYPE = 3 THEN EFF.RATE = FN EFFRT(365)
  IF TYPE = 4 THEN EFF.RATE = EXP(X(4)/100)
  Y(4) = (EFF.RATE-1)*100
  FREQ$ = FREQ$(TYPE)
 REM TOTAL YEARS
  TYEARS = X(2) + X(3)/12
 REM FUTURE WORTH
  Y(1) = X(1)*EFF.RATE^TYEARS
 REM PRINCIPAL & INTEREST
  Y(2) = X(1)
  Y(3) = Y(1) - Y(2)
RETURN

PAINT.SCREEN:
 CLS
 LINE(10,4)-(306,143),2,B
 PAINT (150,60),4,2
 LINE(324,4)-(620,143),2,B
 PAINT (450,60),1,2
 REM LEFT BOX
  COLOR 2,4
  LOCATE 2,11: PRINT "INVESTMENT"
  FOR I=1 TO 4
   LOCATE ROW.LEFT(I),3: PRINT NM$(I);
   PRINT TAB(17) USING F$(F.LEFT(I));X(I)
  NEXT
  LOCATE 8,3: PRINT "Length"
 REM RIGHT BOX
  COLOR 0,1
  LOCATE 2: PRINT PTAB(415)"FUTURE WORTH"
  LOCATE 6,35: PRINT "Total"
  LINE(355,61)-(452,71),5,BF
  COLOR 1,5
  LOCATE 8,37: PRINT "Principal"
  LINE(355,79)-(452,89),6,BF
```

```
      COLOR 1,6
      LOCATE 10,37: PRINT "Interest"
      COLOR 0,1
      LOCATE 13,35: PRINT "Effective"
      LOCATE 14,35: PRINT "Interest Rate"
RETURN

SHOW.SUMMARY:
  COLOR 0,1
  LOCATE 3,36: PRINT SPACE$(25)
  L = LEN(FREQ$)
  LOCATE 3: PRINT PTAB(475-10*L/2);FREQ$
  FOR I=1 TO 4
    LOCATE ROW.RIGHT(I),49
    PRINT USING F$(F.RIGHT(I));Y(I)
  NEXT
RETURN

ASK.TO.CHANGE:
  COLOR 1,0
  LOCATE 18,28: PRINT "Changes ?"
  GOSUB DECIDE
  LOCATE 18,28: PRINT SPACE$(9)
  IF BUTTON = 1 THEN
    CALL HIGHLIGHT(VARIABLE,3)
    COLOR 1,0
    LINE(265,167)-(361,181),0,BF
    LOCATE 19,13: PRINT "Click Mouse on Choice,";
    PRINT " then Hit Return"
    GOSUB CHOOSE
    GOTO ASK.TO.CHANGE
  END IF
RETURN

SUB HIGHLIGHT(V,KOLOR) STATIC
  SHARED NM$(), ROW.LEFT()
  R = ROW.LEFT(V)
  L = LEN(NM$(V))
  X0 = 15: X1 = L*10 + 25
  Y0 = 9*R - 11: Y1 = Y0 + 10
  LINE(X0,Y0)-(X1,Y1),KOLOR,BF
  COLOR KOLOR-2,KOLOR
  LOCATE R,3: PRINT NM$(V)
END SUB

CHOOSE:
  GOSUB GURGLE
  GOSUB CLICKIT
  IF S$ = "" THEN GOSUB LOCATION: GOTO CHOOSE
```

```
 IF ASC(S$) <> 13 THEN CHOOSE
 GOSUB CHANGE
RETURN

GURGLE:
 FREQ = 300
 FOR G=1 TO 5
  FREQ = 500-FREQ
  SOUND FREQ,1,50
 NEXT G
RETURN

LOCATION:
 R = INT(Y/9) + 1
 I=0: V=0
 WHILE V=0 AND I <= 4
  I = I + 1
  IF ROW.LEFT(I) = R THEN V = I
 WEND
 IF X>14 AND X<175 AND V <> 0 THEN
  CALL HIGHLIGHT(VARIABLE,4)
  CALL HIGHLIGHT(V,3)
  VARIABLE = V
 END IF
RETURN

DECIDE:
 BUTTON = 0
 GOSUB DRAWBUTTON
 GOSUB PUSHBUTTON
 COLOR 1,0
RETURN

DRAWBUTTON:
 LINE (265,167)-(361,181),1,BF
 FOR I=1 TO 2
  CIRCLE (XB(I),YB),12,4+I
  PAINT (XB(I),YB),4+I
  COLOR 1,4+I
  LOCATE 20: PRINT PTAB(XB(I)-4);LT$(I);
 NEXT I
RETURN

PUSHBUTTON:
 SOUND 440,2
 GOSUB CLICKIT
 S$ = UCASE$(S$)
 IF S$ = "Y" THEN BUTTON = 1
 IF S$ = "N" THEN BUTTON = 2
```

```
 FOR I=1 TO 2
  XD = ABS(X-XB(I)): YD = ABS(Y-YB)
   IF XD<13 AND YD<7 THEN BUTTON = I: I=2
 NEXT
 IF BUTTON = Ø THEN PUSHBUTTON
RETURN

CHANGE:
 ROW = ROW.LEFT(VARIABLE)
 COLOR 1,Ø
 LOCATE 19,13: PRINT SPACE$(38);
 LOCATE 19,26: LINE INPUT; "New Value ? ";S$
 IF VARIABLE = 2 OR VARIABLE = 3 THEN
  X(VARIABLE) = INT(VAL(S$))
 ELSE
  X(VARIABLE) = VAL(S$)
 END IF
 LOCATE 19,26: PRINT SPACE$(3Ø);
 COLOR 4
 COLOR 2,4: LOCATE ROW,17
 PRINT USING F$(F.LEFT(VARIABLE));X(VARIABLE)
 GOSUB COMPUTE.FW
 GOSUB SHOW.SUMMARY
RETURN
```

Computer Cash Register

If you have a small business, and you're tired of looking at sales-tax tables when you ring up purchases, you'll find this program a joy to use. All you have to do is enter the price of the item, and the computer responds with the total payment due, including tax. After you enter the amount of money received from the customer, the program tells you how much change to give. It's as easy as that.

Before you run the program, however, enter the sales tax of your area into the KEYVALUES subroutine at the beginning of the program. The default value of 4 percent is for the state of Virginia.

When you run the program, the Amiga will paint a colorful cash register on your screen. You can then begin. Enter the price of the item and then press the RETURN key. A total of this transaction, tax included, is displayed. Now, enter the amount given to you by the customer; the Amiga shows how much change to return.

If you make a mistake entering the transaction, don't fret. Just press R for Redo last entry (or click on the appropriate circle at the bottom of the register), and you'll have another chance. No more scratching out entries on the cash register slip. You can even view total sales through any point in time by pressing or clicking on T.

Program 5-4. Computer Cash Register
Save using the filename **REGISTER**

```
REM COMPUTER CASH REGISTER
 GOSUB INITIALIZE
 GOSUB REGISTER
 GOSUB GOODBYE
END

INITIALIZE:
 GOSUB SETSCREEN
 GOSUB KEYVALUES
 GOSUB SETMENUS
 GOSUB SETCOLORS
 GOSUB SHAPES
 GOSUB HEADING
RETURN
```

```
SETSCREEN:
 SCREEN 1,640,200,3,2
 WINDOW 2,"Cash Register",,0,1
RETURN

KEYVALUES:
 DEFINT A-Z: DEFSNG D,K,P,S,T
 DIM CIRCLES(750)
 RANDOMIZE TIMER
 REM SALES TAX (IN PERCENTAGE FORM)
  DATA 4.0
  READ SALES.TAX
  TAX.INDEX = 1+SALES.TAX/100
 REM BUTTON VALUES
  XB(1) = 292: XB(2) = 334: YB = 174
  LT$(1) = "Y": LT$(2) = "N"
 REM CHOICES
  DATA Continue, Redo last entry, Tally totals
  FOR I=1 TO 3
   READ CHOICE$(I)
   CH$(I) = LEFT$(CHOICE$(I),1)
  NEXT
 REM ROWS FOR REGISTER'S DISPLAY
  DATA 3,4,6,7
  FOR I=1 TO 4
   READ R(I)
  NEXT
 REM INITIAL VALUES
  SALES = 0: N = 0: TAXES = 0: C = 0
 REM SHAPE INDICES
  FOR I=1 TO 6
   INDEX(I) = (I-1)*125 + 1
  NEXT
  F$ = "= $$#,#######.##"
RETURN

SETMENUS:
 DATA 2, Instructions, Yes, No
 DATA 5, Register, Brown, Blue, Green
 DATA Lt. Red, Random
 DATA 3, Stop, Go to BASIC
 DATA Go to Finance Menu, Go to System
 FOR I=1 TO 3
  READ NUMBER
  FOR J=0 TO NUMBER
   READ TITLE$
   IF J<>0 THEN TITLE$ = SPACE$(3) + TITLE$
   STATUS = 1
   IF I <> 3 AND J = 1 THEN STATUS = 2
```

```
      MENU I,J,STATUS,TITLE$
   NEXT J,I
   MENU 4,Ø,Ø,""
   INSTRUCTIONS = 1: REGISTER = 1
RETURN

SETCOLORS:
  REM BROWN, BLUE, GREEN, LT. RED
   DATA .67,.45,.33, .36,.57,1
   DATA .26,.59,.47, .78,.4,.43
   FOR I=1 TO 4
    FOR J=1 TO 3
     READ KOLOR(I,J)
   NEXT J,I
  REM BROWN, GREEN, & RED
   PALETTE 4,.67,.45,.33
   PALETTE 5,.14,.43,Ø
   PALETTE 6,.93,.2,Ø
RETURN

SHAPES:
  XØ = 325: YØ = 84
  X1 = XØ-12: X2 = XØ+12: Y1 = YØ-5: Y2 = YØ+5
  REM GREEN & RED
   FOR I=1 TO 2
    FOR J=1 TO 3
     LINE(X1,Y1)-(X2,Y2),1,BF
     CIRCLE(XØ,YØ),12,4+I: PAINT(XØ,YØ),4+I
     COLOR 1,4+I
     LOCATE 1Ø,33: PRINT CH$(J)
     V = (I-1)*3 + J
     GET(X1,Y1)-(X2,Y2),CIRCLES(INDEX(V))
   NEXT J,I
RETURN

HEADING:
  MENU ON
  ON MENU GOSUB OPTIONS
  COLOR 1,Ø
  CLS
  COLOR 3,Ø: LOCATE 18,3Ø:PRINT "then"
  COLOR 1,Ø
  LOCATE 1Ø,21: PRINT "Computer Cash Register"
  LOCATE 17,24:PRINT "Please use menus,"
  LOCATE 19,21:PRINT "Click mouse to continue"
  GOSUB CLICKIT
RETURN
```

```
OPTIONS:
 ID = MENU(Ø): ITEM = MENU(1)
 ON ID GOSUB MENU1,MENU2,GOODBYE
 ITEM = Ø
RETURN

MENU1:
 MENU 1,INSTRUCTIONS,1: MENU 1,ITEM,2
 INSTRUCTIONS = ITEM
RETURN

MENU2:
 K1 = KOLOR(ITEM,1): K2 = KOLOR(ITEM,2)
 K3 = KOLOR(ITEM,3)
 IF ITEM=5 THEN K1=RND: K2=RND: K3=RND
 PALETTE 4,K1,K2,K3
 MENU 2,REGISTER,1: MENU 2,ITEM,2
 REGISTER = ITEM
RETURN

GOODBYE:
 WINDOW CLOSE 2: WINDOW 1: MENU RESET
 SCREEN CLOSE 1
 IF ITEM = 2 THEN RUN "FINANCE"
 IF ITEM = 3 THEN SYSTEM
 COLOR 1,Ø: CLS
 PRINT "Bye-Bye"
 STOP
RETURN

CLICKIT:
 S$ = ""
 WHILE MOUSE(Ø) = Ø AND S$ = ""
  S$ = INKEY$
 WEND
  X = MOUSE(1)
  Y = MOUSE(2)
 WHILE MOUSE(Ø)<> Ø: WEND: REM RESET
RETURN

REGISTER:
 IF INSTRUCTIONS = 1 THEN GOSUB INSTRUCTIONS
 GOSUB DRAW.REGISTER
 GOSUB OPERATE
RETURN

INSTRUCTIONS:
 CLS
 PRINT
```

```
PRINT "    This program turns your Amiga into";
PRINT " a cash register."
PRINT
PRINT "    A sales tax of";SALES.TAX;CHR$(8);
PRINT "% is used in computing the price of"
PRINT " an item."
PRINT
PRINT "    For a different value, go to";
PRINT " BASIC and change the"
PRINT " Data statement in the KEYVALUES";
PRINT " subroutine."
LOCATE 20,26: PRINT "Click Mouse";
GOSUB CLICKIT
RETURN

DRAW.REGISTER:
 CLS
 LINE(113,5)-(513,180),2,B
 LINE(153,14)-(474,65),2,B
 PAINT(313,80),4,2
 LOCATE 3,20: PRINT "Price = $"
 LOCATE 4,17: PRINT "With Tax = $"
 LOCATE 6,18: PRINT "Payment = $"
 LOCATE 7,19: PRINT "Change = $"
 GOSUB BOTTOM
RETURN

BOTTOM:
 COLOR 6,1
 LINE(153,120)-(474,174),2,B
 PAINT(313,130),1,2
 FOR I=1 TO 3
  ROW = 13+I*2
  Y = ROW*9-11
  PUT(233,Y),CIRCLES(INDEX(I)),PSET
  LOCATE ROW,29: PRINT CHOICE$(I)
 NEXT
RETURN

OPERATE:
 GOSUB TRANSACTION
 GOSUB NEXT.ACTION
 REM REDO
  IF R$ = "R" THEN OPERATE
  GOSUB ADD.TO.TOTALS
 REM CONTINUE
  IF R$ = "C" THEN OPERATE
 REM DISPLAY TOTALS
  IF R$ = "T" THEN GOSUB SHOW.TOTALS
```

```
      REM CONTINUE OPERATING
       IF BUTTON = 1 THEN
         GOSUB DRAW.REGISTER
         GOTO OPERATE
       END IF
   RETURN

   TRANSACTION:
    REM BLANK-OUT LINES
       COLOR 1,Ø
       FOR I=1 TO 4
        LOCATE R(I),3Ø: PRINT SPACE$(18)
       NEXT
    REM ENTER PRICE
       PRICE = Ø
       WHILE PRICE <= Ø
        SOUND 9ØØ,2
        LOCATE 3,30: PRINT SPACE$(18)
        LOCATE 3,30: LINE INPUT D$
        PRICE = VAL(D$)
       WEND
       PWT = INT((PRICE*TAX.INDEX + .ØØ5)*1ØØ)/1ØØ
       LOCATE 4,29: PRINT PWT
    REM PAYMENT
       PAYMENT = Ø
       WHILE PAYMENT < PWT
        SOUND 9ØØ,2
        LOCATE 6,3Ø: PRINT SPACE$(18)
        LOCATE 6,3Ø: LINE INPUT D$
        PAYMENT = VAL(D$)
       WEND
    REM CHANGE
       DELTA = INT((PAYMENT - PWT + .ØØ5)*1ØØ)/1ØØ
       LOCATE 7,29: PRINT DELTA
   RETURN

   NEXT.ACTION:
    COLOR 2,4
    LOCATE 13,23: PRINT "PRESS"
     REM RE-SET CIRCLE
     IF C <> Ø THEN
        PUT(233,C*18+1Ø6),CIRCLES(INDEX(C)),PSET
     END IF
   R$ = ""
   WHILE R$ = ""
    GOSUB GURGLE
    GOSUB CLICKIT
    IF S$ = "" THEN GOSUB MOUSEY ELSE GOSUB BOARD
   WEND
```

```
 LOCATE 13,23: PRINT SPACE$(5)
 REM HIGHLIGHT ACTION
  Y = C*18 + 106
  PUT(233,Y),CIRCLES(INDEX(3+C)),PSET
RETURN

GURGLE:
 FREQ = 300
 FOR G=1 TO 5
  FREQ = 500-FREQ
  SOUND FREQ,1,50
 NEXT G
RETURN

MOUSEY:
 C = INT( (Y-120)/18 ) + 1
 IF X > 230 AND X < 260 THEN
  IF C = 1 THEN R$ = "C"
  IF C = 2 THEN R$ = "R"
  IF C = 3 THEN R$ = "T"
 END IF
RETURN

BOARD:
 S$ = UCASE$(S$)
 IF S$ = "C" THEN C = 1: R$ = S$
 IF S$ = "R" THEN C = 2: R$ = S$
 IF S$ = "T" THEN C = 3: R$ = S$
RETURN

ADD.TO.TOTALS:
 SALES = SALES + PRICE
 TAXES = TAXES + (PWT - PRICE)
 N = N+1
RETURN

SHOW.TOTALS:
 COLOR 1,0
 CLS
 LINE(135,5)-(495,100),2,B: PAINT(313,50),1,2
 COLOR 0,1
 LOCATE 2,27: PRINT "TOTAL SALES"
 LOCATE 4,18: PRINT "Number = ";N
 LOCATE 7,18: PRINT "Total Sales";
 PRINT TAB(30) USING F$;SALES+TAXES
 LINE(225,70)-(285,80),5,BF
 COLOR 1,5
 LOCATE 9,24: PRINT "Store";
 COLOR 0,1
```

```
   PRINT TAB(30) USING F$;SALES
   LINE(225,88)-(285,98),6,BF
   COLOR 1,6
   LOCATE 11,24: PRINT "Taxes";
   COLOR Ø,1
   PRINT TAB(30) USING F$;TAXES
   COLOR 1,Ø
   LOCATE 17,12: PRINT "Would you like to keep";
   PRINT " the register on ?"
   GOSUB DECIDE
   C = Ø
RETURN

DECIDE:
  BUTTON = Ø
  GOSUB DRAWBUTTON
  GOSUB PUSHBUTTON
  COLOR 1,Ø
RETURN

DRAWBUTTON:
  LINE (265,167)-(361,181),1,BF
  FOR I=1 TO 2
    CIRCLE (XB(I),YB),12,4+I
    PAINT (XB(I),YB),4+I
    COLOR 1,4+I
    LOCATE 20: PRINT PTAB(XB(I)-4);LT$(I);
  NEXT I
RETURN

PUSHBUTTON:
  SOUND 44Ø,2
  GOSUB CLICKIT
  S$ = UCASE$(S$)
  IF S$ = "Y" THEN BUTTON = 1
  IF S$ = "N" THEN BUTTON = 2
  FOR I=1 TO 2
    XD = ABS(X-XB(I)): YD = ABS(Y-YB)
    IF XD<13 AND YD<7 THEN BUTTON = I: I=2
  NEXT
  IF BUTTON = Ø THEN PUSHBUTTON
RETURN
```

CHAPTER 6

Science and Math

CHAPTER 6

Science and Math

The Amiga's number-crunching capability, colorful graphics, and marvelous mouse make these four programs fun to use. And that's the way it should be, for why make science dull and dreary when it's really entertaining and exciting.

Chemistry Basics. Enables you to review and analyze a wealth of intriguing information on the earth's 103 basic elements. Data items include atomic number, atomic weight, boiling and melting points, density, and date of discovery. You can display elements individually or by family, and you can sort them a number of different ways.

Weather Forecasting. Everybody complains about the weather, but nobody ever does anything about it. Although this program won't change that adage, it will help you make accurate short-range forecasts.

Simultaneous Equation Solver. Solves a set of simultaneous equations for each unknown.

Matrix Manipulator. There are many routines around for adding, subtracting, multiplying, and even inverting matrices. But what if you want to do several operations in succession? "MatMan" is your answer.

Science and Math Menu Driver

Save using the filename **SCIENCE**

```
REM SCIENCE AND MATH
 GOSUB INITIALIZE
 GOSUB MAIN.MENU
 RUN TITLE.SHORT$(PICK)
END

INITIALIZE:
 GOSUB SETSCREEN
 GOSUB KEYVALUES
 GOSUB SETMENUS
 GOSUB SETCOLORS
 GOSUB SHAPES
RETURN

SETSCREEN:
 SCREEN 1,640,200,3,2
```

```
 WINDOW 2,"Science and Math",,0,1
RETURN

KEYVALUES:
 DEFINT A-Z
 N = 4
 DIM TITLE.LONG$(N),TITLE.SHORT$(N),DISCS(250)
 DISC.I(1) = 1: DISC.I(2) = 125
 READ CHAPTER$
 FOR I=1 TO N
  READ TITLE.LONG$(I),TITLE.SHORT$(I)
 NEXT
RETURN

SETMENUS:
 FOR I=2 TO 4
  MENU I,0,0,""
 NEXT
 MENU 1,0,1,"STOP"
 MENU 1,1,1," Go to BASIC"
 MENU 1,2,1," Go to System"
 MENU ON
 ON MENU GOSUB GOODBYE
RETURN

GOODBYE:
 WINDOW CLOSE 2: WINDOW 1: MENU RESET
 SCREEN CLOSE 1
 ITEM = MENU(1)
 IF ITEM = 2 THEN SYSTEM
 CLS
 PRINT "Bye-Bye"
 STOP
RETURN

SETCOLORS:
 REM TAN, GREEN, & RED
  PALETTE 4,.95,.7,.53
  PALETTE 5,.14,.43,0
  PALETTE 6,.93,.2,0
RETURN

SHAPES:
 X=313: Y=80
 LINE(X-12,Y-8)-(X+12,Y+8),4,BF
 FOR I=1 TO 2
  K = 7-I
  CIRCLE(X,Y),12,K: PAINT(X,Y),K
  GET(X-12,Y-8)-(X+12,Y+8),DISCS(DISC.I(I))
```

```
 NEXT
RETURN

MAIN.MENU:
 CLS
 RTN$ = "OFF": PICK = 1
 S$ = CHAPTER$: L = LEN(S$)
 LINE(313-10*L/2-15,15)-(313+10*L/2+15,27),1,B
 PAINT(313,20),6,1
 COLOR 1,6: LOCATE 3: PRINT PTAB(313-10*L/2)S$
 LINE(135,35)-(495,130),2,B: PAINT(313,80),4,2
 COLOR 2,4
 FOR I=1 TO N
  IF I = PICK THEN INX = 2 ELSE INX = 1
  CALL DRAW.CIRCLE(I,INX)
  LOCATE I*2+4,21: PRINT TITLE.LONG$(I)
 NEXT
 LINE(263,141)-(360,153),2,B: PAINT(313,145),3,2
 COLOR 2,3
 LOCATE 17: PRINT PTAB(282)"Return"
 COLOR 1,0
 LOCATE 19,11: PRINT "Click Mouse on Choice,";
 PRINT " then Click on Return"
 GOSUB CHOOSE
RETURN

SUB DRAW.CIRCLE(R,INX) STATIC
 SHARED DISCS(),DISC.I()
 Y = 18*R+22
 PUT(162,Y),DISCS(DISC.I(INX)),PSET
END SUB

CHOOSE:
 GOSUB GURGLE
 GOSUB CLICKIT
 IF S$ = "" THEN GOSUB LOCATION
 IF ASC(S$+" ") <> 13 AND RTN$ = "OFF" THEN
  GOTO CHOOSE
 END IF
RETURN

GURGLE:
 FREQ = 300
 FOR G=1 TO 5
  FREQ = 500 - FREQ
  SOUND FREQ,1,50
 NEXT
RETURN
```

```
CLICKIT:
  S$ = ""
  WHILE MOUSE(Ø) = Ø AND S$ = ""
    S$ = INKEY$
  WEND
    X = MOUSE(1)
    Y = MOUSE(2)
  WHILE MOUSE(Ø)<> Ø: WEND: REM RESET
RETURN

LOCATION:
  IF X>263 AND X<360 AND Y>141 AND Y<153 THEN
    RTN$ = "ON"
  ELSE
    P = INT((Y-39)/18) + 1
    IF X>155 AND X<195 AND P>Ø AND P<= N THEN
      CALL DRAW.CIRCLE(PICK,1)
      CALL DRAW.CIRCLE(P,2)
      PICK = P
    END IF
  END IF
RETURN

REM PROGRAMS
  DATA Science and Math
  DATA Chemistry Basics, CHEMISTRY
  DATA Weather Forecasting, WEATHER
  DATA Simultaneous Equation Solver, SES
  DATA Matrix Manipulator (MatMan), MATMAN
```

Chemistry Basics

Radium is dangerously radioactive. It was discovered in 1898 by Marie and Pierre Curie, and weighs 1783.3 percent more than one carbon atom. Barium is used to coat the stomach for X-rays, gives fireworks a green color, and has a melting point of 714 degrees Celsius (1317 degrees Fahrenheit).

These are a few of the items that you'll have at your fingertips in "Chemistry Basics," a program that enables you to review and analyze a wealth of intriguing information on the earth's 103 elements.

An element, incidentally, is a unique building block in nature which can't, through chemical means, be reduced into a more basic substance. There are 88 natural elements and 15 artificial ones. Together they form compounds which make up all the objects on the earth, including the Amiga computer. Two-thirds of the human body, by the way, is the element oxygen.

Chemistry Basics is what computer scientists call a table-lookup program. It enables you to view a family of elements, view an element in detail, and sort the elements.

An example of the first option is a display of the six inert gases in Figure 6-1. If you'd like the details on an element, just click on a box when you run the program. And to view a different family, use one of the pull-down menus.

In the second option you can select an element by its symbol, number, or name. For example, *H*, *1*, and *Hydrogen* all represent the same element. Figure 6-2 is a closer look at hydrogen.

The third option lets you sort elements by atomic number, atomic weight, boiling point, melting point, density, and year of discovery. If you experiment with this function, you'll learn, among other things, that carbon possesses the highest known melting point of all the elements (3727 degrees Celsius).

Figure 6-1. The Inert Gases

HE	NE	AR	KR	XE	RN

When you run the program, click the mouse on one of the boxes and the Amiga will give you an "up close and personal" view of that element.

Figure 6-2. Facts About Hydrogen

UP CLOSE AND PERSONAL

Boiling Point :   −252.7 Celsius
Melting Point :   −259.2 Celsius
Density   : 0.071 Grams/Milliliter

(1)	HYDROGEN (H)
- Lightest element	
- The sun and stars are almost pure hydrogen	
- Discovered in 1766	
- One (H) atom weighs 91.6% less than one carbon atom	

Finally, you may want to make a game of Chemistry Basics. For example, try to recall which elements belong in a family, or which element is lightest or densest, or has the lowest boiling point. You'll probably find that Chemistry Basics is a lot more fun than staring at a dull table in a textbook.

Basic Chemistry Terms

Atom. From the Greek word *atoma* meaning indivisible. The smallest part of an element capable of existing alone. An atom consists of protons, neutrons, and electrons. The protons and neutrons dwell in a nucleus, and the electrons hover about.

Atomic number. The number of protons in the nucleus of an atom and the numeric value assigned to the corresponding element. An atom of tin, for example, contains 50 protons. Hence, the atomic number for tin is 50.

Atomic weight. The weight of an atom of an element relative to that of an atom of carbon, with the latter taken as 12.011. Hence, an aluminum atom with an atomic weight of 26.982 is slightly more than twice the weight of a carbon atom.

Density. The mass of a substance per unit of volume. In Chemistry Basics the density of an element is measured in grams per milliliter.

Element. A unique building block in nature which can't, through chemical means, be reduced into a more basic substance.

Chemistry Basics Database

Program 6-1A, "Chemistry Basics Database," creates a data file on disk called ELEMENTS for the Chemistry Basics program to run. If you're keying this data in from scratch, a good strategy is to take a break after every 20 or 30 elements you enter. This will cut down on mistakes. Be sure to save the program to disk before running it.

Run Program 6-1A first and only once. Then, whenever you want to use Chemistry Basics, just run Program 6-1B. You don't have to run Program 6-1A again.

Program 6-1A. Chemistry Basics Database
Save using the filename **CHEMISTRY.DATA**

```
REM CHEMISTRY DATA BASE
 GOSUB SETSCREEN
 GOSUB SETMENUS
 GOSUB INSTRUCTIONS
 GOSUB CREATE.FILE
 GOSUB GOODBYE
END

SETSCREEN:
 SCREEN 1,640,200,2,2
 WINDOW 2,"Chemistry Data Base",,0,1
RETURN

SETMENUS:
 FOR I=2 TO 4
  MENU I,0,0,""
 NEXT
 MENU 1,0,1,"STOP"
 MENU 1,1,1," Go to BASIC"
 MENU 1,2,1," Go to System"
 MENU ON
 ON MENU GOSUB GOODBYE
RETURN

GOODBYE:
 WINDOW CLOSE 2: WINDOW 1: MENU RESET
 SCREEN CLOSE 1
 ITEM = MENU(1)
 IF ITEM = 2 THEN SYSTEM
 CLS
 PRINT "Bye-Bye"
 STOP
RETURN

INSTRUCTIONS:
 CLS
 PRINT
 PRINT "   This program creates a data base";
 PRINT " for use in Chemistry"
 PRINT " Basics."
 PRINT
 PRINT "   You need to run this program only";
```

```
  PRINT " once."
  LOCATE 17,26: PRINT "Click Mouse"
  GOSUB CLICKIT
RETURN

CLICKIT:
 S$ = ""
 WHILE MOUSE(Ø) = Ø AND S$ = ""
  S$ = INKEY$
 WEND
  X = MOUSE(1)
  Y = MOUSE(2)
 WHILE MOUSE(Ø)<> Ø: WEND: REM RESET
RETURN

CREATE.FILE:
 DEFINT I,J,N
 N = 1Ø3
 DIM SYM$(N),NM$(N),X(N,5),CM$(N,2)
 GOSUB READ.DATA
 GOSUB SAVE.DATA
RETURN

READ.DATA:
 REM SYMBOL, NAME, ATOMIC WEIGHT, BOILING
 REM & MELTING POINTS, DENSITY, YEAR OF
 REM DISCOVERY, & TWO ONE-LINE COMMENTS
 CLS
 LOCATE 1Ø,24: PRINT "Reading data ..."
 FOR I=1 TO N
  READ SYM$(I),NM$(I)
  FOR J=1 TO 5
   READ X(I,J)
  NEXT J
  READ CM$(I,1),CM$(I,2)
 NEXT I
RETURN

SAVE.DATA:
 LOCATE 1Ø,24: PRINT " Saving data ..."
 FILE$ = "ELEMENTS"
 OPEN "O",#1,FILE$
 FOR I=1 TO N
  WRITE #1,SYM$(I),NM$(I)
  FOR J=1 TO 5
   WRITE #1,X(I,J)
  NEXT J
  WRITE #1,CM$(I,1),CM$(I,2)
 NEXT I
```

```
CLOSE
KILL FILE$ + ".info"
LOCATE 12,23: PRINT "Your file is saved."
LOCATE 19,26: PRINT "Click Mouse"
GOSUB CLICKIT
RETURN

REM ELEMENTS ( 9999 = unknown )
DATA H,Hydrogen,1.008,-252.7,-259.2,0.071,1766
DATA Lightest element
DATA The sun & stars are almost pure hydrogen
DATA He,Helium,4.0026,-268.9,-269.7,0.126,1868
DATA Lighter than air
DATA Used in blimps and ballons
DATA Li,Lithium,6.939,1330,108.5,0.53,1817
DATA From 'Lithos' or stone
DATA Used in treating gout and depression
DATA Be,Beryllium,9.0122,2770,1277,1.85,1798
DATA Note the high melting point
DATA Used in making rocket nose cones
DATA B,Boron,10.811,9999,2030,2.34,1808
DATA Serves as plant food and weed killer
DATA From Bor(ax) and (Carb)on
DATA C,Carbon,12.011,4830,3727,2.26,9999
DATA Used in endless products (like Nylon)
DATA Found in all organic substances
DATA N,Nitrogen,14.007,-195.8,-210,0.81,1772
DATA "Odorless, colorless, gaseous"
DATA Compounds include TNT and laughing gas
DATA O,Oxygen,15.999,-183,-218.8,1.14,1774
DATA The most abundant element
DATA Makes up 2/3 of the human body
DATA F,Fluorine,18.998,-188.2,-219.6,1.11,1771
DATA "Pale, greenish-yellow, pungent"
DATA It corrodes even tough platinum
DATA Ne,Neon,20.183,-246,-248.6,1.2,1898
DATA Famous in electrical display signs
DATA Gives off orange-red light
DATA Na,Sodium,22.990,892,97.8,0.97,1807
DATA Silver-white and highly reactive
DATA Useful compounds include table salt
DATA Mg,Magnesium,24.312,1107,650,1.74,1775
DATA From Magnesia in ancient Asia Minor
DATA Used as a powder in firecrackers
DATA Al,Aluminum,26.982,2450,660,2.7,1827
DATA The earth's most abundant metal
DATA Widely used in alloys
DATA Si,Silicon,28.086,2680,1410,2.33,1823
DATA The second most abundant element
```

```
DATA Makes up 1/4 of the earth's crust
DATA P,Phosphorus,30.974,280,44.2,1.82,1669
DATA Glows in the dark
DATA Is highly flammable
DATA S,Sulfur,32.064,444.6,119,2.07,9999
DATA Pale yellow and nonmetallic
DATA Used in matches and gunpowder
DATA Cl,Chlorine,35.453,-34.7,-101,1.56,1774
DATA A greenish-yellow poison
DATA Used as a bleach and disinfectant
DATA Ar,Argon,39.948,-185.8,-189.4,1.4,1894
DATA Most abundant of the Noble Gases
DATA Used in incandescent lamps
DATA K,Potassium,39.102,760,63.7,0.86,1807
DATA 7th most abundant element
DATA Yields many valuable compounds
DATA Ca,Calcium,40.08,1440,838,1.55,1808
DATA Vital to healthy teeth and bones
DATA Found with chalk and limestone
DATA Sc,Scandium,44.956,2730,1539,3,1879
DATA From Scandinavia
DATA Of little practical use
DATA Ti,Titanium,47.9,3260,1668,4.51,1791
DATA Lightweight yet strong
DATA Used in jet aircraft
DATA V,Vanadium,50.942,3450,1900,6.1,1830
DATA Very tough when added to steel
DATA Used in axles and piston rods
DATA Cr,Chromium,51.996,2665,1875,7.19,1797
DATA Forms tough alloys
DATA Chrome plate on cars
DATA Mn,Manganese,54.938,2150,1245,7.43,1774
DATA Adds toughness to bones
DATA Helps harden steel
DATA Fe,Iron,55.847,3000,1536.7,7.86,9999
DATA From the Old English 'Iren'
DATA Used by early man
DATA Co,Cobalt,58.933,2900,1495,8.9,1735
DATA From 'Kobold' or evil spirit
DATA Alloys used in jet engines
DATA Ni,Nickel,58.71,2730,1453,8.9,1751
DATA Hard and durable
DATA Used in coins and plating
DATA Cu,Copper,63.54,2595,1083,8.96,9999
DATA Great conductor of heat & electricity
DATA Also used in the arts
DATA Zn,Zinc,65.37,906,419.5,7.14,9999
DATA Excellent coating metal
DATA Used in batteries
```

```
DATA Ga,Gallium,69.72,2237,29.8,5.91,1875
DATA Melts in the hand (86 F.)
DATA Expands as it freezes
DATA Ge,Germanium,72.59,2830,937.4,5.32,1886
DATA Named for Germany
DATA First element used for transistors
DATA As,Arsenic,74.922,613,817,5.72,1250
DATA Famed as poison
DATA But also used in medicine
DATA Se,Selenium,78.96,685,217,4.79,1817
DATA Its electrical resist. varies with light
DATA Used in TV cameras
DATA Br,Bromine,79.909,58,-7.2,3.12,1826
DATA Reddish brown with a foul smell
DATA From 'bromos' or stench
DATA Kr,Krypton,83.8,-152,-157.3,2.6,1898
DATA A by-product of nuclear reactors
DATA Helps us track Soviet atomic production
DATA Rb,Rubidium,85.47,688,38.9,1.53,1861
DATA Slightly radioactive
DATA Used to locate brain tumors
DATA Sr,Strontium,87.62,1380,768,2.6,1790
DATA Present in atomic fallout
DATA Destroys bone marrow
DATA Y,Yttrium,88.905,2927,1509,4.47,1794
DATA From Ytterby in Sweden
DATA Used in surgical needles
DATA Zr,Zirconium,91.22,3580,1852,6.49,1780
DATA Unaffected by neutrons
DATA Used as inner lining for nuclear reactors
DATA Nb,Niobium,92.906,3300,2415,8.4,1801
DATA From 'Niobe' of Greek myth
DATA Used in jet engines and rockets
DATA Mo,Molybdenum,95.94,5560,2610,10.2,1778
DATA The world's 5th highest-melting metal
DATA Used in rifle barrels
DATA Tc,Technetium,99,9999,2200,11.5,1937
DATA The first man-made element
DATA A fission product of uranium
DATA Ru,Ruthenium,101.07,4900,2500,12.2,1844
DATA From the Latin 'Ruthenia' for Russia
DATA A first-class hardener
DATA Rh,Rhodium,102.905,4500,1966,12.4,1803
DATA From 'rhodon' or rose
DATA Used in electroplating
DATA Pd,Palladium,106.4,3980,1552,12,1803
DATA Corrosion resistant
DATA Used in surgical instruments
DATA Ag,Silver,107.87,2210,960.8,10.5,9999
```

```
DATA From the Old English 'seolfor'
DATA Best conductor of heat & electricity
DATA Cd,Cadmium,112.4,765,320.9,8.65,1817
DATA Found in zinc ores
DATA Used to control atomic fission
DATA In,Indium,114.82,2000,156.2,7.31,1863
DATA Rare
DATA Soft and malleable
DATA Sn,Tin,118.69,2270,231.9,7.3,9999
DATA Does not rust or corrode
DATA Used to coat cans
DATA Sb,Antimony,121.75,1380,630.5,6.62,1450
DATA "Silver-white, hard, crystalline"
DATA Used in chemistry and in the arts
DATA Te,Tellurium,127.6,989.8,449.5,6.24,1782
DATA From 'tellus' or earth
DATA Its vapor smacks of garlic
DATA I,Iodine,126.9,183,113.7,4.94,1811
DATA Famous as an antiseptic
DATA Supplements the human diet
DATA Xe,Xenon,131.3,-108,-111.9,3.06,1898
DATA Rarest gas in the atmosphere
DATA Produces an intense light
DATA Cs,Cesium,132.905,690,28.7,1.9,1860
DATA The world's softest metal
DATA Liquid at room temperature
DATA Ba,Barium,137.34,1640,714,3.5,1808
DATA Used to coat the stomach for X-rays
DATA Gives fireworks a green color
DATA La,Lanthanum,138.91,3470,920,6.17,1839
DATA Dark lead-gray
DATA Used in high-priced camera lenses
DATA Ce,Cerium,140.12,3468,795,6.67,1803
DATA The most abundant of the rare-earths
DATA Used in alloys for jet-engine parts
DATA Pr,Praseodymium,140.91,3127,935,6.77
DATA 1885
DATA Yellowish white
DATA Used in goggles for glass blowing
DATA Nd,Neodymium,144.24,3027,1024,7,1885
DATA Forms the only bright-purple glass known
DATA Used to take the color out of glass
DATA Pm,Promethium,147,9999,1027,9999,1947
DATA Used in atomic batteries
DATA Named for Prometheus
DATA Sm,Samarium,150.35,1900,1072,7.54,1879
DATA "Hard, brittle, yellowish gray"
DATA Used in lasers
DATA Eu,Europium,151.96,1439,826,5.26,1896
```

```
DATA The most reactive of the rare earths
DATA Used in atomic-reactor control rods
DATA Gd,Gadolinium,157.25,3000,1312,7.89,1880
DATA Named for John Gadolin- chemist
DATA Divides lightweight rare earths from heavy
DATA Tb,Terbium,158.92,2800,1356,8.27,1843
DATA From Ytterby in Sweden
DATA Bursts into flame when heated
DATA Dy,Dysprosium,162.5,2600,1407,8.54,1886
DATA Highly magnetic
DATA Used to 'eat' neutrons
DATA Ho,Holmium,164.93,2600,1461,8.80,1879
DATA Latinized name of Stockholm
DATA Used to absorb neutrons
DATA Er,Erbium,167.26,2900,1497,9.05,1843
DATA From Ytterby in Sweden
DATA Used for pink glaze in ceramics
DATA Tm,Thulium,168.93,1727,1545,9.33,1879
DATA From 'Thule' or Northland
DATA Gives off X-rays
DATA Yb,Ytterbium,173.04,1427,824,6.98,1907
DATA From Ytterby in Sweden
DATA "Rare, and of little practical use"
DATA Lu,Lutetium,174.97,3327,1652,9.84,1907
DATA Heaviest of the rare earths
DATA "Expensive, and of no practical use"
DATA Hf,Hafnium,178.49,5400,2222,13.1,1923
DATA Wonder metal of the atomic age
DATA Absorbs neutrons
DATA Ta,Tantalum,180.948,5425,2996,16.6,1802
DATA Almost immune to corrosion
DATA Vital in human surgery
DATA W,Tungsten,183.85,5930,3410,19.3,1783
DATA Highest melting of metals
DATA Used in high-speed drills
DATA Re,Rhenium,186.2,5900,3180,21,1925
DATA Has second-highest melting point
DATA Used in electrical contact points
DATA Os,Osmium,190.2,5500,2700,22.6,1804
DATA World's densest metal
DATA Used to produce very hard alloys
DATA Ir,Iridium,192.2,5300,2454,22.5,1804
DATA A very hard metal
DATA Used in standard weights/measures
DATA Pt,Platinum,195.09,4530,1769,21.4,9999
DATA From platina or 'little silver'
DATA Used in jewelry
DATA Au,Gold,196.97,2970,1063,19.3,9999
DATA The most malleable metal
```

```
DATA Costs hundreds of dollars per ounce
DATA Hg,Mercury,200.59,357,-38.4,13.6,9999
DATA Used in thermometers
DATA Liquid at ordinary temperatures
DATA Tl,Thallium,204.37,1457,303,11.85,1861
DATA Odorless and tasteless
DATA Its salts are used in rat poison
DATA Pb,Lead,207.19,1725,327.4,11.4,9999
DATA Very durable
DATA Used by Romans for plumbing
DATA Bi,Bismuth,208.98,1560,271.3,9.8,9999
DATA Lustrous and reddish white
DATA Used in medicine and makeup
DATA Po,Polonium,210,9999,254,9.2,1898
DATA Named for Poland
DATA The scarcest natural element
DATA At,Astatine,210,9999,302,9999,1940
DATA Radioactive
DATA Maximum half life is 8 hours
DATA Rn,Radon,222,-61.8,-71,9999,1900
DATA The heaviest gaseous element
DATA Used in cancer therapy
DATA Fr,Francium,223,9999,27,9999,1939
DATA For France
DATA Discovered by one of Marie Curie's helpers
DATA Ra,Radium,226,9999,700,5,1898
DATA Dangerously radioactive
DATA Found by Pierre and Marie Curie
DATA Ac,Actinium,227,9999,1050,9999,1899
DATA The second rarest element
DATA Found in pitchblende
DATA Th,Thorium,232.04,3850,1750,11.7,1828
DATA From the war god 'Thor'
DATA Used to generate atomic energy
DATA Pa,Protactinum,231,9999,1230,15.4,1917
DATA The third rarest element
DATA Radioactive and metallic
DATA U,Uranium,238.03,3818,1132,19.07,1789
DATA Named after the planet Uranus
DATA Used to generate atomic energy
DATA Np,Neptunium,237,9999,637,19.5,1940
DATA Named after the planet Neptune
DATA Artificially produced from uranium
DATA Pu,Plutonium,242,3235,640,9999,1940
DATA Named after the planet Pluto
DATA Used in the first atomic bombs
DATA Am,Americium,243,9999,9999,11.7,1944
DATA Unstable and radioactive
DATA Produced by bombarding plutonium
```

```
DATA Cm,Curium,247,9999,9999,9999,1944
DATA Named for Pierre and Marie Curie
DATA A decay product of americium
DATA Bk,Berkelium,247,9999,9999,9999,1949
DATA Named after Berkeley Calif.
DATA Unstable and radioactive
DATA Cf,Californium,249,9999,9999,9999,1950
DATA Named for the state
DATA Produced by bombarding curium
DATA Es,Einsteinium,254,9999,9999,9999,1952
DATA Named for Albert Einstein
DATA Found in 1952 H-bomb test debris
DATA Fm,Fermium,253,9999,9999,9999,1953
DATA Named for Enrico Fermi
DATA Produced by bombarding Einsteinium
DATA Md,Mendelevium,256,9999,9999,9999,1955
DATA Named after inventor of the Periodic Table
DATA Short-lived and radioactive
DATA No,Nobelium,254,9999,9999,9999,1957
DATA Named for Alfred Noble
DATA Unstable and radioactive
DATA Lw,Lawrencium,257,9999,9999,9999,1961
DATA Named for the U.S. physicist
DATA Latest of the artificial elements
```

Program 6-1B. Chemistry Basics
Save using the filename **CHEMISTRY**

```
REM CHEMISTRY BASICS
 CLEAR ,32000
 GOSUB INITIALIZE
 GOSUB MAIN.MENU
END

INITIALIZE:
 GOSUB SETSCREEN
 GOSUB KEYVALUES
 GOSUB SETMENUS
 GOSUB SETCOLORS
 GOSUB SHAPES
 GOSUB HEADING
 GOSUB GREETING
 GOSUB READ.DATA
RETURN

SETSCREEN:
 SCREEN 1,640,200,3,2
```

```
  WINDOW 2,"Chemistry Basics",,0,1
RETURN

KEYVALUES:
 RANDOMIZE TIMER
 DEFINT I-Z: DEFSNG K,S,X
 N = 103: M = 10
 DIM SYM$(N),NM$(N),X(N,5),CM$(N,2),NF(M)
 DIM FE(M,15),R(M),C(M),SV(N),DISCS(250)
 REM SHAPE INDICES
  DISC.I(1) = 1: DISC.I(2) = 125
 GOSUB MENU.CHOICES
 GOSUB FAMILY.NAMES
 GOSUB FAMILY.ELEMENT.NUMBERS
 GOSUB BOX.COORDINATES
 GOSUB FORMATS
RETURN

MENU.CHOICES:
 REM MAIN MENU
  DATA View a family of elements
  DATA View an element in detail
  DATA Sort the elements
 REM ELEMENT SELECTION
  DATA By its atomic number
  DATA By its symbol { letter(s) }
  DATA By its full name
  FOR I=1 TO 2
   FOR J=1 TO 3
    READ PICK$(I,J)
  NEXT J,I
 REM SORT BY
  DATA Atomic Number, Atomic Weight
  DATA Boiling Point, Melting Point, Density
  DATA Year Discovered
  FOR I=1 TO 6
   READ SORT$(I)
  NEXT
RETURN

FAMILY.NAMES:
 DATA Alkali & Alkaline Earths
 DATA First Transition Metals, The Triads
 DATA Third Transition Metals
 DATA Boron & Carbon Families
 DATA Nitrogen & Oxygen Families
 DATA Hydrogen & the Halogens, The Inert Gases
 DATA The Rare Earths, Actinide Metals
 FOR I=1 TO M
```

```
    READ FM$(I)
  NEXT
  REM ROW & COLUMNS IN EACH FAMILY
    DATA 2,6,2,7,3,3,2,3,2,5,2,5,1,6,1,6,3,5,3,5
    FOR I=1 TO M
      READ R(I),C(I)
      NF(I) = R(I)*C(I)
    NEXT
RETURN

FAMILY.ELEMENT.NUMBERS:
  DATA 3,11,19,37,55,87,4,12,20,38,56,88
  DATA 21,22,23,24,25,39,40,41,42,43,72,73,74,75
  DATA 26,44,76,27,45,77,28,46,78
  DATA 29,47,79,30,48,80
  DATA 5,13,31,49,81,6,14,32,50,82
  DATA 7,15,33,51,83,8,16,34,52,84
  DATA 1,9,17,35,53,85
  DATA 2,10,18,36,54,86
  DATA 57,58,59,60,61,62,63,64,65,66,67,68,69
  DATA 70,71
  DATA 89,90,91,92,93,94,95,96,97,98,99,100
  DATA 101,102,103
  FOR I=1 TO M
    FOR J=1 TO NF(I)
      READ FE(I,J)
  NEXT J,I
RETURN

BOX.COORDINATES:
  REM X
    DATA 164,284,404,0,0,0,0
    DATA 104,194,284,374,464,0,0
    DATA 84,164,244,324,404,484,0
    DATA 54,134,214,294,374,454,534
    FOR J=1 TO 7: READ X.C(3,J): NEXT
    FOR I=5 TO 7
      FOR J=1 TO 7
        READ X.C(I,J)
    NEXT J,I
  REM Y
    DATA 73,0,0
    DATA 46,91,0
    DATA 37,73,109
    FOR I=1 TO 3
      FOR J=1 TO 3
        READ Y.C(I,J)
    NEXT J,I
RETURN
```

```
FORMATS:
 REM CARD
  DATA "Boiling Point :","Melting Point :"
  DATA "Density         :"
  FOR I=1 TO 3
   READ ITEM$(I)
  NEXT
  F.CARD$(1) = "####.# Celsius"
  F.CARD$(2) = F.CARD$(1)
  F.CARD$(3) = "####.# Grams/Milliliter"
 REM SORT
  F.SORT$(1) = SPACE$(4) + "###"
  F.SORT$(2) = SPACE$(2) + "###.###"
  F.SORT$(3) = "#####.# C."
  F.SORT$(4) = "#####.# C."
  F.SORT$(5) = "#####.# g/ml"
  F.SORT$(6) = SPACE$(3) + "####"
RETURN

SETMENUS:
 DATA 5, Color, Tan, Blue, Green, Gray, Random
 DATA 1, Family, Alkali & Alkaline Earths
 DATA 1, Sort, By Atomic Number
 DATA 3, Stop, Go to BASIC
 DATA Go to Science Menu, Go to System
 FOR I=1 TO 4
  READ NUMBER
  FOR J=0 TO NUMBER
   READ TITLE$
   IF J<>0 THEN TITLE$ = SPACE$(3) + TITLE$
    STATUS = 1
    IF I <> 4 AND J = 1 THEN STATUS = 2
   MENU I,J,STATUS,TITLE$
 NEXT J,I
 REM MENU 2
  FOR J=2 TO M
   MENU 2,J,1,SPACE$(3) + FM$(J)
  NEXT
 REM MENU 3
  FOR J=2 TO 6
   MENU 3,J,1,SPACE$(3) + "By " + SORT$(J)
  NEXT
  KOLOR% = 1: FAMILY = 1: SORT% = 1
RETURN

SETCOLORS:
 REM TAN, BLUE, GREEN, GRAY
  DATA .95,.7,.53, .36,.57,1
  DATA .22,.76,.68, .72,.7,.86
```

```
   FOR I=1 TO 4
    FOR J=1 TO 3
      READ KOLOR(I,J)
   NEXT J,I
  REM TAN, GREEN, & RED
   PALETTE 4,.95,.7,.53
   PALETTE 5,.14,.43,0
   PALETTE 6,.93,.2,0
 RETURN

 SHAPES:
  X=313: Y=80
  LINE(X-12,Y-8)-(X+12,Y+8),4,BF
  FOR I=1 TO 2
   K% = 7-I
   CIRCLE(X,Y),12,K%: PAINT(X,Y),K%
   GET(X-12,Y-8)-(X+12,Y+8),DISCS(DISC.I(I))
  NEXT
 RETURN

 HEADING:
  MENU ON
  ON MENU GOSUB OPTIONS
  CLS
  LOCATE 9,24: PRINT "Chemistry Basics"
  COLOR 3,0: LOCATE 14,30: PRINT "then"
  COLOR 1,0
  LOCATE 13,24: PRINT "Please use menus,"
  LOCATE 15,22: PRINT "Click mouse to start"
  GOSUB CLICKIT
 RETURN

 OPTIONS:
  ID = MENU(0): ITEM = MENU(1)
  ON ID GOSUB MENU1,MENU2,MENU3,GOODBYE
  ITEM = 0
 RETURN

 MENU1:
  K1 = KOLOR(ITEM,1): K2 = KOLOR(ITEM,2)
  K3 = KOLOR(ITEM,3)
  IF ITEM = 5 THEN K1=RND: K2=RND: K3=RND
  PALETTE 4,K1,K2,K3
  MENU 1,KOLOR%,1: MENU 1,ITEM,2
  KOLOR% = ITEM
 RETURN

 MENU2:
  MENU 2,FAMILY,1: MENU 2,ITEM,2
```

```
  FAMILY = ITEM
RETURN

MENU3:
 MENU 3,SORT%,1: MENU 3,ITEM,2
 SORT% = ITEM
RETURN

GOODBYE:
 WINDOW CLOSE 2: WINDOW 1: MENU RESET
 SCREEN CLOSE 1
 IF ITEM = 2 THEN RUN "SCIENCE"
 IF ITEM = 3 THEN SYSTEM
 COLOR 1,0: CLS
 PRINT "Bye-Bye"
 STOP
RETURN

GREETING:
 CLS
 PRINT
 PRINT "    This program enables you to review";
 PRINT " and analyze a wealth"
 PRINT " of intriguing information on the";
 PRINT " earth's 103 basic"
 PRINT " elements."
 LOCATE 18,27: PRINT "Click Mouse";
 GOSUB CLICKIT
RETURN

CLICKIT:
 S$ = ""
 WHILE MOUSE(0) = 0 AND S$ = ""
  S$ = INKEY$
 WEND
  X = MOUSE(1)
  Y = MOUSE(2)
 WHILE MOUSE(0)<> 0: WEND: REM RESET
RETURN

READ.DATA:
 CLS
 LOCATE 10,26: PRINT "Reading data"
 OPEN "I",#1,"ELEMENTS"
 FOR I=1 TO N
  INPUT #1,SYM$(I),NM$(I)
  FOR J=1 TO 5
   INPUT #1,X(I,J)
  NEXT J
```

```
    INPUT #1,CM$(I,1),CM$(I,2)
  NEXT I
  CLOSE
RETURN

MAIN.MENU:
  CLS
  LOCATE 3,23: PRINT "Would you like to"
  Z = 1
  GOSUB SHOW.CHOICES
  GOSUB CHOOSE
  ON PICK GOSUB VIEW.FAMILY,VIEW.ELEMENT,SORT
  GOTO MAIN.MENU
RETURN

SHOW.CHOICES:
  PICK = 1: RTN$ = "OFF"
  LINE(135,35)-(495,120),2,B: PAINT(313,80),4,2
  COLOR 2,4
  FOR I=1 TO 3
    IF I = PICK THEN INX = 2 ELSE INX = 1
    CALL DRAW.CIRCLE(I,INX)
    LOCATE I*2+5,21: PRINT PICK$(Z,I)
  NEXT
  LINE(263,141)-(360,153),2,B: PAINT(313,145),3,2
  COLOR 2,3
  LOCATE 17: PRINT PTAB(282)"Return"
  COLOR 1,0
  LOCATE 19,11: PRINT "Click Mouse on Choice,";
  PRINT " then Click on Return"
RETURN

SUB DRAW.CIRCLE(R,INX) STATIC
  SHARED DISCS(),DISC.I()
  Y = 18*R+31
  PUT(162,Y),DISCS(DISC.I(INX)),PSET
END SUB

CHOOSE:
  GOSUB GURGLE
  GOSUB CLICKIT
  IF S$ = "" THEN GOSUB LOCATION
  IF ASC(S$+" ") <> 13 AND RTN$ = "OFF" THEN
    GOTO CHOOSE
  END IF
RETURN

GURGLE:
  FREQ = 300
```

```
  FOR G=1 TO 5
    FREQ = 500-FREQ
    SOUND FREQ,1,50
  NEXT G
RETURN

LOCATION:
  IF X>263 AND X<360 AND Y>141 AND Y<153 THEN
    RTN$ = "ON"
  ELSE
    P = INT((Y-48)/18) + 1
    IF X>155 AND X<195 AND P>0 AND P<4 THEN
      CALL DRAW.CIRCLE(PICK,1)
      CALL DRAW.CIRCLE(P,2)
      PICK = P
    END IF
  END IF
RETURN

VIEW.FAMILY:
  MENU 2,0,0
  RTN$ = "OFF"
  WHILE RTN$ = "OFF"
    GOSUB DISPLAY
    GOSUB SELECT
    IF BOX$ = "ON" THEN
      V = FE(FAMILY,ELEMENT)
      GOSUB SHOW.ELEMENT
    END IF
  WEND
  MENU 2,0,1
RETURN

DISPLAY:
  COLOR 1,0
  CLS
  S$ = FM$(FAMILY): GOSUB PAINT.NAME
  RW = R(FAMILY): CL = C(FAMILY): E = 0
  FOR I=1 TO RW
    FOR J=1 TO CL
      E = E + 1
      ELEMENT = FE(FAMILY,E)
      GOSUB DRAW.BOX
  NEXT J,I
  LINE(263,150)-(360,162),2,B: PAINT(313,155),3,2
  COLOR 2,3
  LOCATE 18: PRINT PTAB(282)"Return"
  COLOR 1,0
  LOCATE 20,22: PRINT "Click Mouse on Choice";
RETURN
```

```
PAINT.NAME:
 L = LEN(S$)
 LINE(313-10*L/2-15,15)-(313+10*L/2+15,27),1,B
 PAINT(313,20),6,1
 COLOR 1,6: LOCATE 3: PRINT PTAB(313-10*L/2)S$
RETURN

DRAW.BOX:
 X = X.C(CL,J): Y = Y.C(RW,I)
 LINE(X,Y)-(X+52,Y+22),6,B
 PAINT(X+25,Y+11),4,6
 R = (Y+17)/9: C = (X+26)/10
 COLOR 2,4
 LOCATE R,C: PRINT SYM$(ELEMENT)
RETURN

SELECT:
 BOX$ = "OFF"
 GOSUB GURGLE
 GOSUB CLICKIT
 IF ASC(S$+" ") = 13 THEN RTN$ = "ON"
 IF S$ = "" THEN
  GOSUB FIND.BOX
  IF BOX$ = "OFF" AND RTN$ = "OFF" THEN SELECT
 END IF
RETURN

FIND.BOX:
 IF X>263 AND X<360 AND Y>150 AND Y<162 THEN
  RTN$ = "ON"
 ELSE
  FOR I=1 TO RW
   FOR J=1 TO CL
    X1 = X.C(CL,J): X2 = X1 + 53
    Y1 = Y.C(RW,I): Y2 = Y1 + 23
    IF X>X1 AND X<X2 AND Y>Y1 AND Y<Y2 THEN
     BOX$ = "ON"
     ELEMENT = (I-1)*CL + J
     J = CL: I = RW
    END IF
   NEXT J,I
 END IF
RETURN

SHOW.ELEMENT:
 CLS
 GOSUB TOP.ITEMS
 GOSUB ELEMENT.NAME
 GOSUB CARD
```

```
 GOSUB CARD.LINES
RETURN

TOP.ITEMS:
 COLOR 1,0
 FOR I=1 TO 3
  LOCATE I+1,6: PRINT ITEM$(I);CHR$(32);
  IF X(V,I+1) <> 9999 THEN
   PRINT USING F.CARD$(I);X(V,I+1)
  ELSE
   PRINT "Unknown"
  END IF
 NEXT
RETURN

ELEMENT.NAME:
 S$ = NM$(V): L = LEN(S$)
 LINE(385-10*L/2-15,51)-(385+10*L/2+15,63),1,B
 PAINT(400,56),6,1
 COLOR 1,6: LOCATE 7: PRINT PTAB(385-10*L/2)S$
RETURN

CARD:
 COLOR 2
 PSET(213,47)
 LINE -STEP(-160,0): LINE -STEP(0,93)
 LINE -STEP(520,0) : LINE -STEP(0,-74)
 LINE -STEP(-360,0): LINE -STEP(0,-19)
 PAINT(313,100),4,2
RETURN

CARD.LINES:
 LINE(73,51)-(193,63),2,B
 PAINT(100,56),5,2
 COLOR 1,5
 S$ = " <" + MID$(STR$(V),2) + ">"
 LOCATE 7,11: PRINT SYM$(V);S$
 COLOR 2,4
 REM COMMENTS
 FOR I=1 TO 2
   LOCATE I*2+7,8: PRINT CM$(V,I)
 NEXT
 REM YEAR OF DISCOVERY
  S$ = "Year of discovery is unknown"
  IF X(V,5) <> 9999 THEN
   S$ = "Discovered in" + STR$(X(V,5))
  END IF
  LOCATE 13,8: PRINT S$
 REM WEIGHT
```

```
    IF X(V,1)<>9999 AND V<>6 THEN GOSUB WEIGHT
   REM CONTINUE
    COLOR 1,Ø
    LOCATE 2Ø,26: PRINT "Click Mouse";
    GOSUB CLICKIT
RETURN

WEIGHT:
 K = (X(V,1)-12)*1ØØ/12
 K = INT(K*1Ø+.5)/1Ø
 S$ = "1 " + SYM$(V) + " atom weighs"
 S$ = S$ + STR$(ABS(K)) + "% "
 A$ = "less": IF K > Ø THEN A$ = "more"
 S$ = S$ + A$ + " than 1 carbon atom"
 LOCATE 15,8: PRINT S$
RETURN

VIEW.ELEMENT:
 GOSUB METHOD.OF.SELECTION
 IF V > Ø AND V <= N THEN
  GOSUB SHOW.ELEMENT
 ELSE
  GOSUB GOOF
  GOTO VIEW.ELEMENT
 END IF
RETURN

METHOD.OF.SELECTION:
 CLS
 V = Ø
 LOCATE 3,17
 PRINT "Method of selecting an element"
 Z = 2
 GOSUB SHOW.CHOICES
 GOSUB CHOOSE
 GOSUB ENTER.ELEMENT
RETURN

ENTER.ELEMENT:
 LINE(263,141)-(36Ø,153),Ø,BF
 LOCATE 19,11: PRINT SPACE$(43)
 GOSUB GURGLE
 LOCATE 16,15: INPUT "Element = ";E$
 E$ = UCASE$(E$)
 REM FIND NUMBER
 V = VAL(E$)
 ON PICK - 1 GOSUB SYMBOL,FULL.NAME
RETURN
```

```
SYMBOL:
 FOR I=1 TO N
   IF E$ = UCASE$(SYM$(I)) THEN V = I: I = N
 NEXT
RETURN

FULL.NAME:
 FOR I=1 TO N
   IF E$ = UCASE$(NM$(I)) THEN V = I: I = N
 NEXT
RETURN

GOOF:
 SOUND 400,3: SOUND 300,3: SOUND 200,3
 LINE(136,151)-(195,161),6,BF
 COLOR 1,6: LOCATE 18,15: PRINT "Sorry"
 COLOR 1,0
 LOCATE 18,22: PRINT "There's no such element !"
 LOCATE 20,26: PRINT "Press any key";
 GOSUB CLICKIT
RETURN

SORT:
 MENU 3,0,0
 GOSUB REARRANGE
 REM DISPLAY
  F$ = F.SORT$(SORT%)
  FOR I=1 TO N STEP 10
    GOSUB TITLE
    GOSUB BODY
  NEXT I
 MENU 3,0,1
RETURN

REARRANGE:
 CLS
 LOCATE 10,29: PRINT "Sorting"
 Q = SORT% - 1
 FOR I=1 TO N
  X(I,0) = I
  SV(I) = X(I,Q)
 NEXT
 SWITCH$ = "ON"
 WHILE SWITCH$ = "ON"
  SWITCH$ = "OFF"
  FOR I = 1 TO N-1
    IF SV(I) > SV(I+1) THEN
      SWAP SV(I),SV(I+1)
      SWAP X(I,0),X(I+1,0)
```

```
      SWITCH$ = "ON"
    END IF
  NEXT
 WEND
RETURN

TITLE:
 CLS
 S$ = "Elements by " + SORT$(Q+1)
 GOSUB PAINT.NAME
 LINE(60,38)-(570,157),2,B: PAINT(313,100),4,2
 COLOR 2,4
 LOCATE 6,14: PRINT "Symbol"
 LOCATE 6,28: PRINT "Name"
 L = LEN(SORT$(Q+1))
 LOCATE 6,52-L: PRINT SORT$(Q+1)
RETURN

BODY:
 ROW = 8
 FOR J = I TO I+9
  IF J <= N THEN
   E = X(J,0)
   LOCATE ROW,16: PRINT SYM$(E)
   LOCATE ROW,27: PRINT NM$(E)
   X = SV(J)
   IF X = 9999 THEN
    LOCATE ROW,43: PRINT "Unknown"
   ELSE
    LOCATE ROW,40: PRINT USING F$;X
   END IF
   ROW = ROW + 1
  END IF
 NEXT J
 COLOR 1,0
 LOCATE 20,26: PRINT "Click Mouse";
 GOSUB CLICKIT
RETURN
```

Weather Forecasting

It's easy to look at a threatening sky and predict that it will rain. But it's not always that easy to tell what the weather will be tomorrow or even later that same day. The National Weather Service has been trying for years, and still, it's impossible to predict with 100 percent accuracy what the weather will be.

You don't have the facilities and huge computers of the National Weather Service, but you do have a computer that you can use to help forecast the weather.

The underlying principle of all weather-prediction computer models, which use hundreds of observations and scores of intricate equations, is simple. If we know what the current weather is and can correlate it with some past experience, then we can use our knowledge of what was to foretell what may be.

This program uses the same idea, but on a much smaller scale. The National Weather Service uses a network of reporting stations and satellites to gather its information. Since you don't have access to these, the best device available to you is a barometer. Barometric pressure along with the wind direction will allow you to make a fairly accurate local forecast.

You can buy an inexpensive barometer at most hardware stores, and a simple wind vane is easy to make. If you don't want to go to this trouble and expense, you can get the same information from the weather report on TV or from your local NOAA Weather Radio Station.

Making Forecasts

To forecast the weather, you'll need to know the current wind direction, the barometric pressure, and whether the barometer is rising or falling. Enter the wind direction by clicking the mouse on one of the points of the weather vane that the Amiga draws on the screen. Then enter barometric pressure using the keyboard, and enter barometric trend with the mouse. For winds out of the south, with barometric pressure 29.7 inches and falling fast, you'll receive this forecast:

Severe storm warning: Windy, with rain in summer and snow in winter.

Local Conditions

The program will work fine as is. But you may want to fine-tune it to reflect weather conditions in your area. This information does not change the operation of the program, but it will change the forecasts.

First, look at the DATA statements near the end of the program under the title MONTHLY WEATHER NORMS. The first three numbers for each month are temperatures in degrees Fahrenheit: the normal high, low, and average for the month. The last two numbers are normal monthly rainfall and snowfall in inches.

Contact a local TV station, newspaper, or National Weather Service reporting station to get the values for your area. Or write NOAA, National Environmental Satellite, Data, and Information Service, National Climatic Data Center, Federal Building, Asheville, NC 28801, and request a copy of the "Local Climatological Data Annual Summary" for your area. Almanacs sometimes include this information as well. *The Weather Almanac*, edited by James A. Ruffner and Frank E. Blair (Avon Books), is available in most libraries.

Changes in barometric pressure and wind direction can imply different forecasts for different parts of the country. See the following technical note if you want to fine-tune the program even more to fit your area.

Technical Note

The subroutine PREDICT does the forecasting, with three variables used:

B = Barometric pressure
W = Wind direction
T = Barometric trend

Barometric trend, in turn, takes on any one of five values:

1 = Steady
2 = Rising slowly
3 = Rising rapidly
4 = Falling slowly
5 = Falling rapidly

The forecasts that appear on the screen are in the DATA statements at the very end of the program. The figure preceding each forecast (1 or 2) represents the number of lines on the screen that the prediction will use. The array variables F.PART1$(i) and F.PART2$(i) store the forecasts.

There are 18 predictions in all, numbered 0 to 17. The variable P in the PREDICT subroutine matches the corresponding prediction in the group of DATA statements. You'll have to do some research at the local library or contact the National Weather Service if you want to modify these forecasts.

Program 6-2. Weather Forecasting
Save using the filename **WEATHER**

```
REM WEATHER FORECASTER
 GOSUB INITIALIZE
 GOSUB MAIN.MENU
END

INITIALIZE:
 GOSUB SETSCREEN
 GOSUB KEYVALUES
 GOSUB SETMENUS
 GOSUB SETCOLORS
 GOSUB READ.DATA
 GOSUB SHAPES
 GOSUB HEADING
 GOSUB GREETING
RETURN

SETSCREEN:
 SCREEN 1,640,200,3,2
 WINDOW 2,"Weather Forecaster",,0,1
RETURN

KEYVALUES:
 RANDOMIZE TIMER
 DEFINT I-Z: DEFSNG B,K,M
 REM NUMBER OF FORECASTS
  DATA 17
  READ N
  DIM MONTH$(12),MW(12,5)
  DIM F.PART1$(N),F.PART2$(N)
 REM SHAPE INDICES
  DIM DISCS(250)
  DISC.I(1) = 1: DISC.I(2) = 125
 REM MENU CHOICES
  DATA Forecast the weather
  DATA Display monthly weather norms
  FOR I=1 TO 2
    READ PICK$(I)
  NEXT
  PICK = 1
 REM VANE COORDINATES
  DATA 386,76,361,51,301,40,241,51,216,76
  DATA 241,101,301,112,361,101
  FOR I=1 TO 8
    READ X(I),Y(I)
  NEXT
 REM DIR. SYMBOLS & COORDINATES (ROW & PTAB)
```

```
    DATA E,10,393, N,6,308, W,10,223, S,14,308
    FOR I=1 TO 7 STEP 2
      READ W$(I),ROW(I),PT(I)
    NEXT
  F1$ = "= ##.# inches"
  F2$ = "= ### degrees F."
  F3$ = "= ###.# inches"
RETURN

SETMENUS:
 DATA 5, Color, Tan, Blue, Green, Gray
 DATA Random
 DATA 3, Stop, Go to BASIC
 DATA Go to Science Menu, Go to System
 FOR I=1 TO 2
  READ NUMBER
  FOR J=0 TO NUMBER
    READ TITLE$
    IF J<>0 THEN TITLE$ = SPACE$(3) + TITLE$
      STATUS = 1
      IF I=1 AND J=1 THEN STATUS = 2
    MENU I,J,STATUS,TITLE$
 NEXT J,I
 MENU 3,0,0,""
 MENU 4,0,0,""
 KOLOR% = 1
RETURN

SETCOLORS:
 REM TAN, BLUE, GREEN, GRAY
  DATA .95,.7,.53, .36,.57,1
  DATA .22,.76,.68, .72,.7,.86
  FOR I=1 TO 4
   FOR J=1 TO 3
     READ KOLOR(I,J)
  NEXT J,I
 REM TAN, GREEN, & RED
  PALETTE 4,.95,.7,.53
  PALETTE 5,.14,.43,0
  PALETTE 6,.93,.2,0
RETURN

READ.DATA:
 REM MONTHLY WEATHER NORMS
  FOR I=1 TO 12
   READ MONTH$(I)
   FOR J=1 TO 5
    READ MW(I,J)
  NEXT J,I
```

```
REM WIND DIRECTION
 FOR I=1 TO 8
  READ D$(I)
 NEXT
REM BAROMETER TREND
 FOR I=1 TO 5
  READ BT$(I)
 NEXT
REM FORECASTS
 FOR I=0 TO N
  READ V, F.PART1$(I)
  IF V = 2 THEN READ F.PART2$(I)
 NEXT
RETURN

SHAPES:
 X=313: Y=80
 FOR I=1 TO 2
  K% = I*5-4
  CIRCLE(X,Y),12,K%: PAINT(X,Y),K%
  GET(X-12,Y-8)-(X+12,Y+8),DISCS(DISC.I(I))
 NEXT
RETURN

HEADING:
 MENU ON
 ON MENU GOSUB OPTIONS
 CLS
 LOCATE 9,23: PRINT "Weather Forecaster"
 COLOR 3,0: LOCATE 14,30: PRINT "then"
 COLOR 1,0
 LOCATE 13,24: PRINT "Please use menus,"
 LOCATE 15,22: PRINT "Click mouse to start"
 GOSUB CLICKIT
RETURN

OPTIONS:
 ID = MENU(0): ITEM = MENU(1)
 ON ID GOSUB MENU1,GOODBYE
 ITEM = 0
RETURN

MENU1:
 K1 = KOLOR(ITEM,1): K2 = KOLOR(ITEM,2)
 K3 = KOLOR(ITEM,3)
 IF ITEM=5 THEN K1=RND: K2=RND: K3=RND
 PALETTE 4,K1,K2,K3
 MENU 1,KOLOR%,1: MENU 1,ITEM,2
 KOLOR% = ITEM
RETURN
```

```
GOODBYE:
 WINDOW CLOSE 2: WINDOW 1: MENU RESET
 SCREEN CLOSE 1
 IF ITEM = 2 THEN RUN "SCIENCE"
 IF ITEM = 3 THEN SYSTEM
 COLOR 1,Ø: CLS
 PRINT "Bye-Bye"
 STOP
RETURN

GREETING:
 CLS
 PRINT
 PRINT "    This program helps you to make";
 PRINT " accurate, short-range"
 PRINT " weather forecasts."
 PRINT
 PRINT "    You'll need to know the current";
 PRINT " wind direction,"
 PRINT " barometric pressure, and whether the";
 PRINT " barometer is rising"
 PRINT " or falling."
 PRINT
 PRINT "    I'll do the rest."
 LOCATE 18,27: PRINT "Click Mouse";
 GOSUB CLICKIT
RETURN

CLICKIT:
 S$ = ""
 WHILE MOUSE(Ø) = Ø AND S$ = ""
  S$ = INKEY$
 WEND
  X = MOUSE(1)
  Y = MOUSE(2)
 WHILE MOUSE(Ø)<> Ø: WEND: REM RESET
RETURN

MAIN.MENU:
 CLS
 RTN$ = "OFF"
 LOCATE 5,23: PRINT "Would you like to"
 FOR I=1 TO 2
  IF I = PICK THEN INX = 2 ELSE INX = 1
  CALL DRAW.CIRCLE(I,INX)
  LOCATE I*2+5,21: PRINT PICK$(I)
 NEXT
 LINE(263,115)-(36Ø,125),5,BF
 COLOR 1,5
```

```
  LOCATE 14,29:.PRINT "Return"
  COLOR 1,Ø
  LOCATE 18,11: PRINT "Click Mouse on Choice,";
  PRINT " then Click on Return"
  GOSUB CHOOSE
  GOTO MAIN.MENU
RETURN

SUB DRAW.CIRCLE(R,INX) STATIC
  SHARED DISCS(),DISC.I()
  Y = 18*R+31
  PUT(162,Y),DISCS(DISC.I(INX)),PSET
END SUB

CHOOSE:
  GOSUB GURGLE
  GOSUB CLICKIT
  IF S$ = "" THEN GOSUB LOCATION
  IF ASC(S$+" ") <> 13 AND RTN$ = "OFF" THEN
    GOTO CHOOSE
  END IF
  ON PICK GOSUB FORECAST,MONTHLY.NORMS
RETURN

GURGLE:
  FREQ = 3ØØ
  FOR G=1 TO 5
    FREQ = 5ØØ-FREQ
    SOUND FREQ,1,5Ø
  NEXT G
RETURN

LOCATION:
  IF X>263 AND X<36Ø AND Y>114 AND Y<125 THEN
    RTN$ = "ON"
  ELSE
    P = INT((Y-48)/18) + 1
    IF X>155 AND X<195 AND P>Ø AND P<3 THEN
      CALL DRAW.CIRCLE(PICK,1)
      CALL DRAW.CIRCLE(P,2)
      PICK = P
    END IF
  END IF
RETURN

FORECAST:
  GOSUB DRAW.VANE
  GOSUB GET.WIND
  GOSUB BAROMETRIC.PRESSURE
```

```
   GOSUB BAROMETRIC.TREND
   GOSUB PREDICT
   GOSUB SHOW.FORECAST
RETURN

DRAW.VANE:
 CLS
 WIND = 3
 LOCATE 3,25: PRINT "WIND DIRECTION"
 XØ=313: YØ=84
 CIRCLE(XØ,YØ),5Ø,4: PAINT(XØ,YØ),4
 LINE(XØ-1,YØ-26)-(XØ+1,YØ+26),2,BF
 LINE(XØ-6Ø,YØ)-(XØ+6Ø,YØ),2
 REM SATELLITES
  FOR I=1 TO 8
   IF I = WIND THEN INX = 2 ELSE INX = 1
   CALL DRAW.SAT(I,INX)
  NEXT
 REM RETURN BAR
  LINE(263,133)-(36Ø,143),5,BF
  COLOR 1,5
  LOCATE 16,29: PRINT "Return"
  RTN$ = "OFF"
RETURN

SUB DRAW.SAT(V,INX) STATIC
 SHARED X(),Y(),DISCS(),DISC.I()
 SHARED ROW(),PT(),W$()
 PUT(X(V),Y(V)),DISCS(DISC.I(INX)),PSET
 COLOR 11-5*INX,5*INX-4
 IF V=1 OR V=3 OR V=5 OR V=7 THEN
  LOCATE ROW(V): PRINT PTAB(PT(V));W$(V)
 END IF
END SUB

GET.WIND:
 COLOR 1,Ø
 LOCATE 19,18:
 PRINT "Click mouse on the direction"
 PRINT TAB(2Ø)"the wind is blowing from";
 WHILE RTN$ = "OFF"
  GOSUB GURGLE
  GOSUB CLICKIT
  IF S$ = "" THEN GOSUB COMPUTE
  IF ASC(S$+" ") = 13 THEN RTN$ = "ON"
 WEND
RETURN
```

```
COMPUTE:
  IF X>262 AND X<361 AND Y>132 AND Y<144 THEN
    RTN$ = "ON"
  ELSE
    FOR I=1 TO 8
      XD = X - X(I)
      YD = Y - Y(I)
      IF XD>0 AND XD<26 AND YD>0 AND YD<18 THEN
        WIND.NEW = I: I = 8
        GOSUB CHANGE.DIR
      END IF
    NEXT
  END IF
RETURN

CHANGE.DIR:
  REM ERASE OLD
    CALL DRAW.SAT(WIND,1)
  REM DRAW NEW
    WIND = WIND.NEW
    CALL DRAW.SAT(WIND,2)
RETURN

BAROMETRIC.PRESSURE:
  COLOR 1,0
  CLS
  LOCATE 2,23: PRINT "BAROMETRIC PRESSURE"
  BP = 0
  LOCATE 4,3
  PRINT "What is the barometric pressure ? "
  WHILE BP <= 0 OR BP > 50
    GOSUB GURGLE
    LOCATE 4,37: PRINT SPACE$(15)
    LOCATE 4,37: INPUT "",S$
    BP = VAL(S$)
  WEND
RETURN

BAROMETRIC.TREND:
  TREND = 1: RTN$ = "OFF"
  LOCATE 6,24: PRINT "Barometric Trend:"
  LINE(213,58)-(413,145),4,BF
  COLOR 2,4
  FOR I=1 TO 5
    IF I = TREND THEN K% = 6 ELSE K% = 4
    CALL HIGHLIGHT(I,K%)
  NEXT
  LINE(263,151)-(360,161),5,BF
  COLOR 1,5
```

```
 LOCATE 18,29: PRINT "Return"
 COLOR 1,0
 LOCATE 20,22: PRINT "Click Mouse on Choice";
 GOSUB SELECT
RETURN

SUB HIGHLIGHT(V,K%) STATIC
 K.F% = 4-.5*K%
 COLOR K.F%,K%
 SHARED BT$()
 ROW = V*2 + 6
 L = LEN(BT$(V))
 X0 = 245: X1 = L*10 + 255
 Y0 = 9*ROW-11: Y1 = Y0+10
 LINE(X0,Y0)-(X1,Y1),K%,BF
 LOCATE ROW,26: PRINT BT$(V)
END SUB

SELECT:
 GOSUB GURGLE
 GOSUB CLICKIT
 IF S$ = "" THEN GOSUB POSITION
 IF ASC(S$+" ") <> 13 AND RTN$="OFF" THEN SELECT
RETURN

POSITION:
 IF X>263 AND X<360 AND Y>150 AND Y<162 THEN
  RTN$ = "ON"
 ELSE
  HORZ = INT(Y/9) + 1
  T = (HORZ-6)/2
  IF X>245 AND X<395 AND T>0 AND T<6 THEN
   CALL HIGHLIGHT(TREND,4)
   CALL HIGHLIGHT(T,6)
   TREND = T
  END IF
 END IF
RETURN

PREDICT:
 B = BP: W = WIND: T = TREND: P = 0
 IF B >= 30.2 THEN
  IF T=4 AND W>=4 AND W<=6 THEN P = 1
  IF T=1 AND W>=4 AND W<=6 THEN P = 2
 END IF
 IF B >= 30.1 AND B < 30.2 THEN
  IF T=1 AND W>=4 AND W<=6 THEN P = 3
  IF T=4 AND W>=4 AND W<=6 THEN P = 4
 END IF
```

```
   IF B >= 30.1 THEN
     IF T=3 AND W>=4 AND W<=6 THEN P = 5
     IF T=5 AND W>=4 AND W<=6 THEN P = 6
     IF T=4 AND W=7 THEN P = 7
     IF T=5 AND W=7 THEN P = 8
     IF T=4 AND (W=2 OR W=1 OR W=8) THEN P = 9
     IF T=5 AND W=8 THEN P = 10
     IF T=5 AND (W=1 OR W=2) THEN P = 11
   END IF
   IF B <= 29.8 THEN
     IF T=5 AND W>=1 AND W<=3 THEN P = 12
     IF T=5 AND (W=8 OR W=7) THEN P = 13
     IF T=3 THEN P = 14
   END IF
   IF B < 30.1 THEN
     IF T=4 AND (W=2 OR W=1 OR W=8) THEN P = 15
   END IF
   IF B > 29.8 AND B < 30.1 THEN
     IF T=5 AND (W=2 OR W=1 OR W=8) THEN P = 16
   END IF
   IF B <= 30.1 THEN
     IF T=2 AND (W=7 OR W=6) THEN P = 17
   END IF
   FT.1$ = F.PART1$(P): FT.2$ = F.PART2$(P)
RETURN

SHOW.FORECAST:
   COLOR 1,0
   CLS
   LINE(219,15)-(400,27),1,B: PAINT(313,20),5,1
   COLOR 1,5
   LOCATE 3,24: PRINT "Weather Forecast"
   LINE(35,35)-(595,135),2,B: PAINT(313,80),4,2
   COLOR 2,4
   LOCATE 6,10: PRINT "Barometric Pressure";
   PRINT TAB(32) USING F1$;B
   LOCATE 8,10: PRINT "Barometric Trend";
   PRINT TAB(32)"= ";BT$(T)
   LOCATE 10,10: PRINT "Wind Direction";
   PRINT TAB(32)"= From the ";D$(W)
   LINE(85,106)-(175,116),6,BF
   COLOR 1,6
   LOCATE 13,10: PRINT "FORECAST"
   COLOR 2,4: LOCATE 13,20: PRINT FT.1$
   LOCATE 14,20: PRINT FT.2$
   COLOR 1,0
   LOCATE 20,26: PRINT "Click Mouse";
   GOSUB CLICKIT
RETURN
```

```
MONTHLY.NORMS:
 GOSUB ENTER.MONTH
 GOSUB DISPLAY.NORMS
RETURN

ENTER.MONTH:
 COLOR 1,Ø
 CLS
 MN% = 1: RTN$ = "OFF"
 LOCATE 2,22: PRINT "Monthly Weather Norms"
 LINE(163,21)-(463,129),4,BF
 COLOR 2,4
 FOR I=1 TO 12
  IF I = MN% THEN K% = 6 ELSE K% = 4
  CALL MONTH(I,K%)
 NEXT
 LINE(263,151)-(36Ø,161),5,BF
 COLOR 1,5
 LOCATE 18,29: PRINT "Return"
 COLOR 1,Ø
 LOCATE 2Ø,22: PRINT "Click Mouse on Choice";
 GOSUB GET.MONTH
RETURN

SUB MONTH(V,K%) STATIC
 K.F% = 4-.5*K%
 COLOR K.F%,K%
 SHARED MONTH$()
 IF V < 7 THEN HALF = 1 ELSE HALF = 2
 IF HALF = 1 THEN ROW = V*2 + 2: COL = 21
 IF HALF = 2 THEN ROW = (V-6)*2 + 2: COL = 36
 L = LEN(MONTH$(V))
 XØ = COL*1Ø-15: X1 = XØ + L*1Ø + 1Ø
 YØ = 9*ROW-11: Y1 = YØ+1Ø
 LINE(XØ,YØ)-(X1,Y1),K%,BF
 LOCATE ROW,COL: PRINT MONTH$(V)
END SUB

GET.MONTH:
 GOSUB GURGLE
 GOSUB CLICKIT
 IF S$ = "" THEN GOSUB NEW.MONTH
 IF ASC(S$+" ") <> 13 AND RTN$="OFF" THEN
  GOTO GET.MONTH
 END IF
RETURN

NEW.MONTH:
 HALF = Ø
```

```
  IF X>263 AND X<360 AND Y>150 AND Y<162 THEN
    RTN$ = "ON"
  ELSE
    IF X>194 AND X<306 THEN HALF = 1
    IF X>344 AND X<456 THEN HALF = 2
    ROW = INT((Y-21)/18) + 1
    IF HALF <> 0 AND ROW > 0 AND ROW < 7 THEN
     M% = ROW: IF HALF = 2 THEN M% = ROW + 6
     CALL MONTH(MN%,4)
     CALL MONTH(M%,6)
     MN% = M%
    END IF
  END IF
RETURN

DISPLAY.NORMS:
 COLOR 1,0
 CLS
 N = MN%
 S$ = MONTH$(N): L = LEN(S$)
 LINE(313-10*L/2-15,15)-(313+10*L/2+15,27),1,B
 PAINT(313,20),6,1
 COLOR 1,6: LOCATE 3: PRINT PTAB(313-10*L/2)S$
 LINE(135,35)-(495,150),2,B: PAINT(313,80),4,2
 LINE(144,43)-(288,53),5,BF
 LINE(144,106)-(288,116),5,BF
 COLOR 1,5
 LOCATE 6,16: PRINT "Temperature"
 LOCATE 13,16: PRINT "Precipitation"
 COLOR 2,4
 LOCATE 8,17: PRINT "Normal high";
 PRINT TAB(33) USING F2$;MW(N,1)
 LOCATE 9,17: PRINT "Normal average";
 PRINT TAB(33) USING F2$;MW(N,3)
 LOCATE 10,17: PRINT "Normal low";
 PRINT TAB(33) USING F2$;MW(N,2)
 LOCATE 15,17: PRINT "Normal rainfall";
 PRINT TAB(33) USING F3$;MW(N,4)
 LOCATE 16,17: PRINT "Normal snowfall";
 PRINT TAB(33) USING F3$;MW(N,5)
 COLOR 1,0
 LOCATE 20,26: PRINT "Click Mouse";
 GOSUB CLICKIT
RETURN

REM MONTHLY WEATHER NORMS
 REM Normal High, Low, & Average; Rain & Snow
 DATA January  ,38,23,30,2.8,9.1
 DATA February ,41,24,32,2.7,9.6
```

```
DATA March      ,51,31,41,3.2,6.5
DATA April      ,64,42,53,3.0,0.3
DATA May        ,75,52,63,3.6,0.0
DATA June       ,83,61,72,3.6,0.0
DATA July       ,87,65,76,3.6,0.0
DATA August     ,85,63,74,3.8,0.0
DATA September,78,56,67,3.2,0.0
DATA October    ,67,45,56,2.8,0.1
DATA November ,53,35,44,2.7,2.1
DATA December ,40,25,33,2.9,7.7

REM WIND DIRECTIONS
DATA East, Northeast, North, Northwest
DATA West, Southwest, South, Southeast

REM BAROMETER TREND
DATA Steady, Rising slowly, Rising fast
DATA Falling slowly, Falling fast

REM FORECASTS
REM Number = Lines for forecast
DATA 2, "Fair, little change in temperature"
 DATA for the next couple of days
DATA 1, Fair and warmer for the next 48 hours
DATA 2, Continued fair with little or no change
 DATA in temperature
DATA 2, "Fair, little change in temperature"
 DATA for the next day or two
DATA 1, "Warmer, rain within 24 to 36 hours"
DATA 2, "Fair today, rainy and warmer within"
 DATA 48 hours
DATA 1, "Warmer, rain within 18 to 24 hours"
DATA 1, Rain within 24 hours
DATA 1, "Windy, rain within 12 to 24 hours"
DATA 1, Rain in 12 to 18 hours
DATA 1, "Windy, rain within 12 hours"
DATA 2, "In summer, rain within 12 to 24 hours."
 DATA "In winter, rain or snow, and windy"
DATA 2, "Heavy rain in summer.  In winter,"
 DATA heavy snow followed by a cold wave.
DATA 2, "Severe storm warning: Windy, with"
 DATA rain in summer and snow in winter
DATA 1, Clearing and colder
DATA 1, Rain for the next day or two
DATA 2, Rain with high winds; clearing and
 DATA cooler within 24 hours
DATA 2, Clearing within a few hours; fair for
DATA the next several days
```

Simultaneous Equation Solver

Remember those math problems where you have to solve *N* equations for *N* unknowns? Well, worry no more, this Amiga program does the solving for you.

While it's important to be able to solve simultaneous equations manually, it's much easier to use this program once you understand the principles involved. Here are two simultaneous equations:

5 * (X1) + 2 * (X2) = 16
3 * (X1) + 4 * (X2) = 18

After telling the Amiga that you have two equations, you enter the column of constants (16 and 18). Then you key in the coefficients on the variable X1 (5 and 3) followed by those on X2 (2 and 4).

The Amiga computes the solution: X1 = 2, and X2 = 3. It's quick and easy with your Amiga, and you're free to interpret the meaning of the numbers and go to the next problem.

Program 6-3. Simultaneous Equation Solver
Save using the filename **SES**

```
REM SIMULTANEOUS EQUATION SOLVER
 CLEAR ,35000&
 GOSUB INITIALIZE
 GOSUB ENTER.NO.EQUATIONS
 GOSUB ENTER.DATA
CONTINUE:
 GOSUB EDIT.DATA
 GOSUB COMPUTE
 IF GOOF = 0 THEN GOSUB SHOW.RESULTS
 IF BUTTON = 1 THEN CONTINUE
 GOSUB GOODBYE
END

INITIALIZE:
 GOSUB SETSCREEN
 GOSUB KEYVALUES
 GOSUB SETMENUS
 GOSUB SETCOLORS
 GOSUB SHAPES
 GOSUB HEADING
 GOSUB INSTRUCTIONS
RETURN
```

```
SETSCREEN:
 SCREEN 1,640,200,3,2
 WINDOW 2,"Simultaneous Equation Solver",,0,1
RETURN

KEYVALUES:
 RANDOMIZE TIMER
 DEFINT A-Z: DEFDBL C,Q,R,S
 REM make X DBL for VERY big or small raw data
  DEFSNG K,X
 REM MAXIMUM NUMBER OF EQUATIONS
  DATA 25
  READ NX
  DIM X(NX,NX),XT(NX,NX),Q(NX,NX),R(NX,NX)
  DIM C(NX),S(NX),V$(NX),CIRCLE.SHAPE%(150)
  V$(0) = "Y"
  FOR I=1 TO NX
   V$(I) = "X" + MID$(STR$(I),2)
  NEXT
 REM BUTTON VALUES
  XB(1) = 292: XB(2) = 334: YB = 165
  LT$(1) = "Y": LT$(2) = "N"
 REM SHAPE INDICES
  INDEX(1) = 1: INDEX(2) = 75
 REM FORMATS FOR OUTPUT
  FOR I=0 TO 6
   F$(I) = STRING$(16-I,"#")
   IF I <> 0 THEN
    F$(I) = F$(I) + "." + STRING$(I,"#")
   END IF
  NEXT
RETURN

SETMENUS:
 DATA 5, Color, Tan, Blue, Green, Gray
 DATA Random
 DATA 7, Decimals, 0 Places, 1 Place, 2 Places
 DATA 3 Places, 4 Places, 5 Places, 6 Places
 DATA 3, Stop, Go to BASIC
 DATA Go to Science Menu, Go to System
 FOR I=1 TO 3
  READ NUMBER
  FOR J=0 TO NUMBER
   READ TITLE$
   IF J<>0 THEN TITLE$ = SPACE$(3) + TITLE$
   STATUS = 1
   IF I = 1 AND J = 1 THEN STATUS = 2
   IF I = 2 AND J = 4 THEN STATUS = 2
   MENU I,J,STATUS,TITLE$
```

```
   NEXT J,I
   MENU 4,Ø,Ø,""
   KOLOR% = 1: DP = 3
   F$ = F$(DP)
RETURN

SETCOLORS:
  REM TAN, BLUE, GREEN, GRAY
    DATA .95,.7,.53, .36,.57,1
    DATA .22,.76,.68, .72,.7,.86
    FOR I=1 TO 4
     FOR J=1 TO 3
       READ KOLOR(I,J)
    NEXT J,I
  REM TAN, GREEN, & RED
    PALETTE 4,.95,.7,.53
    PALETTE 5,.14,.43,Ø
    PALETTE 6,.93,.2,Ø
RETURN

SHAPES:
 X=313: Y=8Ø
 X1 = X-7: X2 = X+7: Y1 = Y-3: Y2 = Y+3
 LINE(X1,Y1)-(X2,Y2),4,BF
 FOR I=1 TO 2
  K = 11-5*I
  CIRCLE(X,Y),7,2: PAINT(X,Y),K,2
  GET(X1,Y1)-(X2,Y2),CIRCLE.SHAPE%(INDEX(I))
 NEXT
RETURN

HEADING:
 MENU ON
 ON MENU GOSUB OPTIONS
 CLS
 COLOR 3,Ø: LOCATE 18,3Ø:PRINT "then"
 COLOR 1,Ø
 LOCATE 1Ø,18
 PRINT "Simultaneous Equation Solver"
 LOCATE 17,24:PRINT "Please use menus,"
 LOCATE 19,21:PRINT "Click mouse to start"
 GOSUB CLICKIT
RETURN

OPTIONS:
 ID = MENU(Ø): ITEM = MENU(1)
 ON ID GOSUB MENU1,MENU2,GOODBYE
 ITEM = Ø
RETURN
```

```
MENU1:
 K1 = KOLOR(ITEM,1): K2 = KOLOR(ITEM,2)
 K3 = KOLOR(ITEM,3)
 IF ITEM=5 THEN K1=RND: K2=RND: K3=RND
 PALETTE 4,K1,K2,K3
 MENU 1,KOLOR%,1: MENU 1,ITEM,2
 KOLOR% = ITEM
RETURN

MENU2:
 MENU 2,DP+1,1: MENU 2,ITEM,2
 DP = ITEM-1
 F$ = F$(DP)
RETURN

GOODBYE:
 WINDOW CLOSE 2: WINDOW 1: MENU RESET
 SCREEN CLOSE 1
 IF ITEM = 2 THEN RUN "SCIENCE"
 IF ITEM = 3 THEN SYSTEM
 COLOR 1,0: CLS
 PRINT "Bye-Bye"
 STOP
RETURN

CLICKIT:
 S$ = ""
 WHILE MOUSE(0) = 0 AND S$ = ""
  S$ = INKEY$
 WEND
  X = MOUSE(1)
  Y = MOUSE(2)
 WHILE MOUSE(0)<> 0: WEND: REM RESET
RETURN

INSTRUCTIONS:
 CLS
 PRINT
 PRINT "    This program solves up to";NX;
 PRINT "equations for";NX;"unknowns."
 PRINT
 PRINT "    Your equations should be independent";
 PRINT " of each other, and"
 PRINT " if they're not, I'll be sure to let";
 PRINT " you know."
 LOCATE 19,27:PRINT "Click Mouse"
 GOSUB CLICKIT
RETURN
```

```
ENTER.NO.EQUATIONS:
 CLS
 PRINT
 PRINT "    Please enter the number of equations";
 PRINT " that you'd like"
 PRINT " to solve.  Up to";NX;"are allowed."
 LOCATE 6,2: PRINT "Number = ? ";
 N = Ø
 WHILE N < 1 OR N > NX
  LOCATE 6,13: PRINT SPACE$(2Ø)
  GOSUB GURGLE
  LOCATE 6,13: INPUT "",N$
  N = VAL(N$)
 WEND
RETURN

ENTER.DATA:
 REM ON Y
  CLS
  PRINT
  PRINT "    Please enter observations on the";
  PRINT " 'Y' variable in each"
  PRINT " equation."
  PRINT
  PRINT "    If 3*(X1) + 5*(X2) = 7, for";
  PRINT " example, then enter 7."
  GOSUB ON.Y
 REM ON COEFFICIENTS
  GOSUB COEFFICIENTS
RETURN

ON.Y:
 GOSUB GURGLE
 LINE(5,52)-(115,62),6,BF
 COLOR 1,6: LOCATE 7,2: PRINT "Value of Y"
 COLOR 1,Ø
 FOR J=1 TO N
  LOCATE 9,3 : PRINT "Equation";J
  LOCATE 9,14: PRINT "=";SPACE$(35)
  LOCATE 9,16: INPUT "",X$
  X(J,Ø) = VAL(X$)
 NEXT
RETURN

COEFFICIENTS:
 FOR I=1 TO N
  CLS
  GOSUB GURGLE
  PRINT
```

370

```
   PRINT "    Please enter the coefficient of";
   PRINT " the ";V$(I);" term in each"
   PRINT " equation."
   LINE(7,34)-(193,44),6,BF
   COLOR 1,6
   LOCATE 5,2: PRINT "Coefficient of ";V$(I)
   COLOR 1,0
   FOR J=1 TO N
     LOCATE 7,3 : PRINT "Equation";J
     LOCATE 7,14: PRINT "=";SPACE$(35)
     LOCATE 7,16: INPUT "",X$
     X(J,I) = VAL(X$)
   NEXT J,I
 RETURN

GURGLE:
 FREQ = 300
 FOR G=1 TO 5
   FREQ = 500-FREQ
   SOUND FREQ,1,50
 NEXT G
RETURN

EDIT.DATA:
 FOR I=0 TO N
   FOR J=1 TO N STEP 10
     GOSUB DISPLAY
     GOSUB CORRECT
 NEXT J,I
RETURN

DISPLAY:
 CLS
 A$ = "values"
 IF I > 0 THEN A$ = "coefficients"
 S$ = "These are " + A$ + " of " + V$(I)
 L = LEN(S$)
 LINE(313-10*L/2-5,7)-(313+10*L/2+5,17),6,BF
 COLOR 1,6
 LOCATE 2: PRINT PTAB(313-L*10/2)S$
 LINE(40,23)-(590,118),4,BF
 COLOR 2,4
 R% = 0: HOLD.ROW = 0
 FOR L = J TO J+9
   IF L <= N THEN
     R% = R%+1
     CALL DRAW.IT(R%,1)
     LOCATE R%+3,10: PRINT "Equation";L
     LOCATE R%+3,22: PRINT "= ";X(L,I)
```

371

```
      END IF
    NEXT L
  RETURN

  SUB DRAW.IT(RW%,INX) STATIC
    SHARED CIRCLE.SHAPE%(),INDEX()
    Y = (RW%+3)*9 - 9
    PUT(65,Y),CIRCLE.SHAPE%(INDEX(INX)),PSET
  END SUB

  CORRECT:
    COLOR 1,Ø
    LOCATE 16,24: PRINT "To make changes,"
    LOCATE 17,13: PRINT "Click mouse on circle,";
    PRINT " then hit Return"
    GOSUB CHOOSE
    IF HOLD.ROW <> Ø THEN
      GOSUB CHANGE: GOTO CORRECT
    END IF
  RETURN

  CHOOSE:
    GOSUB GURGLE
    GOSUB CLICKIT
    IF S$ = "" THEN GOSUB LOCATION
    IF ASC(S$+" ") <> 13 THEN CHOOSE
  RETURN

  LOCATION:
    ROW% = INT(Y/9) - 2
    IF ROW%>Ø AND ROW%<=R% AND X>55 AND X<9Ø THEN
      IF HOLD.ROW <> Ø THEN
        CALL DRAW.IT(HOLD.ROW,1)
      END IF
      CALL DRAW.IT(ROW%,2)
      HOLD.ROW = ROW%
    END IF
  RETURN

  CHANGE:
    LOCATE 16,24: PRINT SPACE$(16)
    LOCATE 17,13: PRINT SPACE$(38)
    LINE(65,133)-(185,143),5,BF
    COLOR 1,5
    LOCATE 16,8: PRINT "New Value ?"
    COLOR 1,Ø
    LOCATE 16,21: INPUT "",V$
    X(J+HOLD.ROW-1,I) = VAL(V$)
    COLOR 2,4
```

```
LOCATE HOLD.ROW+3,24: PRINT SPACE$(30)
LOCATE HOLD.ROW+3,24: PRINT X(J+HOLD.ROW-1,I)
CALL DRAW.IT(HOLD.ROW,1)
HOLD.ROW = Ø
LINE(65,133)-(185,143),Ø,BF
COLOR 1,Ø
LOCATE 16,21: PRINT SPACE$(30)
RETURN

COMPUTE:
 CLS
 LOCATE 10,26: PRINT "Computing ..."
 GOOF = Ø
 GOSUB TRANSFER.DATA
 FOR Z=1 TO N
  GOSUB KEY.ELEMENT.OF.R
  IF GOOF = Ø THEN
   GOSUB COLUMN.OF.Q
   IF Z <> N THEN GOSUB COLUMN.OF.R
   GOSUB ELEMENT.OF.C
   IF Z <> N THEN GOSUB REVISE.X
  ELSE
   GOSUB GOOF
   Z = N
  END IF
 NEXT Z
 IF GOOF = Ø THEN
  S(N) = C(N)/R(N,N)
  IF N <> 1 THEN GOSUB BACKSOLVE
 END IF
RETURN

TRANSFER.DATA:
 FOR I=1 TO N
  FOR J=Ø TO N
   XT(I,J) = X(I,J)
 NEXT J,I
RETURN

KEY.ELEMENT.OF.R:
 R = Ø
 FOR I=1 TO N
  R = R + XT(I,Z)*XT(I,Z)
 NEXT I
 R(Z,Z) = SQR(R)
 IF R(Z,Z) = Ø THEN GOOF = 1
RETURN
```

```
COLUMN.OF.Q:
 FOR I=1 TO N
  Q(I,Z) = XT(I,Z)/R(Z,Z)
 NEXT I
RETURN

COLUMN.OF.R:
 FOR L = Z+1 TO N
  R(Z,L) = Ø
  FOR I=1 TO N
    R(Z,L) = R(Z,L) + XT(I,L)*Q(I,Z)
 NEXT I,L
RETURN

ELEMENT.OF.C:
 C(Z) = Ø
 FOR I=1 TO N
  C(Z) = C(Z) + XT(I,Ø)*Q(I,Z)
 NEXT I
RETURN

REVISE.X:
 FOR I=1 TO N
  FOR L = Z+1 TO N
    XT(I,L) = XT(I,L) - Q(I,Z)*R(Z,L)
 NEXT L,I
RETURN

GOOF:
 CLS
 LINE(82,79)-(15Ø,89),6,BF
 COLOR 1,6
 LOCATE 1Ø,1Ø: PRINT "Sorry:"
 COLOR 1,Ø
 LOCATE 1Ø,18: PRINT "I can't solve your";
 PRINT " equations with"
 LOCATE 11,18: PRINT "the data you've";
 PRINT " entered."
 LOCATE 17,28: PRINT "Continue ?"
 GOSUB GURGLE
 GOSUB DECIDE
RETURN

DECIDE:
 BUTTON = Ø
 GOSUB DRAWBUTTON
 GOSUB PUSHBUTTON
 COLOR 1,Ø
RETURN
```

```
DRAWBUTTON:
 LINE (265,158)-(361,172),1,BF
 FOR I=1 TO 2
  CIRCLE(XB(I),YB),12,4+I
  PAINT(XB(I),YB),4+I
  COLOR 1,4+I
  LOCATE 19: PRINT PTAB(XB(I)-4);LT$(I);
 NEXT I
RETURN

PUSHBUTTON:
 SOUND 44Ø,2
 GOSUB CLICKIT
 S$ = UCASE$(S$)
 IF S$ = "Y" THEN BUTTON = 1
 IF S$ = "N" THEN BUTTON = 2
 FOR I=1 TO 2
  XD = ABS(X-XB(I)): YD = ABS(Y-YB)
  IF XD<13 AND YD<7 THEN BUTTON = I: I=2
 NEXT
 IF BUTTON = Ø THEN PUSHBUTTON
RETURN

BACKSOLVE:
 FOR I = N-1 TO 1 STEP -1
  REM LEFT-SIDE SUM
   S = Ø
   FOR J = I+1 TO N
    S = S + R(I,J)*S(J)
   NEXT J
  REM SOLUTION
   S(I) = (C(I)-S)/R(I,I)
 NEXT I
RETURN

SHOW.RESULTS:
 FOR I=1 TO N STEP 1Ø
  GOSUB PAINT.SCREEN
  GOSUB SHOW.VALUES
  COLOR 1,Ø
  LOCATE 17,26: PRINT "Press any key"
  GOSUB CLICKIT
 NEXT I
 LOCATE 17,25: PRINT "Compute again ?"
 GOSUB DECIDE
RETURN

PAINT.SCREEN:
 CLS
```

```
  LINE(100,30)-(530,130),2,B
  PAINT(313,80),4,2
  LINE(264,6)-(356,18),1,B
  PAINT(313,10),6,1
  COLOR 1,6
  LOCATE 2,28: PRINT "SOLUTION"
RETURN

SHOW.VALUES:
  COLOR 2,4
  ROW% = 0
  FOR J = I TO I+9
   IF J <= N THEN
    ROW% = ROW% + 1
    LOCATE 4+ROW%,21: PRINT V$(J)
    LOCATE 4+ROW%,25: PRINT "= ";
    PRINT USING F$;S(J)
   END IF
  NEXT J
RETURN
```

Matrix Manipulator

If you've ever wanted to add two matrices, multiply the sum by a third, and invert the product, you'll be pleased with "Matrix Manipulator" (MatMan). MatMan can add, subtract, transpose, and invert any two matrices, X and Y. It stores the result in Z. MatMan can even perform further operations using X or Y or Z.

The example in Figure 6-3 is quite complex. Three distinct operations are required to evaluate this expression: addition, scalar multiplication (multiplying by a single number rather than by a matrix), and matrix multiplication.

When you run Program 6-4, use a pull-down menu to place values in both matrix X and matrix Y. Notice that the Amiga lets you edit your entries. And notice that other pull-down menus allow you to view intermediate results and to change the number of decimal places in an answer.

Now ask MatMan to add matrices X and Y. Figure 6-4 shows the response you'll get.

You're not through yet, however. Ask MatMan to scalar-multiply matrix Z by 3. As before, you'll see the results of this computation, and you'll continue to see answers as long as the Results Menu is set to Show.

Here's the tricky part. You need to multiply what is now in matrix Z by the vector at the far right (2's). No problem. First store the 2's in matrix X, then ask MatMan to compute the product Z*X. Remember that the Z should come first in this case. Figure 6-5 shows the final answer.

As you can see, MatMan is versatile, fast, and easy to use.

Figure 6-3. Complex Operations

$$3* \left\{ \begin{bmatrix} 7 & 17 \\ -20 & 512 \end{bmatrix} + \begin{bmatrix} 32 & 9 \\ 1 & 18 \end{bmatrix} \right\} * \begin{bmatrix} 2 \\ 2 \end{bmatrix}$$

$$\qquad\quad X \qquad\qquad\quad Y$$

Figure 6-4. MatMan Adds

$$\begin{bmatrix} 7 & 17 \\ -20 & 512 \end{bmatrix} + \begin{bmatrix} 32 & 9 \\ 1 & 18 \end{bmatrix} + \begin{bmatrix} 39 & 26 \\ -19 & 530 \end{bmatrix}$$

$$\quad\quad X \quad\quad\quad\quad Y \quad\quad\quad\quad Z$$

Figure 6-5. Final Result

$$\begin{bmatrix} 390 \\ 3066 \end{bmatrix}$$

Program 6-4. Matrix Manipulator
Save using the filename **MATMAN**

```
REM MATMAN
 CLEAR ,30000
 GOSUB INITIALIZE
 GOSUB MAIN.MENU
END

INITIALIZE:
 GOSUB SETSCREEN
 GOSUB KEYVALUES
 GOSUB SETMENUS
 GOSUB SETCOLORS
 GOSUB SHAPES
 GOSUB HEADING
 GOSUB GREETING
RETURN

SETSCREEN:
 SCREEN 1,640,200,3,2
 WINDOW 2,"MatMan",,0,1
RETURN

KEYVALUES:
 RANDOMIZE TIMER
 DEFINT A-J,L-Z: DEFDBL F,S,Z
 REM make W,X,Y DBL for VERY big or small data
 DEFSNG W,X,Y
 REM MAX. MATRIX ORDER (ROWS & COLUMNS)
  DATA 15
```

```
    READ MAX.SIZE
    V = MAX.SIZE
    DIM X(V,V),Y(V,V),Z(V,V),F(V,2*V),S(V,V)
    DIM DISCS(250),CIRCLES(150)
REM SHAPE INDICES
    DISC.I(1) = 1: DISC.I(2) = 125
    CIRCLE.I(1) = 1: CIRCLE.I(2) = 75
M$(1) = "Matrix X"
M$(2) = "Matrix Y"
GOSUB OUTPUT.FORMATS
GOSUB MENU.CHOICES
GOSUB ERROR.CODES
ZERO$ = STRING$(10,"0")
REM INITIAL MATRIX SIZES (X,Y,Z)
    FOR I=1 TO 3
      R(I)=0: C(I)=0
      NEXT
RETURN

OUTPUT.FORMATS:
  FOR I=0 TO 6
    F$(I) = STRING$(16-I,"#")
    IF I <> 0 THEN
      F$(I) = F$(I) + "." + STRING$(I,"#")
    END IF
  NEXT
RETURN

MENU.CHOICES:
  DATA Add, Subtract, Multiply, Scalar-multiply
  DATA Invert, Transpose
  FOR I=1 TO 6
    READ PICK$(I)
  NEXT
RETURN

ERROR.CODES:
  DATA I can't add different-sized matrices
  DATA I can't subtract different-sized matrices
  DATA I can't multiply your matrices
  DATA I can't invert a non-square matrix
  DATA Your matrix has no dimension
  DATA I can't invert a singular matrix
  FOR I=1 TO 6
    READ ERROR.CODE$(I)
  NEXT
RETURN
```

```
SETMENUS:
 DATA 5, Color, Tan, Blue, Green, Gray
 DATA Random
 DATA 4, "Data", "Enter Data on X"
 DATA "Enter Data on Y", ** Edit X **
 DATA ** Edit Y **
 DATA 2, Results, Show, Don't Show
 DATA 7, Decimals, 0 Places, 1 Place, 2 Places
 DATA 3 Places, 4 Places, 5 Places, 6 Places
 DATA 3, Stop, Go to BASIC
 DATA Go to Science Menu, Go to System
 FOR I=1 TO 5
  READ NUMBER
  FOR J=0 TO NUMBER
   READ TITLE$
   IF J<>0 THEN TITLE$ = SPACE$(3) + TITLE$
    STATUS = 1
    IF I=1 AND J=1 THEN STATUS = 2
    IF I=3 AND J=1 THEN STATUS = 2
    IF I=4 AND J=4 THEN STATUS = 2
   MENU I,J,STATUS,TITLE$
 NEXT J,I
 MENU 2,0,0
 KOLOR% = 1: RESULTS = 1: DP = 3
 FT$ = F$(3)
RETURN

SETCOLORS:
 REM TAN, BLUE, GREEN, GRAY
  DATA .95,.7,.53, .36,.57,1
  DATA .22,.76,.68, .72,.7,.86
  FOR I=1 TO 4
   FOR J=1 TO 3
    READ KOLOR(I,J)
  NEXT J,I
 REM TAN, GREEN, & RED
  PALETTE 4,.95,.7,.53
  PALETTE 5,.14,.43,0
  PALETTE 6,.93,.2,0
RETURN

SHAPES:
 REM DISCS
  X=313: Y=80
  FOR I=1 TO 2
   K% = I*5-4
   CIRCLE(X,Y),12,K%: PAINT(X,Y),K%
   GET(X-12,Y-8)-(X+12,Y+8),DISCS(DISC.I(I))
  NEXT
```

```
 REM CIRCLES
  CLS
  X1 =X-7: X2 = X+7: Y1 = Y-3: Y2 = Y+3
  LINE(X1,Y1)-(X2,Y2),4,BF
  FOR I=1 TO 2
   K% = 11-5*I
   CIRCLE(X,Y),7,2: PAINT(X,Y),K%,2
   GET(X1,Y1)-(X2,Y2),CIRCLES(CIRCLE.I(I))
  NEXT
RETURN

HEADING:
 MENU ON
 ON MENU GOSUB OPTIONS
 CLS
 LINE(193,60)-(213,90),6,BF
 LINE(205,65)-(213,85),0,BF
 LINE(413,60)-(433,90),6,BF
 LINE(413,65)-(421,85),0,BF
 LOCATE 9: PRINT PTAB(223)"Matrix Manipulator"
 COLOR 3,0: LOCATE 14: PRINT PTAB(295)"then"
 COLOR 1,0
 LOCATE 13: PRINT PTAB(232)"Please use menus,"
 LOCATE 15: PRINT PTAB(215)"Click mouse to start"
 GOSUB CLICKIT
RETURN

OPTIONS:
 ID = MENU(0): ITEM = MENU(1)
 ON ID GOSUB MENU1,MENU2,MENU3,MENU4,GOODBYE
 ITEM = 0
RETURN

MENU1:
 K1 = KOLOR(ITEM,1): K2 = KOLOR(ITEM,2)
 K3 = KOLOR(ITEM,3)
 IF ITEM=5 THEN K1=RND: K2=RND: K3=RND
 PALETTE 4,K1,K2,K3
 MENU 1,KOLOR%,1: MENU 1,ITEM,2
 KOLOR% = ITEM
RETURN

MENU2:
 ACTION = ITEM
 PICK = ITEM + 6
 S$ = CHR$(13)
RETURN
```

```
MENU3:
 MENU 3,RESULTS,1: MENU 3,ITEM,2
 RESULTS = ITEM
RETURN

MENU4:
 MENU 4,DP+1,1: MENU 4,ITEM,2
 DP = ITEM-1
 FT$ = F$(DP)
RETURN

GOODBYE:
 WINDOW CLOSE 2: WINDOW 1: MENU RESET
 SCREEN CLOSE 1
 IF ITEM = 2 THEN RUN "SCIENCE"
 IF ITEM = 3 THEN SYSTEM
 COLOR 1,Ø: CLS
 PRINT "Bye-Bye"
 STOP
RETURN

GREETING:
 CLS
 PRINT
 PRINT "   MatMan adds, subtracts,";
 PRINT " multiplies, transposes, and"
 PRINT " inverts any two matrices."
 PRINT
 PRINT "   He stores the result in Z.";
 PRINT "  Further operations using"
 PRINT " X, Y, and Z are then allowed."
 LOCATE 18,27: PRINT "Click Mouse";
 GOSUB CLICKIT
RETURN

CLICKIT:
 S$ = "": ACTION = Ø
 WHILE MOUSE(Ø) = Ø AND S$ = "" AND ACTION = Ø
  S$ = INKEY$
 WEND
  X = MOUSE(1)
  Y = MOUSE(2)
 WHILE MOUSE(Ø)<> Ø: WEND: REM RESET
RETURN

MAIN.MENU:
 MENU 2,Ø,1
 PICK = 1: GOOF = Ø
 CLS
```

```
    LOCATE 3,23: PRINT "Would you like to"
    FOR I=1 TO 6
      IF I = PICK THEN INX = 2 ELSE INX = 1
      CALL DRAW.CIRCLE(I,INX)
      LOCATE I*2+3,28: PRINT PICK$(I)
    NEXT
    LOCATE 19,13: PRINT "Click Mouse on Choice,";
    PRINT " then Hit Return"
    GOSUB CHOOSE
    GOTO MAIN.MENU
RETURN

SUB DRAW.CIRCLE(R,INX) STATIC
  SHARED DISCS(),DISC.I()
  Y = 18*R+13
  PUT(232,Y),DISCS(DISC.I(INX)),PSET
END SUB

CHOOSE:
  GOSUB GURGLE
  GOSUB CLICKIT
  IF S$ = "" THEN GOSUB LOCATION
  IF ASC(S$+" ") <> 13 THEN CHOOSE
  MENU 2,0,0
  IF PICK <= 6 THEN GOSUB CALCULATE
  IF PICK=7 OR PICK=8  THEN GOSUB ENTER.DATA
  IF PICK=9 OR PICK=10 THEN GOSUB EDIT.DATA
RETURN

GURGLE:
  FREQ = 300
  FOR G=1 TO 5
    FREQ = 500-FREQ
    SOUND FREQ,1,50
  NEXT G
RETURN

LOCATION:
  P = INT((Y-30)/18) + 1
  IF X>225 AND X<265 AND P>0 AND P<7 THEN
    CALL DRAW.CIRCLE(PICK,1)
    CALL DRAW.CIRCLE(P,2)
    PICK = P
  END IF
RETURN

ENTER.DATA:
  M = PICK - 6
  GOSUB MAT.SIZE
```

```
  IF N <> -9 THEN GOSUB OBSERVATIONS
RETURN

MAT.SIZE:
 CLS
 LOCATE 2,3
 PRINT "Please enter the size of ";M$(M)".";
 PRINT "  Enter -9 to exit."
 LINE(125,25)-(510,35),1,BF
 COLOR 0,1
 LOCATE 4,14: PRINT "Current Size: ";
 PRINT "Rows =";R(M);TAB(37)", Columns =";C(M)
 LINE(17,52)-(95,62),5,BF
 LINE(17,70)-(95,80),5,BF
 COLOR 1,5
 LOCATE 7,6: PRINT "Rows"
 LOCATE 9,3: PRINT "Columns"
 COLOR 1,0
 FOR I=1 TO 2
  N=0
  WHILE ( N<1 OR N>MAX.SIZE ) AND N <> -9
   GOSUB GURGLE
   LOCATE I*2+5,12: PRINT SPACE$(30)
   LOCATE I*2+5,12: INPUT "",V$
   N = VAL(V$)
  WEND
  IF N = -9 THEN I = 2
  N(I) = N
 NEXT I
 IF N <> -9 THEN R(M) = N(1): C(M) = N(2)
RETURN

OBSERVATIONS:
 FOR I=1 TO C(M)
  CLS
  GOSUB GURGLE
  PRINT
  PRINT "    Please enter data on ";M$(M);"."
  LINE(7,34)-(149,44),6,BF
  COLOR 1,6
  LOCATE 5,2: PRINT "Column No.";I
  COLOR 1,0
  FOR J=1 TO R(M)
   LOCATE 7,4 : PRINT "Row No.";J
   LOCATE 7,14: PRINT "=";SPACE$(35)
   LOCATE 7,16: INPUT "",V$
   IF M = 1 THEN
    X(J,I) = VAL(V$)
   ELSE
```

```
        Y(J,I) = VAL(V$)
      END IF
   NEXT J,I
 RETURN

 EDIT.DATA:
  M = PICK - 8
  FOR I=1 TO C(M)
   FOR J=1 TO R(M) STEP 10
     GOSUB DISPLAY
     GOSUB CORRECT
  NEXT J,I
 RETURN

 DISPLAY:
  CLS
  LINE(106,7)-(510,17),6,BF
  COLOR 1,6: LOCATE 2,12
  PRINT "These are values of ";M$(M);
  PRINT ", Column";I
  LINE(40,23)-(590,118),4,BF
  COLOR 2,4
  R = 0: HOLD.ROW = 0
  FOR L = J TO J+9
   IF L <= R(M) THEN
    R = R+1
    CALL DRAW.IT(R,1)
    LOCATE R+3,10: PRINT "Row No.";L
    LOCATE R+3,21: PRINT "= ";
    IF M = 1 THEN
      PRINT X(L,I)
    ELSE
      PRINT Y(L,I)
    END IF
   END IF
  NEXT L
 RETURN

 SUB DRAW.IT(RW,INX) STATIC
  SHARED CIRCLES(),CIRCLE.I()
  Y = (RW+3)*9 - 9
  PUT(65,Y),CIRCLES(CIRCLE.I(INX)),PSET
 END SUB

 CORRECT:
  COLOR 1,0
  LOCATE 16,24: PRINT "To make changes,"
  LOCATE 17,13: PRINT "Click mouse on circle,";
  PRINT " then hit Return"
```

```
  GOSUB SELECT
  IF HOLD.ROW <> Ø THEN
    GOSUB CHANGE: GOTO CORRECT
  END IF
RETURN

SELECT:
  GOSUB GURGLE
  GOSUB CLICKIT
  IF S$ = "" THEN GOSUB POSITION
  IF ASC(S$+" ") <> 13 THEN SELECT
RETURN

POSITION:
  ROW = INT(Y/9) - 2
  IF ROW>Ø AND ROW<=R AND X>55 AND X<9Ø THEN
    IF HOLD.ROW <> Ø THEN
      CALL DRAW.IT(HOLD.ROW,1)
    END IF
    CALL DRAW.IT(ROW,2)
    HOLD.ROW = ROW
  END IF
RETURN

CHANGE:
  LOCATE 16,24: PRINT SPACE$(16)
  LOCATE 17,13: PRINT SPACE$(38)
  LINE(65,133)-(185,143),5,BF
  COLOR 1,5
  LOCATE 16,8: PRINT "New Value ?"
  COLOR 1,Ø
  Q = J + HOLD.ROW - 1
  LOCATE 16,21: INPUT "",V$
  IF M=1 THEN X(Q,I)=VAL(V$) ELSE Y(Q,I)=VAL(V$)
  COLOR 2,4
  LOCATE HOLD.ROW+3,23: PRINT SPACE$(3Ø)
  LOCATE HOLD.ROW+3,23: PRINT VAL(V$)
  CALL DRAW.IT(HOLD.ROW,1)
  HOLD.ROW = Ø
  LINE(65,133)-(185,143),Ø,BF
  COLOR 1,Ø
  LOCATE 16,21: PRINT SPACE$(3Ø)
RETURN

CALCULATE:
  GOSUB MATRIX.NAMES
  GOSUB DIMENSIONS
  GOSUB CONFORMABILITY
  IF GOOF <> Ø THEN
```

```
    GOSUB GOOF
   ELSE
    GOSUB TRANSFER.VALUES
    LOCATE 12,28
    IF PICK <> 4 THEN PRINT "Computing"
    ON PICK GOSUB MAT1,MAT1,MAT2,MAT3,MAT4,MAT5
    IF RESULTS=1 AND GOOF=Ø THEN GOSUB RESULTS
   END IF
RETURN

MATRIX.NAMES:
 A$ = "matrix"
 IF PICK < 4 THEN A$ = "matrices"
 CLS
 LOCATE 2,3: PRINT "Please enter the ";A$;
 PRINT " to ";PICK$(PICK);"."
 LOCATE 5,3: PRINT "Matrices: X, Y, or Z"
 REM FIRST
  LOCATE 7,4: PRINT "First = ? _";
  GOSUB ENTER.NAME
  FIRST% = A
 REM SECOND
  IF PICK < 4 THEN
   LOCATE 9,3: PRINT "Second = ? _";
   GOSUB ENTER.NAME
   SECOND% = A
  END IF
RETURN

ENTER.NAME:
 A = Ø
 WHILE A < 88 OR A > 9Ø
  GOSUB GURGLE
  S$ = ""
  WHILE S$ = "": S$ = INKEY$: WEND
  A = ASC( UCASE$(S$) + " " )
 WEND
 PRINT CHR$(8);CHR$(A)
RETURN

DIMENSIONS:
 REM FIRST
  RF = R(FIRST%-87)
  CF = C(FIRST%-87)
 REM SECOND
  IF PICK < 4 THEN
   RS = R(SECOND%-87)
   CS = C(SECOND%-87)
  END IF
RETURN
```

```
CONFORMABILITY:
 REM + AND -
  IF PICK = 1 OR PICK = 2 THEN
   IF RF<>RS OR CF<>CS THEN GOOF = PICK
  END IF
 REM *
  IF PICK = 3 THEN
   IF CF <> RS THEN GOOF = 3
  END IF
 REM INVERSION
  IF PICK = 5 THEN
   IF RF <> CF THEN GOOF = 4
  END IF
 REM ZERO DIMENSION
  IF RF=Ø OR CF=Ø THEN GOOF = 5
RETURN

GOOF:
 CLS
 SOUND 400,3: SOUND 300,3: SOUND 200,3
 COLOR 1,6
 LINE(283,61)-(335,71),6,BF
 LOCATE 8,30: PRINT "Goof"
 S$ = ERROR.CODE$(GOOF)
 COLOR 1,Ø
 LOCATE 10: PRINT PTAB(313-10*LEN(S$)/2)S$
 LOCATE 17,26: PRINT "Press any key"
 GOSUB CLICKIT
RETURN

TRANSFER.VALUES:
 REM DOUBLE PRECISION
 REM FIRST
  FOR I=1 TO RF
   FOR J=1 TO CF
    IF FIRST% = 88 THEN W = X(I,J)
    IF FIRST% = 89 THEN W = Y(I,J)
    IF FIRST% = 90 THEN W = Z(I,J)
    IF W < Ø THEN SG% = -1 ELSE SG% = 1
    F(I,J) = SG%*VAL( ZERO$+STR$(ABS(W)) )
   NEXT J,I
 REM SECOND
  IF PICK < 4 THEN
   FOR I=1 TO RS
    FOR J=1 TO CS
     IF SECOND% = 88 THEN W = X(I,J)
     IF SECOND% = 89 THEN W = Y(I,J)
     IF SECOND% = 90 THEN W = Z(I,J)
     IF W < Ø THEN SG% = -1 ELSE SG% = 1
```

```
      S(I,J) = SG%*VAL( ZERO$+STR$(ABS(W)) )
    NEXT J,I
   END IF
RETURN

MAT1:
 FOR I=1 TO RF
  FOR J=1 TO CF
   IF PICK=1 THEN Z(I,J) = F(I,J) + S(I,J)
   IF PICK=2 THEN Z(I,J) = F(I,J) - S(I,J)
 NEXT J,I
 R(3) = RF: C(3) = CF
RETURN

MAT2:
 FOR I=1 TO RF
  FOR J=1 TO CS
   Z(I,J) = Ø
   FOR L=1 TO CF
    Z(I,J) = Z(I,J) + F(I,L)*S(L,J)
 NEXT L,J,I
 R(3) = RF: C(3) = CS
RETURN

MAT3:
 CLS
 GOSUB GURGLE
 LOCATE 2,3
 INPUT "What is the value of your scalar ";S$
 SK = VAL(S$)
 LOCATE 10,26: PRINT "Computing ..."
 FOR I=1 TO RF
  FOR J=1 TO CF
   Z(I,J) = F(I,J)*SK
 NEXT J,I
 R(3) = RF: C(3) = CF
RETURN

MAT4:
 GOSUB TACK.ON.I
 GOSUB INVERT
 IF GOOF = Ø THEN
  GOSUB MOVE.MATRIX
 ELSE
  GOSUB GOOF
 END IF
RETURN
```

```
TACK.ON.I:
 FOR I=1 TO RF
  FOR J=1 TO RF
   F(I,RF+J) = Ø
   IF J = I THEN F(I,RF+J) = 1
 NEXT J,I
RETURN

INVERT:
 FOR I=1 TO RF
  S = F(I,I)
  IF S = Ø THEN
   GOOF = 6: I = RF
  ELSE
   REM ADJUST KEY ROW
    FOR J = I TO 2*RF
     F(I,J) = F(I,J)/S
    NEXT J
   REM ADJUST REMAINING ROWS
    FOR J=1 TO RF
     Z = F(J,I)
     FOR L = I TO 2*RF
      IF J <> I THEN F(J,L) = F(J,L) - Z*F(I,L)
    NEXT L,J
  END IF
 NEXT I
RETURN

MOVE.MATRIX:
 FOR I=1 TO RF
  FOR J=1 TO CF
   Z(I,J) = F(I,RF+J)
 NEXT J,I
 R(3) = RF: C(3) = CF
RETURN

MAT5:
 FOR I=1 TO CF
  FOR J=1 TO RF
   Z(I,J) = F(J,I)
 NEXT J,I
 R(3) = CF: C(3) = RF
RETURN

RESULTS:
 R = R(3): C = C(3)
 FOR Q=1 TO R STEP 1Ø
  FOR I=1 TO C STEP 2
   GOSUB PAINT.SCREEN
```

```
     GOSUB BODY
  NEXT I,Q
RETURN

PAINT.SCREEN:
 CLS
 LINE(265,6)-(355,18),1,B: PAINT(313,1Ø),6,1
 COLOR 1,6: LOCATE 2,28: PRINT "Matrix Z"
 LINE(35,3Ø)-(595,147),4,BF
 REM COLUMN HEADING
  COLOR 2,4
  COL = 27
  FOR L = I TO I+1
   IF L <= C THEN
    LOCATE 5,COL: PRINT "Column";L
    COL = COL + 23
   END IF
  NEXT L
RETURN

BODY:
 ROW = 7
 FOR J = Q TO Q+9
  IF J <= R THEN
   LOCATE ROW,7: PRINT USING "Row##";J;
   COL = 18
   FOR L = I TO I+1
    IF L <= C THEN
     LOCATE ROW,COL
     PRINT USING FT$;Z(J,L)
     COL = COL + 23
    END IF
   NEXT L
  END IF
  ROW = ROW + 1
 NEXT J
 COLOR 1,Ø
 LOCATE 2Ø,26: PRINT "Press any key";
 GOSUB CLICKIT
RETURN
```

CHAPTER 7

Statistics

CHAPTER 7

Statistics

We all see a large quantity of numerical information each day, everything from batting averages to stock market prices to monthly utility bills. Here are a couple of programs that will help you transform your raw data into useful, understandable form.

Scatter Diagram. This program draws a line of best fit through a set of observations plotted on an X-Y grid. With "Scatter Diagram" you can view all the quadrants of the graph or just the first, you can predict Y for any value of X, and you can estimate four types of curves. And you can do all this without having to enter data more than once.

Super Curve-Fitter. With this program, you can perform multiple linear regression analysis on a set of data. Edit your entries by using the mouse. With "Super Curve-Fitter" you get some of the same capability normally found on much bigger statistical packages for mainframe computers, and you'll find Curve-Fitter far easier to use.

Statistics Menu Driver
Save using the filename **STATISTICS**

```
REM STATISTICS
 GOSUB INITIALIZE
 GOSUB MAIN.MENU
 RUN TITLE.SHORT$(PICK)
END

INITIALIZE:
 GOSUB SETSCREEN
 GOSUB KEYVALUES
 GOSUB SETMENUS
 GOSUB SETCOLORS
 GOSUB SHAPES
RETURN

SETSCREEN:
 SCREEN 1,640,200,3,2
 WINDOW 2,"Statistics",,0,1
RETURN
```

```
KEYVALUES:
 DEFINT A-Z
 N = 2
 DIM TITLE.LONG$(N),TITLE.SHORT$(N),DISCS(250)
 DISC.I(1) = 1: DISC.I(2) = 125
 READ CHAPTER$
 FOR I=1 TO N
  READ TITLE.LONG$(I),TITLE.SHORT$(I)
 NEXT
RETURN

SETMENUS:
 FOR I=2 TO 4
  MENU I,0,0,""
 NEXT
 MENU 1,0,1,"STOP"
 MENU 1,1,1," Go to BASIC"
 MENU 1,2,1," Go to System"
 MENU ON
 ON MENU GOSUB GOODBYE
RETURN

GOODBYE:
 WINDOW CLOSE 2: WINDOW 1: MENU RESET
 SCREEN CLOSE 1
 ITEM = MENU(1)
 IF ITEM = 2 THEN SYSTEM
 CLS
 PRINT "Bye-Bye"
 STOP
RETURN

SETCOLORS:
 REM TAN, GREEN, & RED
  PALETTE 4,.95,.7,.53
  PALETTE 5,.14,.43,0
  PALETTE 6,.93,.2,0
RETURN

SHAPES:
 X=313: Y=80
 LINE(X-12,Y-8)-(X+12,Y+8),4,BF
 FOR I=1 TO 2
  K = 7-I
  CIRCLE(X,Y),12,K: PAINT(X,Y),K
  GET(X-12,Y-8)-(X+12,Y+8),DISCS(DISC.I(I))
 NEXT
RETURN
```

```
MAIN.MENU:
 CLS
 RTN$ = "OFF": PICK = 1
 S$ = CHAPTER$: L = LEN(S$)
 LINE(313-10*L/2-15,15)-(313+10*L/2+15,27),1,B
 PAINT(313,20),6,1
 COLOR 1,6: LOCATE 3: PRINT PTAB(313-10*L/2)S$
 LINE(135,35)-(495,130),2,B: PAINT(313,80),4,2
 COLOR 2,4
 FOR I=1 TO N
  IF I = PICK THEN INX = 2 ELSE INX = 1
  CALL DRAW.CIRCLE(I,INX)
  LOCATE I*2+4,21: PRINT TITLE.LONG$(I)
 NEXT
 LINE(263,141)-(360,153),2,B: PAINT(313,145),3,2
 COLOR 2,3
 LOCATE 17: PRINT PTAB(282)"Return"
 COLOR 1,0
 LOCATE 19,11: PRINT "Click Mouse on Choice,";
 PRINT " then Click on Return"
 GOSUB CHOOSE
RETURN

SUB DRAW.CIRCLE(R,INX) STATIC
 SHARED DISCS(),DISC.I()
 Y = 18*R+22
 PUT(162,Y),DISCS(DISC.I(INX)),PSET
END SUB

CHOOSE:
 GOSUB GURGLE
 GOSUB CLICKIT
 IF S$ = "" THEN GOSUB LOCATION
 IF ASC(S$+" ") <> 13 AND RTN$ = "OFF" THEN
  GOTO CHOOSE
 END IF
RETURN

GURGLE:
 FREQ = 300
 FOR G=1 TO 5
  FREQ = 500 - FREQ
  SOUND FREQ,1,50
 NEXT
RETURN

CLICKIT:
 S$ = ""
 WHILE MOUSE(0) = 0 AND S$ = ""
```

```
   S$ = INKEY$
  WEND
   X = MOUSE(1)
   Y = MOUSE(2)
  WHILE MOUSE(Ø)<> Ø: WEND: REM RESET
 RETURN

 LOCATION:
  IF X>263 AND X<36Ø AND Y>141 AND Y<153 THEN
   RTN$ = "ON"
  ELSE
   P = INT((Y-39)/18) + 1
   IF X>155 AND X<195 AND P>Ø AND P<= N THEN
    CALL DRAW.CIRCLE(PICK,1)
    CALL DRAW.CIRCLE(P,2)
    PICK = P
   END IF
  END IF
 RETURN

 REM PROGRAMS
  DATA Statistics
  DATA Scatter Diagram, SCATTER
  DATA Super Curve-Fitter, SUPER
```

Scatter Diagram

Almost everyone sometimes has the urge to do it. You see a plot of points between two variables and you want to draw a line of best fit through them to depict the apparent trend.

With Scatter Diagram this urge is easy to satisfy. Namely, enter and edit your data. Then gape admiringly as Scatter Diagram draws an X-Y grid on your screen, then scales and labels axes, plots your points, and computes and draws a least-squares regression line.

And this is just the beginning. For with Scatter Diagram you can zoom in on the first quadrant of the graph, scale axes to fit your fancy, compute Y for any value of X, and estimate three other curves besides the commonplace straight line. And you can do all this without having to enter data more than once.

Perhaps a good way to introduce Scatter Diagram is with an example. You'll see how to choose an equation to estimate, select a quadrant to view, and display regression results.

Victories and Turnovers

Pro football coaches, sportscasters, and Sunday afternoon armchair quarterbacks are concerned about turnovers. To win football games, the adage says, "don't beat yourselves." In other words, force the opponent to make a mistake while playing error-free football on offense.

But is this conventional wisdom right? To find out, let's use Scatter Diagram to explore the statistical relationship between victories and turnovers.

Table 7-1 presents grist for our curve-plotting mill. Percent wins is denoted by Y and net turnovers by X.

After you enter this data into the Amiga, Scatter Diagram asks which type of equation you'd like to estimate. Figure 7-1 presents the choices. Let's select the popular linear equation since this is the easiest to estimate. Since some of our observations are negative, use the pull-down menu to tell the Amiga to show all four quadrants of the X-Y grid.

Based on the range of observations on Y and X, Scatter Diagram automatically computes tick intervals for our plot and uses these in Figure 7-2. As suspected, the most successful teams in the NFL tend to be those with the most net turnovers per game.

Regression Results

Now the real power of Scatter Diagram comes into play. With points plotted and curve fitted, we can repeatedly exercise a host of handy options simply by using the pull-down menu labeled Options. Three of the choices enable us to see and use the results of our regression run: Show Equation, Show R-Squared, and Predict Value of Y.

Showing the equation, for example, gives the result $Y = 50.000 + 10.743 * X$. Hence, a team with a net turnover figure of zero should win half its games, or 50 percent. And every one-unit increase in net turnovers per game should lead to 10.743 percent more victories during the season.

Exploring some more, we find that the R-squared value of our equation is 0.302. This means that 30 percent of the variation in victories is explained by turnovers.

In predicting percent victories, we simply enter a value for net turnovers. One net turnover per game, for example, suggests that a team will win 60.7 percent of the time.

Embellish the Picture

To embellish our plot, try the Show Title and Draw Grid options. In the latter, the Amiga draws little dashes across the screen. This is particularly useful for very precise work, that is, when we're interested in knowing exactly where an observation or regression line lies.

X and Y Axes Tick Marks

If you don't like the values the Amiga chooses for intervals along the X and Y axes, don't worry. Simply choose the menu option for changing tick marks. Then enter any new value you like, up to half a million. The Amiga will automatically redraw your graph.

This option can be useful in determining what an equation will look like for values of X that are much larger than those used to estimate the regression equation.

Selecting an Equation

If a plot of your data suggests that the association between Y and X is nonlinear, use the Estimate a New Equation option to return to the main menu. You can then choose to fit a power, exponential, or reciprocal equation to your data. It's usually a good idea to begin with the commonplace linear function, however. This is the simplest case, and gives a good baseline for further analysis.

A word of warning. The reciprocal equation always generates a rectangular hyperbola. Hence, two separate curves that are asymptotic with respect to the Y axis will appear when you plot a full picture. In most cases you'll probably want to ignore the curve on the left. Finally, don't worry about values of X for which a curve is undefined. Scatter Diagram jumps over these.

Scatter Diagram is a powerful statistical tool for plotting points and drawing trend lines. With it you can scale axes, view all the quadrants of a graph or just the first, and compute several types of regression equations. You may want to use Scatter Diagram as a prelude to a full-blown multiple linear regression analysis, covered next in this chapter.

Table 7-1. Victories and Turnovers

(First 10 Games of the 1983 Season)

Team	Percent Wins	Net Turnovers Per Game
Washington	80	2.5
Seattle	60	1.8
Minnesota	60	1.7
Miami	70	1.0
Dallas	90	0.9
Baltimore	60	0.7
Kansas City	40	0.7
San Francisco	60	0.7
Pittsburgh	80	0.5
Atlanta	40	0.4
Denver	60	0.3
Tampa Bay	10	0.3
Cincinnati	40	0.2
Buffalo	60	0.1
New England	50	−0.1
Detroit	50	−0.4
New Orleans	60	−0.4
L.A. Rams	60	−0.5
N.Y. Jets	40	−0.5
Philadelphia	40	−0.5
Cleveland	50	−0.7
N.Y. Giants	25	−0.7
Chicago	30	−1.0
St. Louis	35	−1.0
Green Bay	50	−1.3
L.A. Raiders	70	−1.4
San Diego	30	−1.6
Houston	0	−1.7

Note: Net Turnovers = fumbles and interceptions recovered minus number committed.

Figure 7-1. Equation to Estimate

Linear	$Y = a + b*X$
Power	$Y = a*X\hat{\ }b$
Exponential	$Y = a*e\hat{\ }(b*X)$
Reciprocal	$Y = a + b/X$

Figure 7-2. Scatter Diagram

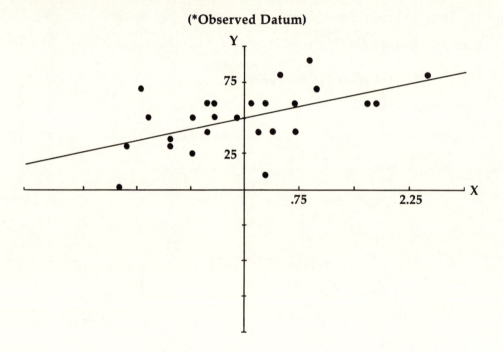

(*Observed Datum)

Program 7-1. Scatter Diagram
Save using the filename **SCATTER**

```
REM SCATTER DIAGRAM
  GOSUB INITIALIZE
  GOSUB ENTER.DATA
  GOSUB EDIT.DATA
  GOSUB SCALE.AXES
  GOSUB MAIN.MENU
RETURN
```

```
INITIALIZE:
 GOSUB SETSCREEN
 GOSUB KEYVALUES
 GOSUB SETMENUS
 GOSUB SETCOLORS
 GOSUB SHAPES
 GOSUB HEADING
 GOSUB INSTRUCTIONS
RETURN

SETSCREEN:
 SCREEN 1,640,200,3,2
 WINDOW 2,"Scatter Diagram",,0,1
RETURN

KEYVALUES:
 RANDOMIZE TIMER
 DEFINT A-J,L-W: DEFDBL A,B,M,S
 REM MAXIMUM NUMBER OF OBSERVATIONS
  DATA 100
  READ NX
  OPTION BASE 1
  DIM X(NX,2),XT(NX),YT(NX)
  DIM DISCS(200),CIRCLES(150)
 REM SHAPE INDICES
  DISC.I(1) = 1: DISC.I(2) = 100
  CIRCLE.I(1) = 1: CIRCLE.I(2) = 75
 GOSUB OUTPUT.FORMATS
 GOSUB MENU.CHOICES
 GOSUB ERROR.CODES
 GOSUB GRID.DATA
 V$(1) = "Y": V$(2) = "X"
 REM MAX VALUE FOR AXIS INCREMENTS
  MAX.VALUE = 500000&
RETURN

OUTPUT.FORMATS.
 FOR I=2 TO 6
  S$ = STRING$(12-I,"#")
  F$(I) = S$ + "." + STRING$(I,"#")
 NEXT
RETURN

MENU.CHOICES:
 REM EQUATIONS
  DATA Y = a + b*X, Linear, Y = a*X^b, Power
  DATA Y = a*e^(b*X), Exponential
  DATA Y = a + b/X, Reciprocal
  FOR I=1 TO 4
```

```
    READ PICK.EQ$(I), PICK.NM$(I)
   NEXT
  REM GRAPH
   DATA Show Title, Draw Grid
   DATA Change Axis Intervals
   DATA Show Equation, Show R-Squared
   DATA Predict Value of Y
   DATA Estimate a New Equation
   FOR I=1 TO 7
    READ GRAPH$(I)
   NEXT
RETURN

ERROR.CODES:
 DATA I can't take the log of zero
 DATA I can't divide by zero
 DATA I can't estimate your equation
 FOR I=1 TO 3
  READ ERROR.CODE$(I)
 NEXT
RETURN

GRID.DATA:
 REM ORIGIN
  DATA 110,138
  DATA 305,84
  FOR I=1 TO 2
   READ CX(I),CY(I)
  NEXT
 REM PLOT VALUES
  DATA 12,156,18,45,565,65
  READ YF%,YL%,YT%,XF%,XL%,XT%
 REM ACTUAL-TO-SCREEN COORDINATES
  DEF FN YS(V!) = CY - 18/YD*V!
  DEF FN XS(V!) = CX + 65/XD*V!
RETURN

SETMENUS:
 DATA 5, Color, Tan, Blue, Green, Gray
 DATA Random
 DATA 2, Quadrant, View the First
 DATA View them All
 DATA 1, Options, Show Title
 DATA 5, Decimals, 2 Places, 3 Places, 4 Places
 DATA 5 Places, 6 Places
 DATA 3, Stop, Go to BASIC
 DATA Go to Statistics Menu, Go to System
 FOR I=1 TO 5
  READ NUMBER
```

```
   FOR J=Ø TO NUMBER
     READ TITLE$
     IF J<>Ø THEN TITLE$ = SPACE$(3) + TITLE$
     STATUS = 1
     IF I=1 OR I=2 OR I=4 THEN
       IF J = 1 THEN STATUS = 2
     END IF
     MENU I,J,STATUS,TITLE$
   NEXT J,I
   FOR I=2 TO 7
     MENU 3,I,1,SPACE$(3) + GRAPH$(I)
   NEXT
   MENU 3,Ø,Ø
   KOLOR% = 1: QUADRANT = 1: DP = 2
   F$ = F$(DP)
RETURN

SETCOLORS:
 REM TAN, BLUE, GREEN, GRAY
  DATA .95,.7,.53,  .36,.57,1
  DATA .22,.76,.68,  .72,.7,.86
  FOR I=1 TO 4
    FOR J=1 TO 3
      READ KOLOR(I,J)
  NEXT J,I
 REM TAN, GREEN, & RED
  PALETTE 4,.95,.7,.53
  PALETTE 5,.14,.43,Ø
  PALETTE 6,.93,.2,Ø
RETURN

SHAPES:
 REM DISCS
  X=313: Y=8Ø
  LINE(X-12,Y-5)-(X+12,Y+5),4,BF
  FOR I=1 TO 2
   K% = 7-I
   CIRCLE(X,Y),12,K%: PAINT(X,Y),K%
   GET(X-12,Y-5)-(X+12,Y+5),DISCS(DISC.I(I))
  NEXT
 REM CIRCLES
  CLS
  X1 =X-7: X2 = X+7: Y1 = Y-3: Y2 = Y+3
  LINE(X1,Y1)-(X2,Y2),4,BF
  FOR I=1 TO 2
   K% = 11-5*I
   CIRCLE(X,Y),7,2: PAINT(X,Y),K%,2
   GET(X1,Y1)-(X2,Y2),CIRCLES(CIRCLE.I(I))
  NEXT
RETURN
```

```
HEADING:
 MENU ON
 ON MENU GOSUB OPTIONS
 CLS
 COLOR 3,Ø: LOCATE 18,3Ø:PRINT "then"
 COLOR 1,Ø
 LOCATE 1Ø,24: PRINT "Scatter Diagram"
 LOCATE 17,24: PRINT "Please use menus,"
 LOCATE 19,21: PRINT "Click mouse to start"
 GOSUB CLICKIT
RETURN

OPTIONS:
 ID = MENU(Ø): ITEM = MENU(1)
 ON ID GOSUB MENU1,MENU2,MENU3,MENU4,GOODBYE
 ITEM = Ø
RETURN

MENU1:
 K1 = KOLOR(ITEM,1): K2 = KOLOR(ITEM,2)
 K3 = KOLOR(ITEM,3)
 IF ITEM=5 THEN K1=RND: K2=RND: K3=RND
 PALETTE 4,K1,K2,K3
 MENU 1,KOLOR%,1: MENU 1,ITEM,2
 KOLOR% = ITEM
RETURN

MENU2:
 MENU 2,QUADRANT,1: MENU 2,ITEM,2
 QUADRANT = ITEM
 ACTION% = 8
RETURN

MENU3:
 ACTION% = ITEM
RETURN

MENU4:
 MENU 4,DP-1,1: MENU 4,ITEM,2
 DP = ITEM + 1
 F$ = F$(DP)
RETURN

GOODBYE:
 WINDOW CLOSE 2: WINDOW 1: MENU RESET
 SCREEN CLOSE 1
 IF ITEM = 2 THEN RUN "STATISTICS"
 IF ITEM = 3 THEN SYSTEM
 COLOR 1,Ø: CLS
```

```
 PRINT "Bye-Bye"
 STOP
RETURN

CLICKIT:
 S$ = ""
 WHILE MOUSE(Ø) = Ø AND S$ = ""
  S$ = INKEY$
 WEND
  X = MOUSE(1)
  Y = MOUSE(2)
 WHILE MOUSE(Ø)<> Ø: WEND: REM RESET
RETURN

INSTRUCTIONS:
 CLS
 PRINT
 PRINT "    Scatter Diagram draws a line of";
 PRINT " best-fit through a set"
 PRINT " of observations plotted on an";
 PRINT " X-Y grid."
 PRINT
 PRINT "    And this is just the beginning.";
 PRINT "  For with Scatter Diagram"
 PRINT " you can"
 PRINT
 PRINT TAB(12)
 PRINT "-- View all the quadrants or just";
 PRINT " the first,"
 PRINT TAB(12)
 PRINT "-- Predict Y for any value of X, and"
 PRINT TAB(12)
 PRINT "-- Estimate four types of curves."
 PRINT
 PRINT "    And you can do all this without";
 PRINT " having to enter data"
 PRINT " more than once."
 LOCATE 19,27:PRINT "Click Mouse"
 GOSUB CLICKIT
RETURN

ENTER.DATA:
 REM Y
  CLS
  PRINT
  PRINT "    Please enter observations on the";
  PRINT " dependent variable, Y."
  PRINT " Hit RETURN when you're through."
  GOSUB ON.Y
```

407

```
  REM X
    GOSUB ON.X
RETURN

ON.Y:
 GOSUB GURGLE
 N = NX
 FOR J=1 TO NX
  LOCATE 5,14: PRINT SPACE$(30)
  LOCATE 5,3: PRINT "Y(";J
  LOCATE 5,9: PRINT ")= ? ";
  INPUT "",X$
  IF X$ = "" THEN
   N = J-1
   J = NX
  ELSE
   X(J,1) = VAL(X$)
  END IF
 NEXT
 REM DEGREES OF FREEDOM
  IF N < 2 THEN
    LOCATE 18,10: PRINT "I need at least 2";
    PRINT " observations ¦  Try again."
    GOTO ON.Y
  END IF
RETURN

GURGLE:
 FREQ = 300
 FOR G=1 TO 5
  FREQ = 500-FREQ
  SOUND FREQ,1,50
 NEXT G
RETURN

ON.X:
 CLS
 GOSUB GURGLE
 PRINT
 PRINT "   Please enter data on the explanatory";
 PRINT " variable, X."
 FOR J=1 TO N
  LOCATE 4,14: PRINT SPACE$(30)
  LOCATE 4,3: PRINT "X(";J
  LOCATE 4,9: PRINT ")= ? ";
  INPUT "",X$
  X(J,2) = VAL(X$)
 NEXT
RETURN
```

```
EDIT.DATA:
 FOR I=1 TO 2
  FOR J=1 TO N STEP 1Ø
   GOSUB DISPLAY
   GOSUB CORRECT
 NEXT J,I
RETURN

DISPLAY:
 CLS
 LINE(2ØØ,7)-(43Ø,17),6,BF
 COLOR 1,6
 LOCATE 2,22
 PRINT "These are values of " + V$(I)
 LINE (4Ø,22)-(59Ø,119),2,B: PAINT(313,8Ø),4,2
 COLOR 2,4
 R = Ø: H.ROW = Ø
 FOR L = J TO J+9
  IF L <= N THEN
   R = R+1
   CALL DRAW.IT(R,1)
   LOCATE R+3,1Ø: PRINT V$(I);"(";MID$(STR$(L),2)
   LOCATE R+3,15: PRINT ")= ";X(L,I)
  END IF
 NEXT L
RETURN

SUB DRAW.IT(RW,INX) STATIC
 SHARED CIRCLES(),CIRCLE.I()
 Y = (RW+3)*9 - 9
 PUT(65,Y),CIRCLES(CIRCLE.I(INX)),PSET
END SUB

CORRECT:
 LINE(262,132)-(36Ø,144),2,B: PAINT(313,137),3,2
 COLOR 2,3
 LOCATE 16: PRINT PTAB(282)"Return"
 COLOR 1,Ø
 LOCATE 19,9: PRINT "Click on Circle to";
 PRINT " Edit, then Click on Return."
 GOSUB CHOOSE
 IF H.ROW <> Ø THEN
  GOSUB CHANGE: GOTO CORRECT
 END IF
RETURN

CHOOSE:
 RTN$ = "OFF"
 GOSUB GURGLE
```

```
    GOSUB CLICKIT
    IF S$ = "" THEN GOSUB LOCATION
    IF ASC(S$+" ") <> 13 AND RTN$ = "OFF" THEN
     GOTO CHOOSE
    END IF
  RETURN

  LOCATION:
    IF X>263 AND X<360 AND Y>131 AND Y<145 THEN
     RTN$ = "ON"
    ELSE
     ROW = INT(Y/9) - 2
     IF ROW>0 AND ROW<=R AND X>55 AND X<90 THEN
      IF H.ROW <> 0 THEN CALL DRAW.IT(H.ROW,1)
      CALL DRAW.IT(ROW,2)
      H.ROW = ROW
     END IF
    END IF
  RETURN

  CHANGE:
   LINE(262,132)-(360,144),0,BF
   LINE(65,133)-(185,143),5,BF
   COLOR 1,5
   LOCATE 16,8: PRINT "New Value ?"
   COLOR 1,0
   LOCATE 16,21: INPUT "",V$
   X(J+H.ROW-1,I) = VAL(V$)
   COLOR 2,4
   LOCATE H.ROW+3,18: PRINT SPACE$(30)
   LOCATE H.ROW+3,18: PRINT X(J+H.ROW-1,I)
   CALL DRAW.IT(H.ROW,1)
   H.ROW = 0
   LINE(65,133)-(185,143),0,BF
   COLOR 1,0
   LOCATE 16,21: PRINT SPACE$(30)
  RETURN

  SCALE.AXES:
   GOSUB HIGH.LOW
   Q = QUADRANT
   GOSUB TIC.MARKS
  RETURN

  HIGH.LOW:
   HY! = -1E+10: HX! = HY!
   LY! =  1E+10: LX! = LY!
   FOR J=1 TO N
    IF X(J,1) > HY! THEN HY! = X(J,1)
```

```
    IF X(J,2) > HX! THEN HX! = X(J,2)
    IF X(J,1) < LY! THEN LY! = X(J,1)
    IF X(J,2) < LX! THEN LX! = X(J,2)
  NEXT
RETURN

TIC.MARKS:
  IF Q = 1 THEN D = 6 ELSE D = 3
  REM Y AXIS
  H! = ABS(HY!): L! = ABS(LY!)
  IF H! >= L! THEN Y = H!
  IF L! >  H! THEN Y = L!
  YD = INT(Y/D + .5)
  REM X AXIS
  H! = ABS(HX!): L! = ABS(LX!)
  IF H! >= L! THEN X = H!
  IF L! >  H! THEN X = L!
  XD = INT(X/D + .5)
  GOSUB CHECK.BOUNDS
RETURN

CHECK.BOUNDS:
  IF YD = Ø THEN YD = .5
  IF YD > MAX.VALUE THEN YD = MAX.VALUE
  IF XD = Ø THEN XD = .5
  IF XD > MAX.VALUE THEN XD = MAX.VALUE
RETURN

MAIN.MENU:
  PICK = 1: RTN$ = "OFF": GOOF = Ø
  GOSUB SHOW.CHOICES
  GOSUB SELECT
  IF Q <> QUADRANT THEN GOSUB SCALE.AXES
  GOSUB COMPUTE
  GOTO MAIN.MENU
RETURN

SHOW.CHOICES:
  COLOR 1,Ø
  CLS
  LOCATE 3: PRINT PTAB(215)"Equation to Estimate"
  LINE(135,35)-(495,12Ø),2,B: PAINT(313,8Ø),4,2
  COLOR 2,4
  FOR I=1 TO 4
    IF I = PICK THEN INX = 2 ELSE INX = 1
    CALL DRAW.CIRCLE(I,INX)
    LOCATE I*2+4,21: PRINT PICK.EQ$(I);
    PRINT TAB(37)PICK.NM$(I)
  NEXT
```

411

```
   LINE(262,141)-(360,153),2,B: PAINT(313,145),3,2
   COLOR 2,3
   LOCATE 17: PRINT PTAB(282)"Return"
   COLOR 1,0
   LOCATE 19,11: PRINT "Click Mouse on Choice,";
   PRINT " then Click on Return"
 RETURN

 SUB DRAW.CIRCLE(R,INX) STATIC
  SHARED DISCS(),DISC.I()
  Y = 18*R+22
  PUT(162,Y),DISCS(DISC.I(INX)),PSET
 END SUB

 SELECT:
  GOSUB GURGLE
  GOSUB CLICKIT
  IF S$ = "" THEN GOSUB POSITION
  IF ASC(S$+" ") <> 13 AND RTN$ = "OFF" THEN
   GOTO SELECT
  END IF
 RETURN

 POSITION:
  IF X>263 AND X<360 AND Y>141 AND Y<153 THEN
   RTN$ = "ON"
  ELSE
   P = INT((Y-39)/18) + 1
   IF X>155 AND X<195 AND P>0 AND P<5 THEN
    CALL DRAW.CIRCLE(PICK,1)
    CALL DRAW.CIRCLE(P,2)
    PICK = P
   END IF
  END IF
 RETURN

 COMPUTE:
  COLOR 1,0
  CLS
  LOCATE 10,27: PRINT "Computing"
  REM TRANSFORM DATA
   ON PICK GOSUB LINEAR,POWER,EXPNL,RECPRL
  REM ESTIMATE EQUATION & SHOW RESULTS
   IF GOOF = 0 THEN GOSUB ESTIMATE
   IF GOOF = 0 THEN GOSUB DRAW.GRAPH
   IF GOOF = 0 THEN GOSUB NEXT.ACTION
  REM ERROR
   IF GOOF <> 0 THEN GOSUB GOOF
 RETURN
```

```
LINEAR:
 FOR I=1 TO N
  YT(I) = X(I,1)
  XT(I) = X(I,2)
 NEXT
RETURN

POWER:
 FOR I=1 TO N
  IF X(I,1) > Ø THEN
   YT(I) = LOG( X(I,1) )
  ELSE
   GOOF = 1: I = N
  END IF
  IF X(I,2) > Ø THEN
   XT(I) = LOG( X(I,2) )
  ELSE
   GOOF = 1: I = N
  END IF
 NEXT
RETURN

GOOF:
 CLS
 SOUND 4ØØ,3: SOUND 3ØØ,3: SOUND 2ØØ,3
 COLOR 1,6
 LINE(283,61)-(335,71),6,BF
 LOCATE 8,3Ø: PRINT "Goof"
 S$ = ERROR.CODE$(GOOF)
 COLOR 1,Ø
 LOCATE 1Ø: PRINT PTAB(313-1Ø*LEN(S$)/2)S$
 LOCATE 17,26: PRINT "Press any key"
 GOSUB CLICKIT
RETURN

EXPNL:
 FOR I=1 TO N
  XT(I) = X(I,2)
  IF X(I,1) > Ø THEN
   YT(I) = LOG( X(I,1) )
  ELSE
   GOOF = 1: I = N
  END IF
 NEXT
RETURN

RECPRL:
 FOR I=1 TO N
  YT(I) = X(I,1)
```

413

```
   IF X(I,2) <> Ø THEN
    XT(I) = 1/X(I,2)
   ELSE
    GOOF = 2: I = N
   END IF
  NEXT
 RETURN

 ESTIMATE:
  REM KEY SUMS
   SX=Ø: SY=Ø: SQ.X=Ø: SQ.Y=Ø: CP# = Ø
   FOR I=1 TO N
    SX    = SX    + XT(I)
    SY    = SY    + YT(I)
    SQ.X = SQ.X + XT(I)^2
    SQ.Y = SQ.Y + YT(I)^2
    CP#  = CP#   + XT(I)*YT(I)
   NEXT
  REM KEY DENOMINATOR
   DMT# = N*SQ.X - SX*SX
   IF DMT# = Ø THEN GOOF = 3
  REM EQUATION
   IF GOOF = Ø THEN
    B = (N*CP# - SX*SY)/DMT#
    A = (SY - B*SX)/N
    IF PICK = 2 OR PICK = 3 THEN A = EXP(A)
   END IF
  REM R-SQUARED
   SS.TOTAL = SQ.Y - SY*SY/N
   SS.REGRN = B*(CP# - SX*SY/N)
   IF SS.TOTAL <> Ø THEN
    RSQ! = SS.REGRN/SS.TOTAL
   ELSE
    GOOF = 3
   END IF
 RETURN

 DRAW.GRAPH:
  GOSUB DRAW.AXES
  GOSUB LABEL.AXES
  GOSUB PLOT.POINTS
  GOSUB DRAW.CURVE
 RETURN

 DRAW.AXES:
  CLS
  LINE(6,3)-(62Ø,16Ø),6,B: PAINT(313,8Ø),4,6
  CX = CX(Q): CY = CY(Q)
  REM Y AXIS
```

```
    COLOR 2,4
    FOR I = CX-1 TO CX+1
      LINE(I,YF%)-(I,YL%)
    NEXT
    FOR I = YF% TO YL% STEP YT%
      LINE(CX-2,I)-(CX+2,I)
    NEXT
  REM X AXIS
    LINE(XF%,CY)-(XL%,CY)
    FOR I = XF% TO XL% STEP XT%
      FOR J = I-1 TO I+1
      LINE(J,CY-1)-(J,CY+1)
    NEXT J,I
RETURN

LABEL.AXES:
  REM Y AXIS
    YD = ABS(YD)
    FOR I=1 TO 10-3*Q
      Y = YD*I
      L = LEN(STR$(Y))
      LOCATE 22-6*Q-2*I,19*Q-9-L: PRINT Y
    NEXT
  REM X AXIS
    XD = ABS(XD)
    FOR I=1 TO 7-2*Q STEP 2
      X = XD*I
      L = LEN(STR$(X))
      IF Q = 1 THEN
        LOCATE 17: PRINT PTAB(105+65*I-L*10/2);X
      ELSE
        LOCATE 11: PRINT PTAB(300+65*I-L*10/2);X
      END IF
    NEXT
    LOCATE 22-6*Q: PRINT PTAB(570)"x"
    LOCATE 17: PRINT PTAB(CX-20)"y"
RETURN

PLOT.POINTS:
  FOR I=1 TO N
    Y = FN YS(X(I,1))
    X = FN XS(X(I,2))
    X$ = "OFF": Y$ = "OFF"
    IF X >= XF% AND X <= XL% THEN X$ = "OK"
    IF Y >= YF% AND Y <= YL% THEN Y$ = "OK"
    IF X$ = "OK" AND Y$ = "OK" THEN
      CIRCLE(X,Y),3,6: PAINT(X,Y),6
    END IF
  NEXT
RETURN
```

```
DRAW.CURVE:
 XB = XD*(XF% - CX)/65
 XE = XD*(XL% - CX)/65
 DL! = (XE-XB)/200
 HOLD$ = "OFF"
 FOR X = XB TO XE STEP DL!
   COLOR 1,0: LOCATE 20,29: PRINT "X =";
   PRINT INT(X*10+.5)/10;SPACE$(7);
   COLOR 0,4
   E$ = "OFF"
   ON PICK GOSUB EQ1,EQ2,EQ3,EQ4: REM Y-HAT
   X1 = FN XS(X): Y1 = FN YS(Y)
   IF E$ = "ON" OR Y1 < YF% OR Y1 > YL% THEN
    HOLD$ = "OFF"
   ELSE
    IF HOLD$ = "ON" THEN LINE(HX!,HY!)-(X1,Y1)
    IF HOLD$ = "OFF" THEN PSET(X1,Y1)
    HX! = X1: HY! = Y1: HOLD$ = "ON"
   END IF
 NEXT X
RETURN

EQ1:
 Y = A + B*X
RETURN

EQ2:
 IF X <= 0 THEN E$ = "ON" ELSE Y = A*X^B
RETURN

EQ3:
 Y = A*EXP(B*X)
RETURN

EQ4:
 IF X = 0 THEN E$ = "ON" ELSE Y = A + B/X
RETURN

NEXT.ACTION:
 MENU 3,0,1
 COLOR 1,0
 LOCATE 20,23: PRINT "Use the Options Menu";
 ACTION% = 0
 WHILE ACTION% = 0: WEND
 GOSUB CLEAR.BOTTOM
 IF ACTION% = 1 THEN GOSUB TITLE
 IF ACTION% = 2 THEN GOSUB GRID
 IF ACTION% = 3 THEN GOSUB AXES
 IF ACTION% = 4 THEN GOSUB EQUATION
```

416

```
 IF ACTION% = 5 THEN GOSUB RSQUARED
 IF ACTION% = 6 THEN GOSUB PREDICT
 IF ACTION% = 8 THEN GOSUB NEW.QUADRANT
 IF ACTION% <> 7 THEN NEXT.ACTION
 MENU 3,0,0
RETURN

CLEAR.BOTTOM:
 FOR I=1 TO 2
   LOCATE 18+I,3: PRINT SPACE$(40);
 NEXT I
RETURN

TITLE:
 IF Q = 2 THEN
   LINE(303,12)-(307,29),4,BF
 END IF
 S$ = PICK.NM$(PICK) + " Function: "
 S$ = S$ + PICK.EQ$(PICK)
 L = LEN(S$)
 LINE(313-10*L/2-15,6)-(313+10*L/2+15,18),2,B
 PAINT(313,12),6,2
 COLOR 1,6: LOCATE 2: PRINT PTAB(313-10*L/2)S$
RETURN

GRID:
 IF Q = 1 THEN
   X1% = XF% + 2*XT%
   Y2% = YL% - 2*YT%
 ELSE
   X1% = XF%
   Y2% = YL%
 END IF
 FOR I = YF%+YT% TO Y2% STEP YT%
   FOR J = X1% TO XL% STEP XT%
     LINE(J-2,I)-(J+2,I),2
 NEXT J,I
RETURN

AXES:
 FOR I=1 TO 2
   S$ = "New " + CHR$(87+I)
   S$ = S$ + "-Axis Increment = "
   GOSUB GURGLE
   LOCATE 20,5: PRINT S$;
   LINE INPUT ;"? ";S$
   LOCATE 20,30: PRINT SPACE$(15);
   IF I = 1 THEN XD = VAL(S$) ELSE YD = VAL(S$)
 NEXT I
```

417

```
      GOSUB CHECK.BOUNDS
      GOSUB DRAW.GRAPH
RETURN

EQUATION:
  LOCATE 19,3: PRINT "a =";
  PRINT USING F$;A
  LOCATE 20,3: PRINT "b =";
  PRINT USING F$;B;
RETURN

RSQUARED:
  LOCATE 20,3: PRINT "RSq =";
  PRINT USING MID$(F$,5);RSQ!;
RETURN

PREDICT:
  LOCATE 19,3: PRINT "Value of X = ";
  GOSUB GURGLE
  LINE INPUT ;"? ";X$
  X = VAL(X$)
  E$ = "OFF"
  ON PICK GOSUB EQ1,EQ2,EQ3,EQ4
  IF E$ <> "ON" THEN
   LOCATE 20,3: PRINT "Y =";
   PRINT USING F$;Y;
  ELSE
   LOCATE 20,3: PRINT "Y is undefined !";
  END IF
RETURN

NEW.QUADRANT:
  GOSUB SCALE.AXES
  GOSUB DRAW.GRAPH
RETURN
```

Super Curve-Fitter

Super Curve-Fitter is a multiple linear regression routine that enables you to estimate, in numerical form, the cause-and-effect relationship between variables.

Suppose, for example, that we want to explain the volume of immigration to the United States from 1889 to 1918, as shown in Table 7-2. Our hypothesis is twofold: (1) that immigration depends upon income, and (2) that World War I may have affected the flow of citizens from foreign nations into America.

To test these suppositions, first key in data on the three variables: Immigration, Gross National Product (GNP), and Wartime. The yearly volume of immigration is called the dependent variable in the equation and is denoted by Y.

Enter 444 for the year 1889, 455 for 1890, and so on. Then enter observations on the two explanatory variables, GNP and Wartime, denoted by X1 and X2, respectively.

After all of the observations are entered, the computer asks us to edit the data. Click the mouse on the circle beside each number you see when you run the program. Then enter the corrected value. When you don't have any more entries to edit, click the mouse on the Return bar at the bottom of the screen or simply press RETURN on the keyboard.

The Amiga estimates the regression equation and displays the results (Figure 7-3).

The estimated values 9.779 and −901.862 are called regression coefficients. They measure the impact on Y of a one-unit change in the value of an explanatory variable, with all other X's held constant. Since X1 is the variable on GNP, the 9.779 means that each $1 billion increase in real income in the U.S. induced roughly 9.8 thousand more immigrants to enter America per annum.

Similarly, the figure −901.862 means that the war induced roughly 901 thousand would-be immigrants to stay home. In short, then, immigration increased when the U.S. economy was healthy and decreased when the country was embattled.

A *t-ratio* is the value of a term divided by its estimated standard error. As a rough rule of thumb, a t-value of 2 or more means that an explanatory variable is statistically significant in explaining changes in Y, as are GNP and Wartime in the example.

The total variation in the dependent variable about its mean is called the Total Sum of Squares. It equals the *regression sum of squares* (the variation in Y explained by the regression equation) plus the *residual sum of squares* (the unexplained variation in Y).

The next three figures are called *goodness-of-fit* statistics. The *coefficient of determination*, or *R-squared*, is the proportion of variation in the dependent variable explained by the regression equation. In the example, roughly 70 percent of the fluctuation in yearly immigration is explained by changes in real GNP and by World War I.

The *F-Statistic* measures the power of the regression equation in explaining Y. As a rough rule of thumb, an F value of 4 or more means that the X's explain Y well.

The *Standard Error of the Estimate* is, roughly speaking, the average error made in predicting immigration based on X1 and X2. That is, the predictions are off by roughly 192 thousand persons per year on average.

Finally, the *Durbin-Watson statistic* is used in testing for something called *first-order serial correlation*, or for linear association between successive regression residuals (a residual is the observed minus the predicted value of Y).

Figure 7-3. Regression Equation

Term	Estimated Value	t-Ratio
B0	−174.488	−1.366
B1	9.779	6.951
B2	−901.862	−7.239

Summary Values

Sum of Squares

Total	3374698.300
Regression	2379656.446
Residual	995041.854

Goodness-of-Fit Statistics

R-Squared = 0.705
F-Statistic = 32.285
Standard Error of
the Estimate = 191.972

Serial Correlation Statistics

Durbin-Watson
Statistic = 0.798

First-Order Serial
Correlation Coefficient = 0.613

Table 7-2. Immigration Data

Year	Number of Immigrants (thousands)	Gross National Product (billions $)	Wartime Variable (0 = peace and 1 = war)
1889	444	49.1	0
1890	455	52.7	0
1891	560	55.1	0
1892	580	60.4	0
1893	440	57.5	0
1894	286	55.9	0
1895	259	62.6	0
1896	343	61.3	0
1897	231	67.1	0
1898	229	68.6	0
1899	312	74.8	0
1900	449	76.9	0
1901	488	85.7	0
1902	649	86.5	0
1903	857	90.8	0
1904	813	89.7	0
1905	1026	96.3	0
1906	1101	107.5	0
1907	1285	109.2	0
1908	783	100.2	0
1909	752	116.8	0
1910	1042	120.1	0
1911	879	123.2	0
1912	838	130.2	0
1913	1198	131.4	0
1914	1218	125.6	0
1915	327	124.5	1
1916	299	134.3	1
1917	295	135.2	1
1918	111	151.8	1

Note: GNP, or national income, is in constant 1958 prices.

Program 7-2. Super Curve-Fitter
Save using the filename **SUPER**

```
REM SUPER CURVE-FITTER
 CLEAR ,32000
 GOSUB INITIALIZE
 GOSUB ENTER.DATA
CONTINUE:
 GOSUB EDIT.DATA
 GOSUB COMPUTE
 IF GOOF = 0 THEN
  GOSUB SHOW.RESULTS
 ELSE
  IF CNT$ = "YES" THEN CONTINUE
 END IF
 GOSUB GOODBYE
END

INITIALIZE:
 GOSUB SETSCREEN
 GOSUB KEYVALUES
 GOSUB SETMENUS
 GOSUB SETCOLORS
 GOSUB SHAPES
 GOSUB HEADING
 IF INSTRUCTIONS = 1 THEN GOSUB INSTRUCTIONS
RETURN

SETSCREEN:
 SCREEN 1,640,200,3,2
 WINDOW 2,"Super Curve-Fitter",,0,1
RETURN

KEYVALUES:
 RANDOMIZE TIMER
 DEFINT A-Z: DEFDBL B-F,Q-W
 REM make X DBL for VERY big or small raw data
  DEFSNG X
 REM MAXIMUM NUMBER OF OBSERVATIONS & X'S
  DATA 75,6
  READ NX,KX
  M = KX + 1
  DIM B(M),C(M),B$(M),V$(M),R(M,M),V(M,M)
  DIM Q(NX,M),X(NX,M),XT#(NX,M)
  DIM CIRCLES%(150)
 REM BUTTON VALUES
  XB(1) = 292: XB(2) = 334: YB = 165
  LT$(1) = "Y": LT$(2) = "N"
 REM SHAPE INDICES
```

```
   INDEX(1) = 1: INDEX(2) = 75
  GOSUB CREATE.SYMBOLS
  GOSUB OUTPUT.FORMATS
  ZERO$ = STRING$(1Ø,"Ø")
RETURN

CREATE.SYMBOLS:
  V$(Ø) = "Y": B$(Ø) = "BØ"
  FOR I=1 TO KX
   V$(I) = "X" + MID$(STR$(I),2)
   B$(I) = "B" + MID$(STR$(I),2)
  NEXT
RETURN

OUTPUT.FORMATS:
   FOR I=2 TO 6
    F$(I) = STRING$(14-I,"#")
    F$(I) = F$(I) + "." + STRING$(I,"#")
   NEXT
RETURN

SETMENUS:
  DATA 2, Instructions, Yes, No
  DATA 5, Color, Tan, Blue, Green, Gray
  DATA Random
  DATA 5, Decimals, 2 Places, 3 Places, 4 Places
  DATA 5 Places, 6 Places
  DATA 3, Stop, Go to BASIC
  DATA Go to Statistics Menu, Go to System
  FOR I=1 TO 4
   READ NUMBER
   FOR J=Ø TO NUMBER
    READ TITLE$
    IF J<>Ø THEN TITLE$ = SPACE$(3) + TITLE$
    STATUS = 1
    IF I < 3 AND J = 1 THEN STATUS = 2
    IF I = 3 AND J = 2 THEN STATUS = 2
    MENU I,J,STATUS,TITLE$
  NEXT J,I
  INSTRUCTIONS = 1: KOLOR = 1: DP% = 3
  F$ = F$(DP%)
  F.SHORT$ = MID$(F$,5)
RETURN

SETCOLORS:
  REM TAN, BLUE, GREEN, GRAY
   DATA .95,.7,.53, .36,.57,1
   DATA .22,.76,.68, .72,.7,.86
   FOR I=1 TO 4
```

```
   FOR J=1 TO 3
     READ KOLOR!(I,J)
   NEXT J,I
 REM TAN, GREEN, & RED
   PALETTE 4,.95,.7,.53
   PALETTE 5,.14,.43,0
   PALETTE 6,.93,.2,0
RETURN

SHAPES:
 X=313: Y=80
 X1 = X-7: X2 = X+7: Y1 = Y-3: Y2 = Y+3
 LINE(X1,Y1)-(X2,Y2),4,BF
 CIRCLE(X,Y),7,2: PAINT(X,Y),6,2
 GET(X1,Y1)-(X2,Y2),CIRCLES%(1)
 CIRCLE(X,Y),7,2: PAINT(X,Y),1,2
 GET(X1,Y1)-(X2,Y2),CIRCLES%(75)
RETURN

HEADING:
 MENU ON
 ON MENU GOSUB OPTIONS
 CLS
 COLOR 3,0: LOCATE 18,30:PRINT "then"
 COLOR 1,0
 LOCATE 10,23: PRINT "Super Curve-Fitter"
 LOCATE 17,24: PRINT "Please use menus,"
 LOCATE 19,21: PRINT "Click mouse to compute"
 GOSUB CLICKIT
RETURN

OPTIONS:
 ID = MENU(0): ITEM = MENU(1)
 ON ID GOSUB MENU1,MENU2,MENU3,GOODBYE
 ITEM = 0
RETURN

MENU1:
 MENU 1,INSTRUCTIONS,1: MENU 1,ITEM,2
 INSTRUCTIONS = ITEM
RETURN

MENU2:
 K1! = KOLOR!(ITEM,1): K2! = KOLOR!(ITEM,2)
 K3! = KOLOR!(ITEM,3)
 IF ITEM = 5 THEN K1!=RND: K2!=RND: K3!=RND
 PALETTE 4,K1!,K2!,K3!
 MENU 2,KOLOR,1: MENU 2,ITEM,2
 KOLOR = ITEM
RETURN
```

```
MENU3:
 MENU 3,DP%-1,1: MENU 3,ITEM,2
 DP% = ITEM + 1
 F$ = F$(DP%)
 F.SHORT$ = MID$(F$,5)
RETURN

GOODBYE:
 WINDOW CLOSE 2: WINDOW 1: MENU RESET
 SCREEN CLOSE 1
 IF ITEM = 2 THEN RUN "STATISTICS"
 IF ITEM = 3 THEN SYSTEM
 COLOR 1,Ø: CLS
 PRINT "Bye-Bye"
 STOP
RETURN

CLICKIT:
 S$ = ""
 WHILE MOUSE(Ø) = Ø AND S$ = ""
  S$ = INKEY$
 WEND
  X = MOUSE(1)
  Y = MOUSE(2)
 WHILE MOUSE(Ø)<> Ø: WEND: REM RESET
RETURN

INSTRUCTIONS:
 CLS
 PRINT
 PRINT "    This program estimates a multiple";
 PRINT " linear regression"
 PRINT " equation."
 PRINT
 PRINT "    The maximum numbers of";
 PRINT " observations and explanatory"
 PRINT " variables allowed are:"
 LOCATE 9,1Ø : PRINT "Observations    =";NX
 LOCATE 1Ø,1Ø: PRINT "Variables (X's) =";KX
 LOCATE 19,27:PRINT "Click Mouse";
 GOSUB CLICKIT
RETURN

ENTER.DATA:
 GOSUB EQUATION.SIZE
 REM DEPENDENT VARIABLE
  CLS
  PRINT
  PRINT "    Please enter observations on the";
```

```
    PRINT " dependent variable, Y."
    PRINT " Hit RETURN when you're through."
     GOSUB ON.Y
   REM EXPLANATORY VARIABLES
     FOR I=1 TO K
      GOSUB ON.X
     NEXT I
RETURN

EQUATION.SIZE:
  CLS
  PRINT
  PRINT "    Please enter the number of";
  PRINT " explanatory variables (X's)"
  PRINT " in your regression equation.  Up to";
  PRINT KX;"are allowed."
  K = Ø
  WHILE K < 1 OR K > KX
   LOCATE 6,13: PRINT SPACE$(1Ø);
   GOSUB GURGLE
   LOCATE 6,2: INPUT "Number = ";K$
   K = VAL(K$)
  WEND
RETURN

GURGLE:
  FREQ = 3ØØ
  FOR G=1 TO 5
   FREQ = 5ØØ-FREQ
   SOUND FREQ,1,5Ø
  NEXT G
RETURN

ON.Y:
  GOSUB GURGLE
  N = NX
  FOR J=1 TO NX
   LOCATE 5,14: PRINT SPACE$(3Ø)
   LOCATE 5,3: PRINT "Y(";J
   LOCATE 5,9: PRINT ")= ? ";
   INPUT "",X$
   IF X$ = "" THEN
    N = J-1
    J = NX
   ELSE
    X(J,Ø) = VAL(X$)
   END IF
  NEXT
  REM DEGREES OF FREEDOM
```

```
   P = N - K - 1
  IF P < 1 THEN
   LOCATE 18,7: PRINT "I need at least 1";
   PRINT " degree of freedom I  Try again."
   GOTO ON.Y
  END IF
RETURN

ON.X:
 CLS
 GOSUB GURGLE
 PRINT
 PRINT "  Please enter data on ";V$(I);"."
 FOR J=1 TO N
  LOCATE 4,16: PRINT SPACE$(30)
  LOCATE 4,3: PRINT V$(I);TAB(6)"(";J
  LOCATE 4,11: PRINT ")= ? ";
  INPUT "",X$
  X(J,I) = VAL(X$)
 NEXT J
RETURN

EDIT.DATA:
 FOR I=0 TO K
  FOR J=1 TO N STEP 10
   GOSUB DISPLAY
   GOSUB CORRECT
 NEXT J,I
RETURN

DISPLAY:
 CLS
 SYM$ = V$(I)
 SYM$ = STRING$(2-LEN(SYM$)," ") + SYM$
 S$ = "These are values of " + V$(I)
 L = LEN(S$)
 LINE(313-10*L/2-15,6)-(313+10*L/2+15,18),1,B
 PAINT(313,10),6,1
 COLOR 1,6: LOCATE 2: PRINT PTAB(313-10*L/2)S$
 LINE (40,25)-(590,116),4,BF
 COLOR 2,4
 R% = 0: H.ROW = 0
 FOR L = J TO J+9
  IF L <= N THEN
   R% = R% + 1
   CALL DRAW.IT(R%,1)
   LOCATE R%+3,10: PRINT SYM$;"(";MID$(STR$(L),2)
   LOCATE R%+3,16: PRINT ")= ";X(L,I)
  END IF
```

```
  NEXT L
 RETURN

 SUB DRAW.IT(RW%,INX) STATIC
  SHARED CIRCLES%(),INDEX()
  Y = (RW%+3)*9 - 9
  PUT(65,Y),CIRCLES%(INDEX(INX)),PSET
 END SUB

 CORRECT:
  LINE(262,132)-(360,144),2,B: PAINT(313,137),3,2
  COLOR 2,3
  LOCATE 16: PRINT PTAB(282)"Return"
  COLOR 1,0
  LOCATE 19,9: PRINT "Click on Circle to";
  PRINT " Edit, then Click on Return."
  GOSUB CHOOSE
  IF H.ROW <> 0 THEN
   GOSUB CHANGE: GOTO CORRECT
  END IF
 RETURN

 CHOOSE:
  RTN$ = "OFF"
  GOSUB GURGLE
  GOSUB CLICKIT
  IF S$ = "" THEN GOSUB LOCATION
  IF ASC(S$+" ") <> 13 AND RTN$ = "OFF" THEN
   GOTO CHOOSE
  END IF
 RETURN

 LOCATION:
  IF X>263 AND X<360 AND Y>131 AND Y<145 THEN
   RTN$ = "ON"
  ELSE
   ROW% = INT(Y/9) - 2
   IF ROW%>0 AND ROW%<=R% AND X>55 AND X<90 THEN
    IF H.ROW <> 0 THEN CALL DRAW.IT(H.ROW,1)
    CALL DRAW.IT(ROW%,2)
    H.ROW = ROW%
   END IF
  END IF
 RETURN

 CHANGE:
  LINE(262,132)-(360,144),0,BF
  LINE(65,133)-(185,143),5,BF
  COLOR 1,5
```

```
     LOCATE 16,8: PRINT "New Value ?"
     COLOR 1,0
     LOCATE 16,21: INPUT "",V$
     X(J+H.ROW-1,I) = VAL(V$)
     COLOR 2,4
     LOCATE H.ROW+3,19: PRINT SPACE$(30)
     LOCATE H.ROW+3,19: PRINT X(J+H.ROW-1,I)
     CALL DRAW.IT(H.ROW,1)
     H.ROW = 0
     LINE(65,133)-(185,143),0,BF
     COLOR 1,0
     LOCATE 16,21: PRINT SPACE$(30)
RETURN

COMPUTE:
     GOOF = 0
     COLOR 1,0
     CLS
     LOCATE 10,26: PRINT "Computing ..."
     GOSUB TRANSFER.DATA
     GOSUB ORTHOGONALIZATION
     IF GOOF = 0 THEN GOSUB BACKSOLVE
     IF GOOF = 0 THEN GOSUB VAR.COV.MATRIX
     IF GOOF = 0 THEN GOSUB OTHER.STATISTICS
RETURN

TRANSFER.DATA:
     REM CONSTANT TERM
      FOR I=1 TO N
       XT#(I,1) = 1
      NEXT
     REM X'S (MAKE ROOM FOR CONSTANT TERM)
      FOR I=1 TO K
       FOR J=1 TO N
        W = X(J,I)
        IF W < 0 THEN SG% = -1 ELSE SG% = 1
        XT#(J,I+1) = SG%*VAL( ZERO$+STR$(ABS(W)) )
      NEXT J,I
      M = K + 1
RETURN

ORTHOGONALIZATION:
     FOR Z=1 TO M
      GOSUB KEY.ELEMENT.OF.R
      IF GOOF = 0 THEN
       GOSUB COLUMN.OF.Q
       IF Z <> M THEN GOSUB COLUMN.OF.R
       GOSUB ELEMENT.OF.C
       IF Z <> M THEN GOSUB REVISE.X
```

429

```
       ELSE
         GOSUB GOOF
         Z = M
       END IF
     NEXT Z
   RETURN

   KEY.ELEMENT.OF.R:
    R = Ø
    FOR I=1 TO N
      R = R + XT#(I,Z)*XT#(I,Z)
    NEXT I
    R(Z,Z) = SQR(R)
    IF R(Z,Z) = Ø THEN GOOF = 1
   RETURN

   COLUMN.OF.Q:
    FOR I=1 TO N
      Q(I,Z) = XT#(I,Z)/R(Z,Z)
    NEXT I
   RETURN

   COLUMN.OF.R:
    FOR L = Z+1 TO M
      R(Z,L) = Ø
      FOR I=1 TO N
        R(Z,L) = R(Z,L) + XT#(I,L)*Q(I,Z)
    NEXT I,L
   RETURN

   ELEMENT.OF.C:
    C(Z) = Ø
    FOR I=1 TO N
      C(Z) = C(Z) + X(I,Ø)*Q(I,Z)
    NEXT I
   RETURN

   REVISE.X:
    FOR I=1 TO N
      FOR L = Z+1 TO M
        XT#(I,L) = XT#(I,L) - Q(I,Z)*R(Z,L)
    NEXT L,I
   RETURN

   GOOF:
    CLS
    LINE(82,79)-(150,89),6,BF
    COLOR 1,6
    LOCATE 10,10: PRINT "Sorry:"
```

```
   COLOR 1,0
   LOCATE 10,17: PRINT "I can't estimate";
   PRINT " a regression equation"
   LOCATE 11,17: PRINT "with the data you've";
   PRINT " entered."
   LOCATE 17,28: PRINT "Continue ?"
   GOSUB GURGLE
   GOSUB DECIDE
   CNT$ = "NO"
   IF BUTTON% = 1 THEN CNT$ = "YES"
RETURN

DECIDE:
  BUTTON% = 0
  GOSUB DRAWBUTTON
  GOSUB PUSHBUTTON
  COLOR 1,0
RETURN

DRAWBUTTON:
  LINE (265,158)-(361,172),1,BF
  FOR I=1 TO 2
   CIRCLE (XB(I),YB),12,4+I
   PAINT (XB(I),YB),4+I
   COLOR 1,4+I
   LOCATE 19: PRINT PTAB(XB(I)-4);LT$(I);
  NEXT I
RETURN

PUSHBUTTON:
  SOUND 440,2
  GOSUB CLICKIT
  S$ = UCASE$(S$)
  IF S$ = "Y" THEN BUTTON% = 1
  IF S$ = "N" THEN BUTTON% = 2
  FOR I=1 TO 2
   XD = ABS(X-XB(I)): YD = ABS(Y-YB)
   IF XD<13 AND YD<7 THEN BUTTON% = I: I=2
  NEXT
  IF BUTTON% = 0 THEN PUSHBUTTON
RETURN

BACKSOLVE:
  B(M) = C(M)/R(M,M)
  FOR I = M-1 TO 1 STEP -1
   REM LEFT-SIDE SUM
     S = 0
     FOR J = I+1 TO M
      S = S + R(I,J)*B(J)
```

```
    NEXT J
   REM SOLUTION
    B(I) = (C(I)-S)/R(I,I)
  NEXT I
RETURN

VAR.COV.MATRIX:
  GOSUB ERROR.VARIANCE
  GOSUB INVERT.R
  GOSUB UNSCALED.VAR.COV.MAT
RETURN

ERROR.VARIANCE:
  REM RESIDUALS = Y - Q*C
   FOR I=1 TO N
    S = Ø
    FOR J=1 TO M
     S = S + Q(I,J)*C(J)
    NEXT J
    Q(I,Ø) = X(I,Ø) - S
   NEXT I
  REM ERROR VARIANCE
   ESS = Ø
   FOR I=1 TO N
   ESS = ESS + Q(I,Ø)*Q(I,Ø)
   NEXT
   EV = ESS/P
RETURN

INVERT.R:
  FOR I=1 TO M
   V(I,I) = 1/R(I,I)
  NEXT
  FOR I = M-1 TO 1 STEP -1
   FOR J = I+1 TO M
    S = Ø
    FOR L = I+1 TO J
     S = S + R(I,L)*V(L,J)
    NEXT L
    V(I,J) = -S/R(I,I)
  NEXT J,I
RETURN

UNSCALED.VAR.COV.MAT:
  FOR I=1 TO M
   FOR J=1 TO M
    R(I,J) = Ø
    FOR L=1 TO M
     R(I,J) = R(I,J) + V(I,L)*V(J,L)
```

```
  NEXT L,J,I
RETURN

OTHER.STATISTICS:
 GOSUB ANOVA
 GOSUB DW.STATISTIC
 GOSUB RHO
RETURN

ANOVA:
 REM TOTAL SUM OF SQUARES
  S = Ø: SS = Ø
  FOR I=1 TO N
   S  =  S + X(I,Ø)
   SS = SS + X(I,Ø)^2
  NEXT
  TSS = SS - S*S/N
 REM REGRESSION SUM OF SQUARES
  RSS = TSS - ESS
 REM GOODNESS-OF-FIT STATISTICS
  RSQ  = RSS/TSS
  F    = RSS/(M-1)/EV
RETURN

DW.STATISTIC:
 S = Ø
 FOR I=2 TO N
  S = S + (Q(I,Ø)-Q(I-1,Ø))^2
 NEXT
 DW = S/ESS
RETURN

RHO:
 REM NUMERATOR
  S = Ø
  FOR I=2 TO N
   S = S + Q(I,Ø)*Q(I-1,Ø)
  NEXT
 REM DENOMINATOR
  D = Ø
  FOR I=2 TO N-1
   D = D + Q(I,Ø)^2
  NEXT
  RHO = S/D
RETURN

SHOW.RESULTS:
 GOSUB SCREEN.EQUATION
 GOSUB SHOW.EQUATION
```

```
    GOSUB  SCREEN.ANOVA
    GOSUB  SHOW.ANOVA
    GOSUB  DW.RHO
RETURN

SCREEN.EQUATION:
 CLS
 LINE(35,3)-(595,60+9*M),2,B
 PAINT(313,50),4,2
 COLOR 2,4
 LOCATE 2,23: PRINT "REGRESSION RESULTS"
 COLOR 1,6
 LINE(65,25)-(115,35),6,BF
 LOCATE 4,8: PRINT "Term"
 LINE(215,25)-(375,35),6,BF
 LOCATE 4,23: PRINT "Estimated Value"
 LINE(455,25)-(575,35),6,BF
 LOCATE 4,47: PRINT "t-Statistic"
RETURN

SHOW.EQUATION:
 COLOR 2,4
 LOCATE 6,1
 FOR I=1 TO M
  SE = SQR(EV*R(I,I))
  PRINT TAB(9);B$(I-1);TAB(21) USING F$;B(I);
  PRINT TAB(41) USING F$;B(I)/SE
 NEXT
 COLOR 1,0
 LOCATE 19,26: PRINT "Click Mouse"
 GOSUB CLICKIT
RETURN

SCREEN.ANOVA:
 CLS
 LINE(35,3)-(595,160),2,B
 PAINT(313,50),4,2
 COLOR 2,4
 LOCATE 2,25: PRINT "SUMMARY VALUES"
 LINE(115,25)-(266,35),5,BF
 COLOR 1,5
 LOCATE 4,13: PRINT "Sum of Squares"
 LINE(115,88)-(385,98),5,BF
 COLOR 1,5
 LOCATE 11,13: PRINT "Goodness-of-Fit Statistics"
 COLOR 2,4
RETURN
```

```
SHOW.ANOVA:
 LOCATE 6,15: PRINT "Total";TAB(31)"=";
 PRINT USING F$;TSS
 LOCATE 7,15: PRINT "Regression";TAB(31)"=";
 PRINT USING F$;RSS
 LOCATE 8,15: PRINT "Residual";TAB(31)"=";
 PRINT USING F$;ESS
 LOCATE 13,15: PRINT "R-Squared       =";
 PRINT USING F$;RSQ
 LOCATE 14,15: PRINT "F-Statistic     =";
 PRINT USING F$;F
 LOCATE 16,15: PRINT "Standard Error"
 LOCATE 17,15: PRINT "of the Estimate =";
 PRINT USING F$;SQR(EV)
 COLOR 1,0
 LOCATE 20,26: PRINT "Click Mouse";
 GOSUB CLICKIT
RETURN

DW.RHO:
 CLS
 LINE(35,3)-(595,100),2,B
 PAINT(313,50),4,2
 COLOR 2,4
 LOCATE 2,17:
 PRINT "SERIAL CORRELATION STATISTICS"
 LOCATE 5,14: PRINT "Durbin-Watson Statistic =";
 PRINT USING F$;DW
 LOCATE 8,14: PRINT "First-Order Serial"
 LOCATE 9,14: PRINT "Correlation Coefficient =";
 PRINT USING F$;RHO
 COLOR 1,0
 LOCATE 17,26: PRINT "Click Mouse"
 GOSUB CLICKIT
RETURN
```

Index

addition 148
Amiga BASIC 3, 5
Amiga Extras disk 6
atom 330
atomic number 330
atomic weight 330
barometer 352
barometric pressure 352
"Bunny's and Piglet's Tic-Tac-Toe" program 10, 114–27
business and finance 261
"Business and Finance Menu Driver" program 262–64
button bar 5
calculator, multifunction 236
cells 265
"Chemistry Basics" program 325, 329, 331–51
    Program A (Chemistry Basics Database) 331–39
    Program B (Chemistry Basics) 339–51
coefficient of determination 420
columns, sixty 5
common denominators 131, 181
"Computer Cash Register" 261, 314–21
COMPUTE!'s Amiga Applications disk 4
    using the disk 6
constant dollars 217
counting 135
"Crazy Critters" program 131, 135–47
cryptography 14
current dollars 217
DATA statements 4
definition of shapes, menus, and variables 4
denominator 181
density 330
dollars
    constant 217
    current 217
Durbin-Watson statistic 420
electron 330
"Electronic Spreadsheet" program 3, 261, 265, 268–90
element 330
"Elementary, Watson" program 9, 26, 27–38
elements 325, 329
"Enigma" program 9, 14, 15–25
equation, selecting 400
equipment required 3
exponential equation 400, 402
"Falstaff" program 9, 73, 74–85
FICA (Federal Insurance Contributions Act) 249
first-order serial correlation 420
"Foreign Language Flash Cards" program 131, 198–209
fractions 131, 181
f-statistic 420
"Fun with Fractions" program 131, 181–97

future worth 305
"Future Worth" program 261, 305–13
games of skill 9, 10
"Games of Skill Menu Driver" program 10–13
goodness-of-fit statistics 420
"Hi-Q" program 10, 96–104
household helpers 213
"Household Helpers Menu Driver" program 213–16
icon names 4
individual retirement account. See IRA
investment 305
IRA 213, 217, 265
"IRA Planner" program 213, 217, 218–24
KEYVALUES routine 4
Kickstart 1.1 disk 3
"Knights Errant" program 9, 39, 40–51
"Least-Squares Forecasting" program 261, 291, 293–304
least-squares regression line 399
"Let's Add and Subtract" program 131, 148–64
"Let's Multiply" program 131, 165–80
linear equation 399
line of best fit 395, 399
loading a program 4, 5
"Loan Payments" program 213, 225, 226–35
"Local Climatological Data Annual Summary" 353
main routine 4
matrices 325, 377
"Matrix Manipulator" program 325, 377, 378–91
"Menu Driver" program 4
modular design 4
money-market certificate 305
"Mosaic Puzzle" program 9, 86, 87–95
"Multifunction Calculator" program 213, 236, 237–48
multiple linear regression analysis 395
multiple linear regression routine 419
multiplication tables 131, 165
multiply 131
National Weather Service 353
neutron 330
NOAA 353
nucleus 330
numerator 181
operating system 3
"Paycheck Analysis" program 213, 249, 250–57
"Pharaoh's Pyramid" program 9, 52, 53–61
power equation 400, 402
PREDICT subroutine 353
Preferences drawer 5
program names (table) 5
programs
    typing in 4
    loading and running 4, 5
proton 330
pull-down menu 5

rainfall 353
RAM (random access memory) 3
reciprocal equation 400, 402
rectangular hyperbola 400, 402
regression 400
regression coefficients 419
regression sum of squares 420
residuals 420
residual sum of squares 420
"Roman Checkers" program 9, 62, 63–72
R-squared 420
running a program 4, 5
sales tax 314
scalar multiplication 377
"Scatter Diagram" program 395, 399, 402–18
science and math 325
"Science and Math Menu Driver" program 325–28
SETSCREEN routine 4
"Simultaneous Equation Solver" program 325, 366–76
sliding-square puzzles 86
slope 291
snowfall 353
Social Security 249
"Solitaire Checkers" program 10, 105–13
spreadsheet 265
   formulas 267
   labels 265
   printing 267
   saving 268
   tallying 267

Standard and Poor's Index 91
standard error of the estimate 420
statistics 395
"Statistics Menu Driver" program 395–98, 419, 422–35
stock market 291
stock prices and interest rates (table) 292
"Stop, Look, and Learn Menu Driver" program 132–34
string 265
subroutines, series of 4
subtraction 148
"Super Curve-Fitter" 395
temperature 353
tick intervals 399
tick marks 400
total sum of squares 420
t-ratio 419
Treasury Bill rate 291
typing in programs 4
variables 419
vocabulary lists 131
Weather Almanac, The 353
"Weather Forecasting" program 325, 352, 354–65
white bar 5
wind direction 352
Workbench disk 3, 5

To order your copy of *Amiga Applications Disk*, call our toll-free US order line: 1-800-346-6767 (in NY 212-887-8525) or send your prepaid order to:

Amiga Applications Disk
COMPUTE! Publications
P.O. Box 5038
F.D.R. Station
New York, NY 10150

Send ____ copies of *Amiga Applications Disk* at $15.95 per copy.

All orders must be prepaid (check, charge, or money order). NC residents add 4.5% sales tax.

Subtotal $_____

Shipping and Handling: $2.00/disk $_____

Sales tax (if applicable) $_____

Total payment enclosed $_____

□ Payment enclosed
□ Charge □ Visa □ MasterCard □ American Express

Acct. No. _____ Exp. Date _____
(Required)

Name _____

Address _____

City _____ State _____ Zip _____

Please allow 4-5 weeks for delivery.

COMPUTE! Books

Ask your retailer for these **COMPUTE! Books** or order directly from **COMPUTE!**.

Call toll free (in US) **1-800-346-6767** (in NY 212-887-8525) or write COMPUTE! Books, P.O. Box 5038, F.D.R. Station, New York, NY 10150.

Quantity	Title	Price*	Total
_____	COMPUTE!'s Beginner's Guide to the Amiga (025-4)	**$16.95**	_____
_____	COMPUTE!'s AmigaDOS Reference Guide (047-5)	**$14.95**	_____
_____	Elementary Amiga BASIC (041-6)	**$14.95**	_____
_____	COMPUTE!'s Amiga Programmer's Guide (028-9)	**$16.95**	_____
_____	COMPUTE!'s Kids and the Amiga (048-3)	**$14.95**	_____
_____	Inside Amiga Graphics (040-8)	**$16.95**	_____
_____	Advanced Amiga BASIC (045-9)	**$16.95**	_____
_____	COMPUTE!'s Amiga Applications (053-X)	**$16.95**	_____

*Add $2.00 per book for shipping and handling.
Outside US add $5.00 air mail or $2.00 surface mail.

NC residents add 4.5% sales tax _____
Shipping & handling: $2.00/book _____
Total payment _____

All orders must be prepaid (check, charge, or money order).
All payments must be in US funds.
NC residents add 4.5% sales tax.
☐ Payment enclosed.
Charge   ☐ Visa   ☐ MasterCard   ☐ American Express

Acct. No._____ Exp. Date_____

Name_____

Address_____

City_____ State _____ Zip_____

*Allow 4–5 weeks for delivery.
Prices and availability subject to change.
Current catalog available upon request.